Bad Gays

Bad Gays

A Homosexual History

Huw Lemmey
and
Ben Miller

VERSO
London • New York

This paperback edition first published by Verso 2023
First published by Verso 2022
© Huw Lemmey, Ben Miller 2022, 2023

3 5 7 9 10 8 6 4 2

Verso
UK: 6 Meard Street, London W1F 0EG
US: 388 Atlantic Avenue, Brooklyn, NY 11217
versobooks.com

Verso is the imprint of New Left Books

ISBN-13: 978-1-83976-328-1
ISBN-13: 978-1-83976-330-4 (US EBK)
ISBN-13: 978-1-83976-329-8 (UK EBK)

British Library Cataloguing in Publication Data
A catalogue record for this book is available from the British Library

The Library of Congress Has Cataloged the Hardback Edition as Follows:

Names: Lemmey, Huw, author. | Miller, Ben (Historian), author.
Title: Bad gays : a homosexual history / Huw Lemmey and Ben Miller.
Description: London ; New York : Verso, 2022. | Includes bibliographical
references and index.
Identifiers: LCCN 2022002156 (print) | LCCN 2022002157 (ebook) | ISBN
9781839763274 (hardback) | ISBN 9781839763304 (ebk)
Subjects: LCSH: Homosexuality – History. | Gay men – History. |
Lesbians – History.
Classification: LCC HQ76.25 .L45 2022 (print) | LCC HQ76.25 (ebook) | DDC
306.76/609 – dc23/eng/20220321
LC record available at https://lccn.loc.gov/2022002156
LC ebook record available at https://lccn.loc.gov/2022002157

Typeset in Sabon by MJ & N Gavan, Truro, Cornwall
Printed and bound by CPI Group (UK) Ltd, Croydon, CRO 4YY

For our friends Virgil and Michael

[H]omosexuals are ... widely consigned to the same category of things as drugs, the category of illicit dirty things that people have to be protected from ... since the homosexual is continually taught by the world around him that his natural home is the sewer, the homosexual is uniquely equipped to discover what truly belongs and doesn't belong in the sewer ...

Gary Indiana, *Three-Month Fever*

Contents

Introduction

In 1891, Oscar Wilde's star was on the rise. For a decade he had been the talk of London, a literary wit who pioneered the fashion and philosophy of aestheticism. He had successfully published works of prose and collections of poetry, and was preparing his first novel, *The Picture of Dorian Gray*, for publication, a masterful account of a Faustian bargain dripping with desire, vanity, and corruption. England regarded this sparkling Irishman with a combination of fascination, admiration, and horror, but no one could deny he was becoming a titan of the national culture. Yet within five years, Wilde's reputation, and his health, were destroyed. Sentenced to two years of backbreaking hard labour, Wilde was spat at by strangers as he was transported via train to jail. Upon release, he fled into exile, living in penury under an assumed name. Nobody wanted to be known as his friend. Less than a decade after he had reached the heights of literary stardom, Wilde was dead.

It's right and proper that we remember the role Wilde played within an otherwise staid and repressive Victorian culture, as well as the important, pioneering work he did describing, in public, a form of same-sex desire that otherwise lay hidden and criminalised on the margins. Wilde was one of the first men in British society to give a creative form to a sexuality that barely yet understood itself, let alone was understood or discussed by straight people. For that, conservative forces succeeded in destroying him. But at the core of Wilde's story is his love for a terrible young man, a love that drove him close to madness and sparked the wildfire of events that led to his ruin.

That boy, a petulant and cruel son of the British aristocracy, was Lord Alfred Douglas, known by his affectionate nickname 'Bosie'. Wilde and Bosie first met in 1891, when Bosie was a twenty-one-year-old undergraduate at Wilde's alma mater, Magdalen College, Oxford. Bosie was an archetypal twink, popular and athletic, who cared more about his writing and activities in the new 'Uranian poetry' movement, which idolized pederastic relationships between older and younger men, than his studies, which he never completed. In Wilde he found his ideal older lover and benefactor, whose work and plays he had already praised in Uranian journals.

Their tempestuous affair pushed Wilde's homosexuality from the realm of flirtatious literary innuendo into that of reckless public identity. Besotted with the young poet, Wilde fell in with Bosie's lifestyle and indulged his demands. The two lovers drank and partied together and became the subject of scurrilous rumours. They began to host wild sex parties with young working-class men, who they paid to fuck (or get fucked by). Wilde's public image – an educated and charming raconteur, married with children – clashed with his private life, and while the conflict could hold for a few years, it wasn't long before the inevitable happened. Wilde was expecting it. In a letter to Bosie after his release from jail, he wrote:

> It was like feasting with panthers. The danger was half the excitement. I used to feel as the snake-charmer must feel when he lures the cobra. They were to me the brightest of gilded snakes. Their poison was part of their perfection.[1]

After clashing with Bosie's father, the Marquess of Queensberry, Wilde was left a calling card from the Marquess accusing him of being a sodomite. Queensberry, having two homosexual sons whom he regarded as having been corrupted by 'snob queers' such as Wilde and then–prime minister Archibald Primrose, 5th Earl of Rosebery, was obsessed with homosexuality. Wilde's friends told him to leave the case well alone, but, pushed by an impetuous and jealous Bosie, who hated his father, Wilde sued. There was a fatal hole in Wilde's case – he *was* a sodomite, and Queensberry could prove it. The civil trial not only humiliated Wilde in the eyes of a homophobic Victorian public, but instigated a further criminal trial for gross indecency. Wilde was found guilty and sentenced to hard labour, which, in the end, indirectly killed him.

Wilde's imprisonment, as awful and scandalous as it was, came at what was both a dangerous and an auspicious time for the new figure of the 'homosexual' in Europe. Within certain, albeit small, literary and scientific circles, a new identity was forming. Sexologists described a 'third sex' somewhere between male and female. In cities thronging with the new proletarian masses and enriched by colonial plunder, a group of people became the first generation of activists pursuing something we might recognize as 'gay rights'. They discussed same-sex desire with sensitivity, even respect, calling themselves 'Uranians', 'Urnings', or even 'Homosexuals'. For such people, Wilde's trial was an important moment in the development of what would, in the ensuing decades, become something like a coherent movement. Scandals, after all, brought public attention. The newspapers wrote about the dangerous homosexuals, and more people began to recognize themselves as such and be endangered, and intrigued, by what that recognition might mean.

Wilde's utopian vision of love between men remains, in Britain and beyond, a creation myth of the public male homosexual identity. Speaking at his trial Wilde launched a passionate defence of homosexual desire:

> It is in this century misunderstood, so much misunderstood that it may be described as 'the love that dare not speak its name', and on that account of it I am placed where I am now. It is beautiful, it is fine, it is the noblest form of affection. There is nothing unnatural about it.[2]

Such a statement can almost be seen as a rallying cry for the century of LGBTQ rights activism that was to follow, and Wilde became one of its first martyrs.

Bosie became a footnote in the story: an embodiment of 'evil twink energy', a poisoned apple whose path through life left a wake of destruction that led to the great hero's downfall. Yet Bosie – the man, his desires, his attitudes, and his foibles – was just as integral to the eruption of homosexuality into the public sphere as was Wilde. Bosie set the trial in motion. Indeed, it was actually Bosie, and not Wilde, who had coined the term 'the love that dare not speak its name' in one of his poems. No less than Wilde, Bosie shaped and was shaped by the sexual attitudes and cultures of his time, and Bosie's later life of far-right political involvement is just as unpleasant and illuminating as his years with Oscar.

After Wilde's death, Bosie married a bisexual poet named Olive Custance, and when their marriage went downhill he converted to Catholicism and began espousing increasingly anti-Semitic views. He wrote articles for the anti-Semitic magazine *Vigilante* accusing various people of plots to undermine British masculinity with Jewish homosexuality, and in 1920 co-founded a magazine called *Plain English* that advertised copies of the anti-Semitic conspiracy theory *The Protocols of the Elders of Zion*, defamed leftists and the Irish, and accused figures as right-wing and conventionally masculine as Winston Churchill of being involved in Jewish conspiracies to undermine the war effort. (Churchill eventually sued, and won). After a period of imprisonment, Bosie died poor and obscure in 1945. Only two people attended his funeral.[3]

For years, gay people have remembered Oscar as one of their own, but neglected Bosie as someone who has anything to tell us about how homosexuality came to be. Why do we choose to remember the witty and glamorous Wilde, and to forget the Machiavellian, anti-Semitic, and louche Bosie? And more crucially, why do we assume that Wilde's life and attitudes shaped the track record of the project of homosexuality better than Bosie's? Bosie was hardly the first gay to become obsessed with far-right and racist politics, or to confuse liberation with the freedom to live out his own desires and elevated class status.

Bad Gays is a book about such characters, a book about the gay people in history who do not flatter us, and whom we cannot make into heroes: the liars, the powerful, the criminal, and the successful. From Alexander the Great to J. Edgar Hoover, our history is littered with them. Unlike our heroes, however – people like Oscar Wilde, Audre Lorde, and Alan Turing – we rarely remember them as gay. And yet their sexuality was just as important an influence on their lives as those whom we celebrate, and their stories have much to tell us about how the sexual identities we understand today came to exist.

Over the course of this book we will profile these evil and complicated queers from our history. Among their ranks are emperors and criminals, fascist thugs and famous artists, austere puritans and debauched bon viveurs, yet all of them have one thing in common – they engaged in same-sex behaviour that, in the context of today's society, we might understand as, somehow, *gay*. By examining the interplay of their lives and their sexualities, this book investigates the failure of homosexuality as an identity and a political project.

'Failure' seems like a harsh word, and this assessment, while our primary argument in this book, is of course incomplete. There is indeed hope for queer forms, and our history contains many vital, living histories of struggle, alliance, and solidarity. In the conclusion we will think a bit about how these histories and the darker stories we've spent the book telling might exist in productive tension as we think about the future of gay lives in Europe and the United States.[4]

The failure, however, of mainstream, actually existing white male homosexuality to enact liberation and its embrace instead of full integration into the burning house of the couple-form, the family unit, and what we might hopefully call late-stage capitalism is real, and it is arranged on three primary axes: first, its separation from and fear of gender non-conformity; second, its simultaneous appropriation of the bodies and sexualities of racialized people and denial of those people's full humanity, political participation, and equality; and third, its incessant focus on the bourgeois project of 'sexuality' itself.

The first theme is explored in the scholarly work of people like Susan Stryker, who have pointed out that homosexuality's project of self-justification has often depended on claiming normalcy at the expense of a gender non-conforming Other: the trans woman, the street queen, the person not respectable enough to 'pass'.[5] The second is examined by people like C. Riley Snorton, Jules Gill-Peterson, Ann Stoler, and Anne McClintock, who have described the ways that the bodies of racialized and colonized people and ideas about their social organization have served as the literal substance of white metropolitan homosexual and transgender subjectivities and identities.[6] And the third has been discussed by a variety of queer Marxist scholars, from gay liberationists themselves,[7] to classic texts on the emergence of gay identity and its relationship to capitalism,[8] to Christopher Chitty's recent intervention into the correspondence between crises of capitalism and the persecution of poor and working-class sodomites.[9] This book aims to explore these themes not through scholarly argument, but through storytelling: by retelling the stories of a set of queer lives that are individually fascinating and horrifying, and that collectively communicate a version – *our version* – of the story of the evolution and failure of white male homosexual identities.

It can be very easy to assume that the way we think about identities has always been the same. Our race, gender, sexual orientation, or nationality can seem like such an important, intrinsic part of ourselves that we assume they must have been important for people living in the past as well. But identities are, as Stryker has said, 'where the rubber of larger social and cultural systems hits the road of lived experience'.[10] They are constantly changing and being changed by the shifting structural realities of life, by systems of production and exchange, by the ways that we relate to one another.[11]

Even the idea that people have a specific 'sexuality' is remarkably recent – perhaps only 150 years old, emerging out of the rapidly industrializing colonial metropolises of Europe.[12] The rigid segmentation of time into separated zones of work and leisure, along with moral panics about 'backwards' people intended to justify colonial expansion and incursions into the supposedly immoral private lives of the working classes, inculcated the idea that who you fucked made you who you were.[13] Even after the invention of 'homosexuality' (and 'heterosexuality') in the late nineteenth century, most people who felt same-sex love and desire did not want to convert their feelings into identities, to subscribe to being medicalized and set apart.[14]

These feelings were, instead, sources of shame, crimes for which they could be punished, and social taboos. As some people began to fight for their recognition and against medicalizing systems, movements began to emerge. The people who led these movements – at least, the ones that have succeeded in winning state recognition – were often not working-class or people of colour, but instead members of the emerging bourgeoisie who sought to assign positive values to their sexual acts within the prevailing value systems of their time.[15] And often, as we will see in this book, to bad ends.

At the same time, working-class people, colonized people, and people of colour have consistently lived, fought for, manifested, and expressed forms of social and sexual expression that have challenged both social prejudice towards sexual and gender minorities *and* the bourgeois politics of the gay elite.[16] These challenges have often been bitterly resisted by that elite in their time, while still – owing to their embrace of mass politics and disruptive organizing – having far-reaching effects in our queer lives. Often, after the fact, the queer elite will belatedly acknowledge these people, movements, moments, and struggles in an attempt to incorporate them into the dominant story of what it means to be gay or lesbian or trans, as though the working-class gays and sex workers, drag queens, and trans women of colour at the Stonewall Inn in New York City's West Village threw bricks at cops in order to win marriage equality for the gay and lesbian donor class.[17]

It is this process of struggle and contestation that has *created* the very idea of what being gay or queer is – it has marked the production of queer cultures, the discussion of queer lives, and queer people's search for historical examples to justify their own acts and identities. Even the term 'gay' has changed; fifty years ago, the term had a broader meaning that included queer and bisexual people, transgender people, transvestites, and more: anyone who lived openly outside the heterosexual and cissexist norms of a more conservative society, and suffered as a result. Today, it tends to refer to a more limited idea of same-gender sexual attraction. These definitions, too, are sites of struggle and negotiation.[18]

It can be difficult, therefore, to find the right terminology to discuss people who might fit into such a category today, when such ideas and identities did not exist in their society. Can you call someone like James VI and I, a man who almost certainly had sex with other men, a *homosexual*, when that identity did not even exist as a concept at the time? When he was ruling England and Scotland, and beginning his campaigns of colonization in Ireland and America, nobody thought who they *fucked* had anything to do with who they *were*. So what does it mean to call James, or the Emperor Hadrian, or any number of nefarious nellies from history, 'gay'?

We have decided to use that present-day term as a way of putting today's homosexuality under a microscope and figuring out why it is troubled and incomplete, and why it failed to live up to its utopian promises of liberation. By discussing these people and their shared behaviours in relation to each other, we can begin to draw out characteristics and stories that might shed a light on how a contemporary gay identity came to exist – from ideas of what it means to be 'a man', to how same-sex desire has influenced major historical events, to how the dreaded heterosexuals came to exist, to understand themselves as opposed to queers, and to fear, police, and repress us. Our subjects may not have held a 'gay' identity, but their lives can tell us so much about why we do.

If 'gay' is an imprecise term of convenience, so is 'bad'. While some of the folks in the book are, without doubt, *bad* – fascists, murderers, and other such scumbags – many are a bit more complicated. We can start to look at their lives in the context of the times in which they lived, and see how, within that context, their decisions influenced or were influenced by their sex lives.

Many were profoundly traumatized by the guilt they felt as a result of their sexual desires: pushed by society into lives they found themselves unable to lead, they made strange choices, or ended up damaging the world in their efforts to reform it. Nonetheless, the links between their negative actions and their sexual desires are worth exploring, worth expanding upon. For example: can we really understand Roy Cohn's aggressive political witch-hunting and fear of secret subversion outside the context of his own negative feelings regarding his homosexuality? It's for these reasons we use the categories of 'bad' and 'gay' – as provocations to talk more deeply about what we understand both words to mean.

If it is not clear enough that we are not writing as homophobes, ask our boyfriends, our lovers, our friends. Both of us are deeply shaped by homosexuality but also deeply unsatisfied by it. This is why we have subtitled this book 'A Homosexual History', and we mean that precisely: not (just) that we are homosexuals or that this is (only) a history of homosexuality or homosexual behaviours, but that this book is a dance through homosexuality's usable and abusable pasts. We learn from the broad spectrum of theory by and about queer and trans people, and write from our position as white gay men, about a series of people whose behaviours, attitudes, and actions can help us understand why and how white male homosexuality, as a political, identitarian, and emancipatory project, has failed.

The Birth of Homosexuality

When we say 'gays didn't exist before the nineteenth century', we do not mean, of course, that men were not getting it on with men, or women with women; or that people were not living or understanding their gender differently from how it was assigned at birth or how their society understood it. In fact, when LGBTQ people in Europe and the US in the twentieth century started searching back through history for their queer antecedents, there was plenty of documentary evidence that same-sex fucking and loving had a long history – mostly from antiquity, from anthropological and ethnographic records from the colonies, and through the records and transcripts of crime and punishment. Sex between men in Europe has been punished for centuries, of course; biblical law lays down explicitly that it is forbidden. But the way people think about it, and what they think is *wrong* with it, has changed.

In Europe, throughout the Middle Ages sex between two men was known as sodomy. Unlike today, when sodomy means anal sex, for most of the mediaeval period it simply referred to sexual acts which would not or could not result in procreation. In fact, if a woman sucked a man's dick in mediaeval England, she could be regarded as a sodomite. The reason, therefore, for the prohibition of sodomy was that it was *unnatural*, against God's plan for mankind to 'be fruitful, and multiply'.

Sometimes this can make it difficult to discern whether accusations of sodomy and sinful behaviour thrown at kings or noblemen at the time were supposed to imply they were fucking other men or just fucking around. As this behaviour was a sin, its prosecution was left up to the powerful church courts. In the early mediaeval period sodomy between two men was not singled out as a special sin; like all others, it carried its penance. It was only later in mediaeval Europe that same-sex sex acts accreted a unique stigma. Around the 1300s the Italian city-states began to implement the first civil laws against such behaviour, and in the early fourteenth century Philip of France realised how useful the accusation of sodomy could be in repressing the powerful Knights Templar, to whom he owed a large sum of money he could not pay back. It wasn't until 1533 that English law had its first anti-sodomy legislation. The public sentiment around sodomy, along with the usefulness of accusations in riling up the masses in the service of reaction, was too great to remain in the hands of the church courts, so it moved into the realm of the civil courts.

With the invention of such civil laws, sodomy stopped simply being just a sin and became a crime as well. With it, a new wave of stigmatization began to emerge around it, one that proved remarkably useful for the monarchs and politicians who could wield the laws in their own favour. For Henry VIII, who implemented the 1533 Buggery Act, the accusation of same-sex behaviour became a useful tool for prosecuting monks and priests who had long been associated, in the public mind, with lewd man-on-man action. Henry VIII's desire to crush the clergy was not simply about his own sex life; he was also trying to seize their lands and enclose common lands, wrestling power and wealth from the hands of the Church. Therefore, the punishment named in the Buggery Act was not only execution (priests and monks could not even be executed for murder at this time) but also the seizure of their land and property by the monarch. Throughout the early modern period, many people still regarded men sleeping with men, and women with women, to be sinful, but it was also solidified in the popular imagination as a crime. Society was rapidly changing; the enclosures started by Henry continued over the sixteenth and seventeenth centuries. Cities, as a result, exploded in size. When the Buggery Act was passed there were fifty thousand people living in London; within seventy years there were almost a quarter of a million, and by the end of the Victorian era there were over 6 million people living in the largest city the world had ever seen. The increasing urbanisation across Europe was accompanied by worries about just what this new 'working class' was getting up to in their sparse free time, living in close quarters and, in the eyes of the emerging bourgeoisie, worryingly lacking in moral scruples.

Alongside wider moral panics about aberrant sexual behaviour and prostitution, the ruling classes in Victorian England became increasingly worried about same-sex sexual acts taking place in their cities. As well as reinforcing anti-sodomy legislation with the 1861 Offences Against the Person Act (which, although removing the rarely implemented death sentence for buggery, introduced a new punishment of ten-years-to-life in penal servitude), in 1885 they also passed the Criminal Law Amendment Act, criminalising, for the first time, not just anal sex but all forms of sexual activity between men, including the solicitation of sex, between men. Cruising, kissing, chatting up,

slapping arses – all banned. It was with this law that they perse-
cuted Wilde, and Alan Turing too, more than half a century later.

When colonizers first reached the shores of Africa and the Americas, and began to murder the people they found there and steal
their land and resources, they encountered societies that tended
to have varying social functions for people engaging in behaviour
Europeans considered to be 'same-sex' or gender-transgressive.
These identities were often rooted in the close connection between
sex and kinship and sometimes had religious, political, or social-
reproductive functions. The presence of people whom colonists
could call sodomites and cross-dressers provided a useful religious
and political justification for their murder and subjugation.

At the same time, stories of these strange colonial sins (in
French, 'doing it colonial-style' came to be slang for sodomy)
became encoded into the fabric of European discourse, even
becoming sources of haunted, deadly inspiration for some European homosexual figures.[19] Same-sex sexual activity in France
had been decriminalised after the revolution when sodomy laws,
as with many other laws regulating the behaviour of the popular
classes, were left out of the 1791 penal code; and that principle was imposed in most territories (including the Netherlands
and much of pre-unification Germany) that came under French
control, although legal harassment and moral opprobrium still
often targeted people who engaged in same-sex acts there. (Post-
unification, Germany adopted the Prussian legal code of 1870,
making sodomy illegal.) Turkey had also decriminalised same-
sex behaviour under the Ottoman Empire.

It was in the mid-nineteenth century that, for the first time,
groups of doctors, scientists, sociologists, and queer people
themselves began to formulate their own theories about what all
this sexual desire might *be*, might *mean*. As colonialism and race
science were beginning to create taxonomies of humans based on
traits and behaviours, sex theorists began to conceptualise into
life a new type of human – the homosexual.

In Germany the lawyer and writer Karl Heinrich Ulrichs
acknowledged to his friends and family that he was *that way*, so
to speak, in the 1860s. He began to write a series of pamphlets

under the collective title 'Studies on the Riddle of Male-Male Love', in which he developed the theory that, rather than same-sex acts being a *thing* people did, instead the desire to *do those things* was, in itself, part of some people's nature. This was a theory not just of sex, but of sexuality. Ulrichs described same-sex-loving men as 'Urnings' and women as 'Urinden'. More than that, he campaigned publicly in his role as a lawyer for the repeal of anti-sodomy legislation in Prussia, and began correspondence with other sexologists interested in his ideas.[20]

One such man was the Hungarian journalist and campaigner Karl-Maria Kertbeny, who wrote his own texts calling for legal reform arguing that these urges were innate. Claiming solely an 'anthropological interest' in the subject (*whatever you say, queen*), he coined new terms to describe the phenomenon – among them, the term 'homosexual'. Importantly, he also looked back into history for examples of homosexual men with which to argue that this phenomenon was not new: an early example of a gay history. Sexologists and campaigners such as Ulrichs, Kertbeny and, later, the psychiatrist Richard von Krafft-Ebing began to popularise the idea that homosexuality should be understood as neither sin nor crime but in clinical terms, as a medical condition some are born into.[21]

The stage was set for our contemporary understanding of homosexuality. Today, Krafft-Ebing's psychiatric model is, with some amendments, still regarded by many as a sufficient 'explanation' for the gays, while political campaigning and cultural changes have slowly begun to push back the notion that homosexuality is either a sin or a crime. Likewise, the idea of homosexuality as a holistic and inherent part of one's *identity*, rather than just a type of sex anyone could have, is now established as a norm. The political model built on the back of it – that, as gays do what they do because it's who they are, and we can't help who we are, it would be cruel and illiberal to repress their nature or withhold their civil rights – still holds sway. Indeed, in much of the West the idea that homosexuality is an immutable characteristic is now so ingrained that 'Born this Way', once a stigmatizing medical explanation, is now both a rallying cry and pop anthem, rising up in opposition to conservative notions that homosexuality is an acquired deviance that can be 'cured' with 'therapy'.

This binary model of thinking about homosexuality is so deeply internalised that to suggest that one might choose homosexuality as a positive choice, or even be able to have some control over the shaping of your own desires, is regarded as hate speech. Within liberal circles, even when homosexuality is okay, even when it comes with pension rights and military service and a lovely flat with a balcony and a little dog, it's still an *affliction*.

Homosexuality's Career

However, it would take more than the detached, clinical and pejorative analysis of Krafft-Ebing to produce the shift from the crime of sodomy to the identity of homosexuality. Throughout the late nineteenth century, inspired by increasing discussion and organisation around the subject of 'Urnings', 'Uranians' and 'homosexuals', writers such as Wilde, John Addington Symonds, Walt Whitman, and Edward Carpenter helped try to flesh out, with varying degrees of success, the subjectivity of homosexuality – not just what it was, but how it felt, and what it might mean. Meanwhile, in Germany, the sexologist Magnus Hirschfeld, himself a gay man, established the 'Scientific-Humanitarian Committee' in 1897 and Institute for Sexual Science in 1919 to help support LGBTQ people and campaign for legal reform and social understanding. Lesbian activists, artists, and writers like Claire Waldoff, Johanna Elberskirchen and Lotte Hahm also thrived. Many transgender people found a refuge in Hirschfeld's institute; it provided police protection for dressing differently than their assigned gender at birth, and even rudimentary surgical and hormonal gender confirmation treatment – although Hirschfeld also attempted crude anti-trans 'corrective' surgeries, as we'll discuss later in the book.

Thus, from the turn of the century to the Nazi seizure of power, and especially in the time of the Weimar Republic (1919–33) after the end of the First World War, Germany sustained not just a political campaign for reform but a thriving queer social and cultural scene. With an understanding of homosexuality as a political and social identity, a social culture attached to that political understanding, and a variety of organizations – including some mass organizations – fighting for and defending legal rights, Germany during the Weimar years saw the first iteration of what we might call a popular LGBTQ movement. As with many such movements, there were disagreements – between masculinists and feminists, between socialists and anarchists and far-right fascists – but, fascinatingly, virtually all these writers and thinkers emphasized ethnographic records from colonized peoples as central to their understanding of who homosexuals were and what their culture might become.

Weimar-era gay magazines were full of references to colonized people and their supposedly exotic sexualities: from Native Americans to Africans (classified as 'nature-peoples' by racist anthropology) to the civilizations of India and China ('culture-peoples'), these writers thought same-sex activity in these cultures had been natural and socially accepted. It was only in European civilization that it had been outlawed and banned. This worldview combined potentially subversive critiques of European civilization's supposed superiority with fundamentally racist understandings of the differences between places, peoples, and cultures.

These movements were obliterated by fascism. Approximately one hundred thousand suspected homosexuals were arrested under the Nazi regime, of whom fifty thousand were sent to camps, where thousands died. Many hundreds of thousands more suppressed their lives, and thousands moved into exile. Clubs and bars were closed, and the archives of Hirschfeld's Institute for Sexual Science were among the first thrown into the flames during the infamous book burnings. After the war, in West Germany, things hardly improved: the Nazis' sharpening of anti-sodomy laws was not repealed by the West German government until 1969, and prison terms served in concentration camps were not considered to have been properly served at all. Gay men were freed from camps and sent directly back to jail, where tens of thousands of newly arrested men joined them.

The gay rights movements re-emerged in the 1950s. Many men and women had experienced same-sex environments for the first time during the Second World War and liked what they found there. Ideas that had been banned in Germany spread through émigrés and refugees. In the United States, as the movements began to emerge, the state also cracked down hard on both the emergent gay rights movement and on homosexuality more generally. As part of a widespread paranoia fabricated by the right, the government associated homosexuality with communism and understood it a national security threat. Thousands of queer men and women mostly living 'in the closet' had their private lives investigated and were fired from federal employment and blacklisted from their professions. The gay rights movement, still a largely underground network of small groups and publications, received both a fresh intake of activists and renewed repression. In many organisations, leftists, communists, and community organisers were purged by other LGBTQ activists worried about government infiltration and desperate to remain 'respectable'. The reverse was also true.

It wasn't until the late 1960s, after a six-day insurrection at Stonewall by largely working-class LGBTQ people, including many people of colour, that the middle-class, gradualist homophile organizations (which had albeit started with a surge of Communist activity in Los Angeles in the 1950s before turning sharply right) were superseded by a new generation of activists. Rather than advocating for incremental civil rights victories achieved by respectable political campaigning, this new movement demanded gay liberation now. Gays (at this time more of an umbrella term covering all manner of sexual and gender identities) would no longer live in the shadows and request toleration – they would 'come out' as their true selves and win their rights by being unmistakably themselves.

The huge social movement that followed, driven by a core belief in the value of self-actualization, advanced the idea that to overcome political oppression queer people also had to overcome their personal shame. Within this context, writers, poets, and artists looked back through history to find examples to prove that *we had always been here*, and that our lives need not be lived cloaked in shame or fear. If Oscar Wilde, Sappho, Langston Hughes, Federico García Lorca, Lucía Sánchez Saornil, Leonardo da Vinci, Billie Holiday, and Alexander the Great could be gay, and if they could be gay and live their lives to the fullest, then so could you. These people may have had their true selves repressed, both by their peers and by history, but by uncovering it LGBTQ people were building their own histories.

The Death (and Life) of Homosexuality

This was important work, helping people who were raised in fear and self-hatred to live happily, fully, and *with pride*. But is it not time we also look at those whom the early gay rights pioneers were less keen to claim as *family*, as *one of us*? Or the people among those pioneers – the people who helped bake the cake of identity and desire that now defines our lives – who perhaps irreparably harmed the substance of 'gay' itself? Within their lives, buffeted by the winds of history and social circumstance, many same-sex-loving and gender non-conforming chose terrible paths and inflicted appalling damage upon others.

If we are to accept that some of the greatest artists, activists, and poets of history were guided and motivated by their sexuality, why not the criminals, despots, and bigots? Within their lives are valuable lessons regarding how we came to understand ourselves, about the challenges LGBTQ people have faced – not always honourably – through history, and how sex, love, and desire have led people to make world-changing decisions. It is not simply that these are fascinating, complex lives that compel us towards understanding homosexuality. They also ask us to pose the question of the whole notion of gay heroes: why do we choose to remember, and why do we choose to forget?

When a gay man becomes a fascist, how does his homosexuality affect his attraction to the politics of venerating the state as though it were a go-go boy dancing on a box? When a king takes young male lovers and is then blackmailed, and when the process of forcing peasants off their land is tied to the same moral opprobrium that threatens the king, what are the transactions of power and influence at play? When a bisexual anthropologist relies on primitivist projections of colonized Others to find answers for how she might live now, in a society that sees her queerness as terrifying and backwards and a threat to the modern, how might her desires have affected the mythic nostalgia of her work and thus the course of twentieth-century anthropological thinking? Why do configurations of identity and desire that seem to have expired continue to hold such power over so many people, including us, the authors? Why can't we finally kill or abandon homosexuality and do something else, something better, instead?

Ultimately, this book is a project of demystification and an act of love. 'Gay is good,' went the old slogan, but it's no good at all on its own. As you will see, many of the queers with the very worst political goals have wanted to position themselves as heirs to a secret or magical kingdom, as the sons of a long line of heroes. The process of making the movement and the identity has often involved reifying, recreating, and worshipping power and evil in their most brute forms. Maybe it is time that homosexuality itself dies, that we find new and more functional and more appropriate configurations for our politics and desires. Or maybe being queer is just as transitory and incomplete as anything else. Maybe all of us are lost and scared, subject to forces beyond our control, and trying to figure out how to configure our unruly desires and our politics into an ethical way of being in the world.

If there is anything of homosexuality to be saved, it is its reconstruction of the concept of the family. Not born into fixed kin, we get to choose ours. This can be a project of socialization but also of politicization, of understanding to which kind of political 'we' we wish to belong. Understanding how we became a 'we' in the first place – and interrogating the extent to which that 'we' even makes sense, given how different 'we' have been from one another and how terribly 'we' have often been treated by one another – might help more of us choose better. Then the real work begins.

1

Hadrian

Hadrian was born the son of empire. His father was a high-ranking and wealthy Roman senator who, as a soldier, had fought in the Roman provinces in modern-day North Africa, and was the cousin of the future emperor Trajan. Hadrian, like his father and Trajan, was probably born in Italica, the first Roman city to be built outside Italy, near modern-day Seville, in January of AD 76.

Hadrian's family had settled in the Roman province of Hispania Baetica hundreds of years before he was born. An ancestor, probably an Italian who had fought to conquer the region for Rome, was given some land in the newly subdued territory upon his retirement. He married a local woman and became a farmer, a common story typical of Rome's strategy of colonization and empire-building. To control the territory was not enough: an empire was built on cultural dominance, and the Romanisation of new provinces happened by ensuring the ruling elites of those territories were acculturated into Roman habits, tastes, and values, often through marriage. Baths and amphitheatres were built, gladiatorial games introduced, and (in much of the empire) Latin adopted as the official and primary language. From these colonies new generations of soldiers could be raised, resources could be extracted, and in time the people would come to regard themselves not as vanquished, but as Roman. At the same time, the colonies could have an influence back at the centre of Rome – some desired, some more insidious – including new ideas around sexuality.

Hadrian's family, like Trajan's, held political power, providing senators for Rome going back over five generations. Mr and Mrs Hadrianus were an exemplary provincial family in this regard, and their son, little Publius Aelius, may have expected to follow this tradition of making war and retiring into minor public service. The growth of the empire meant that the senate was now populated with senators from further afield than Italy and Rome, especially Spain, with its prosperous silver resources, and Greece, whose classical culture was hugely influential in Rome itself.

But trauma at a young age diverted Hadrian from his family's well-worn path. In AD 86, when Hadrian was just ten years old, both of his parents died. According to Roman custom, the young orphan and his sister were then adopted by a wealthy male relative; it was just Hadrian's luck that his new guardians were an official named Publius Acilius Attianus, and his father's cousin, a young military officer named Marcus Ulpius Traianus, the future emperor Trajan. Ostensibly, this guardianship was for the safe protection of the orphan's inherited property until he was old enough to take care of it himself, but it seems Trajan extended his role into a more paternal one, and set about planning the education of Hadrian. When Hadrian turned fourteen, Trajan sent for him in Rome.

The Roman Empire was barely 100 years old when Hadrian arrived. Just twenty-five years earlier the city had been devastated by a great fire under Nero; during Hadrian's lifetime the Colosseum was opened, the volcano of Vesuvius erupted, burying Pompeii, and numerous military victories were achieved on the empire's northern border in the Dacian Wars. It was a golden age, with a great flourishing of economic and cultural wealth. Even for a youth as well travelled as Hadrian, it must have been a thrilling place to find himself.

Hadrian took to his education well; he had a taste for earlier writers such as Cato the Elder, rather than the preferred statesman of his tutors, Cicero.[1] But most notably, even at that young age, he fell in love with Greek culture, a love affair that would shape both his life and the Roman Empire. His passion for Greek literature and history was intense enough to earn him the nick-name *Graeculus*, or 'Greekling', which was not entirely flattering. Greece had been a dominant Mediterranean power long before the rise of Rome, and what was known as 'Hellenistic Greece', a loose affiliation of sometimes warring, sometimes allied city-states and leagues, survived right through the period of the Roman Republic. It was not until the time of the first emperor, Augustus, that Greece was finally annexed in 27 BCE. By this stage, Greek influence was already deeply seated in Roman art, philosophy, architecture, administration, banking, and literature. Trade between the two cultures was long established, and young Roman men were sent to Greek cities to learn from the schools there. Many Romans could speak Greek, facilitated by the large numbers of Greeks, freemen and traders as well as slaves, who lived in Rome.

Despite their nascent strength as a republic, and Greek's waning influence in the region, there was something in Greek culture that the Romans not only admired but aspired to. In the third Century BCE, the Roman nobility became increasingly Greek in their habits, a phenomenon known as 'Hellenization', and those with a particular taste for Greek culture were known as 'philhellenic'. Under the rule of the emperor Nero, a notorious tyrant who, incidentally, was said to have twice been in a same-sex union (a truly Bad Gay), philhellenism became even more pronounced.

Yet there was also an ambivalence in this relationship. The Romans, after all, had conquered the Greeks, and to what extent could you truly want to replicate a loser's culture? They filled their homes with Greek sculptures; but they were looted sculp-tures, their display as much a mark of subjugation as respect. When Greek-speaking Romans addressed the Senate, their words were translated into Latin, as much as a sign of inferiority as to help with comprehension. Even within the more Hellenistic aristocracy, there were significant figures who saw Greece as a moral threat, if not a military one. Indeed, Cato the Elder, whom Hadrian studied enthusiastically, was one such figure. Greece, Cato felt, was a degenerate and decadent culture and its adoption would bring trouble for the Romans, whom he saw as a people of noble simplicity and strength. Addressing his own child he said, 'I shall speak of those Greeks in a suitable place, son Marcus, telling what I learned at Athens, and what benefit it is to look into their books, – not to master them. I shall prove them a most worthless and unteachable race. Believe that this is uttered by a prophet: whenever that folk impart its literature, it will corrupt everything.'[2]

This Roman ambivalence, that the Greeks were both wise and decadent, worthy of study but worth being wary of, rang down through history, and has had a significant impact on the history of homosexuality. As the classical literature of the Greeks and Romans was supposedly 'rediscovered' by scholars in western Europe in the Renaissance, many adopted the same prejudices and intellectual arguments that were being fought almost two millennia earlier. Greek attitudes towards same-sex relationships were known about, and were hard for good Christian academics to square with their otherwise fulsome admiration of the virtues of classical Greece. While most Victorian scholars were disgusted by the 'unspeakable vice of the Greeks', as the uptight Mr Cornwallis refers to it in E.M. Forster's *Maurice*, those who found their desires drifting in a similar direction found in Greek culture a heroic example that *their sort* had indeed always existed, and began mining Greek literature for heroes and storylines that might serve as a defence of the unspeakable vice. The works of Greeks like Plutarch and Plato were used to help imagine a positive model for male and female same-sex relationships, although, as we'll see, neither the Greeks nor the Victorians had quite the same concept of the 'homosexual' that we have today.

For the Greeks, the concept did not meaningfully exist at all; the social identities we today understand in the West as a gay man or a bisexual woman, for example, simply weren't something that people recognised. Greece was not a single political entity with a set of laws and customs that everybody followed; different city-states developed different sexual cultures. Across Greece, sexual activity between men was common; the important prohibitions were not focused on gender, but status (and hence age).

In Plato's *Symposium*, Aristophanes uses a myth to demonstrate the nature of love, explaining that lovers are the two reunited components of single souls split in two by Zeus. This myth of soulmates is not as structured around ideas of heterosexual compatibility as you might presume. Aristophanes explicitly mentions same-sex relationships, but the important qualification is that they are between men of different *ages*. For Aristophanes, if not necessarily for Plato, sex between men and boys was not merely tolerable, but noble in itself. Of such people, Aristophanes says that 'while they are boys … they fall in love with men, they enjoy sex with men and they like to be embraced by men. These boys are the ones who are outstanding in their childhood and youth, because they're inherently more manly than others. I know they sometimes get called immoral, but that's wrong: their actions aren't prompted by immorality but by courage, manliness, and masculinity. They incline towards their own characteristics in others.'[3] Worryingly for us, he says such men go on to become politicians.

What is fundamental to understand, of course, is that this form of relationship is *only* seen as good and honourable between men and teenage boys, while sexual behaviour between men of the same age was taboo. This is an inversion of our own social norms. Today the defining characteristic of such a relationship to observers would be the abusive power imbalance. In the same manner, in Greek society it would also be the age difference that would be regarded as the core characteristic of the relationship, although in a positive way, and not the gender roles.

This form of pederastic relationship was seen to have many qualities; in the *Symposium*, Phaedrus suggests that the loyalty between male lovers and their aversion to being shamed in front of each other by acts of cowardice offered them a unique advantage in organising a society, claiming that 'the best possible organisation [for a] battalion would be for it to consist of lovers and their boyfriends … A handful of such men, fighting side by side, could conquer the whole world'.[4] In fact, such a battalion *did* exist in the city-state of Thebes. The Sacred Band of Thebes was a military unit made up of 150 pairs of male lovers and was regarded as the most elite unit in the Theban army, its soldiers being of unusual bravery and moral character.

Still, the acceptance of a certain type of same-sex behaviour is littered with qualifications concerning status. Often, sexual relationships between men involving anything up the bum were frowned upon, because anal sex is too close to penis-in-vagina sex. This would make the receptive partner in anal sex something like a woman or a prostitute, as in many circumstances 'homosexual anal penetration [was] treated neither as an expression of love nor as a response to the stimulus of beauty, but as an aggressive act demonstrating the superiority of the active to the passive partner', a drop in status too humiliating to be sanctioned.[5]

To be the receptive partner in anal sex was regarded as being *kinaidos*, or effeminate: there's no escaping it, bottom-shaming is as old as European civilization itself, baked into the deep misogyny of patriarchal societies. This prohibition on anal did not apply to men visiting male sex workers, or men having sex with enslaved males, so long as the man of higher status was the one doing the penetrating, a good illustration of how, in Greek society, status was the key determinant of the nature of sexual activity.

This early history of same-sex relationships in Greece and Rome is vital to understanding Hadrian's story. The philhellenic Romans took up many of the same concepts and attitudes towards homosexuality, but with an important difference. While for the Greeks the pederastic relationship had a pedagogical and philosophical basis – to ensure the induction of noble males into the intellectual and political society they were to dominate – for the Romans the focus was instead on the sensual.

Roman culture was openly celebratory of male dominance and power. There are no European cultures for whom the hard cock was such a symbol of worship; indeed the Vestal Virgins, the priestesses of Vesta, the goddess of the hearth, literally attended to the cult of Fascinus, a deity depicted as a disembodied erect penis, usually with wings. Their role was to tend to the holy fire at the centre of Rome, from which any Roman citizen could light their own fire. As such, the fire symbolised the continuance of

Rome and the integrity of the state. That a hard cock was one of the subjects of the Vestal's adoration is no coincidence, as the integrity of the male body was a symbol of a free Roman's political status.[6]

That's because for a free man, a citizen of Rome, to be the penetrated partner in a same-sex act was, in some way, a violation of the integrity of his body. To be a free Roman meant your body *could not* be violated. In the words of historian Amy Richlin, 'To be penetrated, for a Roman, was degrading both in a physical sense of invasion, rupture, and contamination, and in a class sense: the penetrated person's body was likened to the body of a slave.'[7] This emphasis on virility and conquest is slightly different to the Greeks' obsession with pederasty and pedagogy, but to much the same ends, and, as we will see in later chapters, becomes part of the dynamic of the politics of masculinity, and the masculinity of politics, throughout modern European history.

When Marcus Calpurnius Bibulus accused his enemy and co-consul Julius Caesar of being 'Queen of Bithynia', the accusation was not that that Caesar was gay, but that he had been fucked in his younger days by Nicomedes IV, the king of Bithynia. These accusations clearly stuck. Even in Caesar's moment of triumph, having crushed the Gauls in the Gallic Wars, a popular rhyme in Rome began '*Gallias Caesar subegit, Caesarem Nicomedes*' (Caesar subjugated the Gauls, Nicomedes subjugated Caesar). It seems to be true what the senator Haterius said, that 'unchastity (*impudicitia*: allowing anal penetration) is a source of accusation for a freeborn (male), a necessity for a slave, and a duty for a freed slave'.[8]

Status and freedom, then, were vital to Roman conceptions of both sexuality and society. Indeed, after his education, Hadrian took his first official appointment, as a member of a *decemviri*, a ten-man commission that ruled upon the formal status of people. It was a minor role but accepted as a fitting first step into a future senatorial career. From there, he took up the role of a military tribune with the Legio II Adiutrix, a military legion stationed in Aquincum (modern-day Budapest).[9] A military tribune was a high-ranking officer who was organisationally, although not militarily, second-in-command of the legion. An appointed position, it required administrative skill, but it was also a position for young members of the senatorial rank to learn the qualities and competencies deemed necessary for future service as a senator.

It was expected that most young men on such a career path would become a military tribune for a short time. Hadrian, however, served in the role three times, for three different legions, giving him significant political advantages in the future. More than this, according to his biographer, Anthony Birley, it was in Aquincum that Hadrian developed his lifelong ability to talk to people across the class system.[10]

When Hadrian was twenty-two, serving his second tour as a tribune, Emperor Domitian, a ruthless and moralistic autocrat, was assassinated in a palace coup. His enemies in the Senate damned his memory, melting down his statues and pulling down his victory arches, and replaced him with a safe pair of hands, Nerva. The toppling of Domitian had been unpopular with his elite Praetorian Guard, and Nerva was probably a compromise candidate between the guard and the Senate, not least because, being old and childless. He left the door open for either side to make the political manoeuvrings to secure their own candidate not too far down the line. Nerva attempted to soothe both sides, but pleased no one. His authority was fatally compromised, so he named a successor in the hope that this might buoy up his flagging regime. He chose a popular young general who was busy fighting for the empire on its Germanic borders, Marcus Ulpius Traianus. In the *Historia Augusta*, the general was said to have been told the news by a special messenger dispatched to Upper Germany: the future Hadrian.[11] It's no surprise Hadrian wanted to bring these good tidings, for Marcus Ulpius Traianus was his adoptive guardian: Trajan.

Trajan did not have to wait long to become emperor. The following year Nerva suffered a stroke and died, and with his death, new opportunities opened up to the young Hadrian.

By age twenty-five he was back in Rome, acting as go-between for the emperor and the Senate. In short order he became first the Senate record-keeper, and then the tribune of the plebs.

Originally this role had been reserved for non-noble Romans, and was elected by their assembly. Among their rights and duties was the ability to lay the demands of the people before the aristocrats in the Senate, to intercede on the people's behalf in disputes with the magistrates, and to propose legislation. For the next decade or so, Hadrian ping-ponged between working in Rome, including as a praetor, and fighting on the empire's northern borders in what is now eastern Europe.

In Rome, Hadrian managed to integrate himself even further into Trajan's life, becoming increasingly close with the emperor's family, especially his wife, Pompeia Plotina. Plotina was, like Hadrian, born in Hispania, and was a keen advocate of Greek culture and values. It was probably Plotina who found him his political roles on Trajan's staff, and it was almost certainly she who arranged for him to be married into the family, to Trajan's grand-niece Vibia Sabina.[12] Sabina had been raised by her mother in Trajan's household since she was a baby, following the death of her father.

Given what we know already of Roman obsession with status and sexual mores, it should come as no surprise that marriages within the senatorial rank tended to be political rather than romantic, but Hadrian's was far from a love match. Sabina was intelligent and educated, but she and Hadrian were said not to get on, and he treated her shabbily throughout their marriage. This was not helped by the fact that Hadrian clearly preferred boys, and Sabina was, according to some sources, the lover of her best friend, Julia Balbilla.[13] This lavender marriage produced no children, but she performed her political duty and stayed close to Hadrian's side for most of his life, eventually dying just a year before him.

Some such arrangements work surprisingly well, but theirs was a cold and cruel marriage. It probably didn't help that Hadrian's love for younger men, in the Greek manner of *erastes* and *eromenos*, the ancient equivalent of a daddy top and twink bottom, was already a key part of his sex life, and was getting him in trouble. It seems that, as a younger man working for Trajan, he overstepped the bounds and started hitting on boys that the emperor himself regarded as his, demonstrating how deeply the pederastic model ran through the upper reaches of the empire. But he didn't leave it at that; in fact, one of the key criticisms of Hadrian was not merely that he had sex with younger men, something the philhellenic Romans tolerated, but that he fucked adult men, his peers, too.[14]

The twink theft of the perpetually horny Hadrian did not go unanswered and caused a serious rift between him and his benefactor, a situation that had repercussions later. Waiting for more benefaction, he received neither a job as a consul nor the expected announcement that he was 'Caesar', the heir to the emperor.

In the meantime, his location was not certain, but it seems likely that he was sent to Greece around 109, a trip that must have greatly excited and influenced him. It was an important time for the empire, and the focus of its cultural and military might was turning east. The Parthian Empire, which stretched from Armenia to the Hindu Kush, had ruled its territory for over three hundred years and had been pushing its borders up against the empire. The Parthians had long fought with Rome over both territory and client states, and Trajan wished to suppress and conquer them. He had already extended Roman territory into the Middle East, turning former client kingdoms into Roman provinces. Athens was rising in prominence and importance, and it was clear the empire needed another centre of power in the East.

Like every gay who goes on holiday to Greece, Hadrian grew a beard (distinguishing himself from the clean-shaven Romans), wined and dined with Athenian society, took in lectures and talked with philosophers, and became smitten with the culture. The feeling was mutual: Athens made him a citizen and in 112 he was made eponymous archon, the position of magistrate and ruler of the city, which he held for a year. The trip was clearly influential on him, imbuing in him not just a desire to further Hellenize the Roman Empire as a whole (and not just the aristocrats in the city of Rome), but also a desire to travel, and to rule directly.

Yet his stay in Greece was brief. In 114 Trajan began his military campaign against the Parthians, and Hadrian took control of a legion as a legate. Trajan's war was far more successful than previous Roman campaigns, allowing the empire to push into Mesopotamia for the first time. But it was undermined by a wave of rebellions throughout the eastern part of the empire, including a rebellion of Jews in the Kitos War, the suppression of which drew resources from the Parthian campaign and fatally undermined Roman attempts to finish them off. In 117, on campaign, Trajan had a stroke. He had made the empire larger than it had ever been, but also stretched to its limits, and, catastrophically, without an heir.

This was a crucial moment. As he lay on his deathbed, without a named successor, the fate of the empire hung in the balance. Luckily, a woman was at hand to sort things out. Plotina announced that her husband had named his heir, and it was to be her favourite, Hadrian. We will leave aside that Trajan himself never formally adopted Hadrian as his successor; the important thing was that the empire was not left leaderless. Hadrian informed the Senate in a letter that travelled with the dead emperor's ashes that the job was done, and he had the support of the troops of the eastern legions who felt Rome could not be left leaderless a second longer.[15] The Senate confirmed him, and he rewarded the soldiers with a bonus. He never forgot Plotina's role in his accession; upon her death four years later, she was, like her husband the emperor, deified and made part of the official imperial cult.

Hadrian's position was hardly safe. He had influential enemies and a demoralised army along its vast borders, spreading from modern-day Scotland to the Black Sea, from the Arabian Peninsula to the Straits of Gibraltar and beyond. He faced rebellions, insurrections, and incursions. Acquiring new territories was out of the question. So, instead, Hadrian marked his reign by consolidating what he had, attempting to create an integrated empire with a shared cultural foundation in Hellenism, and by building. And boy, did he build!

Hadrian's legacy is in his buildings, a project deeply tied in with his campaign to pacify and consolidate the empire. Wherever he travelled, he left everything from enormous fortifications to new temple complexes, walls, arches, and gates, even whole new cities. While most Roman emperors stayed in Rome, too paranoid to leave their scheming senators or Praetorian Guard unattended, Hadrian spent the majority of his rule travelling outside Italy. But before his campaign to turn the empire into a stable, peaceful polity could begin, he had to pacify the frontiers. With the help of his Greek friend (but of course), the fabulously named Marcius Turbo, as his closest, more trusted military adviser, he crushed the Jewish revolt in Roman Judea. Crushing more rebellions in North Africa, he left Turbo in charge of two provinces on the Mediterranean coast, returning to Rome to try and clean up a different mess. At home his Praetorian Guard had put down an alleged conspiracy against Hadrian in Rome with astonishing swiftness and brutality, a move that forever tarnished his relationship with the Senate.

He then began a series of sweeping reforms, both to sort Roman finances and win some political capital. New systems for child support and help for widows were announced, and a system for funding magistrates' travels from central coffers, rather than on the back of local communities, were introduced. But most significantly of all, Hadrian organised a forgiveness of private debt, symbolically burning the records of debt in the centre of the city. This not only won him friends, but effectively served as an economic stimulus package, putting money back into the pockets of Roman consumers.[16]

Pacification also included bold new building projects, such as a temple, altar, and basilica dedicated to his recently departed and much beloved mother-in-law, Matidia, and a temple to his adoptive father, Trajan. Also, the Pantheon, a temple to all the gods, to replace the one that had burnt down in the reign of Trajan. The new Pantheon was an architectural marvel, with a rotunda some 150 Roman feet wide and 150 Roman feet tall. When it was built, with its oculus that allows in light, air, and rain, it was the world's largest unreinforced concrete dome, a record it still holds almost two thousand years later.

Having settled disquiet at home, Hadrian began to visit his empire, leaving his old friend Marcius Turbo in charge of the Praetorian Guard, overseeing the city. He travelled first to the Germanic borders, where he set about restoring discipline with new sets of military codes that removed the luxuries that had set in.[17] It seems likely that while this new regime was not popular with the officers, it might have gone well with the lowly *legionarii*, especially when Hadrian himself renounced the luxuries of his position and joined them in the mud, eating the same basic meals and wearing a simple uniform. He aimed to project an image as a good, fair, and honest military leader, who led from the front and was imbued with all the qualities of his best predecessors.

Not just to keep the German tribes *out* but also to keep the Romans *in*, Hadrian ordered that a vast palisade wall across the Germanic frontier be built of huge wooden posts to delineate and fix the border. The message was set quite literally in stone when Hadrian visited Britain in 122 with Sabina. Veteran soldiers were to be made citizens, and, in a move common across his reign, the land's incarnation in the form of a woman – in this case, Britannia – was deified, and a shrine built in her honour. He also continued the consolidation of territorial gains, the firming up of the borders: in this case, by commissioning the construction of a wall that crossed the entire country.

Hadrian's Wall is a perfect symbol for the man's reign, demonstrating his desire to ensure internal peace as a priority over expansion, and demonstrating that stability and his own personal power through the metaphor of stone. The Wall is colossal in its ambition, the most impressive frontier defence of the Roman world. It was over seventy miles long, stretching from coast to coast, splitting the island in two. But for the emperor, it was more than a fortification; it was a statement of political intent for the course of his reign, to literally build peace by preparing for war. Hadrian left within the year, and the wall would be completed about six years later. In the meantime, however, he was about to embark on a relationship that would change his life.

After his time in Britain, Hadrian continued his travels, including returning to his homeland of Hispania. He then travelled back towards the Black Sea and the Middle East, aiming to reach an agreement and end hostilities with the Parthian Empire. It's highly possible that it was while in Nicomedia, a Greek city in modern-day Turkey, that he first set his eyes on a youth named Antinous.

Antinous was from a Greek family who lived in the nearby city of Claudiopolis, named after the Roman emperor Claudius. Hadrian craved the Hellenic, and his feelings towards Antinous were no different. He was greedy for the Greek boy and yearned to possess what he had to offer: beauty and youth. Antinous was probably in his early teens when they met; Hadrian was in his late forties. There is some dispute over whether they knew each other so early, but according to Royston Lambert, the evidence points to that summer of 123.[18]

It is unlikely that Hadrian's desire was instantaneous, or if it was, that he consummated their relationship at that point. Instead, following the Greek model of pedagogy and pederasty, Hadrian decided to send the young man to Rome for an education, just as he had been sent thirty years before. Meanwhile, the emperor continued on his travels through Asia Minor and North Africa. He again helped shore up the overstretched military, and contributed funds, as he had throughout his reign, to rebuilding cities devastated by the Jewish revolts or by natural disasters. He then spent a year in Greece, succeeding in bringing the aristocracy into a closer political alignment with their Roman conquerors.

Despite Roman supremacy, the old elite and their political systems were still largely intact. Hadrian, an admirer of their system, persuaded two Greek noblemen to join the Roman Senate for the first time. He encouraged the citizens of Athens to start funding their own civic infrastructure, in part by himself establishing two foundations to support Athens's popular public games, including a horse race among athletic younger men. Out of the goodness of his heart, he decided to attend the boys' race personally and preside over them: truly, when it came to helping support muscular young men, his generosity knew no limits.[19] He built temples and a huge library for the city of Athens. He even ensured the completion of the enormous Olympieion, the temple to the Olympian god Zeus. The building was begun seven centuries before Hadrian but he ensured, at vast expense, that it was completed on his watch. His generosity and affection for the Greeks was mutual; he was rewarded not just with statues, but with the nickname 'Hadrianos Sebastos Zeus Olympios', with some identifying him with no less than the God of Gods himself.[20]

Hadrian returned to Rome. In 126 he began to fall ill, and it seems it was at this time that he found comfort in the arms of Antinous, who was now in his late teens. Hadrian was, without doubt, a difficult man: tight-lipped and secretive, prone to rage, he made and lost friends quickly. But, for a man who conducted his political life with such austerity, he threw himself into love with grand, high passion.[21] He wrote poems for the boy, while continuing to humiliate Sabina. Later authors, writing a few hundred years after his death, depicted Antinous as 'the slave of Hadrian's lust', his 'husband', and 'the love of his heart'.[22] But was Hadrian's affection and love for Antinous purely paternalistic or platonic, an admiration for his youth and beauty? Put simply: did they fuck?

Given the lascivious nature of both contemporary sources and Hadrian's own words, the depictions of the young man (usually depicted as a muscular, handsome, and radiant youth of twenty) that littered Hadrian's villas, and the contemporary context of both Roman sexuality and philhellenism, it's hard to imagine that they could not have. Such a pederastic relationship would have been familiar, even perhaps expected, by Greek Antinous. Beyond that, though, Hadrian clearly felt something more for Antinous than just desire for his body. On an obelisk he devoted to the youth, Hadrian described him as intelligent and wise, and the two seemed to share an almost spiritual bond. Such infatuation must have been a huge burden for the younger man to bear.

In 128, Hadrian took Antinous to Greece. There they took part together in the Eleusinian Mysteries, a week-long religious initiation ritual into an archaic agrarian cult, probably dating back to Minoan civilization. Performed largely by women, the rituals included feasting, procession, vigil, and pilgrimage, although most of the details, kept secret by initiates upon pain of death, were never revealed. Some modern scholars suggest that the ritual involved the consumption of hallucinogens; coming at the end of such a spectacular ritual, with the initiates being informed of holy mysteries, any trip must have been powerfully intense. Hadrian had already been initiated into the first order on a previous trip, but for Antinous, it was his first time.

The rituals climaxed in a dark, crowded hall on a rocky outcrop overlooking the Gulf of Elefsina. The high priest would appear in a flash of intense light by the altar. In the words of the historian Plutarch, 'Just before the end, the terror is at its worst. There is shivering, trembling, cold sweat, and fear. But the eyes perceive a wonderful light. Purer regions are reached and fields where there is singing and dancing, and sacred words and divine visions inspire a holy awe.'[23]

For Hadrian, this second initiation signalled a rebirth, a rejuvenation. For the much younger Antinous, the vision of death and afterlife may have been more disturbing. From that point on, the relationship between the man and the boy gained an almost religious dimension. Hadrian began to revel in the Greek conception of him as Zeus, and as he grew more philhellenic than ever, an avowed Emperor of the East, the relationship with his young lover became increasingly public and formal. Taken with his role, Hadrian decided to continue the Hellenization of the wider Roman Empire. He decided to found a league of Greek city-states, in emulation of Pericles. He also wanted to emulate the work of Alexander the Great, another Bad Gay whose conquests across Asia Minor and the Middle East had kickstarted a Hellenic culture hundreds of years previously. Hadrian called his project the 'Panhellenion', but it failed as a political project, instead working mainly as a cultural and religious organisation. Still, Hadrian's verve to spread Hellenism was far from dimmed.

Meanwhile, the entire imperial entourage continued their journey onwards towards the Middle East. Arriving in Egypt,

Hadrian set to work on his favourite hobby, rebuilding destroyed monuments. Alexandria was, at this time, still a Greek city, although the rest of Egypt worshipped its old gods, and he was as beguiled by the potential of drawing them into his syncretic religion as Zeus. From Alexandria, the men set out on a lion hunt in Libya. Antinous was no longer a boy, but a young, virile man, handsome but outgrowing the Hellenistic relationship that Hadrian had cultivated. On the hunt the men cornered a ferocious lion and, in an act of strength and bravery, Hadrian killed it just as it seemed to be sure to devour Antinous – or so the stories and monuments commissioned by Hadrian say.

Back in Alexandria, the imperial procession prepared for a trip by boat down the Nile River. The trip was long – around six weeks, and throughout the journey Hadrian and Antinous spent considerable time partaking in the rites and rituals of traditional religions, as well as magic ceremonies. They would have heard the origin myths of a religious practice deeply tied to the Nile, around which Egyptian society literally and symbolically congregated, its annual flooding being the source of life and prosperity for the Egyptian kingdom. These included the story of Osiris, the god of judgement, the bringer of life, who controlled the Nile and who was described as 'He Who Is Permanently Benign and Youthful'. Antinous, himself worshipped by a god-king, must have recognised a kindred spirit in that description; portentously, the story of Osiris ends with his murder, drowned in the very waters of the river.

Antinous drowned in the Nile. More than this, we cannot say for certain. Perhaps it was an accident; Hadrian himself recounts that he fell into the river. Others are not so sure. After all, Hadrian was not merely a scholar of the religious and occult, but a true believer. Antinous, his only true love, was growing physically out of his role. They had experienced a profound, disturbing, and abusive journey together, with both becoming, in Hadrian's eyes, increasingly divine in the process. Perhaps the temptation to offer to the Nile a sacrifice to love, or greatness, was too much. According to Cassius Dio, a historian writing after Hadrian's death, 'Antinous died either by falling into the

Nile, as Hadrian writes, or, as the truth is, by being offered in sacrifice.'[24] According to the Roman historian Sextus Aurelius Victor, Antinous was a sacrifice, but a willing one, prepared to offer his life for the prolongation of his emperor's.

The relationship, disturbing enough to modern ears as it is, takes a profoundly dark turn with these allegations. Each account, accident or sacrifice, is feasible; if it *was* a sacrifice, it suggests both a religiosity and a sense of loyalty and devotion that is hard for us to comprehend, where desire and violence, sex and divinity come together in a relationship of toxic and passionate intensity. One thing we do know is that after his death, Hadrian regarded Antinous as nothing less than a god. He was immediately deified as a god by both Hadrian and the local priesthood, who formed a cult devoted to him and identified him with no lesser a figure than Osiris.

Antnous's deification was extremely unusual, as the deification of people who weren't members of the imperial family was prohibited, and it occurred without the consultation of the Senate. Hadrian also decreed that a city should be built at the site of the young man's death, named Antinoöpolis in his honour. It was the first Hellenic city so far down the Nile, and was the site of worship for a cult that formed around Antinous. The cult became uncommonly popular, spreading throughout the empire; the boy-god was a figure of devotion, with shrines and statues built in his honour, especially in the East. Rumours abound, fittingly, that secret rites in Antinoöpolis included orgies in the dead of night.

While Antinous's cult was to be held in deep affection, and would last for hundreds of years, until eradicated by the Christians, any potential sacrifice towards Hadrian's longevity was in vain. The remainder of his life was taken up fighting a resurgent Jewish insurrection in Judea, the Bar Kokhba revolt. The revolt was largely a result of Hadrian's own hubris: as well as banning the religious practice of circumcision (according to the *Historia Augusta*), he decided to re-establish the holy city of Jerusalem, still in ruins after its destruction sixty years prior, as a Roman colony named Aelia Capitolina (after his family name) and the

Roman god Jupiter. He built a temple to Jupiter in the centre of the new colony – on Temple Mount. The ensuing war, which lasted for around four years, was incredibly bloody. Cassius Dio claims that over half a million Jews were killed; their homes, villages, and farms destroyed; and the name Judea wiped from the map.

By the end of the revolt, still mourning his lover, Hadrian had returned to Rome. He was close to a broken man, in ill health and miserable. His unloved and humiliated wife Sabina was to die soon after his return, followed by his named successor Lucius Aelius Caesar. He tried, and failed, to commit suicide rather than endure further illness, but on the 10th of July in 132, he was to die at his villa outside Rome. He was sixty-two. Fittingly, for a man who devoted his life to building and to stability, he was buried in a colossal mausoleum that he had commissioned for himself. It was the tallest building in Rome upon its completion. Having been converted into a fortress in the mediaeval period, it still stands today, and is known as the Castel Sant'Angelo – the Castle of the Holy Angel.

Hadrian's life is a compelling one. His official biography as an emperor tells a traditional story of the consolidation of an empire, the suppression of rebellion and the building of great structures, the sort of story that has filled history books for hundreds of years. However, behind this desire for order was another less traditional story, one of an overwhelming, all-consuming passion for a beautiful man he quite literally worshipped as a young god. On one level, it's clear that this devotional desire was integral to Hadrian's legacy: to ignore Hadrian's love for Antinous is to ignore the central pillar around which Hadrian built his life. But on another level, Hadrian's story is also hugely illuminating for our understanding of homosexuality through history.

In the Victorian era, European men searching for historical examples of their own same-sex desires would find in the Greek and Roman worlds a new model for their own sexuality, men who loved other men without shame, and who weren't regarded by their peers as aberrant, diseased, and disgusting, as they themselves were. A story was constructed that said homosexual men have always existed. Yet a closer look at the nature of same-sex love in the society in which Hadrian lived, and his obsessive love for a much younger man in particular, complicates the idea of an unchanging thread of homosexuality that passes through history, sometimes suppressed and sometimes celebrated, of same-sex relationships that looked the same and felt the same. As we will see, the designation of gender as the most important distinguishing feature of sexual identity is not historically universal, and the meaning of gender is not fixed through history. Hadrian's story tells us of the importance status, power, education, and sexual role has had in the story of same-sex desire, something that will have a huge impact on the Bad Gays that followed him.

2

Pietro Aretino

The year 1492 is seen in European history as an axis around which the ages turn; in reality, it was perhaps a moment where symbolic events came to stand in for the culmination of some long-developing, grand historical processes, and the beginning of new cycles. In Spain, the year started with the defeat of Muhammad XII, the emir of Granada, marking the end of eight hundred years of Muslim rule in Spain following a campaign of 'Reconquista', or reconquest, that had lasted just as long. The two victorious Catholic kingdoms, Castile and Aragon, united to become Spain through the marriage of their rulers, Isabella I and Ferdinand II respectively, who subsequently expelled all of Spain's Jews. Within a month, the 'Catholic Monarchs' had met with Christopher Columbus to finalise their support for his attempt to reach Asia by travelling west across the Atlantic Ocean, and by the end of the year he had landed in modern-day Cuba, bringing with him the full terror of the colonial project that was to unfold.

For many, it is seen as the year which birthed the modern world. That year, on Good Friday, the holiest day of the Christian calendar, was born one of the most profane gays in history: Pietro Aretino. Aretino would be remembered across Europe for centuries to come as a transgressive writer and sodomite who so revelled in sin that his very name because synonymous with good fucking. For our purposes, however, his life and work is also symbolic of a shift between a mediaeval and a modern way of looking at, talking about, and writing about sex.

Despite arriving on Good Friday, his early years were hardly auspicious. It is thought he was the son of a shoemaker called Luca Buta in Arezzo, a town south of Florence in Tuscany, Italy. His mother was Tita Bonci, a courtesan.[1] Their relationship, if they ever had one, certainly did not last long. His father left for a career in the military, and young Pietro abandoned his father's surname, choosing to be known instead by the demonym of his town, 'Aretino'. He remained estranged from his father for his whole life, but his mother's work was to become an obsession for him in his writing, and in later life he had a portrait of her commissioned, which an adversary suggested was not his mother, but the Virgin Mary, such was the depth of his blasphemy.[2]

He did not stick around in Arezzo for long. In his late teens he left the city in a hurry, having written a poem that was deemed offensive to the Church. So began a career of pissing off all the right people at just the right time, because in Perugia he found a city that he loved, that he regarded as 'my true fatherland because there I grew to manhood', and a new role, training to become a painter.[3] Painting was to become a passion, although there is little evidence he excelled in it. For the remainder of his life, however, he loved the company of other artists.

Attitudes towards sodomy varied across the Italian states. The governing body of Venice had, at the start of the fifteenth century, established a *Collegium sodomitarum* for the purposes of investigating sodomy in the city, resulting in hundreds of public burnings in the Piazzetta San Marco.[4] However, Florence, under the control of the Medici family (to whom Aretino became closely tied), chose to monetize sodomy on a large scale. Christopher Chitty describes this regime as a 'persecution of sodomy [that] represented more of a tax or rent collected from its population than a rabid moral campaign of repression and punishment'. This increased informing and prosecution, given that there was a general understanding that the accused would be fined but not put to death, as the public felt that informing on homosexual behaviour was a simpler, less serious process.

Florence's extensive records suggest that sodomy was widespread, helping to 'secure business deals and patronages' among rich men and 'as a way to form friendships and political affinity groups' among poorer, politically disenfranchised labourers, and the ability to regulate this behaviour (especially cross-class social contact) and monitor it was more politically useful than to stamp it out.[5] Chitty also suggests that one reason for this relatively tolerant position within a continental practice of execution was that the Medicis' hold on power relied upon a high degree of popular consent in a city where sodomy was a regulated civic norm: 'too many convictions, seemingly disproportionate convictions of poor rather than rich men, and punishments that might be perceived as excessive threatened to turn the lower strata of the city against the regime'.[6]

The Florentine experience of sodomy as part of the functioning social system and the rise of both cultures of sodomy and its persecution in the early modern world suggest, in Chitty's reading, an intimate relationship between homosexual sex, class struggle, and the development of capitalism. It also puts paid to many contemporary liberal readings of the persecution of sodomy and homosexuality as some kind of primitive urge that exists in superstitious societies or 'lower classes', with the idea that we are progressing in a straight line through education towards tolerance. Such an understanding of changing attitudes towards homosexual behaviour, Chitty states, tends

> to assume that antihomosexual sentiment is a sort of timeless ideology given vent by social crisis. Tolerance gets negatively conceived as the absence of homophobia; however, the very publicness of cultures of sodomy suggests that something more than the absence of fear and panic allowed such cultures to flourish, something positive or constitutive, perhaps solidarity with sexual outlaws, or opposition to the dominant culture.[7]

A Florentine Renaissance culture where sodomy, encouraged by a rediscovery of earlier Mediterranean homosexual cultures such as the Romans and Greeks, was widespread is a useful tool for us to challenge a popular reading of gay history that sees four thousand years of repression flower into a late twentieth-century golden age of tolerance, largely thanks to Western democracy. The value of your freedom may go down as well as up. It's also useful to help us understand the huge popular acclaim that Aretino garnered in his lifetime, for nothing could describe him better than the phrase 'sexual outlaw in opposition to the dominant culture', and the ordinary people loved him for it.

It was in Perugia, and barely out of his teens, that Aretino published his first collection of poetry, *Opera nova*, in 1512, demonstrating the key talent of the satirist: the ability to ape the styles of others, to inhabit their words with his own mischievous ideas.[8] Emulating the lyrical mode of writers like Pietro Bembo and Plutarch, *Opera nova* was a form of courtly lyric that, presumably, Aretino hoped would open doors to the social circles of the powerful. He soon had the opportunity to try that out as at twenty-four he left the city under a cloud, due to 'an alteration made by him in a picture on a sacred subject',[9] allegedly painting a lute into the hands of a supplicating Mary Magdalene in a painting in a public building.[10]

He headed for Rome, where he took a position in the household of Agostino Chigi, a banker from a prestigious Sienese family. It was quite the city for a young satirist to find himself in. Only three years before, Giovanni di Lorenzo de' Medici had been elected pope in the Papal Conclave of 1513. The second son of the immensely powerful Florentine banker Lorenzo the Magnificent who had ruled that city, Giovanni, now using the papal name Leo X, had lived through the revolutionary tumult that had overturned Florence during the ascendancy of the hellfire prophet and reformer Girolamo Savonarola. Savonarola was a preacher who saw in Florence a pit of sodomy, fornication, and sin. Firing the people of Florence up with his promises of divine retribution, he began a series of 'bonfires of the vanities', burning anything regarded as idolatrous, extravagant, or immodest in order to purify the populace. After Lorenzo died and Florence's old enemy, Charles VII of France, crossed the Alps into Italy, Savonarola took the opportunity to finish the cleansing, overthrowing Giovanni's elder brother, Piero 'the Unfortunate'.

When Piero and Giovanni were forced from the city, Savonarola declared Christ the King of Florence, and continued his campaign to purge the city of vice and tyranny. However, Giovanni, who swiftly became a cardinal, had his revenge. In 1497 Savonarola was excommunicated, and the following year, as popular opinion turned against him and his moral reforms, he was added to the bonfire himself. In 1512, Giovanni recaptured the city with papal soldiers, returning the Medicis to power.

When Giovanni was elected pope the following year, his rule in Rome and, by proxy, in Florence, could not have been more different. Where Savonarola burnt art, Pope Leo commissioned it, and on a vast scale. He spent huge amounts of money on goldsmiths and musicians, he enjoyed 'buffoons', hunting, and parties, and, most differently to Savonarola, it seems likely he practised sodomy himself.[11] He also pushed ahead with work on the great new basilica for the Vatican, St Peter's, under its new architect, Raphael; to fund work, he authorised the sales of even more 'indulgences', a sort of 'get out of purgatory free' card that the wealthy could buy to smooth over their entry to heaven. It was Leo's indulgences that pushed Martin Luther over the edge, and led to him nailing his '95 Theses' to the church door in Wittenberg, leading to a Reformation that, unlike earlier attempts at 'purifying' the Church, actually stuck. For Luther, it wasn't just the indulgences; it was also the man-on-man action that symbolised the collapse of the Roman Church's authority. In 1531 Luther would write of a papal decree or 'bull':

More remarkable yet, in the same bull they decided that a cardinal should not keep as many boys in the future. However, Pope Leo commanded that this be deleted; otherwise it would have been spread throughout the whole world how openly and shamelessly the pope and the cardinals in Rome practice sodomy. I do not wish to mention the pope, but since the knaves will not repent, but condemn the gospel, blaspheme and revile God's word, and excuse their vices, they, in turn, will have to take a whiff of their own terrible filth. This vice is so prevalent among

them that recently a pope caused his own death by means of this
sin and vice. In fact, he died on the spot.[12]

We cannot know how much Luther understood about the mechanisms of anal, but it seems unlikely that Pope Leo X (to whom
he's referring here) was, indeed, fucked to death. Still, it paints a
vivid picture of Rome and the Church during Leo's papal rule,
and the objections to it. What better place for Aretino to make
his mark!

The debauched city, with its courtly intrigue, was the sort of
hothouse in which Aretino thrived. He began to write a series of
pasquinades. The 'Pasquino' is a battered old classical statue that
was dug up in the fifteenth century and sits on a street corner near
the Pantheon. It became a tradition for people to post short poems
and skits on the statue, satirical and political in nature, opposing
injustices and corruption, especially within the Church. A *pasquinade* follows this model, and Aretino revelled in the form.

Following the humanist poets of the Renaissance, who looked
back to classical antiquity for models of purity, much poetry of
Aretino's time was formal, and elevated in tone. Aretino bucked
this trend, adopting an earthy language of the street, a vernacular for ordinary folk that emulated the jokes and smut that
resounded around the taverns and brothels of Rome.[13] His wit
was rapier-sharp, and he took no prisoners in his attacks on the
rich and powerful. It should be no surprise to us to learn that, in
contrast to the humanists' high ideals, this bawdy gutter tongue
was wildly popular amongst working people. In his hands, he
grasped control of the form, so much so that, across Europe,
Aretino *was* Pasquino.[14] The use of this vernacular form suited
his interests; he wrote opportunistically, as a good satirist should,
on the exciting news of the moment. Therein lay an irony: it was
because of this quick, accessible skill that Aretino was so popular
in his life, but that same thing dated him once the context of the
contemporary became history.

One of his most famous alleged satires was published in 1516,
on the death of Pope Leo's beloved elephant, Hanno, a gift from
the king of Portugal. The pope was so upset, he commissioned no

less than Raphael himself to paint Hanno's portrait in fresco, but did not commission Aretino's (anonymously published) pasquinade, which took the form of a 'Last Will and Testament' dictated by Hanno himself. In it 'Hanno' donates parts of his bodies to various cardinals and priests, including his cock to one Cardinal di Grassi, well known for fathering illegitimate children, 'so that he can become more active in the incarnation of bastards', and his bollocks 'to the Most Reverend Cardinal of Senegaia so that he will become more fruitful in progeny, and in the more merry procreation of the Antichrist with the Reverend Julia of the nuns of Saint Catherine of Senegaia'.[15] It was a riotous success, even to the mourning pope; and as a result, Aretino's career began, as he was commissioned to write for Roman aristocrats who were motivated partly by amusement and partly by the fear they might end up on the wrong side of his pen.

Yet life was always a risk for Pietro; soon Leo X followed his beloved elephant to the grave, dying of pneumonia (rather than, as Luther claimed, being fucked to death). A new papal conclave began, and the city was thrilled by the high gossip of the event. Aretino was put on the payroll by one Giulio de' Medici, cousin of the late pope, who himself wanted the top spot. Not only was that a smart decision by de' Medici, it was also a smart decision by Aretino: his man garnered the most support within the conclave. Having his patron become pope would secure his position within the city, and so Aretino set to work in perhaps his most energetic creative burst to date, producing scores of poems daily that lampooned and libelled Giulio de' Medici's competitors.

The plan backfired when de' Medici fluffed his political manoeuvrings, resulting in the election of the dour Dutchman Adriaan Florensz Boeyens as Pope Adrian VI. The dusty Adrian, unlike his fun-loving predecessor, did not see the funny side of Aretino's attacks, demanding the Pasquino statue be hurled into the Tiber when he arrived in the city in August of 1522. Aretino fled the city and returned to Florence, but having so angered Pope Adrian, he brought an unwelcome heat to the Medicis' city, and the pope was demanding they turn him over.[16]

They sent him away, but only to live with a cousin from a secondary branch of the family, Lodovico de' Medici, better known as Giovanni delle Bande Nere. Giovanni was a ruthless man of vicious and unsuppressed appetites, and so inevitably they became firm friends. His new best friend was a *condottiero*, a captain of a group of mercenaries known as the Bande Nere, after their habit of dressing in black to mourn the passing of Pope Leo X. As a thirteen-year-old, Giovanni had been exiled from the city by the post-Savonarola regime for having been the accomplice in the rape of a sixteen-year-old boy, and for accidentally killing another child.[17] He was a teenager when he first went to war, and still in his early twenties when Aretino befriended him a decade later, but with a reputation for being an audacious adventurer. Aretino was also gaining a reputation: for his ability to blackmail and extort the wealthy nobles who lived in fear of his pen, he became known as 'the scourge of princes'.

Yet Adrian's dreary rule was not to last.[18] The following year, in April, he suppressed the Pasquino's feast day, but by September he was dead; by November Giulio de' Medici had been elected as Pope Clement VII, and Aretino could return to the Holy City.[19] Presumably feeling reasonably secure with his old patron on the papal throne, he took up a new writing project: *I Modi*, or *The Ways*. The work was a collaborative one. Alongside erotic illustrations by the engraver Marcantonio Raimondo, Aretino wrote short, bawdy captions.

Like the Renaissance humanists who looked back to the classical world for inspiration, Raimondi and Aretino depicted scenes of mythical Roman and Greek figures: unlike the Renaissance humourists, though, their depictions came complete with engorged penises, women playing with their genitals, and sex acts in various positions (hence the title, *The Ways*). Aretino's sonnets place the asshole, rather than the cunt, as the site of primary pleasure for the participants, with one woman proclaiming in Sonnet 8, 'If I were a man, I wouldn't want cunt.' It is this morphing between male and female, according to academic Keir Elam, that 'transforms the aggressive heterosexuality of the images into a primarily homoerotic literary event'.[20] To translate that into

46

the vernacular which Aretino might have used, we could instead think of him as an ass-man rather than a tits man. Again we see that it is the nature of the sexual act, and not the gender of the lovers, that was at the heart of understanding sexuality.

The erotic drawings were presumably for a private collection. It was not uncommon for nobles to have such 'erotic art' for their own private wank-bank, but Raimondi and Aretino's contribution had significant impact. It is one thing for the cultured elites to stroke one out to high art; quite another to reproduce such images for the ordinary person in mass-produced prints, and these 'postures' were seen as little more than a manual for sex. A former friend turned bitter rival, Cardinal Gian Matteo Giberti, brought an accusation of obscenity against Aretino for his set of pornographic sonnets. Raimondi was thrown into jail and Aretino again had to scuttle out of the city.

He refused to apologise for his work, and it's in this mode that we see Aretino at his best, a sexual libertine who was in a state of permanent revolt against the sexual moralism of Church and society, which he saw as little more than rank hypocrisy and prudishness. He wrote:

> I amused myself by writing the sonnets that are seen beneath the figures, the wanton memory of which I dedicate by leave to the hypocrites, out of patience with their villainous judgment and with the hoggish custom that forbids the eyes what most delights them. What evil is there in seeing a man possess a woman? Why, the beasts would be more free than we! It seems to me that that which is given us by nature for our own preservation ought to be worn round the neck as a pendant and in the hat for a medal.[21]

A hoggish custom indeed. He returned to the service of his friend Giovanni delle Bande Nere for a while, with whom he had stayed in contact by letter. In fact that very year he'd complained to Giovanni that a terrible fate had befallen him: he had fallen for a woman. He told Giovanni that he should not worry, of course, for 'we all return to the ancient great mother, and if I escape with my honour from this madness, will bugger as much as much and as much for me as for my friends'. The sentiment is hardly out of character for a man who described himself as 'a sodomite from birth'.[22]

He also visited his friend the Duke of Mantua, a trusted business adviser who also helped arrange his love life, procuring young men for him in a series of letters in which the Duke apologised for not knowing the particular 'kept boy' that Pietro was after.[23] It was in Mantua that Aretino wished to enter court life, and indeed the dynamics of the Duke's house provided fruitful pickings for his work long after he left, in plays such as *La Cortigiana* (The Courtesan), *La Ipocrita* (The Hypocrite), and especially *Il Marescalco* (The Stableman), in which the Duke of Mantua forces his stablemaster to marry, much to his dismay. The play depicts the homosocial world in which Aretino lived, with the poor, put-upon bride-to-be cast in misogynistic tones. Yet the story has a happy ending when it is revealed that the wedding is a practical joke, and his new 'wife' is a page boy, Carlo da Fano. The stablemaster's relief is palpable: 'Well doesn't it seem better to you, that I see you laughing at a lie, than that you see me crying at the truth?'[24]

Yet Aretino never settled at the court. He was again in Rome in July of 1525, and again writing his *pasquinades*, when Cardinal Giberti attempted his final revenge, sending an assassin who stabbed Aretino five times, damaging his hand, a wound from which he never recovered. That was enough for him, and he left Rome for good. The following year we find him again with his friend's band of mercenaries, the Bande Nere, who were busy fighting in the War of the League of Cognac, where the Holy Roman Emperor Charles V of the House of Habsburg was fighting an alliance of the pope and Francis I, King of France, to drive Charles V from the Italian states.

It was during a battle at the end of 1526 that Giovanni was shot by a small cannon. Aretino was there for the gruesome amputation that followed, writing that when the doctor called for eight or ten men to hold Giovanni down during the procedure to saw through his leg, the man proclaimed, 'Not even twenty would hold me.' He bravely bore the operation, even declaring upon its completion, 'I am healed,' but it was not to be, and he died shortly after in Aretino's arms.[25]

With his closest friend dead, finding himself out of favour with the Duke of Mantua, and in fear of his life in Rome, Aretino fled again, this time to Venice. In this most anti-papal of Italian states, rich in commercial wealth and welcoming to artists, he finally found a place to thrive without (much) fear.

Here, he was at the height of his powers as a satirist and libeller. His pen was now so feared that he commanded great respect not just from the ordinary citizens who read his work, but from the most powerful men in the world. Europe at the time was riven by the feud between Francis I, the King of France, and Charles V, the Holy Roman Emperor. With this crown, plus the crown of Spain, and dominion over the Netherlands and much of Italy, Charles V encircled Francis, who, like many European monarchs, feared the domination of the Habsburg ruler.

Their rivalry was also fiercely personal: a number of times Francis even challenged him to have it out, mano a mano. It was perhaps inevitable that both men would either seek out the help of 'the Divine Aretino', or otherwise become his victim. At one point, according to the historian Jacob Burckhardt, 'Charles V and Francis I both pensioned him at the same time, each hoping that Aretino would do some mischief to the other.'[26] This practice, seemingly devoid of any genuine personal commitment to the politics of the day, was incredibly lucrative, although he could spend it as fast as he earned it. He even took money from Cosimo de' Medici, the Duke of Florence and the son of his late friend Giovanni delle Bande Nere (remember that Giovanni's real name was Lodovico de' Medici), who sent him rolls of cash that had been perfumed.

At the same time, it was an understandably risky affair; as with modern columnists, it was easy to make powerful enemies. Yet Aretino was incredibly skilful as a politician acting for the party of *himself*. A testament to this is that, after only a few years in Venice, the Doge of the Venetian Republic, Andrea Gritti, intervened with the pope on Aretino's behalf. It was a significant milestone for Aretino, and seemingly guaranteed him the support and protection of the republic in which he was to make his home.[27] He wrote in praise to the doge, 'I, who have stricken terror into kings … give myself to you, fathers of your people.'[28] Flattery, Aretino knew, gets you everywhere, and in this case, a pension to live there with.

The doge's support is highly symbolic. It shows that Aretino now enjoyed something more than simply the favour of the powerful, but rather power himself, not through the wealth, titles, or armies that the princes enjoyed, but through the power of his pen. He enjoyed so much public support, he was what might today be called an opinion-maker. All this was possible thanks to the technological innovation of the printing press and the publishing industry. It is this new method of communication of which he was the master, and which ironically was both the cause and solution to so many of his problems: the cause, because while obscene literature previously existed within the ranks of the nobility, publishing allowed Aretino to circulate his writings much more widely, raising the fears of popes and princes; and the solution, because the mass appeal of his work protected him.

It is not too far a stretch to situate Aretino in the same dynamic as Martin Luther, whose success lay not just in the message, but in the skilful way it was disseminated. Both used the printed word to build a base of immense power, understanding literature not simply in the relationship between a text and a reader, but within a wider framework as a commercial venture. Increasing the scale of the dissemination of texts, something that had become easier as the printing press slashed the cost and speed of accessing the written word, meant Aretino could write on the pressing issues of the day and circulate the ideas widely and quickly. He also published well-received collections of his witty letters, and, realising they were what sustained his fame and therefore his power, waived his royalties so that they could be sold cheaper, to more people.[29] Aretino's biographer claimed this made him 'the founder of the European Press', but his interests, as we have seen, lay not just with the politics of the day, but with a more earthy discussion that would see his poems and satires flying from the stands: sex.[30]

Settled in Venice, Aretino began work on a set of writings that became one of his best-known pieces, *The Ragionamenti*. Composed of two separate pieces of prose writings, *The Ragionamenti* take the form of a dialogue. They're meant to parody, to an extent, the hugely popular dialogues of the Renaissance that are modelled on the classical Socratic dialogue, with the main character Nanna, an aging Roman courtesan, discussing three social roles for women with her daughter Pippa, and with her confidante, Antonia. Over the course of three days she explains the paths and opportunities her daughter might enjoy in life.

On day one, she tells of Pippa's possible life as a young nun in a sex-obsessed convent, and the corruption of a church where cardinals fuck nuns in orgiastic gatherings. On the second day, she describes the life of a married woman, too dull to contemplate for a woman with any passion, and on the third, the life of a courtesan and sex worker, which offers freedom and empowerment compared to the previous two. This, she suggests, is a good life for her daughter,[31] and unlike nuns and wives, courtesans are the only ones to stay true to their vows.[32]

It goes without saying that Aretino's vision of the life of women is a thoroughly male one, processed through the eyes of a misogynistic culture. Yet the work is also a sharp deviation from the traditional representations of women within Renaissance culture; as with all his work, he consistently returns the tropes and characters of his work from an idealised, humanistic perspective to an earthy, realistic vernacular. As Nanna says, 'Speak plainly and say "fuck", "prick", "cunt", and "ass" if you want anyone except the scholars at the University of Rome to understand you.'[33] His world is a gritty and material one, where people must do what they will to survive, and where others are as much a vehicle for realising your own needs and wants as they are sources of potential human connection.[34]

It is not hard to see how the talented and puckish son of a humble shoemaker who has talked his way into royal courts, has been stabbed by the assassins of cardinals, has infuriated popes and sweet-talked emperors and finally done good with his own palazzo in Venice, teeming with ducats, might have landed upon such a philosophy. His belief was that the flattery of courtesans and the willingness of sex workers to impress kindness in the service of their own income was a worthy model of, and for, literature.

Finally he was happy, living just off the Grand Canal in a large house called 'Casa dell'Aretino' in which he could entertain his friends, especially his closest friend, the painter Titian, who painted his portrait many times.[35] Tintoretto decorated his ceiling personally, while he bought work from other great painters of the age, like Sebastiano del Piombo and Giorgio Vasari. While he continued to draw fat pensions from across Europe, he was frequently short of cash, because amongst his many virtues he was generous to a fault, giving his money freely to the poor. His big house was full of young women in need, often single mothers or women needing refuge – at one point twenty-two lived with him.

He had relationships with women, including Caterina Sandella, whom he refused to marry, hating the institution, but with whom he had two daughters, Adria and Austria, upon whom he doted, calling Adria 'the most engaging creature imaginable', and saying that 'Austria is as dear to me as life'.[36] There was no need to legitimize their births, he said, for 'they are legitimate in my heart'.[37]

Yet it seems the habit of sodomy was, indeed, lifelong. Towards the end of his life he was accused of blasphemy and sodomy by a Venetian nobleman, and was forced to flee again, briefly. But his friends persuaded authorities to drop the charges, and on his return the ordinary people of Venice gathered along the Grand Canal to cheer him. He also found favour again with the Church, being made a Knight of St Peter by Pope Julius III, but as ever, he was more concerned with the financial reward than the honour. 'A knighthood without revenue', he had written upon being offered a pension-free bauble from Francis I, 'is like a wall without Forbidden signs; everybody commits nuisances there.'[38]

A man of such generosity and earthly tastes was right to be concerned; in 1554 he was evicted from his Venice home after failing to pay rent.[39] Although he became more religious towards the end of his life, writing a number of pious texts, his love of the rough, bawdy vernacular stayed with him to the last. According to popular tradition, in late October 1556, he was told a particularly dirty joke, of which his own sister was the punchline. Finding it hilarious, he died laughing. From contemporary sources, it seems unlikely that this was the case, but for his death to be the subject of such a story suggests he was still held in high esteem amongst ordinary people.[40]

Aretino's legacy is mixed. The tone of the coverage of his life, and especially his writings on sex, tends to fluctuate according to the morals of the age. The Victorian author William Roscoe, with the typical pearl-clutching prudishness of the age, called him 'disgracefully notorious ... unprincipled and licentious' and said his writings displayed a 'depravity of taste and morals'.[41] Even his generous biographer Edward Hutton said the 'man was a monster', but a monster produced by an 'evil' that had swept through Europe during the later Renaissance.[42] Upon his death, Aretino's literary power withered, devoid of the lifeforce – Aretino himself – that had allowed it to thrive, metamorphosising with each change of political and social current. Three years after he died, all his books were added to the *Index Librorum Prohibitorum*, the Catholic Church's list of banned books that emerged in response to both the Reformation and the rise of the printing press. He had a huge influence upon society and literature in the late Renaissance, bringing the vernacular and everyday into the political sphere and countering the refinement of the influence of Latin. Yet he was soon reviled in polite society as little more than a smut-peddler, precisely because his satires, so cutting and timely when written, dated when those circumstances changed.

Ironically, it was his erotic writings that guaranteed his longevity. His works were translated, including into English, and it's certainly possible that both in terms of setting and formal innovations, Shakespeare may well have been influenced by them. Indeed, the only Renaissance artist to whom Shakespeare ever refers (in *The Winter's Tale*) is Aretino's erstwhile collaborator, Giulio Romano. Certainly, the English diarist Samuel Pepys, something of a connoisseur of filthy books, was more than aware of Aretino, claiming that King Charles II's mistress, Barbara Palmer, knew 'all the tricks of Aretin that are to be practised to give pleasure' – a reference to *The Ways*, no doubt.[43]

But while history has deemed him a Bad Gay, perhaps history can also redeem him, for in his life we see a man who understood the hypocrisies of the powerful and pious, and used those hypocrisies against them to give himself the good life of friendship and partying he wanted. Surely that is why they hated him, and what might make him an unusual queer icon.

3

James VI and I

Late one afternoon in 1598 or '99, a crowd of excited Londoners shuffled through the door of the Theatre, an open-roofed playhouse wedged between a horse pond and a garden in Shoreditch. They were there to see a performance of *Henry IV, Part 2*, a new play by the city's hottest playwright, William Shakespeare. Perhaps they'd seen one of his recent popular comedies, *A Midsummer Night's Dream* or *The Comedy of Errors*, or maybe *Romeo and Juliet* or *The Merchant of Venice*, in the previous decade since he had arrived in London. More likely they had seen *Henry IV, Part 1*, and wanted to watch the next instalment of the history play, with characters such as Falstaff and Prince Hal. They might have recognised something of themselves in the milieu of lowlifes in which the young prince found himself, having watched him drinking and fucking his way around Eastcheap, half an hour's walk towards the river, in the previous instalment.

Yet in *Part 2*, Hal was mending his wayward habits. Kingship awaited, and the play made clear to the audience that it was a heavy responsibility. Not that they would have needed the reminder: for the past eighty years Europe had been enduring the turmoil of religious reformation, with attendant political and social transformations. Under the reign of their queen, Elizabeth I, they had seen some degree of religious settlement, but the consequences of the English Crown's break with the Catholic Church under her father Henry VIII were still fresh in people's minds, and many would have remembered the bloody religious strife and persecution that followed his reign, not least when his Catholic daughter and Elizabeth's sister, Queen Mary, had tried to re-establish Catholicism within the kingdom. Queen Elizabeth had surprised not just her detractors but even her allies with the extent of her political and colonial accomplishments and her success in persecuting Catholics. Yet she had continued the tragedy of the Tudor dynasty's neurotic, violent obsession with reproduction, failing to produce an heir.

As the audience left the theatre that evening, they would have been aware that England sat on the edge of chaos. Ten years previously, Elizabeth thwarted the invasion plans of her brother-in-law, Mary's widower Philip II of Spain, by defeating the Spanish Armada with the help of adverse weather. Yet the English had been quite literally paying for their victory ever since through higher taxes levied to support the military, combined with price-fixing by royal favourites bestowed by Her Majesty with monopolies. A series of bad harvests added to the country's woes. The words Shakespeare put into the mouth of Prince Hal's father, Henry IV, as he worried about his own heir and legacy, would therefore have rung true to his audience: 'Uneasy lies the head that wears a crown.'

Her heir, who took the throne when she died in early 1603, knew it to be true. He was just thirty-six years old, yet had already been King of Scotland for thirty-five of them. He was bestowed the crown of England by a queen who had not only forced his own mother, Mary, Queen of Scots, off the Scottish throne, but then imprisoned her for his entire childhood before finally executing her for alleged treason. Worse still, she was a Catholic. Mary's son, James, however, was raised as a Protestant, and made an acceptable heir: family, of sorts, but also loyal to Elizabeth and to her faith.

These tensions – between Scotland and England, between Catholicism and Protestantism, and between his duty to the crowns and his own political survival – were to structure both the Scottish and English reigns of James. But he was not merely a pawn in wider political and economic games. As we will see, over his life James was to make powerful interventions and decisions that shaped the growth of colonialism and capitalism, the development of the early modern state, and ultimately the clash between Parliament and his son Charles I in the English Civil War. Yet all these developments were highly influenced by the ongoing intrigue of his royal court, not least the fallout from his persistent, foolhardy habit of falling head over heels for beautiful, arrogant, and reckless favourites – for James had realised that the unease of the crown-wearing head could be eased significantly if it lay beside a beautiful young man.

James's desire for men was obvious, and a cause for concern, even as a teenager, decades before he took the English throne. Concerns around his upbringing had meant he was surrounded by a rolling retinue of teachers and regents who were to shape the young prince, and both his spiritual and earthly desires. He was born on June 19, 1566, in Edinburgh Castle, to Mary Stuart. Mary had ruled Scotland for more than two decades after her father, King James V, died when she was an infant. Mary inherited her father's deep Catholic faith along with his kingdom, but with her Protestant cousin Elizabeth on the throne across the border, religious struggle both within and without the country would mark her reign.

Mary was promised to Francis, the son of the Catholic French king, Henry II, when they were both children, and lived in the French court for a decade, but he died two years after their wedding. She then married her cousin, Lord Darnley, with whom she had her son, James, but Darnley was to die in mysterious circumstances shortly after; many suspected Mary had a hand in it, thinking Darnley was plotting against her. Those rumours were fuelled when she married his suspected murderer, Lord Bothwell, just four months later. Seeing their chance, Protestant lords raised an army against Mary, Queen of Scots, and her new husband, and her own soldiers deserted her. On 24 July 1567, while held captive in a castle in a loch just north of Edinburgh, she was forced to abdicate, and James, barely a year old, became James I of Scotland. He would never see his mother again, although she would continue to play a significant role in his life. The young queen lived for another twenty years, variously imprisoned and fugitive, her Catholicism and her claim to the throne a constant thorn in the side of the Protestant lords who had toppled her and propelled James to early kingship.

Separated from his mother's influence, the young king was raised within the Protestant faith, with a series of Protestant regents ruling in his stead until he reached his majority. More significantly, he was educated by Protestants, including George Buchanan, a fiercely intelligent and intellectually rigorous theologian and poet who believed, controversially, that political power emanated from the people, to whom the monarch was bound, and any monarch who practised tyranny could be lawfully resisted. A strange choice for a royal tutor, perhaps, but an influential one: James could be said to be the last English monarch to betray anything like an intellectual streak, and went on to write two books on kingship, amongst other writings, although his own theories deviated significantly from Buchanan's.

James's regents were drawn from his own family. The first was his mother's half-brother, the Earl of Moray, James Stewart (the differences in spelling are confusing, but the Stewarts and the Stuarts were, in fact, the same family). A devout Protestant, the Earl of Moray faced an uprising from the old queen who had slipped her Scottish captors just a year into his regency and raised an army to recapture her throne. In the name of her son, the baby king, and defending his own power, he beat Mary in battle and forced her into exile in England. Despite suppressing the uprising, he continued to face opposition from Scottish Catholics still aligned with Mary, and two years later he was assassinated by a gunshot from a window fired by a veteran of the uprising.

Matthew Stewart, James's paternal grandfather and the 4th Earl of Lennox, replaced him and died the next year, shot by loyalists of Mary. Then, the Earl of Mar, who managed a year in the role before being struck down with a mysterious illness after dining with an ambitious noble, James Douglas, 4th Earl of Morton. Clearly, the Scottish regent was a lethal job to have, yet the power it held was considerable, so it should be of little surprise that the Earl of Mar was quickly replaced by none other than James Douglas himself. Douglas lasted longer in the role, and concluded the civil war between the Protestants and the supporters of Queen Mary, yet after six years he'd managed, in this strife-torn land, to make more than his share of enemies.

He stepped back from the role, allowing James, not even yet a teenager, to assert himself. His downfall was nigh; a handsome young French nobleman had arrived at court, and it spelled disaster for Douglas. This thirty-seven year-old Catholic was Esmé Stewart, the cousin of the late Lord Darnley, James's dad. James took a shine to the exciting French relative and he soon became his favourite. Forced from power, Douglas lasted less than two years before an associate of Esmé Stewart accused him of being complicit in Lord Darnley's murder almost fourteen years earlier. Convicted, he was executed on the 'Maiden', a huge, ghastly primitive guillotine the likes of which only the Scots could concoct, and young James, only fourteen years old, was finally able to reign as king in his own right, under the guidance of Esmé.

To say James rewarded Esmé is to put it lightly. Arriving in Scotland holding only a small title in France, Esmé was showered with seven peerages, two earldoms and one dukedom, making him Scotland's only duke. But these were not just gifts of gratitude for political service. The fact that James also gave Esmé Stewart a treasure trove of his mother's jewels might go some way in explaining the nature of his attachment. Despite, or perhaps because of, Esmé being old enough to be James's father, James was immediately attracted to what he himself called Esmé's 'eminent ornaments of body and minde'.[1]

He was, it appears, the whole package. The nature of the relationship seems incredibly difficult to parse from historical accounts mired in the intrigue of court, and because the relationship itself was subject to so many external influences – power and ambition, its semi-incestuous nature, the significant age gap and the implications of a role of authority and care over someone who, legally speaking, is themselves invested with almost absolute authority over their supposed caretaker. But from the sources we have, it is clear that the relationship between James and Esmé was amorous, both emotionally and sexually.

More than that, it's clear that this wasn't a single-direction crush of a younger onto an older man, but instead, as far as we can say, a 'mutual' affection. As complicated and difficult as it might be to discuss today, in the norms of the age that difference in years might not have implied a predatory relationship to observers. Esmé appears to have been as besotted with his second cousin as the king with Esmé.

Predation and exploitation *was* a concern, but not of sexual exploitation of a younger man. Rather, there was a concern that, as with the regents before him, too much power could be held in the hands of this nobleman, and worse, a Catholic noble. In fact, it's in the correspondence of fellow powerbrokers about this danger that we find much of the evidence for the sexual nature of their relationship. English observers in the Scottish court, ever wary of potential Catholic threats on their northern border, noted the incipient danger. English politician Sir Henry Widdrington, writing to the Queen Elizabeth's right-hand man, William Cecil, claimed that Esmé was corrupting the seventeen-year-old James, claiming 'the ministry are informed that the Duke goes about to draw the King to carnal lust'.[2]

The fact that it is only this danger of the usurpation of power that leads to these letters being written does raise an interesting question. Had Esmé not been an ambitious noble, but merely another young man without status, would evidence of their relationship have been a matter of the historical record? And how many other monarchs did engage in such same-sex behaviours, but in a way that didn't challenge the wheels of power, and hence were never written down?

The problem with their relationship for Scottish nobles, and particularly the Protestants, was not so much the same-sex desire they showed for each other, but more that, in their relationship, they saw the consolidation of power in the hands of the king's favourite – a dynamic which became a lifelong concern for James's court – and especially a *Catholic* favourite. The peace in Scotland was fragile, and the Kirk (the Scottish national church, a Presbyterian, protestant institution) was young: only six years older than James himself. For James to be 'in such love with [Esmé] as in the open sight of the people often he will clasp him about the neck with his arms and kiss him' must have seemed like a potential existential threat, not least because within the minds of Protestants there was a link between sodomy and Catholicism.[3]

Across the border Henry VIII had implemented the Buggery Act in 1533 not just as a demonstration of state power (such cases had previously been restricted to ecclesiastical courts), but also as a legal weapon to give his officials 'licence to roam through the monasteries, convents and friaries',[4] taking advantage of the popular (and not unfounded) assumptions that such gender-segregated institutions, far from being places of solemn chastity, were nests of sodomites.[5] This was happening at the exact moment Henry was attempting to dissolve the monasteries and seize as much land, capital, and power for himself, making this link in the minds of the people very handy indeed.

The Protestant religious polemicist John Bale regarded the vow of chastity and the act of sodomy inextricably linked, both a corruption of God's plan for marriage. The Catholic Church, in its insistence upon chastity for the clergy, were corrupters of men, and according to Bale, 'the men in theyr prelacies, priesthodes [and] innumerable kinds of Monkery, for want of women hath brent in theyr lusts [and] done abominations'.[6]

Alongside sectarian assumptions about the relationship between Catholics and sodomy were others fears of corruption. As in the classical Greek and Roman worlds, in early modern Europe many same-sex relationships were structured around hierarchical relationships which were seen to have an educational function, and it was this pedagogical relationship which may have created space for the toleration of sodomy.[7] Yet despite being considerably younger than Esmé, James was not just his king, and Esmé his subject. The implication of superiority, of paternalistic teaching, that went with early modern assumptions of same-sex relationships would, in this instance, have upended the natural ideological order, putting far too much power in Esmé's grasp.

To quell these fears, Esmé converted to Presbyterianism, but it was of little use. Few believed the conversion was sincere, but merely a perfidious Catholic trick, and his role in the execution of the king's last regent, the Earl of Morton, seemed to seal that opinion for the Protestant nobles. Rather than removing him from the king's presence, the nobles decided to remove the king. In the summer of 1582 a group of conspirators known as the 'Lords Enterprisers' effectively kidnapped James in the 'Ruthven Raid', holding him a virtual hostage for a year. It was not strictly a coup d'etat: James remained the king, but the forcible change in his court and advisers altered the nature of the regime. The extravagant court lifestyle was out, replaced by a thrifty, militantly Protestant administration of nobles known as the 'Gowrie Regime', who aimed to correct the suspiciously Catholic tendencies of James under Esmé's influence and, funded by the English, remove all trace of pro-Mary sentiment in the government.

In July 1583 James managed to slip his captors, but Esmé had already been exiled to France, where he continued to send James heartfelt entreaties on his loyalty, claiming his 'faithfulness which is engraved within my heart, which will last forever'.[8] By the time James had reasserted control over his throne, it was too late: Esmé had died in France, confounding his suspicious critics by refusing to renounce Protestantism, and his embalmed heart was returned to his king in Scotland. Full of grief, James penned a poem to his former favourite, comparing him to a phoenix. But the collapse of the Gowrie Regime led to a change in how James approached his governance. He comprehensively rejected the teachings of the Protestant schoolmaster Buchanan, who had attempted to beat his own ideas of kingly moderation into him, and instead imposed upon his kingdom his own understanding of his kingly authority as being derived directly from God.

To resolve the ongoing uncertainty with England, the question of Queen Elizabeth's heir, and the English anxieties about a potential Catholic threat in Scotland, both James and Elizabeth began making diplomatic overtures towards each other. In 1586, the signing of English treaties with the Dutch meant the prospect of a Spanish invasion looked increasing likely, and James and

Elizabeth formalised an Anglo-Scottish treaty, not only providing James with a pension from the English crown, but promising that the English would respect his legal claims and titles, in exchange for Scottish support.

It was by now clear that Elizabeth was not going to produce a child to inherit her throne, and the implications were obvious. The following year Elizabeth somewhat sealed the deal by executing James's mother, Mary Queen of Scots, after many years of holding her imprisoned in England, for an alleged treasonous plot against her throne. While James publicly protested the execution, he benefited from it: Mary and her followers would no longer threaten either throne, and it left James as Elizabeth's closest surviving relative. In letters to Elizabeth he referred to himself as her 'natural son and compatriot of your country', and her as his 'Madame and dearest sister': it was clear he was angling for a peaceful inheritance upon her death.[9]

With his succession to the English throne increasingly likely, his thoughts turned to producing an heir himself. James was well respected in Scotland for not having produced illegitimate children, although the fact he was rumoured to be 'too much carried by young men that lie in his chamber and are his minions' probably made an unwanted pregnancy unlikely, no matter how hard he tried.[10] If he wanted an heir, having sex with a woman might help. Fresh on the European royal marriage market was the fourteen-year-old daughter of King Frederick of Denmark, Anne.

Anne was, in many ways, an excellent match for James. Yes, she may have been Lutheran rather than Calvinist, but she was a protestant, and both the daughter and sister of European kings. After the negotiation of a significant dowry, she took part in a proxy marriage, with one of James's ambassadors, in Denmark on 20 August 1589. Anne immediately prepared to travel to Scotland to meet her new husband, but the voyage was beset by bad fortune. Terrible storms rose in the North Sea, splitting the fleet in which she travelled. The new queen was pushed back to Oslo to take refuge, while on 12 September one of James's emissaries, Lord Dingwall, arrived, and told the king of the storm.

For a month James watched and waited the rough seas, order-ing prayers be said for his new wife's safe voyage, but a month later she managed to get word to him that she was safe, and would winter in Oslo. In a pique of romance, James set out to collect her himself, and spent the winter in Denmark, before braving more storms on the return leg. The storms, the passion, and the impromptu honeymoon in a country where Lutherans were much more attuned to news of demons coming in from Germany raised in James a terrible political and misogynistic paranoia. Scotland had, up to that moment, been reasonably free of the witch panics that had sprung up around Europe through-out the Reformation and Counter-Reformation. However, safely ensconced back in Scotland, James launched an investigation into the causes of the storms that had risked not just the life of his wife, but his chance at an heir.

The investigation dug up some disturbing 'facts', undoubtedly influenced by the allegations of witchcraft spreading around the Danish court. The Danish minister of finance, wanting to indem-nify himself against any claims of incompetence in outfitting the ships for potential storms, claimed witches had raised the bad weather, which led to a witch trial. James sought, and found, the presence of witchcraft in his own land.

In North Berwick, the accusers alleged, some form of unholy and devilish gathering had been held on 31 October, the eve of All Hallows' Day. In attendance was no less than the Devil himself, and it was clear that it was he who rose the stormy seas to prevent James's marriage. A Scottish widow who worked as a healer and midwife, Agnes Sampson, was accused of participat-ing. She denied the accusations until put under terrible torture, and afterwards confessed to her role: she had thrown a chris-tened cat, with parts of a dead human attached, into the sea in order to raise a storm.[11]

The North Berwick Witch Trials of 1590 ignited a passion within James for understanding the nature of witchcraft and rooting it out. It seems, especially in the early days of his obses-sion, that his beliefs were deep and sincere; he had disbelieved accusations against Agnes Sampson until her final confession before him. Yet it also seems undeniable that his paranoia had both a political cause (a childhood being raised around diabolical religious plotting, ending in the recent execution of his mother) and useful political consequences.

One of those implicated in the tortured confessions of the supposed witches was Francis Stewart, the Earl of Bothwell. Bothwell had played a significant role in James's court, even partially standing in for him in governance when the king was away in Denmark. Bothwell's uncle, from whom he inherited the title, was Mary Queen of Scots's third husband, the alleged murderer of James's father. His interest in the occult and his exuberant nature had led him to fall from James's grace, and he was arrested, imprisoned, and eventually escaped, to be cast as an outlaw and to launch raids upon James's life, until finally captured and pardoned.[12]

After the North Berwick Witch Trials, which James attended personally, he threw himself into the science and art of witch-hunting. Witch panics in Scotland had previously been rare, in comparison to the rest of Europe, but in the eight decades following the case, there are thought to have been over two thousand executions for witchcraft in a sparsely populated country: an average of more than twenty-five a year.

There are also wider, more material political implications regarding the rise of the witch hunts than mere court scheming. In *Caliban and the Witch*, Silvia Federici argues that the witch hunts were an integral part of the restructuring of social relations in the early modern period, when a new phase in capitalist development required a new patriarchal order. Federici expands traditional Marxist explanations of this period, during which 'conquest, enslavement, robbery, murder, in short, force, play[ed] the greatest part'. These forms of brutality created a degree of wealth, and a degree of landless impoverishment on the part of ordinary people, which enabled that wealth (invested in industry) and the labour of the poor to come together to produce the capitalist order.[13]

To this process of the enclosure of land and the creation of a proletariat reliant upon waged labour to survive, Federici adds a violent revolution in the sexual order. Traditional bases of power for women, such as healthcare and midwifery, and other parts of the mediaeval sexual order that challenged the new role for women within the wage economy and the sexual division of labour, such as sex work, were suppressed. Rather than being 'the last spark of a dying feudal world', witch panics and concurrent hunts were a key weapon in the violent disciplining of women, and a vital part of the creation of a modern sexual order.[14]

James's opinions on witchcraft are well known, thanks in part to *Daemonologie*, a book he published in 1597, at the height of his obsession with satanic possession. The purpose of the book was 'to proue two things as I haue alreadie said: the one that such diuelish [devilish] artes haue bene and are. The other what exact trial and seuere punishment they merite'.[15] In the book James sets himself up as something of an expert on anti-witch theory and practice, and *Daemonologie* contains the same anxieties that Federici documents about women as unstable, dissolute social agents. Asked in the Daemonologie's 'dialogue' why there are twenty witches for every warlock (a male witch), he replies, 'The reason is easie, for as that sexe is frailer then man is, so is it easier to be intrapped in these grosse snares of the Deuill,' drawing a comparison with the seduction of Eve by the serpent in the Garden of Eden.[16]

Along with the desire to discipline women into this new economic and social order, witch panics were driven by the growth of colonialism. Seeking justification for the subjugation of Indigenous peoples, and trying to likewise discipline those people's into the economic order of the settler colonists, colonists denigrated Indigenous religious and spiritual practices as 'devil-worshipping', and consequently their ideas were both influenced by, and in turn influenced, European witch-hunting in the early modern period. Illustrations in Europe of Indigenous people in the Americas taking part in cannibalistic rituals mirrored those already circulating that portrayed witches' Sabbaths, while colonists sought to depict 'illicit' forms of sex practised in Indigenous societies, such as sodomy, as part of these devilish practices.

These attempts to dehumanise and racialize Indigenous people as somehow gripped by satanic forces went hand in hand with attempts to destroy Indigenous economies and force populations into working in the new silver and mercury mines: an example of how race science, witch-hunting, and colonial dispossession were all interlinked forms of 'primitive accumulation', the violent appropriation of land and resources from ordinary people to enable capitalist economic growth. With regards to sodomy, the tools of race science and the colonial project became vital in later centuries to the creation of an idea of 'homosexuality' as a scientific subject.

Colonialism soon became a key concern for James, because in March 1603 Queen Elizabeth died, and he became the first king of both England and Scotland. He inherited a kingdom that had been going through a so-called Golden Age, with a blooming of cultural talent, an efficient centralised government, and new colonies being established in the Americas. Yet it was also a country still wracked with sectarian division and, particularly, a huge legacy of debt from almost twenty years of war with Spain, and from the Nine Years' War in Ireland, where English attempts to colonize the country faced resistance from Irish nobles.[17]

A new king bought peace with Spain, but the desire of the Spanish for the freedom of Catholic worship in his kingdom was something James was unwilling to cede.[18] England, meanwhile, still had its own share of Catholics worshipping in secret, many of whom prayed, and plotted, for liberation from the Protestant yoke by the hand of Spanish invasion. One such Catholic was a young Yorkshireman who had already fought for Spain against Dutch protestant reformers for control of the Spanish Netherlands in the Eighty Years' War. He had then travelled to Spain in a futile attempt to rustle up support for another Spanish invasion of England, an escapade that found little enthusiasm in a country still struggling to repay the debts of its numerous failed armadas.[19] His name was Guy (Guido) Fawkes, and if he could not gain the support of Spain in an invasion, he would have to foment a rebellion inside the country instead.

Joined in England with a group of fellow Catholic plotters, Fawkes and the conspirators formulated a plan whereby the new English king would be blown up in a spectacular attack on the Houses of Parliament while he was in attendance, followed by a revolt of Catholics through which the king's daughter, Elizabeth, would be put upon the throne. The plot was foiled when an anonymous letter warning of the scheme was allegedly sent to a Catholic peer, Lord Monteagle, who handed it to the king. The undercroft of the Houses of Parliament were then searched. In the midst of the search, they caught Guy Fawkes, using the alias 'John Johnson', red-handed with a lantern and fuses.

The torture of Fawkes, still claiming to be John Johnson, was horrifically brutal, and carried out on the orders of James himself, who demanded that 'the gentler tortures' be first used on him in the Tower of London, and if they did not work, 'by degree proceeding to the worst'. Fawkes was laid out upon the rack, which stretched his limbs until they popped from their sockets, his ligaments tearing and muscles stretching.[20] Within days he had revealed not just his own identity, but the identities of fellow conspirators; one reason we can surmise the rack was used is the signature on his dictated confession is a barely legible scrawl, suggesting he had been maimed by the torture.

Along with seven co-conspirators, Fawkes was tried and found guilty of treason. The following January he was dragged by horse through the streets, sentenced to be hanged but mutilated whilst still alive, his genitals cut from his body and burned before him, disembowelled and his heart removed, his head chopped off and his body cut into parts for public display. He avoided this grizzly fate by jumping from the scaffold while the noose was around his neck, killing him instantly, but many of his fellow plotters endured the whole ghastly public spectacle.

The plot, having been foiled, proved useful for James, allowing him to become closer to Parliament. Popular mood was behind him, buoyed by widespread sympathy for the royal family after the recent attempted assassination. Taking into account the anti-Catholic mood, James passed new laws further suppressing the rights of Catholics. Parliament passed the 'Popish Recusants Act' the year after the attempted insurrection, giving it the power to force Catholics to swear allegiance to the king, which made explicit the idea that the pope did not possess the authority to overthrow a king.

James also took the opportunity to counter anti-Catholic laws with new demands on hardline Protestants, enforcing conformity on so-called dissenters: early Puritans. He much preferred the Anglican model, which saw the king as 'Supreme Governor' and gave him a certain degree of power through a system of bishops, over the Scottish model of the Kirk, which does away with the episcopacy (the rule of bishops) in favour of a Presbyterian model.

James's most important weapon in this strategy of conformity, and marginalising radicals on both sides, was the commissioning of a new translation of a bible, which would be an 'authorised version': the only one permitted to be read in churches. Launching the endeavour after a conference he had convened in 1604, James would carefully oversee this new English translation, ensuring that, amongst other things, it removed much of the commentary from earlier Protestant translations which challenged his position on kingly supremacy. This new bible, known as the 'King James Version', is still used widely today, and regarded as a cornerstone book in the English language, rivalling Shakespeare for the number of phrases that have become everyday English idioms.

James's concern with ensuring the power of the monarchy to rule unencumbered descended from his belief in the divine right of kings, by which the authority of a monarch to rule was granted not by the population but instead by God. This was not a new idea by any means, but James developed it considerably as an intellectual theory, and it would go on to play a significant role in the tragedies of the Stuart dynasty. He laid out his theories in a treatise, *The True Law of Free Monarchies*, and in a book, the *Basilikon Doron*, both written before he took the English throne. The *Basilikon Doron* was effectively a manual for kingship intended for his firstborn son and heir, Henry, which stressed to him that there were two types of kings, good kings and tyrants, and 'the one acknowledgeth himselfe ordained for his people, hauing receaued from God a burthen of gouernment where of he must be countable: the other thinketh his people ordayned for him, apray to his passions & inordinate appetites, as the fruites of his magnanimitie.'[21]

If his tone with his son was paternal, his tone with his parliament was patrician. While he vowed to rule justly, he would brook no quarter to challenges to his authority from the House. This assertion of his rights, as if he were himself a god, went down as well as you might expect in England, which had long fought for the rights of Parliament against unjust kings. Part of the English Parliament's resistance to James's belief in the absolute power of the king was not just his attempt to sideline them, but also the system of patronage which he used to bestow gifts of land, title, and power to people who pleased him personally.

This would have been bad enough were he a king with only an eye for the ladies, but given that James's tastes lay elsewhere, it gave young, ambitious, and presumably sexy men the opportunity to acquire significant power by making themselves available to his advances. There is power in being the king who sits upon the throne, but sometimes there is more power in being the throne on whom the king sits.

A young Scot named Robert Carr, descended from wealthy landowners, Catholics, and supporters of Mary, Queen of Scots, was the first to take advantage of this opening. According to one of James's biographers, Bryan Bevan, Carr had 'little intellectual ability', but was 'athletic and skillful at games, aristocratic in appearance, handsome with flaxen hair, a small beard and moustache, [and] possessed an air of stupid arrogance'.[22] Let's face it, any of us could have made James's mistake. We can add to the list a certain vulnerability, as James first saw Carr as an adult at a jousting competition in 1607, when before James this handsome twenty-one-year-old was thrown from his horse. James immediately took a shine to him, even though he was some two decades older, and helped nurse him through his convalescence.

Carr quickly rose to become the king's 'favourite', and was handsomely rewarded with a knighthood. He was then gifted the right to live in Sherborne Castle, which the king had taken from Sir Walter Raleigh, who was languishing in the Tower, having been involved in a plot against him. Acting upon the advice of his lifelong friend, the poet Thomas Overbury, Carr used the king's affections to manoeuvre himself into a considerable position of power, earning himself bad favour with Queen Anne, and also with Prince Henry, the king's heir and only seven years younger than himself.

The death of Prince Henry from typhoid fever in 1612 changed the balance of power at court. The king grew more distant from his wife, and closer to an emboldened Carr, whom he created the Earl of Somerset the following year. But Carr was also in love, and not with the king. Instead he had fallen for a married woman, Frances Howard, the wife of the Earl of Essex. She complained their marriage had never been consummated, a humiliation for young Essex, and their marriage was annulled with the king's intervention, leaving Carr free to marry in a lavish ceremony paid for by the king. Yet Carr had lost control of himself. Not only had he lost the strategic advice of Thomas Overbury, who had opposed his love match and ended up in the Tower himself, having fallen foul of James, but his passion for Frances Howard had led him to spurn the king, being openly rude to him, forcing James into begging for his affections. James wrote to Carr complaining of his 'long creeping back and withdrawing ... from lying in my chamber, notwithstanding my many hundred times earnest soliciting you to the contrary'.[23]

When Carr and his wife were accused of having arranged for Overbury to be poisoned in the Tower, the game was up; yet James, ever the romantic, commuted their death sentences and would go on to pardon them. Frances's first husband, the Earl of Essex, would have his own revenge against the king for his humiliation, later becoming the first chief commander of the Parliamentarian Army when it took to the field against Charles I, James's son.

Although undoubtedly wounded by Carr's cruelty, James had a new lover boy, George Villiers, a handsome young man from the country whom James's privy councillors, wishing to counter

Carr's influence, had dolled up with a new wardrobe and pushed into the king's line of sight at the Royal Stables. Having been made the King's Cupbearer, and with Carr out of the picture, Villiers began a meteoric rise through the royal appointments that gave James's system of patronage so much power. Already a gentleman of the Bedchamber, in 1616, the year of Carr's conviction, Villiers was made Master of the Horse and given a peerage. A year later, he was upgraded to an earl and became the king's private secretary, and a year after that, the Marquess of Buckingham and a privy councillor in both England and Scotland.[24] In 1619 he was made the Lord High Admiral of England. In 1623, still just thirty-one years old, he was made the Duke of Buckingham. Unlike Carr, he stayed close to other members of the royal family, accompanying Prince Charles on an ill-fated escapade to Spain to win the hand of the Catholic princess, the Infanta Maria Anna, in marriage. The question of whether James's relationship with Buckingham was sexual or not has been one of historical debate, although a debate where biographers seem keen to let the benefit of doubt fall on the side of 'not'. But undoubtedly James has form, and given that, it hardly seems reckless to suggest something physical when, for example, Buckingham sent James letters asking if he still loved him like he did 'at Farnham, where the bed's head could not be found between the master and his dog'.[25]

The poet Alexander Gill the Younger described James as 'the old fool', a refrain that has followed older men who fall hopelessly for handsome younger men down through the centuries. Gill compared Buckingham to Ganymede, the eternally youthful cupbearer for Zeus who was a symbol of homosexuality in Renaissance Europe: indeed, it is from the Latinized version of Ganymede, Catamitus, from which we get the English word *catamite*, meaning the younger, passive sexual partner in a pederastic relationship. As we saw in earlier chapters, this was the model through which Greeks and Romans formalised same-sex desire, and was re-emerging with the Renaissance readings of classical antiquity culture. In a poem Gill asked that God save 'my sovereign from a Ganymede / Whose Whorish breath hath power to lead / His Majesty which way it list'.[26]

Concerns around James's patronage and his lovers were not restricted to the life of court alone. Despite the best efforts of Buckingham, by now the most powerful politician and courtier in the land, James was forced by problems in Europe to convene a new Parliament in 1621 after a hiatus of seven years, leading to renewed calls for yearly parliaments. The Parliament allowed the landowning classes to address some of their major grievances emerging from James's absolutist rule.

The system of monopolies, whereby the king could grant his favourites the total control of certain commodities, was attacked, and with it those courtiers and advisers who had pushed the system. The lord chancellor, the philosopher Sir Francis Bacon, was impeached for corruption, fined, and stripped of his titles, although he was something of a fall guy for Buckingham.[27] But it was clear that this was an inevitable conflict between a form of mercantile capitalism that demanded representation through Parliament, and a form of absolutism which saw no authority in the landowning class outside of its subservience to a generous king. James's regime was, writes Perry Anderson, 'contemptuous and uncomprehending of Parliament [and] made no attempt to assuage the growing oppositional temper of the English gentry'.[28]

Buckingham was also a source of grievances for Parliament owing to his acquisitions in Ireland. Both the protestant merchant class and the king had engaged with full hearts in the colonization of Ireland, and in particular the plantation of Ulster. Even before he took to the English throne, James had justified colonial conquest and advocated plantations in order to create a Protestant 'ascendancy' in the country and take control of the land. Yet Buckingham's attempts to secure wealth for his family and heirs had led to the creation of a new English aristocracy in Ireland supported by a corrupt system of subsidies and other privileges, of which Buckingham and the Villiers family were scraping off the cream. As the scheme unfolded, it was clear that attempts at colonization had become a drain upon the English Parliament.

The English colonial project was turbocharged during James's reign, with the foundation of England's first permanent, surviving colony in North America at Jamestown, and the settlement of Bermuda and Newfoundland, all driven by the same mercantile interests that were rapidly losing patience with James. Likewise, the *Mayflower* Pilgrims, settler colonists whose voyage and survival at the Plymouth Colony in Massachusetts became a foundation myth of the United States of America, were puritan protestants who left England in part through dissatisfaction with James's attempts to moderate religion and enforce conformity in the Church of England.

As James grew older and more infirm, Buckingham's power grew, but unlike Carr, the affection and love between the two held fast, despite the protestations of courtiers and Parliament. Towards the end of his life, in December 1623, James wrote to Buckingham

> praying God that I may have a joyful and comfortable meeting with you and that we may make at this Christmas a new marriage ever to be kept hereafter; for, God so love me, as I desire only to live in this world for your sake, and that I had rather live banished in any part of the earth with you than live a sorrowful widow's life without you. And so God bless you, my sweet child and wife, and grant that ye may ever be a comfort to your dear dad and husband.
>
> James R.[29]

In the early months of 1625 his ill health got the better of him; following a stroke and an attack of dysentery, he died on 27 March, with Buckingham in attendance. Buckingham remained a powerful force in the court of James's son, Charles I, but was so unpopular he lasted barely three more years before he was assassinated by a disgruntled soldier, who was hailed as a hero for the deed.

James's contempt for a parliament that represented the emergent mercantile class and belief in an absolutist monarchy was inherited by his son, Charles I. Yet the divine right of kings couldn't survive the English Civil Wars, Charles's execution, and the Interregnum. James's love of the court as a profligate and flamboyant spectacle powered by intrigue and sexual desire, however, would live on in his grandson, Charles II, resulting on that occasion in innumerable illegitimate children, but no heir. It was James's inability to decisively settle the religious divisions in the country, and the continued suspicions that his family had never truly renounced the Catholicism of his mother, Mary Queen of Scots, that led to the end of his dynasty in the so-called Glorious Revolution of 1688. This 'revolution', which would see the overthrow of his second grandson, James VII and II, saw England settle on an ideology of Protestantism and constitutional monarchy, and commit to continuing the dual project of colonialism and domination of Catholic European countries: in short, the creation of the world we live in today. That combination of Protestantism, white supremacy, and colonialism would prove a violently toxic mix. Amongst the many repercussions of its system of exploitation and extraction would be a drive towards a scientific rationalism that swept up same-sex desire into the world of crime and disease, making the sort of easy, open attitude that James appeared to show towards the men he loved unimaginable.

4

Frederick the Great

In 2011, in Berlin, Vanessa de Senarclens, a scholar of the Enlightenment who currently teaches at Bard College, discovered a 1740 poem entitled 'La Jouissance' – 'the pleasure', perhaps, or 'the orgasm'.[1] Addressed to Francesco Algarotti, a Venetian poet, art critic, and sodomite, the poem reads, in part:

> That night, vigorous desire in full measure,
> Algarotti wallowed in a sea of pleasure.
> A body not even a Praxiteles[2] fashions
> Redoubled his senses and imbued his passions
> Everything that speaks to eyes and touches hearts
> Was found in the fond object that inflamed his parts.[3]

While readers who are familiar with Berlin may think that passage describes an average Saturday night in the German capital, this letter caused a stir because of who appeared to have written it: Friedrich II, King of Prussia and Elector of Brandenburg, known in English as 'Frederick the Great' and in German as the diminutive 'Alte Fritz'. Such a man turned the insignificant electorate of Brandenburg, known as the 'sandbox of Europe' for its moory and unproductive terrain, into the centrepiece of a vast and powerful empire. He was also a pioneer of an enlightened style of monarchic rule that combined military campaigning with artistic and intellectual patronage. A self-styled philosopher-king, he wrote a hundred flute sonatas and four symphonies, and hobnobbed with Voltaire and Bach, who wrote the *Musical Offering* for him in 1747, based off one of the king's original themes.

Frederick's sexuality has been the source of heated debate both during his life and later, around the turn of the twentieth century. After Germany unified and sought in the history of its new Prussian overlords examples of both heroic warriors and enlightened philosophers, Frederick's legend only grew. At the same time, new ideas and understandings of sexuality were being developed by sexologists and activists in that sandy bog from which Frederick once conquered vast swaths of Europe. This combination makes his memory uniquely complicated: a man who could simultaneously serve as an object of masculinist gay identification and, among his supporters, face the marring of a legacy of statecraft and militarism because of his supposedly effeminate ways.

During his life, however, this appears to have been less of a conflict. Frederick's story helps us understand the complex and shifting relationship between the same-sex erotic and masculinist, military power: how different that relationship could be and feel across time, how historical memory could transform and be shaped by it, and how the making of the modern homosexual was less a taking-up of queer fictions of the past than a scrambling and re-writing of them. Christopher Chitty encourages us to think about the history of homosexuality less as a story of how people did or did not deviate from transhistorical norms and more in terms of their relationship with power.[4] Frederick – in his life and his memory – helps us do just that.

Brandenburg, the province that surrounds the city of Berlin, forms part of the flat Polish plain that separates the Western German territories and Russia. Misty and marshy, with sandy soil, this land had never been rich. 'Apart from Libya', Frederick would write to Voltaire in 1776, 'there are few states that can equal ours when it comes to sand.'[5] Since the Middle Ages, Prussia's core territory was ruled through a feudal, manorial system. A small number of nobles, known as *junkers* (short for *jung Herr*, or 'young lord'), ruled over vast swaths of swampy and unproductive land from one- or two-story brick houses – similar, say, to the system of French *chateaux*, but without the wealth that made those *chateaux* sites of opulent luxury. Marx would call these nobles the 'cabbage-Junkers', a reactionary and brutish class of petty minor aristocrats dreaming of their imagined origins as Teutonic crusading knights civilizing Slavic land.

It was here, on 24 January 1712, in Berlin, then just a small provincial capital where the Prussian rulers had their winter palace, that Frederick was born to Frederick William I, then the crown prince of Prussia, and his wife, Sophia Dorothea of Hanover. A year later, Frederick William I ascended to the throne.

Although both Frederick William I and his son Frederick the Great proved to be influential rulers who helped transform Prussia from a backwater into a fearsome power, it is inaccurate to say that the process began entirely with them. The Thirty Years' War, from 1618 to 1648, had torn Europe (and Germany) asunder as the absolutist Catholic Habsburgs tried to put down the Protestant rebels to the north.[6] Frederick William's father, Frederick I, had tried to turn muddy Berlin into a proper court, building baroque palaces and wide, tree-lined boulevards, founding a court orchestra, the Staatskapelle, that exists to this day, and inviting Jews (to whom he extended limited tolerance) and Huguenots to settle the city in an aim to grow it. Frederick William – short and gout-riddled – had no time for these niceties upon ascending the throne. 'The new king', he told his father's courtiers, 'bids you all to go to hell.'[7]

He also ended a long-standing practice in which the excess sons of the Junkers travelled to serve as mercenaries in other armies across Europe. Instead, he decreed, these men had to serve in *his* army, the ranks of which began to swell. Generals replaced courtiers in the ranks of precedence that defined court life, and the various fineries of the baroque court – powdered wigs, champagne, sumptuous fabrics – were replaced with cabbage and beer.

Accordingly, Frederick William had aimed to raise his son as a relentlessly practical young general, assigning him Huguenot tutors to teach him a religious and practical education in both German and French. From a young age, however, young

Frederick had other plans, secreting away an enormous library of philosophy, poetry, and the classics. One story from his sixth birthday will strike a chord with any homo who's ever had to navigate the fraught space between parental expectations and forbidden desires that come when presents are opened: after receiving an enormous set of toy lead soldiers, the young prince ignored the gift, opened up his book of French melodies, and began serenading the court ladies with his lute.[8]

Father and son would never get along. Frederick William's illnesses only worsened – nightmares, swollen genitals, digestive disruptions, intense pain – as would his campaign to fashion his son into a man he was most certainly not. The young Frederick received no praise, no warmth. He was derided by his father for his effeminacy, for his free thinking, for his incompetence at riding and shooting. In 1728 he wrote to his father complaining of the 'cruel hatred' between them. In response, his father denounced him. Physical violence increased: Frederick William beat his son with a cane, threw him to the ground, and forced him to kiss his feet.[9]

As he took refuge with his friends – once, at seventeen, writing, 'I play my flute, I read, and I love my friends more than I do myself' – Frederick became closer and closer to Hans Hermann von Katte, a young Junker with strikingly bushy black eyebrows eight years Frederick's senior who hailed from the Brandenburg village of Wust.[10] Katte had travelled in his youth, studying in the Netherlands before joining the Prussian army. He shared Frederick's interests in poetry and flautistry, and the two men rapidly became closer as they studied philosophy and mathematics. Meanwhile, Frederick William ruled from a 'tobacco parliament' in his hunting lodge, a gloomy affair decorated with stag antlers and full of drunken generals.

It is not easy to categorize the budding relationship that was forming between Katte and Frederick. As we have already discussed, the identity category of 'gay' as we understand it now, and even the idea of a coherent sexual identity, both date to the late nineteenth century. This does not mean that Frederick's effeminacy or supposed affinity for 'Greek' love went uncommented, merely that such things were considered, in the immortal words of Michel Foucault, an 'aberration' rather than evidence that the person committing such acts was of a different 'species'.[11] Accordingly, state regulation of these acts focused on the acts themselves: the Prussian sodomy statutes were strengthened by Frederick William during his reign, who turned it into a capital offense (as well as ordering the strangling of all the Roma/Sinti in his kingdom in a 1725 edict). Both the differences and the continuities between the forms of the regulation of same-sex erotic behaviour then and now are instructive. In 1721, to use one unhappy example, a married former military officer, Anastasius Lagrantius Rosenstengel, was discovered to have been assigned female at birth, and to have 'simulated' the male role in intercourse with 'a penis of stuffed leather ... tied to [his] pubes with a leather strap'.[12] Frederick William personally intervened to ensure Rosenstengel's execution and his wife's lifelong imprisonment.

Only one year after meeting Katte, the young prince revealed his plan: to flee to Great Britain, which he thought of as a land of liberal enlightenment. This meant not only the abandonment of his throne but also a treasonous defection to the enemy, and it was part of a complex game of diplomacy and subterfuge in which both Britain and France were attempting to install and influence a more compliant and liberal Prussian ruler. Katte advised against Frederick leaving, but he could not be moved. Courtiers spoiled the plot, revealing both Frederick's plan, which was to flee from a royal tour of various other German principalities, and Katte's involvement.

According to his daughter Wilhelmina, Frederick William threatened to kill his son upon finding out about the plan, and had to be implored to spare his life. The prince and Katte were both locked up like common deserters in the military fortress at Küstrin, each in solitary confinement.[13] The two men were court-martialled. The implications seem to have been clear to Frederick William as well, who reportedly asked Frederick if he had 'seduced Katte ... or did Katte seduce you?'[14] Frederick William at first insisted that Katte have his tongue ripped out with red-hot tongs and then be hanged, which was then the Prussian punishment for *lèse-majesté*, but, owing to the nobility of Katte's birth, eventually accepted a simple beheading.[15] Frederick was forced to watch. As Katte was marched up onto the executioner's platform, Frederick cried out, 'I beg of you, a thousand apologies!' Katte replied, 'Monseigneur, you owe me nothing,' and when the sword hit his neck, the young prince fainted, spent three days inconsolable, and then never spoke of Katte again.[16]

Part of the complex diplomatic machinations around Frederick's planned escape had to do with the question of the young prince's marriage: he had first gotten the idea to go to Britain from his mother's attempt to marry him off to her niece Princess Amelia, the daughter of King George II. Despite Frederick's own inclination towards marrying one of several powerful and imposing women – including Maria Theresa of Austria, who would become the only female Habsburg regent and for whom he was willing to give up his succession – his father insisted on marrying him off to Elisabeth-Christine of Brunswick-Bevern, a distant Protestant cousin. Frederick was distraught. 'There can be neither love nor friendship between us,' he wrote to a friend. In another letter, he wrote: 'If I am forced to marry her, I will reject her away as soon as I am master ... No man can blame me for it, knowing that I was made to do something that was totally against my inclinations ... I feel myself too flighty, and insufficiently attracted to the female sex.'[17]

At this point he was still being imprisoned in Küstrin, and was only released when he agreed to the match, realizing that once married he could ensure his liberty, and see his new bride as infrequently as possible. He set up court in the Brandenburg town of Ruppin and focused on garden remodelling, home and interior decoration, the creation of an orchestra, and the building of architectural follies in the Greek style. Careful to keep his spending habits a secret from his father, he developed at this time a reputation for having rapacious and libertine sexual appetites. The two men slowly reconciled and when Frederick William I died at the end of May of 1740, Frederick was able to credit him with having died 'with the steadfastness of a philosopher and the resignation of a Christian'.[18] Upon his assumption of the throne, the first problem Frederick busied himself with was his wife, to whom he wrote, on the first of June, 'When you arrive [in Berlin] you will go first to the Queen [Mother] to pay your respects, and you will try to make a better job of it than in the past; after that you may remain here, your presence being necessary, until I write to tell you what to do.'[19] Queen Elizabeth would live out her days in a palace in Schönhausen, eighty kilometers (and a full day's carriage ride) from Frederick's palace in Potsdam, which she would only see once, and briefly, in 1751. While he paid her bills, he ignored their anniversaries, refused to refer to her as his wife, and the two never had children. Frederick turned over many official court duties to his wife's court at Schönhausen while neglecting and underfunding it; nevertheless, she made lifelong donations of significantly more than half her income to charity.

At Ruppin, Frederick's right-hand man became Michael Gabriel Fredersdorf, for whom he immediately purchased a nearby estate and who became his lifelong privy treasurer – attending to money matters, home life, interior decorations, music, and essentially managing the outside world for the king. He served as 'a kind of prime minister';[20] Voltaire called him Frederick's 'grand factotum'.[21] Fredersdorf oversaw the construction and opening of Frederick's new summer palace Sanssouci, a yellow-pink confection with lavishly painted and panelled rooms decorated to various themes, featuring an enormous staircase of terraced fruit vines, set in a palace park including thousands of fruit trees, statuary, obelisks, rococo follies, and a Temple of Friendship, built in honour of his sister, which celebrated the manly love of the Greeks. 'He has a very pretty face,' Frederick wrote of Fredersdorf, who Voltaire once described as 'young, handsome, well-made', saying he 'served to entertain [Frederick] in more than one fashion'.[22]

Around the same time he became king, Frederick met and became infatuated with Francesco Algarotti, the philosopher to whom he wrote a poem as an answer to the charge that northern Europeans lacked passion (the same poem that appears at the beginning of this chapter). Partially in response to rumours about this affair, the artist William Hogarth painted *The Toilette*, in which a flute player (perhaps Frederick?) is positioned next to a painting of Ganymede being pursued by Zeus; Giles MacDonogh, one of Frederick's biographers, understands this as a joke about Frederick's (homo)sexuality.[23]

So far, so gay, right? Yes, and no: while it seems clear that Frederick had significant erotic and romantic attachments to men and virtually none to women – 'fortune has it in for me', he once wrote, 'alas, she is a woman, and I am not that way inclined' – it is also important to remember that our contemporary regimes of sexuality are just that.[24] Looking back with today's eyes, we put two and two together and make four: which is fair. But it is also fair to note, as Bodie Ashton does in a recent article on Frederick, that something as complicated and historically contingent as sexuality can't be solved as if it were simple arithmetic. It seems that Frederick's homoerotic predilections, along with his love of gardening and music and literature, were actually understood as *part* of a 'constant definition of Prussian masculine character', and being a proper Prussian man '*required* a man to embody "sensitive" traits that later generations would come to view as "effeminate"'.[25] If it would have been beyond the pale – illegal, even – for a king to be openly practicing sodomy, a bit of flute-playing and some temples to Greek Love fit right in. Understood as embodying a kind of Attic masculinity, Frederick would become part of a vision of Berlin as the 'Athens of the Spree' (referring to Berlin's Spree river) in the nineteenth century, a city dedicated to humanistic pursuits at the centre of a militaristic empire.

Of course, the expanding empire was just as important as the palatial rococo repose. Frederick William's conscription of the Junker failsons had made the Prussian army enormous: 1 in 80 were soldiers, as opposed to only 1 in 300 in Great Britain. In addition to Brandenburg, Frederick inherited the prosperous city of Magdeburg along with several other cities near what is now the German border with the Netherlands. Another duchy, centred around the city of Königsberg farther east, had been consolidated under Prussian control in 1770.

Frederick's first rapid territorial expansion came immediately after ascending to the throne, when he invaded and occupied Silesia, then ruled by Austria, which had just been taken over by Maria Theresa, the Habsburg empress whom Frederick had once attempted to wed. His troops rapidly overtook the indebted and poorly trained Austrians, and after several years of squabbling, in 1745 he signed the Treaty of Dresden, firmly placing Silesia in his control.

After the collapse of the alliance between Austria and Great Britain, Frederick aligned Prussia with England against the Catholic alliance of France and Austria, and launched the Seven Years' War in 1756 by attacking Saxony and forcibly incorporating the Saxon forces into his own army. While Frederick didn't manage to hold on to any of his initial conquests, the broader geopolitical effects of the Seven Years' War were vast. This was a truly global conflict defined by squabbles between France, Britain, and their proxies on several continents, including the French-Indian War in North America, and became a key tipping point for both the French and American Revolutions. The absolutist monarchies of France and Austria could not compete with the dynamic, early modern capitalist economy of Britain, which Frederick greatly admired and towards which he sought to reform the Prussian state.

At home, between the wars, Frederick continued to rule over a court of at least partial and self-understood enlightenment. His court modulated between British liberalism and the ancient traditions of continental European monarchy. Freed from his father's restrictions on spending, Frederick was able to engage the best musicians in Europe for his court orchestra, including CPE Bach, the son of JS, as his harpsichordist. In 1747, JS Bach visited Sanssouci to see his son and was, upon his arrival, immediately summoned to the court of the great king.

Frederick greeted Bach by sitting down at his piano and playing a theme. Frederick then asked Bach to write him a fugue in three parts, a complex composition in which a given musical theme is introduced, repeated, and transformed. Certain kinds of themes, like the one Frederick suggested to Bach, are particularly difficult to set as they cannot be combined with other themes in canons without breaking the rules of functional harmony. It would be, to paraphrase the historian James R. Gaines, like giving a poet a line with which to begin a rhymed poem that ended with 'salad'.[26] Bach sat himself down at the piano and immediately improvised a three-part fugue. (Again, this would be as impressive as a poet hearing a line ending with 'salad' and immediately improvising a villanelle.) Frederick, taken aback, demanded a six-part fugue. Bach indicated that he needed some time, but ended up composing in two weeks *The Musical Offering*, a collection of keyboard music ending with a 'Prussian Fugue' in six parts, which, like the rest of these pieces of music, are all based on Frederick's impossible theme. Musicologists and historians, including Gaines, have deduced extramusical meanings in the work: Bach, deeply religious and suspicious of the secularist clarity of the enlightenment, had transformed the king's provocation into the godly music of the spheres.

Speaking of godless secularism, Voltaire was a regular at Sanssouci: he and Frederick had kept up their correspondence since Frederick's young adulthood and it was Voltaire who first referred to Frederick as 'the Great'.[27] Voltaire was, of course, an icon of enlightenment, and admired many of Frederick's legal reforms. This new legal code, finished in 1780 but not published until 1794, when the king had already died, attempted to moderate between feudalism and capitalism, curbing the absolute power of the monarch and maintaining the privileges of the aristocracy while introducing more principles of equality under the law, to the horror of the Junkers.[28] During his reign, Frederick supported a relatively free press, the abolition of torture, the admission of non-nobles to the highest levels of the bureaucracy and judiciary, the reorganization of the Prussian Academy of Science, and severe restrictions on the death penalty.

But Voltaire was also a vicious satirist, and Frederick still an absolutist monarch. Voltaire began writing his memoirs in 1750, including sections detailing Frederick's homosexual exploits. 'He sent for two or three minions', Voltaire wrote, 'lieutenants, pages … or young cadets, and took coffee with them. The one to whom he threw a handkerchief remained alone with him for an hour.'[29] When these descriptions made it from Voltaire's memoirs into the realm of public gossip – eventually appearing in altered form in a pamphlet published in London in 1752 – the two men's friendship significantly cooled, although they had reconciled by Frederick's death.

As Frederick grew older, he became increasingly solitary; as friends died, including his beloved Fredersdorf, he made few new ones. Shying away from people, he preferred to spend his days with his flute and with his Italian greyhounds. As early as 1747, he had made requests for Italian greyhounds to be sent from England; the diplomat Thomas Villiers reported back that this would be difficult: 'That sort of dog is rare and much desired ... Few have any but Ladies, and it is not to be expected that they will part with what is fitted to their laps.'[30]

These dogs, and his horse Condé, were his most faithful companions as he grew old, gouty, and began to exhibit some of the same signs of illness that had plagued his father. He died, unattended by either his wife or any clergyman, on 17 August 1786.

Despite all the art and music that Frederick enjoyed at his court, it was opulent only compared to the austere standards of his father (and of course, to the daily life of most people who have ever lived). In fact, he inherited from his father somewhat of a suspicion of the overly padded French and Austrian aristocratic courts, with complex hierarchies of state and precedence and backstabbing. Therefore, when Frederick died, leaving no heir, he requested that he be buried in a simple grave next to Sanssouci, with his beloved greyhounds. He also desired that his resting site be next to a statue of Antinous for which he had a particular fondness; Antinous, as Blanning points out, 'had sacrificed himself for his lover' just as Katte had done for Frederick.[31] His nephew, who ascended the throne as King Frederick William II of Prussia, disregarded these instructions, as he would disregard many of Frederick's enlightenment legacies. Attempting to shore up the monarchy after the threat of the French Revolution made the guillotine seem a real threat to Europe's pampered aristocrats, the new king dulled many of the liberal innovations in Frederick's legal code and was content to fritter away his time gambling while the Junkers ran the country and even the military. He insisted that Frederick the Great be buried in state next to Frederick William I in the Garrison Church in Potsdam, where his tomb became, throughout the nineteenth century, a regular symbol of Prussian and later German nationalism.

As the eighteenth century rolled into the nineteenth, industrialization and the accompanying economic transformations associated with it – urbanization, the separation of the peasants from the land, the increasing power of the bourgeoisie and the reactionary response of the Junkers – only increased the pressure on the cluster of small principalities and kingdoms that made up what we now call Germany. By the 1840s, small uprisings and protests were regular affairs, and liberals and radicals were regularly publishing political programs calling for the reunification of the German nation along the lines of equality and brotherly love. Liberals overtook radicals in 1848 – Marx and other 'stagist' leftists controversially supported this, believing that the bourgeoisie needed its turn at the wheel before the proletariat could be formed, and then take power – and were themselves overtaken by monarchists who put down the uprisings. When Germany eventually did reunify, after the Franco-Prussian War of 1870, it was under the same line of Prussian kings, with the same class of reactionary Junkers rising swiftly into key military and political leadership roles.

By this time, however, significant changes had occurred in the dominant regimes of masculinity and sexuality. If Berlin still liked to think of itself as the 'Athens of the Spree', Frederick's Attic masculinity, in which homoerotic and homosocial signifiers could be a point of amusement or even scandal but not define him as unmanly or seriously threaten his rule, was no longer possible. The increasing movement of people off the land and into cities created new living arrangements and classes of people, urban dwellers with disposable income and the ability to make their own lives. This only increased the amount of same-sex erotic and romantic contact, much of which happened on dangerous and difficult-to-control streets and in the new spaces created by mass urban life. Sexologists and psychiatrists, newly empowered with the method and the mission to peer into the souls of the masses and try to make them better and more productive workers – and to reproduce the next generation in highly policed nuclear families – began to transform these rebels against the sexual order into a class of being: the homosexual.

From the beginning in the late 1800s, the homosexual was constructed together with the figure of the worker and the savage – theorized as backwards, inverted, or primitive, he/it was distanced from the 'straight time' of productive work.[32] In a world in which men were increasingly seen as industrial labour machines, with a similarly mechanistic and nationalistic understanding of history rolling inexorably forwards, the homosexual was anti-national and anti-progress. This led to several complex memory cultures growing up around Frederick: a culture of shame in which his supposed homosexuality was suppressed or dismissed in order to make him a more attractive national/nationalist hero, and a culture of homosexual masculinism that pioneered a misogynistic celebration of his homosexual-inclusive masculinity.

For the devoted Prussian nationalists, Frederick's homosexuality became an embarrassment even as his legacy grew. The German nationalism of the late nineteenth-century reunified empire was conservative, anti-liberal, and anti-Catholic: the Junkers' myths of Teutonic glory, of the subjugation of the savage Slavs, only increased. Given that the German-speaking lands (with the exception of Austria) were reunified under the Protestant Prussians, it became important for Frederick the Great to become, according to the historian Hagen Schulze, 'the model for a German hero ... who, in Goethe's words, had "saved the honour of part of the Germans against an allied world"'.[33]

It did not matter, Schulze points out, that Frederick's actual life found him opposed to German culture, favouring the French, and inhabiting a glittering and homoromantic intellectual world. 'The Frederick myth still had a profound effect', Schulze writes, 'especially among the *Reich's* young men ... who felt "Fritzisch" – as the young Goethe did.'[34] Schoolbooks included pictures of

Frederick's court and of the great man on horseback, placing him at the heart of Germany's national heritage. He was presented as the predecessor to the political system that developed under Bismarck and the Kaiser, in which monarchy was combined with modernity and militarist discipline. If, as Bodie Ashton points out, in the era of his rule Frederick's homosexuality did not stand in the way of his becoming 'Great' – a ruler, a national hero – after the reunification it was dismissed by historians as so much malicious gossip-mongering.[35]

For the subset of homosexual men in reunified Germany who wished to identify with their maleness, however, Frederick the Great became a key figure. Even before the First World War, the German homosexual movement had divided. While they still shared many publishing outlets, and both movements were vanguardist and relatively small, some homosexual men, like the 1870s pioneers in the terminology of homosexuality Karl-Maria Kertbeny and Karl Heinrich Ulrichs, preferred to think of homosexuality as a form of gender inversion, a framework that survived into Magnus Hirschfeld's early twentieth-century model of sexual 'steps in-between'. Others, however, preferred to understand homosexuality as a form of hypermasculine comradeship.

Adolf Brand's small anarchist group, the 'Community of the Self-Possessed', idealized war and male bonding as a spiritual plateau, looking back to ancient Greece as their model. Often misogynist and anti-Semitic, these men framed Frederick as a model for homosexual integration into, and leadership of, the Nation and its specific form of history. Later, in the 1920s, a homosexual writer named Friedrich Radszuweit would attempt to use Frederick's image along these lines to defend the national honour of homosexuals.[36]

Frederick's tomb, and indeed the Garrison Church in Potsdam, became a key site of national identification for the Nazis. After Hitler was elevated by conservatives to the chancellorship in 1933, he chose to open his first session of Parliament outside the Garrison Church, the site of Frederick's burial, where he was greeted solemnly by then president Paul von Hindenburg. Hitler personally glorified Frederick, calming himself down from political defeat by reminding himself of Frederick's losses and keeping an oil painting of Frederick above his desk in his bunker throughout the war. Goebbels and other Nazi propagandists repeatedly portrayed Frederick as the predecessor to the glorious German empire they were trying to build.[37] At the end of the war, Hitler had Frederick exhumed and moved to a salt mine lest bombs destroy the Garrison Church.

The Church survived the war but was demolished in 1968 by the East German Communists, who saw it as a site of right-wing nationalism. Frederick's body was then spirited off to West Germany to a family castle during the years that Germany was divided. In 1991, after reunification and on the 205th anniversary of his death, Frederick was laid to rest in his chosen spot of the side terrace at Sanssouci, in a tomb marked with only a small plaque, where his greyhounds had once been interred.

5

Jack Saul

In 1881 London was the largest metropolis the world had ever seen. More people resided in its central boroughs than even today, with great contrasts between the lives and lifestyles of the poor and the wealthy. The city was enjoying the spoils of the British Empire, leading to a boom in consumer culture. Anything could be bought, if you had the money, but for those who did not, there were only miserable choices: the workhouse, crime, and the concomitant risks of prison, transportation, and death. Victorian London has been described as the beating heart of the empire, that pumped capital, troops, and power around the world; it might just as well be described as the drain of empire, into which the material and human wealth of the colonies flowed.

One of those humans was a young Irish immigrant who, were it not for his immense boldness, may well have passed into history unnamed and unremembered. We meet him first in the introduction to a book he wrote allegedly at the tender age of twenty-three, putting his life to date on paper. The gentleman introducing the book describes their first encounter, which is well worth quoting at length:

> The writer of these notes was walking through Leicester Square one sunny afternoon last November, when his attention was particularly taken by an effeminate, but very good-looking young fellow, who was walking in front of him, looking in shop-windows from time to time, and now and then looking round as if to attract my attention.

Dressed in tight-fitting clothes, which set off his Adonis-like figure to the best advantage, especially about what snobs call the fork of his trousers where evidently he was favoured by nature by a very extraordinary development of the male appendages; he had small and elegant feet, set off by pretty patent leather boots, a fresh looking beardless face, with almost feminine features, auburn hair, and sparkling blue eyes, which spoke as plainly as possible to my senses, and told me that the handsome youth must indeed be one of the 'Mary-Ann's' of London, who I had heard were often to be seen sauntering in the neighbourhood of Regent Street, or the Haymarket, on fine afternoons or evenings.

Presently the object of my curiosity almost halted and stood facing the writer as he took off his hat, and wiped his face with a beautiful white silk handkerchief. That lump in his trousers had quite a fascinating effect upon me. Was it natural or made up by some artificial means? If real, what a size when excited; how I should like to handle such a manly jewel, etc. All this ran through my mind, and determined me to make his acquaintance, in order to unravel the real and naked truth; also, if possible, to glean what I could of his antecedents and mode of life, which I felt sure must be extraordinarily interesting.[1]

The introduction ends, after a little mutual masturbation into an open fire, with the writer suggesting to the young man that he write down the history of his sexual experiences. What follows is an eye-watering pornographic memoir of sodomy, oral sex, and prostitution. Some regard the book, titled *The Sins of the Cities of the Plain* (a reference to the Old Testament story of Sodom and Gomorrah, the two cities supposedly destroyed by God in punishment for their practicing of anal sex, from where we get the word 'sodomy'), as fiction, and perhaps the first entirely homosexual erotic fiction, but the subject of the memoir, Jack Saul, was a very real person. He was born into a working-class Catholic Irish family in Dublin in 1857, only five years after the Great Hunger, a devastating famine caused by potato blight and which British colonizers orchestrated into widespread death and dispossession. It is thought that a quarter of the country's population either died or emigrated during the Great Hunger, and it followed on an earlier famine in 1841 in which the country's population had already fallen by 20 percent. His parents and grandparents were one of the many people from the rural population that were forced from their ancestral homes, and had moved to the south of the city from County Wicklow; many millions more migrated overseas, especially to North America.[2]

It seems fairly certain that Saul's early life was a tough one, living in cramped tenements on Duke Street, surrounded by a large extended family. His father drove a horse-drawn cab around the city, which was not a hugely profitable endeavour. His mother was illiterate, and like most working-class people of the time, he lost brothers and sisters early in childhood.[3] Opportunities were hard to come by, and you had to make your own luck.

As a port city that also contained a very large British garrison, Dublin was home to one of Europe's largest red-light districts at the time, known as 'Monto', after Montgomery Street. According to a local legend, the future British king, Edward VI, even lost his virginity in the neighbourhood, and later took his son and heir, Prince Albert Victor, to the district in disguise. Prostitution and brothels were an intrinsic part of most Victorian cities; while not respectable, they were at least very visible, and the coalition of the state and moral reformers had not yet coalesced, as it would in the 1870s and '80s, to shut down prostitution, cruising, and other sex cultures as 'vice'.[4]

While Monto offered a large population of female sex workers, the presence of the barracks meant there were many poorly paid working-class young soldiers who boosted their income through selling sex. The idea that the British army contained a culture of sex work might surprise a modern reader, but well into the twentieth-century London's Wellington Barracks, home to the Foot Guards and conveniently located near a number of large parks, was a site where men could pick up working-class soldiers for sex.[5]

Certainly, the working-class Jack, still a teen, would have been more than aware of the presence not just of sex workers, but also clients. When he was seventeen he met a soldier named Martin Kirwan, a well-off member of the Irish Protestant gentry whose family had prospered during the Protestant ascendancy. Kirwan was twenty-eight, and, like Saul, raised in the city, enough a part of the daily fabric of life that, amongst the homosexual community, he was known as 'Lizzie'.[6] They began an affair, and Kirwan was the key to a door that opened up Dublin's well-to-do queer community. Through him Saul met Gustavus Cornwall, secretary of the General Post Office, an older, well-respected British official who lived in a large house at 17 Harcourt Street, just off St Stephen's Green. Whether he was well respected within Dublin's homosexual demi-monde is another question; it's hard to tell the degree to which his nickname, 'The Duchess', was a term of affection or mockery.

Jack began attending the parties held by this well-off coterie, where, according to both the tastes and norms of the age, younger working-class men, soldiers, and police recruits attended alongside men from the richer colonial class. Jack began to make friends with fellow rent boys at these parties, as well as with other men of standing, such as James Ellis French, a senior detective with the Royal Irish Constabulary, part of the British administration that worked out of Dublin Castle.

With such important new friends, Jack could see a way out of poverty, if only they could find him a job. It was probably The Duchess who helped him get a job on the same street he lived on, at 82 Harcourt Street, as servant to a young Catholic medical doctor, Dr John Joseph Cranny.[7] Yet Jack remained friends with his old rent boy colleagues, especially with one called Bill Clarke, and probably still moonlighted in sex work. It was with Clarke that Jack was arrested in October of 1878, in mysterious circumstances that looked like the theft of a coat from Dr Cranny's house. Although the two were sent to a remand prison awaiting trial, they were ultimately acquitted as it became unclear whose coat had been stolen in the first place.[8]

Still, unsurprisingly, Saul lost his job and decided to emigrate to London. There was not much chance of domestic service there, not without a reference and with an Irish accent, and so he took to prostitution again, working the streets around Piccadilly, where homosexual men cruised for sex. For a while he lived with another man, Charles Hammond, and his wife, with Hammond acting as a sort of pimp. He returned to Dublin for a few months following his father's death in 1880, but was soon back in London, living in Soho at 36 Lisle Street, barely a minute's walk from Leicester Square. It was 1881, and it is at this moment that the young man, still in his early twenties, begins to write his memoirs.

While *The Sins of the Cities of the Plains* is (still) a remarkable and effective piece of pornography, it should be read with a pinch of salt. For a start, Saul's account of his early life is entirely different from reality, turning him from a working-class Dubliner to a well-to-do young man from Suffolk. However, that might be expected, for there were numerous reasons why a young sex worker in Victorian England might wish to disguise his identity a little. And even if many of the sex scenes had been accentuated for dramatic effect, perhaps even written by a different hand (it seems likely that the publisher, William Lazenby, at the very least helped shape the work), they still offer interesting insights into the Victorian homosexual underworld, insights supported by other sources.

For example, the descriptions of the trafficking of children for sexual exploitation matched those offered just four years later by the provocative campaigning journalist W. T. Stead in his four-part special, 'The Maiden Tribute of Modern Babylon,' written for the *Pall Mall Gazette*.[9] Stead's work, part investigative journalism, part moral panic and part plausibly deniable pornography, became part of a wider campaign of public outrage by early feminists and anti-vice campaigners for a change in the law regarding sexual offences.

Much of the action of *The Sins of the Cities of the Plains* describes real-life places that are barely disguised with new names, but would be instantly recognisable to the urbane London gentlemen who were, presumably, the audience for the book. For example, the shop the author names 'Cygnet and Ego' is very clearly a stand-in for an actual high-end drapery named

'Swan and Edgar' that sat in Piccadilly Circus, on the corners of Regent Street and Piccadilly. It is after Saul (or 'Saul') is fired from Cygnet and Ego that he becomes more acquainted with London's homosexual life thanks to a high-end sex club, and through which we learn of his supposed encounter with two notorious queer figures of Victorian life, Thomas Boulton and Frederick Park.

The club is located just off Portland Place, and cost 100 guineas to join: a colossal sum at the time, almost a year's wage for a skilled tradesman.[10] Arriving there, another young rent boy regales Saul with stories of gang-bangs with clergymen and his time as a soldier, and 'considerably opened my eyes as to how the sin of Sodom was regularly practised in the Modern Babylon'. The rent boy then prepares him for his first fucking in the club, by dressing him in 'a charming female costume. He acted as lady's maid, fitted my bust with a pair of false bubbies, frizzed my hair with curling irons, and fixed me up by adding a profusion of false plaits behind.'[11]

The club's owner, the fortuitously named 'Mr Inslip', then takes them to a room with ten men and eight other 'women'. Saul is assigned to an elderly man who, as the night progresses, plies him with booze before reaching under his dress to fondle his cock. Then, at 2 a.m., the lights are extinguished, and the action begins, with the old man 'lifting up my skirts behind he knelt down and kissed my bottom, buggering me with his tongue till the hole was well moistened; then getting up, I felt a fine prick brought up to the charge. It hurt me a little; but he was soon in, then passing his hands round my buttocks he frigged me most deliciously as he worked furiously in my bum.'[12] And so it continues, with the partners swapping multiple times, until the sun rises.

Saul recounts that such sex parties became regular occurrences for him. He was even, he claims, at a party with actors Thomas Boulton and Frederick Park, and Lord Arthur Clinton at Haxell's Hotel on the Strand. The story of Boulton and Park is a fascinating one that sheds much light onto contemporary Victorian attitudes towards homosexuality and gender, but it throws doubt on the veracity of Saul's 'memoir', as Lord Arthur Clinton, an important player in the story, had died (possibly at his own hand) in June of 1870, when the historical Jack Saul had not even reached his teens.

The author describes how, at the party, Boulton and Lord Clinton retreated to a private room, and Saul kneeled to watch through the keyhole as they exchanged blow jobs, before Clinton rimmed Boulton then fucked him. The sight, he recalls, excited him, and through his friendship with the two he is granted access to the highest echelons of society, resulting in him, still dressed in women's attire, getting a blow job at a party hosted by the Prince of Wales (the future Edward VII). While it's impossible that Saul could have been involved in such circles, it's not impossible that *someone* – the potential author or co-author of the book – was, not least because those were the circles that Lord Arthur Clinton, MP for Newark and brother of the Prince of Wales's mistress, did indeed move in.

Thomas Boulton and Frederick Park had been raised in reasonably well-off circumstances. Unlike Saul's account of his own period of crossdressing, it doesn't seem that they took up crossdressing as an accessory to prostitution, but for their own personal reasons, and they did not just dress in what was regarded as 'women's attire' for sex alone, but dressed in their day-to-day life, attending public events such as boat races and the theatre. As with homosexual history, it's extremely difficult to retroactively assign to them a specific transgender identity as we might understand it today. But by the same token, it's very clear that they lived lives where their identities as Stella and Fanny, as they were addressed, were meaningful parts of their lives, and that in living those identities they transgressed the understood boundaries of sex and gender in the society they lived in, despite the significant danger were they to be 'uncovered'.

They took a room in Mrs Stacey's 'house of accommodation' in Wakefield Street.[13] Most establishments that fell under that title were little more that flop-houses where sex workers who worked the streets could take a john, but Mrs Stacey's was quite different, and was a place where people like Boulton and Park could change into women's clothing. More importantly, they could store their clothing, wigs, and makeup there, a necessity considering that many, like Boulton, still lived with their parents.[14] Although still in their early twenties, they had maintained this way of life for many years, both in the street and onstage, where as actors they performed women's roles.

It was in a touring theatre production that they met Lord Clinton, and Stella Boulton soon became his lover. The two spent most of their time together, regarding themselves as sisters, consistently using female pronouns or titles (something, as we saw in Dublin, that cisgender gay men also did). However, considering how provocative it would be were they to be uncovered, unlike the majority of cisgender gay men their public persona was clearly deviating from the established gender and sex norms. Considering that the two were both indiscreet in their behaviour and reckless in the paper trail they left behind, including letters and photographs of themselves as Fanny and Stella, it seemed inevitable they would end up in trouble.[15]

Sometime around 1869 a policeman named Detective Officer Chamberlain had begun a year-long surveillance of the pair, gathering evidence of whatever crimes he could in order to prosecute them. In April of 1870 the two decided to visit the theatre with two gentlemen, not knowing their house on Wakefield Street had been under close surveillance for the past two weeks.[16] Inside the theatre, and drunk, the two behaved rather badly, making lewd gestures at other theatregoers from their private box, and causing a scene in the public bar.[17] As they were leaving the theatre, they were seized by police officers, and hauled off to Bow Street police station. There they were subject to a humiliating inspection by the police, and the next morning, still in their crinoline dresses, although with makeup rather dishevelled, they were dragged through a cruel and baying mob of observers to attend their remand hearing.

They were charged with sodomy, conspiracy to commit sodomy, and outraging public decency, and held in prison, following another degrading physical inspection by a quack doctor who regarded their rectums to have been permanently dilated by anal sex; their penises were also deemed unusually long. Asked to explain why, the doctor replied that 'traction might produce elongation of the penis and testicles'.[18] Nonsense of course, as other doctors later testified, but a symptom of the deep body horror that sodomy induced in many respectable figures at the time.

Lord Arthur Clinton died of scarlet fever before the court case, although police suspected that he had actually faked his own death, escaping to the continent or the United States. It was not the first time, nor the last, that an aristocrat implicated, accused, or even convicted in this damnable sin did a runner; even Oscar Wilde, when he was eventually freed from Reading Gaol, escaped to France, where the laws and social attitudes were considerably less strict.

If Clinton had faked his own death, he need not have bothered. Despite the odds being stacked against them in terms of social attitudes, the prosecution fluffed its case, and Fanny and Stella were acquitted as actually *proving* that sodomy took place was a difficult task. They dropped their 'not guilty' pleas on the morals charges, allowing them to be 'bound over' for two years: essentially, they were to agree not to get into any more trouble. They both left the country for the United States, where they continued to perform. Boulton lived until the first decade of the twentieth century, dying in England, while Park died just a decade later, around the time that the historic Saul arrived in London.

The Boulton and Park case is remarkable as it landed just as the concept of a homosexual identity and subculture was emerging both between the new discipline of sexologists and in wider society, both in the UK and in Germany and the rest of continental Europe, and as moral panics about this new type of man started to grow, tied to worries about prostitution and immorality. It also happened in a strange interlude between two periods where the state had tough tools with which to discipline same-sex activity. The increased suppression of same-sex activity and gender variance during these moral panics played a significant role in growing public awareness of sexually deviant behaviour.

Anal sex had been outlawed by the Buggery Act of 1533, but that did not specify sex between two men, merely non-productive sex, and was used to prosecute same-sex and opposite-sex offences, often non-consensual. The law, therefore, was an attempt to prosecute criminal *acts* rather than to define a criminal *type* of person, and this was the only law on the books that pertained to men who had sex with men. The crime, however, was a capital offence, and men were executed for consensual anal sex right up until the 1830s.

There was an attempt to reform the law in 1841, undertaken by Lord John Russell, which failed due to a lack of parliamentary backing, but increasingly judges were refusing to enact the death sentence as was required. A compromise had to be reached; for legal sentences not to be carried out made a mockery of the law. In 1861 Parliament passed the Offences Against the Person Act, making the penalty for buggery a minimum of ten years of hard labour: for many, in Victorian prisons equipped with the punishing treadmill, a virtual death sentence anyway.

Yet as the nineteenth century progressed, cases like Boulton and Park opened the eyes to a homosexual subculture that was identified in the popular mind with male prostitution, which put new pressures on authorities to crack down. Historian Jeffrey Weeks suggests that, during the trial, there was significant uncertainty as to what the actual crime consisted of, and that various doctors on the case could come to no agreement as to what physical proof of sodomy might look like: they simply had not seen enough cases. He writes that 'as late as 1871, concepts of homosexuality were extremely underdeveloped, both in the Metropolitan Police and in high medical and legal circles, suggesting the absence of any clear notion of a homosexual category or of any social awareness of what a homosexual identity might consist of'. Even if there was a general awareness that a subculture around male prostitution existed, in court, married men were less likely to be found guilty of buggery than unmarried men.[19]

To put it simply, the authorities knew what Boulton and Park were up to was *wrong*, even if they did not know exactly what that consisted of. They were clearly transgressing certain gender and sexual boundaries, however, and something had to be done.

It is unsurprising there was not much understanding of homosexuality as a distinct sexual identity amongst society's higher echelons. The word 'homosexual' had only been coined in 1869, and even then in a limited-run pamphlet published anonymously, and in German, by the Austrian writer Karl-Maria Kertbeny. The Austro-German psychiatrist Richard von Krafft-Ebing documented homosexuality extensively in his 1886 book on sexual paraphilias, *Psychopathia Sexualis*, but it was not until the very end of the century, 1897, that the first English book on the subject, Henry Havelock Ellis's *Sexual Inversion*, was published.

The idea of 'Sexual inversion' – that a homosexual had inverted the 'normal' sexual characteristics, and the idea that these attributes were congenital – was not developed on the psychiatrist's couch or in the medical lab alone. These were already concepts that were swimming round the social circles of some upper-class men, including poets. Indeed, Havelock Ellis's co-author of *Sexual Inversion* was the poet and literary critic John Addington Symonds, who had earlier published *A Problem in Greek Ethics* in 1873. Symonds's book, partially inspired by the homoerotic poetry of American poet Walt Whitman, examined the role of pederasty and homosexual desire in ancient Greece, a model which had been used to justify and explain sex between men since the time of Hadrian.

Others adopted the same approach. This model of inversion, positing that homosexual men were female souls 'trapped' in male bodies through accident of birth, and the notion that pederastic relationships was a worthy tradition inherited from classical civilization were also taken up by the 'Uranian Poets', a loose group of poets and writers working in Britain in the second half of the nineteenth century. This third sex, many believed, offered a noble form of love between equals, and found further expression in the work of Edward Carpenter, Oscar Wilde, and his wretched boyfriend, Lord Alfred Douglas. Wilde takes this approach in his testimony for his trial in 1895, stating:

'The Love that dare not speak its name' in this century is such a great affection of an elder for a younger man as there was between David and Jonathan, such as Plato made the very basis of his philosophy, and such as you find in the sonnets of Michelangelo and Shakespeare. It is that deep, spiritual affection that is as pure as it is perfect. It dictates and pervades great works of art like those of Shakespeare and Michelangelo, and those two letters of mine, such as they are. It is in this century misunderstood, so much misunderstood that it may be described as the 'Love that dare not speak its name', and on account of it I am placed where I am now. It is beautiful, it is fine, it is the noblest form of affection. There is nothing unnatural about it. It is intellectual, and it repeatedly exists between an elder and a younger man, when the elder man has intellect, and the younger man has all the joy, hope and glamour of life before him. That it should be so the world does not understand. The world mocks at it and sometimes puts one in the pillory for it.[20]

This figure of the invert, a literary and spiritual 'third sex' that existed within the social elites and medical establishment, was joined by the complementary figure of the pervert, as it was coming to be understood by the legal system. Perverts had no innate problem that drove them to sex with other men; they simply lacked the moral framework to resist the opportunity of a quick fuck. The division was explicitly class-based, and inter-linked with the fear of prostitution, as the offer of money, for a working-class young man, was a surefire road to corruption and perversion.[21] It's not for nothing that even today, working-class men who do not 'present' as homosexual, yet are still open for sexual encounters with upper- and middle-class men, are, whether or not money is actually exchanged, often known as 'trade', a usage that came to be in the 1870s.[22] While inverts were a subject for treatment, sympathy, and even poetry, perverts could expect little more than for the long arm of the law to feel them up.

This link was already emerging at the conclusion of the Boulton and Park trial, and there was concern that current laws weren't sufficient to deal with this rising moral threat to the empire's youth. In his summing up, Lord Chief Justice Cockburn lamented the lack of legal tools he had as a judge to deal with the problem, saying,

> It is one of those instances to which the provisions of a most useful act for the prevention of public indecency might be extended. If the law cannot reach it as it is, it ought to be made the subject of such legislation, and a punishment of two or three months' imprisonment, with the treadmill attached to it, with, in case of repetition of the offence, a little wholesome corporal discipline, would, I think, be effective, not only in such cases, but in all cases of outrage against public decency.[23]

Cockburn got his way, but not until 1885, when the public outcry following W. T. Stead's exposé on child sex trafficking forced the government to act. The government's response was to expedite the Criminal Law Amendment Bill, which had been languishing in the doldrums of the committee stages for the past few years. The new act was primarily focused on the subject of Stead's exposé, addressing prostitution and child trafficking.

But Stead also contacted the Liberal MP Henry Labouchère, a theatre owner, drawing his attention to the phenomenon of homosexuality, and Labouchère introduced an amendment to the bill that would criminalise all acts of 'gross indecency' between two men. The crime of buggery, as was clear from the Boulton and Park case, was extremely hard to prove, and the horrific sentence made prosecutions rare. Gross indecency, however, was never defined in law, which meant that the lower sentencing provisions, although still horrific (up to two years, with or without hard labour), could encourage more prosecutions.

It certainly did. Although the amendment was discussed for mere minutes, tens of thousands of men would be prosecuted for consensual sex acts with other adult men over the next eighty-two years that it remained law in England, and longer still in Scotland and Northern Ireland. Those convicted included Oscar Wilde himself, as well as Alan Turing. It invested a huge amount of power in the hands of law enforcement and the judiciary, with very little clarity as to what constituted either 'gross indecency' or 'procuring' sex.

Before, anal sex resulting in ejaculation was prohibited; now, everything that manifested desire between men was pulled into the remit of the law, including flirting, propositioning, and kissing. It was the first law to explicitly target sex between men, rather than merely the act of anal sex, regardless of gender, and it was also incorporated into penal codes across the British Empire. Indeed, even today, the provision remains in penal codes across the world, from Section 377A of the Penal Code of Singapore to Section 165 of the Kenyan Penal Code, in almost identical wording to the Labouchere Amendment, testament to the long and brutal relationship between colonialism and the moral fear of homosexual behaviour.

These laws resulting from the moral panic around emergent homosexual identities and prostitution had a powerful effect upon Jack Saul's life. In 1884, just before the Criminal Law Amendment Act went through Parliament, Jack was called by police to return to Dublin. Back in Ireland two prominent British officials had been accused of sodomy in the newspaper *United Ireland* by its publisher, William O'Brien. *United Ireland* had been established by the Irish nationalist political party the Irish National League, founded by Charles Stewart Parnell. The accusations were clearly politically motivated: accusations of sodomy served as ways for both the Brits and the Irish to attempt to discredit the agents of the opposition, as we shall see again in later chapters. The potency of such allegations with the public were such that men were frequently blackmailed for fear that their secrets might be leaked, often by the lower-class young men they had sex with, and sometimes paid for. Yet it was allegations from *within* the same social class that could cause the most damage.

United Ireland's rumours were not unfounded, given that the two men accused were Gustavus 'The Duchess' Cornwall, secretary of the General Post Office, and James Ellis French, the Royal Irish Constabulary detective, both of whom were well known amongst the homosexual underground social scenes of Dublin.

French and Cornwall both decided to sue their accuser. But they were ill-advised to do so, because a libel trial is likely to raise all sorts of stories about your sex life, most of them true. The jury found in favour of O'Brien, and again, as the trial of Oscar Wilde revealed, the stories raised in the civil court made a criminal trial almost inevitable. Politically speaking, the libel trial had been serious news: not only was the British soldier Martin Kirwan bought up as a witness, but numerous other soldiers were implicated in the sex parties and general debauchery.[24]

Jack had avoided giving a deposition in the libel trial, although private investigators had almost certainly sought one from him. At the second trial, however, Martin Kirwan was also to face justice, alongside others, including the chairman of the Dublin Stock Exchange, policemen, merchants, and soldiers.[25] Saul's close relationship with Kirwan meant he was bound to be called at some point. As in many of these cases, the implication of the police was clear: testify against your clients of higher social standing, or face the same, or even worse, fate. Yet, despite giving a deposition, the prosecution never called Saul, presumably because too much time had passed between the crime and the trial. Kirwan and Cornwall were both acquitted because the Crown could not prove its case – always a tricky task when it was one man's word against the other – but their lives and reputations were destroyed. Jack, however, could return to London and his job.

Scandal, however, seemed to follow Saul. Back in London, he made contact again with his old friend and erstwhile pimp, Charles Hammond. In 1887 he moved into a house that Hammond ran at 19 Cleveland Street.[26] The house was tall and thin, and, facing the Middlesex Hospital which dominated the area of north Soho, abutted a house for young nurses. Hammond ran an unusual establishment. Not only did the house function as a brothel for male sex workers, rare enough for the time, but it was extremely tastefully decorated, making it the ideal place for a well-heeled gentleman of a certain persuasion with a taste for younger men, rough trade, or soldiers, but who did not wish to spend his evening kneeling in the mud and dark at Hyde Park.

The services offered made this discrete venue a popular place for upper-class men, and for a few years it operated largely under the radar of the authorities. That state of affairs did not last for long, thanks to an incident across the city, at the Central Telegraph Office just behind St Paul's Cathedral.

At that time large amounts of money were sent by post, and the post office employed a veritable squadron of teenage boys as messengers, carrying mail and telegraphs around the City of London. The post office reported a theft from its building, and Police Constable Luke Hanks was tasked with investigating this not-uncommon offence. He suspected a fifteen-year-old telegraph messenger, Charles Swinscow. He found fourteen shillings on Swinscow, and was sure he had nabbed his offender, whose weekly pay was only a couple of shillings.[27] However, pressed on how he got the money, the boy admitted he had earned it himself from one Mr Charles Hammond of 19 Cleveland Street, saying, 'I will tell you the truth. I got the money for going to bed with gentlemen at his house.' Not only this, but Swinscow told the police that another messenger boy named Henry Newlove was also working there. This passing admission proved explosive.

Not only was the running of a male brothel a serious offence, but the fact that post office employees were implicated was even more worrying. Hanks passed the case up his chain of command until it reached the Metropolitan Police commissioner, who himself assigned Detective Frank Abberline to the case, an indication of just how seriously they took it: just two years earlier Abberline had been the detective in charge of the investigation into the serial murderer Jack the Ripper. Abberline obtained a warrant to search the Cleveland Street house and arrest Hammond, but Hammond had been tipped off and left the country. Newlove protested to the police that he was facing prosecution while 'men in high positions are allowed to walk about free', and named a series of important figures as clients of Cleveland Street, including Lord Arthur Somerset and the Earl of Euston.[28]

This made the case a sensitive political issue. Lord Arthur Somerset was no minor aristocrat. His father was the former

Conservative MP turned peer and privy councillor, the Duke of Beaufort, and Arthur himself managed the stables of the Prince of Wales. Lord Somerset was, it seems, 'allowed' to slip out of the country before a trial could commence, but he paid for a lawyer to represent Newlove and another of Hammond's men. The Met commissioner was keen to see Somerset charged, but upon his return to England no less a figure than the Lord Chancellor vetoed him.

But why was Somerset allowed to go free when it was quite clear, as in Dublin, that the British state *was* prepared to crack down on sodomy? Perhaps the answer is in a letter the assistant public prosecutor, whose responsibility it was to draw up charges, wrote to his boss, saying, 'I am told that Newton [the defendant's lawyer] has boasted that if we go on a very distinguished person will be involved (PAV). I don't mean to say that I for one instant credit it – but in such circumstances as this one never knows what may be said, be concocted or be true.'[29]

Some historians, including the venerable historian of gay life in Britain H. Montgomery Hyde, suggest that 'PAV' stands (rather convincingly) for 'Prince Albert Victor', the son of the Prince of Wales and second in line to the British throne, known to friends and family as 'Eddy'. Indeed, while abroad, Lord Somerset would write to a friend:

> I cannot see what good it would do Prince Eddy if I went into court. I might do him harm because if I was asked if I ever heard anything against him – whom from? – has any person mentioned with whom he went there etc? – the question would be very awkward. I have never mentioned the boy's name (PAV) except to (Sir Dighton) Probyn, (Oliver) Montagu and (Francis) Knollys. Had they been wise, hearing what I knew and therefore what others knew, they ought to have hushed the matter up, instead of stirring it up as they did with all the authorities.[30]

You might recall that the Prince of Wales had once allegedly taken his son Eddy to the Monto in Dublin, presumably to shore up his heterosexuality and give him a taste of the world:

the thought of his son and heir being publicly implicated in a homosexual scandal would have been beyond appalling to the British Royal family. Eddy's brother, who became George V (Eddy died before his father became king) and Elizabeth II's grandfather, once remarked on the case of another outed homosexual aristocrat, some fifty years later, 'I thought men like that shot themselves.' Yet the attempt at a discreet coverup collapsed when Ernest Parke, of the radical *North London Press*, was tipped off. He named the Earl of Euston as party to the affair, and wrote, 'These men have been allowed to leave the country, and thus defeat the ends of justice, because their prosecution would disclose the fact that a far more distinguished and more highly placed personage than themselves was inculpated in these disgusting crimes.'[31]

The Earl had not, in fact, left the country, and he started libel proceedings against Parke. It was at this trial that Jack Saul appeared as a witness for the defence. It was here that he provided the testimony that shocked Victorian London. His testimony was frank and open, including descriptions of the Earl's sexual habits, including his taste for ejaculating onto boys' stomachs. He described picking him up on Piccadilly before taking a cab with him to Cleveland Street, the warning the Earl gave him not to talk to him if he saw him on the street, and the Earl's return visits to Cleveland Street – although not to see Saul.[32]

The court was shocked to hear Saul's ungilded descriptions of male prostitution in London. The judge was shocked to discover that Saul had already divulged this information, including the names of prominent clients like the MP and Judge Advocate General George Cavendish-Bentinck, and no action had been taken. Everybody was shocked by his claim that the police 'shut their eyes' not just to his behaviour, as a lifelong male sex worker, but to much more of the same.[33] In the end, the judge was inclined towards the Earl, to nobody's surprise, describing Saul to the jury as a 'revolting creature' whose testimony was not to be believed.[34]

Parke was convicted and sentenced to twelve months hard labour, and Saul's name was dragged through the mud by the press, many of whom called for him to be tried, either for sodomy or perjury. Other newspapers, such as *Reynold's News*, might have thought Saul 'a filthy, loathsome, detestable beast', but pointed out that while the Earl's account of how he ended up at Cleveland Street just once, accidentally, was uncorroborated, many others had witnessed him there several times. Why were they to be disbelieved, just because they were 'persons in a very low grade in life. Surely he did not expect that the Archbishop of Canterbury would appear in the box and testify to having met the Earl coming to or from that den of infamy.'[35]

Newspapers also criticised the injustice of the young men being prosecuted while aristocrats escaped, highlighting the contemporary discourses of homosexuality that associated it with the perversion of the working class by middle- and upper-class inverts generally, and prostitution more specifically. 'What, then, is the conclusion to come to?' asked *Reynold's News* the following week. 'Why, that the authorities are more anxious to conceal the names of those who patronised the horrible den of vice, than punish the principal patrons of the hideous place? ... Why were the wretched telegraph boys taken to the Old Bailey ... while Lord Arthur Somerset, being duly warned of what had occurred, duly made his escape, and is now living in clover abroad?'[36]

One MP *did* address this clearly unjust situation in Parliament, going as far as to implicate the young Prince Eddy and his father, the Prince of Wales, although not going so far as to mention them by name. He accused the prime minister, Lord Salisbury, and his cabinet, of having attempted to cover up the activities of 'a gentleman of very high position' at Cleveland Street. He stated that

> it is the common talk in the workshops of this country respecting the case that the law is not fairly administered as between the rich man and the poor man, that justice is not fairly meted out between man and man, regardless of rank and social position, and thus great harm has been done by the course which has been adopted. We have heard a good deal lately about criminal conspiracy. What is this case but a criminal conspiracy by the very

guardians of public morality and law, with the Prime Minister at
their head, to defeat the ends of justice?[37]

That MP was Henry Labouchère, whose amendment to the
Criminal Law Amendment Act five years earlier had created the
offence of gross indecency which was at the heart of the case.
There's a certain irony at play here, and not just that he was
the creator of the sloppy law he now felt was unfairly applied.
While he was concerned with equality in the eyes of the law,
and the unfair way in which working-class homosexuals were
treated in comparison with the wealthy, as when England partially decriminalised homosexual acts in the Sexual Offences Act
in 1967, that commitment to equality wasn't reflected in the law
itself, which required that if men do have sex, it occurred in a
private dwelling in which they were alone – a situation which
brings with it certain class restrictions for those who did not
own or rent a private house.

As late as 1998, consenting men in the UK were being prosecuted for having sex in the presence of other consenting adults,
as this violated this clause of the Sexual Offences Act. Indeed, the
1957 Wolfenden Report, which led to the 1967 Sexual Offences
Act, was a publication of the findings of the Departmental Committee on Homosexual Offences and Prostitution, its conclusions
indicating that the link between prostitution and homosexuality
was still firmly in the minds of the public and lawmakers. It
was the treatment of the well-off friends of Lord Montagu, and
especially the testimony of his Oxford University colleague Peter
Wildeblood, who was jailed in 1954 for having had gay sex two
years before on Lord Montagu's estate, that was integral in convincing the committee that the law should be changed. Like the
Labouchere Amendment, the 1967 Act was an attempt to reform
the law but not necessarily to improve the lives of homosexual
men; it even failed to reduce sentences, as after its passage prosecutions of gay men rose considerably, just as, post-1885, tens of
thousands of men were prosecuted, and countless more became
subject to blackmail.

All this was too late for Jack Saul, anyway. Unlike the aristocrats, there was nobody to document the life of an old Irish working-class queer. He took a job at the Marlborough Hotel at number 23, Villiers Street, just by Charing Cross railway station.[38] A few years later he moved back to Dublin, and there are a few traces of him in the census at addresses like Poolbeg Street and Luke Street, before his death was recorded at Our Lady's Hospice on 28 August 1904, from tuberculosis.[39]

6

Roger Casement

At the height of his career, the dashing Irish diplomat and humanitarian Roger Casement was a national hero in the United Kingdom, and knighted for his service to the realm by King George V. When he died in 1916, he was infamous as a traitor and a pervert: executed by hanging in Pentonville Prison before being buried in quicklime in an unmarked grave. Casement is the most uncomplicatedly good man that we are discussing in this book: someone motivated by a deep and profound compassion and solidarity with oppressed people who used his voice and his status to combat the violent colonization and subordination of Black and brown people in the Global South.

As we will see, this was all very well and good for the British state as long as it aligned with the national interest – as long as the barbaric practices he was describing could be safely ascribed to other, supposedly less-enlightened, Europeans. Once he began to materially assist people rebelling against *British* rule, however, he was blackmailed and defamed using his own diaries – his homosexuality, which was joyous and Whitmanesque if sometimes problematic in its elision of the power dynamics between Casement and his subaltern suitors, became a millstone hung around his neck.

Roger Casement was born in 1864 in Sandycove, a seaside suburb of Dublin with rocky beaches and clear blue water. Roger's family was deeply embedded in the British colonial project. His grandfather Hugh ran a prosperous shipping business out of Belfast, and his father had been a captain in the Royal Dragoons in the 1842 Anglo-Afghan war. For the first two hundred years of British colonization on the Indian subcontinent, wars of conquest were fought not by the state alone but by the British East India Company, a joint-stock company with private armies and navies that cooperated with the state ones, when needed.[1] In 1800, the British East India Company's private army numbered 250,000 men – double the size of the British army.

If Casement's father was by dint of colonial service and Protestant birth an exemplar of the British colonial state, his family, like many Anglo-Irish families, was often characterized by conflict around nationality and religion. His father insisted he was born in Ulster instead of Dublin; when Roger was four, his mother allegedly had Roger baptized into the Catholic faith while on holiday in Wales. Roger would come to believe that she had always been a Catholic, but a cousin claimed that his mother had converted, having 'revolted from the coldness of the Protestant faith'.[2]

The young Roger, like many of the sensitive boys in this book, always preferred the company of his vivacious and warm mother to that of his disciplinarian father. But when Roger was only nine years old she died, sending his father into a deep depression. After some years of moving around – and a notable episode when Roger, aged eleven, appeared in court in London alongside his older brother for the crime of having stolen books from a newsstand – he, his brother, and their two siblings were sent to live with his father's uncle and aunt in the family home of Magherintemple House, near Ballycastle, on the Northern Irish coastline. His father lived, grief-stricken by the loss of his wife, in a hotel forty miles away and, when Roger was twelve, died of tuberculosis.

The boy was then shipped off to the Diocesan School in Ballymena, studying classics and French. One of only six boarders at the school, he played cricket and began to love – and to write his own – poetry. Casement loved swimming in the nude on the rocky beaches near his school, seemingly as much for the opportunity to eye, and score with, local trade as for the exercise. The young Roger was torn between his family identity as an Anglo-Irish Protestant and a heartfelt association with and belief in Catholicism and Irish nationalism. As a teenager, he became interested in politics by following the career of Charles Stewart Parnell, an Irish nationalist and part of the Irish Parliamentary Party who sought to overthrow English landlords, support tenant farmers being starved off their land by genocidal British politics, and advocate for home rule. At the same time, his uncle Edward Bannister, a Liverpudlian who worked in shipping, regaled the young lad with stories about travel to South America and the Congo. And so at fifteen, when Roger finished his schooling, he took a job at the Elder Dempster company, a shipping line operating between Liverpool and the West Coast of Africa.

At this time, in 1881, the late Victorian imperialist world system was just kicking into its highest gear.[3] The Seven Years' War and American Revolution had drawn to a close the first wave of European colonization, while the Congress of Vienna after Napoleon's defeat established a new European diplomatic order. The Industrial Revolution led to growth and urbanization in liberal Britain, which spent the nineteenth century consolidating colonial and naval power and building up industry and infrastructure.[4] By the 1870s, other European countries, including Germany, which reunified under the Prussian Hohenzollern family that counted Frederick the Great among its number, had begun to challenge British hegemony and develop projects of heavy industry and colonization to match.

Africa had, before this time, only seen piecemeal colonization: while the transatlantic slave trade, pioneered by and then ineffectually condemned by the British, had devastating impacts on African lives and politics, very little of the continent was under direct European control. All of this changed over the next ten years, enabled by the second Industrial Revolution and key accompanying technologies such as railways, steamboats, the telegraph, and the medical discovery that quinine could treat malaria. Economic necessity – capitalism always needs new front lines of primitive accumulation – combined with race science and Christian missionary zeal in what became known as the 'Scramble for Africa'.[5]

In 1876, at a conference ostensibly about humanitarian projects, King Leopold II of Belgium formed the 'International Association for the Exploration and Civilization of Central Africa', a front organization for violent colonization with members from many European nations. The fact that Central Africa was neither unexplored nor uncivilized – millions of people lived in the areas around the Congo river, and many kingdoms and states there had signed treaties with European nations – did not slow down these wild-eyed, genocidal ideologues one bit.

As different European powers began to colonize different parts of Africa and war seemed possible, in 1884, Otto von Bismarck, chancellor of Germany, organized the Berlin Conference, at which Africa was divided up between the various European powers with an active and racist disregard for the lives, desires, and humanity of the people who lived there. The conference was intended only to prevent conflict between Europeans and to ensure that each nation got supposedly 'fair' pieces of Africa, as though Africa were a cake to be distributed. The principle established in Berlin in 1884 was that of 'effective occupation': a given colonizer's supposed 'right' to land depended on its ability to subjugate, control, and establish administration of the people who already lived there.[6] Given control over a piece of land relatively contiguous to the borders of the present-day Democratic Republic of the Congo, the 'International Association ...' established the Congo Free State, which became King Leopold's personal fiefdom.

The year of the Berlin Conference, Casement left his job as a ship's purser and began to work for the International Association in the Congo. Why was King Leopold so intent on getting his hands on this piece of property? Industrial machinery in Europe required rubber, and the land in the Congo was perfect for the cultivation of rubber vines. All the humanitarian talk was cover for Leopold's cold desire for personal enrichment, and conviction that Black people's lives, freedom, and dignity mattered less than his personal fortune. Casement's initial job was to help survey the land between the shoreline and two hundred miles up the Congo river; this waterway, not navigable because of waterfalls, stood between the site of potentially lucrative rubber plantations and the ships to take the crop to market in Europe.

While there, Casement met two men who would be very significant to his life. First, he met another young explorer named Herbert Ward, who became a fast and lifelong friend and praised Casement's muscle and bone, sun-tanned face, and blue eyes. Casement was, in fact, an astonishingly beautiful man; however, it seems that he and Ward were never anything more than friends. Ward went on to become a sculptor in Paris, and died from injuries sustained assisting French soldiers at the front during the First World War.

Casement also met the British-Polish merchant marine named Joseph Conrad; like Roger, he had come to the Congo motivated by racist greed and the ideology of 'civilizing' the region through trade and forced religious conversions, and like Roger, he began to become horrified by the project of colonization upon seeing the ways in which the Congo Free State was administered.[7] In 1899, Conrad published *Heart of Darkness*, a novel set against the background of the colonization of the Congo, which offers a penetrating critique of the colonial project and was itself critiqued by the Nigerian novelist Chinua Achebe for its repetition and re-instantiation of racist visions of Africans as 'primitives' and Africa as an 'other' onto which white Europe could project its racial and spiritual anxieties.[8]

Casement, too, would step away from the Congo Free State and instead sign up to work for the British Colonial Office. In 1895 he was made Her Majesty's Consul in Maputo, in what is today Mozambique; and in 1901 he was transferred to the French Congo. Two years later, he was commissioned by the Balfour government in Britain to write a report about human rights in the Congo Free State. The British Empire was, at the time, invested in its self-image as more progressive and liberal than the monarchies of 'old' continental Europe; even in its colonization practices, it argued, it aimed to spread free trade and liberation.

These myths were lies then and they remain lies today: British colonization was a process in which a wealthy few were enriched through the shedding of unquantifiable volumes of blood. Anti-colonial resistance against the British was put down with harsh violence, and the British operated with near-total disregard for the lives, choices, autonomy, and self-determination of the peoples they conquered and governed. The fact of resistance, and of the importation of that resistance into progressive and liberationist political movements in the European metropolis (as scholars such as Leela Gandhi and Priyamvada Gopal have described), does not excuse or whitewash the actions of white European elites.[9] Just as some British commentators today seek to excuse British actions then by comparing them to those of other colonizers – a fool's game – the British state then aimed to do the same. This is how such a report was ever commissioned: the British wanted to establish themselves as comparatively good and moral colonizers in comparison with even worse others.

But none of this meant that what was going on in the Congo Free State – which Casement knew well, having worked there for years – was not an atrocity. Casement spent weeks travelling around the region interviewing workers and soldiers. As a private colony, Congo was governed by King Leopold's personal decree. He had instituted a system of statute labour. The invention and patenting of the tire by John Dunlop in 1887 and Édouard Michelin in 1891 increased the demand for rubber for bicycle and, eventually, automobile tires. To meet this demand, by decree, the Congo Free State dictated that any land without a house or cultivated garden was the property of the state. Leopold then allocated the land, rich in natural resources and particularly rubber, to private companies as concessions.[10] In this way the commons of the people of the Congo were stolen and converted into private European property.

On the plantations, law did not govern the treatment of labourers. The demand for labour was high, so the state demanded labour from Congolese people as a form of taxation, creating the 'Red Rubber system' – essentially a slave society, where people were forced to work. Local officials called *capitas* were recruited to organise the labour, but quotas for production were imposed from the central authority, with little consideration of the situation on the ground, meaning they were essentially unmeetable. The Free State also organised a military force to oversee production, called the 'Force Publique', in which the officers were white, while the soldiers were recruited from specific ethnic groups selected to inflame ethnic tensions. Overseers beat workers with hippopotamus-hide whips.[11]

The Red Rubber system was one of extreme brutality, with mass rape among its methods. The white authorities began to worry that the ammunition supplied to Force Publique soldiers, imported at great expense, was being used for hunting. So they implemented a new system for ensuring labourers worked, and no ammunition was wasted; if the quota was not met, plantation managers were commanded to supply the severed hands of those punished for underproduction. The quota of severed hands became easier to meet than the quota of rubber. The mutilation or murder of workers, the seizure of land, and the forced labour meant families could not produce enough food to survive, and famine ensued. The white colonizers then kidnapped the orphaned children of their victims and forced them into child colonies, where they would be raised as more reserve labour.

Casement documented all these abuses, and worse. He made a very conservative estimate that 3 million people had died or been murdered under Leopold's regime; Casement's collaborator, the journalist E. D. Morel, claimed 20 million. The Congolese historian Georges Nzongola-Ntalaja describes these as 'heinous crimes against humanity … Villages unwilling or unable to meet the assigned daily quotas of production were subject to rape, arson, bodily mutilation, and murder … It resulted in a death toll of holocaust proportions.'[12] In 1880, between 20 and 30 million people lived in the Congo; by 1911, 8.5 million did. The survivors were, to quote Nzongola-Ntalaja, 'enslaved subjects of a sovereign they never saw'.[13] The profits flowed into magnificent construction projects in Belgium, both fitting out Leopold's private residences and projects of public improvement. While many historians have shied away from the term 'genocide' because the overarching goal was profit rather than ethnic cleansing, this hardly reduces the ethical stain or the ongoing obligations for reparations.

The Casement report caused an outcry, although many business owners trading with the Free State refused to change their policies. Published in 1904, his was not the first such report – the Black American historian and journalist George Washington Williams first published a report describing Leopold's regime as committing 'crimes against humanity' in 1890, while the Black American reverend William Henry Sheppard co-founded, with the Reverend Samuel Lapsley, the American Presbyterian Congo Mission in 1891.[14] Reports from these men and Casement led to the creation of the Congo Reform Association, which succeeded in pressuring major powers to end Leopold's one-man regime. Nzongola-Ntalaja points out that the CRA was still concerned with 'reforming colonialism, not abolishing it ... The Leopoldian system was [to be] replaced by a colonial regime that was just as oppressive, albeit in a less brutal manner.'[15] The Belgian government took control of the Free State in 1908, but it was not until 1960 that the Congo achieved independence. Its first prime minister, the leftist nationalist and anti-colonial activist leader Patrice Lumumba, was assassinated by firing squad less than a year after a CIA-involved coup.

Casement was appointed in 1906 by the Foreign Office to a commission to investigate the Peruvian Amazon Company, a rubber extraction company that was registered in the UK with British shareholders and directors. Allegations had been made that, in its Peruvian plantations in Putumayo, workers were treated as virtual slaves; and some of those workers were Barbadians, who were British subjects, giving Casement the right to investigate. In letters and diaries, he resolved also to write about the 'poor, docile forest tribes of Indians' who according to rumours were being forced into slave labour.[16]

Casement interviewed workers and discovered a regime of brutality, casual murder, sexual abuse, and beatings. In interviews, white colonizers cheerfully admitted 'owning' Native labourers 'with the willing support of the Lima government which regard any such "conquest" of a new tribe as a patriotic act'.[17] Seizing Indians as slaves 'for any so called public "need"' was 'done openly'.[18] Casement found stocks in which workers were tortured by having their legs locked into cages too small to hold them; in a report about the use of pillories as punishment for workers, he wrote, 'Men, women, and children were confined in them for days, weeks, and often months ... Whole families ... were imprisoned – fathers, mothers, and children, and many cases were reported of parents dying thus, either from starvation or from wounds caused by flogging, while their offspring were attached alongside of them to watch in misery themselves the dying agonies of their parents.'[19]

His final report, published in 1912, combined journalistic observation with interviews with victims – one of the first times that the voices of the victims of colonial violence had been presented in an official Western government report. Casement was praised at Westminster Abbey and in the London *Times*; a year later, he returned to check on promised improvements and found that there were none.

However, alongside the diaries in which he was compiling detailed notes on the atrocities he found in the Amazon, Casement kept a second set of diaries. Later, when they were discovered, these came to be known as the 'Black' Diaries (as opposed to the virtuous and journalistic 'White' Diaries); in them, Casement chronicled his sexual subjectivity, including sexual encounters with, and sexualized observations of, the people he was meeting on his travels. 'Captain's steward an Indian boy of 19, broad face, thin. Huge soft long one. Also Engineer's steward, big too,' went one characteristic entry, from 20 November 1910.[20] Casement used the code 'X' to indicate sodomy; writing, on 13 January 1910: 'Gabriel Ramos – X Deep to hilt ... Gabriel *querido* waiting at Barca gate! *Palpito*. In very deep thrusts.'[21] His meticulous notation would indicate both the size of the relevant cock – Casement was, it must be said, a size queen – as well as any money that changed hands during the encounter; it seems that in port cities, he was willing and able to pay for trade, although he appears to have had the same almost reverent attitude towards the men he was sleeping with whether he was paying them or not.

On 28 February 1910, in Rio de Janeiro, he wrote, 'Deep screw and to hilt. X "poquino." Mario in Rio 81/2+6' 40$ ... lovely, young 18 and glorious. Biggest since Lisbon July 1904 ... Perfectly huge.'[22] Three days later, having headed to São Paolo as part of his approach to the Peruvian Amazon, he wrote, 'Antonio. 10$ Rua Dierita. Dark followed and hard ... breathed and quick, enormous push. Loved mightily, to hilt deep X.'[23] Ten days later, in Buenos Aires, Casement spent a 'morning in Avenida de Mayo. Splendid erections. Ramon $7. 10" at least. X In.'[24]

These are complicated relations, both because of the racial hierarchies of the societies he was moving in, the wealth and power discrepancies, and the fact Casement usually paid for sex. Yet the accounts are marked by a tenderness and a refusal of many of the racial distinctions made at the time. But again, here there is an ability to choose, to cast certain bodies as desirable, as fetishized, that occurred within the framework of colonial and racial power. W. G. Sebald once wrote that 'it was precisely Casement's homosexuality that sensitized him to the continuing oppression, exploitation and destruction, across the borders of social class and race, of those who were furthest from the centres of power'.[25] The historian Leela Gandhi describes this as a politics of friendship, in which homosexuality (alongside other forms of late nineteenth-century radicalism she describes) was understood as a 'ground for ... strange affinities with foreigners', a 'source of ... ethical and political capacity'.[26] Other such men included the utopian socialist and fellow handsome devil Edward Carpenter.

It is interesting here to think about homosexuality as a path towards anti-colonial alliance, and about the shared births of colonialism and homosexuality in the modern West. Many scholars of colonialism, including Silvia Federici, have established the mind-body binary as a central problem of colonial capitalist epistemology, in which bourgeois Protestant discourses of the mind-body binary led to two parallel phenomena: the colonization of the imagined 'body' by the imagined 'mind,' and the colonization of non-European peoples who were seen to be simply body. The obsession with hygiene and bodily regulation that accompanied the development of bourgeois hegemony in Europe reached its peak with investments in colonial hygiene and bodily regulation through forced conversions, cultural genocide, and public health programmes.[27]

These technologies of regulation were then imported back into the metropolis, where they were imposed on new urban proletarian populations seen as similar to the colonized in their resistance to both disciplined work and moral discipline. Casement was part of a group of gay men – not a group that understood itself necessarily as such, but a group we can definitely think of as relatively coherent in hindsight – who understood their homosexuality as part of a broader project of metropolitan anticolonial radicalism.

The literary scholar Javier Uriarte has argued persuasively that the twinned diaries – documenting Casement's sexual interests and the atrocities of colonial domination – share key ways of looking. Uriarte defines this as 'cruising', a word queers use to describe both looking for casual sex and the particular attentiveness to detail combined with openness to possibility that characterizes a way of moving through the world.[28] There is, queer scholars and activists have argued, a utopian and revolutionary possibility in this way of looking.[29]

Cruising's codes are often quite strict even though they are learned socially; Uriarte writes that cruising, 'looking and reading the body, the gaze, the gestures, and the movements of others … are precisely the activities that lay at the centre of Casement's investigative travels'.[30] The same attentive eye that documented the beaten and bruised bodies of labourers, or a torture device defying a colonial administrator's testimony that no such thing existed, also documented the pleasures and connections available beneath the surface. Uriarte argues that it was *both* the tortured and pleasure-seeking bodies that led Casement to increasingly understand himself as a victim of British colonization and to radicalize his anti-colonial stance. In contrast to narratives of the Amazon as a woman to be deflowered, Casement's Amazonian sex was connected to anti-imperialism.

Casement would eventually be granted a Companion of the Order of St Michael and St George for his work in the Congo and, in 1911, a knighthood for his work in Peru. Why was Casement receiving these gongs from an imperialist power like Great Britain? Partly because his investigations were obviously aimed at Britain's rivals, and because his work in Peru and the Amazon was seen to be in defence of British subjects – that is, their colonial subjects. But it's also worth pointing out that within Britain at the time there was some form of popular moral and political opposition to colonialism, especially in the aftermath of the Boer War.

In 1902 the liberal economist J. A. Hobson had written his economic treatise *Imperialism*, which had positioned imperialism as a result of imbalances within capitalist society and not an offshoot of nationalist pride. Hobson also separated imperialism as a necessary corollary or development of capitalism, unlike, say, Lenin, who published his *Imperialism, the Highest Stage of Capitalism* in 1917, but both included a moral critique of the crimes of imperialism.[31] Hobson was additionally anti-Semitic, especially in his explanation of the causes of war in South Africa.

This sentiment was echoed in socialist politicians of the time, including in the speeches of Keir Hardie, the founder of the Labour Party. That the critique of imperialism and colonialism at the time was a moral one should not obscure that it was often, if not usually, deeply paternalistic, if not racist. Much of the Christian moral critique revolved around a sort of racist idea of a duty of care to lesser races, a mirror of the White Man's Burden that was a justification for colonialism in the first place. Critiques like Hobson's, while opposing imperialism, still revolved around a social Darwinism, an advocacy of eugenics: in Hobson's words, there were 'important differences which should affect our conduct towards countries inhabited by what appear to be definitely low-typed unproductive races ... and countries like China and India, where an old civilization of a high type ... exists'.[32]

All this puts the lie to the idea that imperialist racism went unopposed in its day, a lie that serves to whitewash the reputation of racists like the politician and mining baron Cecil Rhodes.[33] Even if there was a default racism cutting across society at the time, it was possible to take a stand against racism, imperialism and colonialism. While Cecil Rhodes was advocating white supremacism, Casement was writing in a letter home: 'What has civilisation itself been to them? ... A thing of horror – of smoking rifles and pillaged homes – of murdered fathers, violated mothers and enslaved children.'[34] If Casement's writings of the time are unusual in their foregrounding of Indigenous voices and disruption of the racist concept of the 'civilizing mission', some scholars have argued for a more complex understanding of the transactions at play in his depictions of and interactions with subaltern peoples.

Casement did not travel alone back to the United Kingdom – he brought with him two Indigenous young people from Putumayo, living examples of the violence and abuse described in his report. These men were featured in tours, photographed, and sat for portraits; this, argues the critic Leslie Wylie, placed Casement squarely within the long-standing metropolitan tradition of exhibiting picturesque 'living curiosities and "native types"' that postcolonial theory has long argued is part of the machinery of colonialism.[35]

In 1913, Casement retired from the British consular service and immediately threw himself into the Irish struggle for national liberation. He had been a member of the Irish nationalist party Sinn Féin since 1905. In November of 1913 he co-founded the nationalist militia the Irish Volunteers, and travelled to the United States on their behalf to build up support and make connections with exiled nationalists. As tensions in Europe began to rise in the run-up to the First World War, in July of 1914 Casement organised and helped fund the illegal importation of 1,500 rifles from Germany into Howth harbour, to arm the volunteers. Some of these guns were used in the Easter Rising of 1916.

In October of 1914, with Britain now at war with Germany, Casement disguised himself and travelled, via Norway, to Germany. He saw himself as an ambassador for a nascent independent Ireland. In Germany, Casement negotiated with the

Germans and achieved an agreement in the scenario of a German invasion of Britain and Ireland, agreeing that Germany could land troops in Ireland 'not as an army of invaders ... but as the forces of a Government that is inspired by goodwill towards a country and people for whom Germany desires only national prosperity and national freedom'.[36] Even if, as was likely, the Kaiserreich was less interested in Irish national freedom than sticking it to the British, this was still a major diplomatic achievement at a time when the defeat of Britain seemed possible in a way that would have enabled Irish freedom.

Casement then visited the German prisoner of war camps, where he tried to organise Irish POWs into an 'Irish Brigade'. He did not get much luck: the threat of execution if Britain were to win the war was probably too strong, as well as the fact that many troops, having fought on the front line, maintained their loyalty to Britain. But he did manage to persuade the Germans to provide twenty thousand rifles and ten machine guns in addition to other forms of support.

Casement had learned of the upcoming Easter Rising and wanted to reach Ireland before it started in April 1916 so that he could delay it in advance of the arms shipment, which would enable a more decisive and effective attack. He had a German U-boat drop him in County Kerry but, upon landing, he suffered a relapse of the malaria he had picked up in the Congo. He retreated to a fort, too sick to travel. The Irish Volunteers refused to save him, worried about taking any action in advance of the Rising that might jeopardize their supplies or plans. Casement was charged with sabotage, espionage, and high treason; meanwhile, the arms shipment never arrived, having been intercepted by the Royal Navy. Casement was taken to London and held in Brixton Prison to await trial.

The trial was complicated; arcane legal arguments meant there was some confusion as to whether someone outside the country could commit treason. Argument revolved around whether an unpunctuated sentence in the original law implied that the crime had to be committed in the country, or whether it was enough for the crime to have impacts within the country. The decision went against Casement. Meanwhile the prosecution had uncovered more incriminating evidence – not of treachery, but of homosexuality. His 'Black Diaries' came to light, and were used as evidence of his general degeneracy in addition to treachery.

A government memorandum of the time read that 'he has for years been addicted to the grossest sodomitical practices. Of late years he seems to have completed the full cycle of sexual degeneracy and from a pervert has become an invert – a woman or pathic who derives his satisfaction from attracting men and inducing them to use him.'[37] The government leaked transcribed, typed copies of some of the most incriminating pages of the diaries. This hugely undermined Casement's support, not just amongst British friends who might have been able to overlook some of his political activities, but amongst his allies in the Irish nationalist movement. His old friends, Joseph Conrad and Herbert Ward, disowned him. Casement's reputation was besmirched for a generation, his role as a martyr destroyed before it could be built.

It would become almost an article of faith among some conservative Irish nationalists that the diaries had been forged. Some pointed to the large numbers of homosexuals involved in British intelligence during the First and Second World Wars; theories as to their supposed secret author include Sir Frank Ezra Adcock, who, before taking up a professorship in ancient history at Cambridge, had broken ciphers for the British military. Adcock was himself certainly gay, but there is no evidence that he or any other spooks faked four complete, day-to-day perfect diaries in Casement's own handwriting.[38]

But for the new Irish state, dominated by the Roman Catholic Church, Casement's case was a problematic one. A national hero killed by the British and therefore a martyr to the cause – but also a queer. The Irish nationalist William Maloney argued that the diaries had been faked to discredit Casement, arguing in a 1936 book that the diary was actually written by a man Casement was investigating. On the basis of this book, W. B. Yeats wrote an angry poem about Casement's treatment, and in 1965 a book about Casement that included excerpts from the diaries and accepted them as fact was banned from being published by the Irish Censorship of Publications Board for obscenity. As recently as 2013, Angus Mitchell – who edited and helped publish the 'White Diaries' – published a book arguing that the Black Diaries were forged, and Irish media approvingly discussed the apparent forgeries.[39] In his critical biography of Casement, which includes the texts of the Black Diaries in their entirety, the historian Jeffrey Dudgeon lays out a comprehensive provenance of the diaries, making it clear that Casement wrote them and that none of the supposed irregularities that congealed into conspiracy theories about their originality hold the slightest bit of water. The handwriting has been multiply analysed and proven to be authentic.[40]

During Casement's trial, the prosecution actually offered a plea bargain, with the diaries used as evidence that Casement was guilty but insane, and he'd therefore avoid hanging. Casement refused the offer. Supporters, including Arthur Conan Doyle, Yeats, and George Bernard Shaw, made appeals for clemency, but to no avail. He lost his appeal, was stripped of his knighthood, and was sentenced to death. He was hanged by the British state in Pentonville Prison on 3 August 1916, at the age of fifty-one.

Father Carey, the Catholic priest who attended to Casement in his prison cell on the day of his execution, said Roger 'marched to the scaffold with the dignity of a prince.'[41] The executioner, Albert Ellis, later said: 'He appeared to me the bravest man it fell to my unhappy lot to execute.'[42] Found among the diaries was this poem by Casement, called 'The Nameless One':

> I sought by love alone to go
> Where God had writ an awful no.
> Pride gave a guilty God to hell
> I have no pride – by love I fell.[43]

7

Lawrence of Arabia

What does the name 'Lawrence of Arabia' bring to mind? Do you immediately think of the impossibly beautiful, impossibly blond Peter O'Toole in the title role of David Lean's 1962 CinemaScope spectacular? There he is, face framed in white robes, staring firmly into the distant desert horizon; riding a camel; screaming, 'No prisoners!' as his men take vengeance on the Turkish army that has just massacred the residents of Tafas.

These images renewed the idea of 'Arabia' for a generation of credulous Western adventure-seekers, images constructing the Middle East as a place of dark passions, proud natives, and tragic beauty, with a sympathetic white leader at the centre to lead the people towards their freedom. The film had its queer fans, as well. Noel Coward joked that 'if O'Toole were any prettier, the film would have been called "Florence of Arabia"'.[1] As with many mid-century Technicolor epics, *Lawrence of Arabia* featured a sizzling on-screen romance with sexual tension sublimated into wisecracks and innuendo. In this case, however, the lovers were both men, with O'Toole's Lawrence playing opposite the equally delicious Omar Sharif, in the role of Sharif Husayn bin Ali of the Harith.

White gay men have long had a haunted relationship with the politics of empire. Some of the first justifications for European colonization were charges that Black and brown people committed acts of sexual immorality such as sodomy. Tibira do Maranhão, for example, a Tupinambá Native man, was executed in 1614 for sodomy, one of the first people in the New

World to be so executed, and tales of his execution and deeds were circulated in Europe. These charges served as evidence for Europeans that Indigenous people were immoral and unworthy political subjects, and required harsh penalties and paternalistic rule. Colonies were seen as a place of sexual license: in French slang, for example, *faire passer son brevet colonial* meant 'doing it colonial-style' – or to be initiated into sodomy.[2]

The first modern associations for the practice of anthropology were founded in 1869 in Germany, the same year that the term 'homosexuality' was coined there. Through images and stories from the colonies and anthropological and ethnographic data, ideas about sexuality and gender formed in the colonies ended up weaving themselves into the ways that Europeans thought about those things. Some people desired to separate themselves from colonized people by preserving strict standards of heterosexual morality, while some others, like the homosexuals beginning to recognise themselves and be noticed in European cities in the late nineteenth century, began identifying with these othered people. Sometimes, those homosexual encounters in the colonies led to ambivalence towards, or even explicit criticism of, European imperialism. As it turns out, the true story of T. E. Lawrence ends up revealing a lot about how these themes worked themselves out in the context of British military adventure in the Middle East.

Thomas Edward Lawrence was born in August 1888 in Wales, the illegitimate son of the nobleman Sir Thomas Chapman and a Scottish governess, Sarah Junner. Chapman, who liked drinking and the hunt more than family life with his wife and four daughters on their estate in County Westmeath, ran off with Junner after the birth of their first illegitimate child, Montagu Robert, leading his wife to issue an ultimatum. Giving up his estate and fortune, Chapman and Junner adopted the name Lawrence and moved around Wales and Scotland with their ever-growing brood of boys: after Thomas Edward, known in childhood as Ned, came Will, Frank, and Arnold.

The young Ned was plagued by fears about his illegitimacy, which was not confirmed until the 1920s. In the Victorian era such illegitimacy, especially in the upper-middle classes to which the derogated Lawrences now belonged, was cause for great scandal. Chapman left a letter for his sons to be opened only after his death, explaining the situation in which he had left them (the letter is quoted in Anthony Sattin's excellent biography *The Young T. E. Lawrence*, which is repeatedly cited throughout this chapter):

> You can imagine or try to imagine, how your Mother and I have suffered all these years, not knowing what day we might be recognized by someone ... You can think with what delight we saw each of you growing up to manhood, for men are valued for themselves and not for their family history, except of course under particular circumstances ... The ways of transgressors are hard.[3]

This uncertainty spurred repeated moves, the family constantly worried that new neighbours or friends might discover their secret. Only the need to provide a good education for their boys – the kind of education that might help them overcome a murky pedigree – drew them to settle in Oxford. By this time, Chapman had settled his estate and received an annual income that kept the family comfortably afloat.

Whether inspired by this experience of uprootedness or not, from a young age, Ned was fascinated by antiquarian objects, cycling around Oxfordshire with schoolmates and making rubbings of local churches and their monuments, and monitoring building sites for archaeological finds, which they presented to Oxford's famed Ashmolean Museum. With his friend CFC Beeson, he collected old shards and fragments of pottery and reassembled them. A 1906 trip with Beeson to the south of France yielded weeks of cycling to ruined medieval churches.

While he adored his father, from whom he inherited a love for photography and shooting, rumours about his illegitimacy made him fear for his future and think of his mother as a hypocritical woman who 'held his father as her trophy of power'.[4] Perhaps as a consequence, at Oxford High School, where he studied, the young Lawrence chafed against strict discipline and lessons he thought were beneath him. At Oxford University, where he read history and wrote a thesis on medieval military history, he was an erratic if motivated pupil, who decided to conduct the archival research of French military and religious architecture himself on his bicycle, spending the summer of 1908 riding 2,400 miles across the French countryside to document the architecture. Continuing these interests, he followed up his graduation by touring crusader castles in Ottoman Syria on foot. English antiquarians at this time were often thought to be morbidly, queerly obsessed with old objects and the past, much as some decadent orientalists used fantasies of mysterious and magical other lands to escape bourgeois life.[5]

Back in England, Lawrence was shunned for having been born out of wedlock, and homosexual sex was still an illegal offence; for him, the Middle East seems to have opened up a new world of exotic, and erotic, experiences. These experiences were and continued to be, however, predicated on a view of the native population as 'noble savages' – representatives of romanticized primitive man, free to express themselves without the corrupting influences of civilisation. A 2014 monograph by Joseph Boone focusing on homosexuality and orientalism in late nineteenth- and early twentieth-century anglophone literary cultures argues that 'Western fantasies of the "Orient"' contained 'the potential for unexpected eruptions of sex between men that ... disrupt European norms of masculinity and heterosexual priority'.[6]

The experience of the homosexual erotic could be, and for Lawrence seems to have been, that of an ecstatic dissolution of boundaries. Remembering this time later in his autobiography, Lawrence wrote,

> The efforts for those years to live in the dress of an Arab, and to imitate their mental foundation, quitted me of my English self, and let me look at the West and its conventions with new eyes: they destroyed it all for me. At the same time I could not sincerely take on the Arab skin: it was an affectation only.[7]

This self-awareness, one which was not reproduced in uncritical media celebrations of the dashing Lawrence having 'gone native', accompanied him throughout his life and adds complexity to our understanding of this troubled colonial figure unable or unwilling to shed himself of his dominant status and the privileges it brought him. Even as he argued for more Arabs' independence, he always referred to them as being 'clean' and 'uncontaminated', words recalling the Victorian view of children requiring guidance and direction and implying a pre-civilizational innocence.[8]

That summer of 1909, on foot and alone, he walked first along the path of the railway being constructed through Palestine and Lebanon. Like many British men of this period, Lawrence assumed that British colonization was superior to that of other imperial powers, including the Ottomans, who until after the First World War maintained, at least nominally, rule over Syria and Lebanon, which they had conquered in 1516. British and American missionaries did, at least, enable some Arabs to study abroad, many of whom returned and began to seed nationalist movements for which Lawrence always had a great deal of sympathy.

This new generation of educated Arabs (one of whom Lawrence described, in a letter home, as 'a-most-civilized-French-speaking-disciple-of-the-Herbert-Spencer-Free-Masonic-Mohammedan-Young Turk,' in a display of the dizzying array of intellectual influences on these growing movements) became his friends, collaborators, and the kind of men he increasingly believed should lead a return of Arab lands to Arab rule.[9] As he travelled and studied the military strategy of both the crusaders and of their Indigenous opponents, he began to refine ideas about guerrilla warfare that he would later be credited with inventing, although in fact he merely introduced these military tactics into Western practice for the first time. Returning to Oxford several stone lighter – some assumed he had been severely ill, or did not recognize him – he finished his thesis and graduated in the spring of 1910.

The next December, Lawrence travelled back to Syria to

study Arabic and work on archaeological digs under Leonard Woolley; he also worked with R. Campbell Thompson of the British Museum. It was while working on these digs that he met the teenage Selim Ahmed, known as Dahoum, a native-born assistant on an archaeological dig. He took to the boy quickly, and by 1913 the sixteen-year-old Dahoum was a senior member of the dig team.

Lawrence, like many colonialists obsessed with what they saw as the noble beauty of native peoples, praised Dahoum for his simplicity and honesty. They lived together in the dig camp and Lawrence carved what Woolley later called 'a queer crouching figure ... in the soft local limestone' in his likeness. The implication was that Lawrence had a sexual relationship with Dahoum. Woolley wrote: 'To portray a naked figure was proof ... of evil of another sort. The scandal about Lawrence was widely spread and firmly believed.'[10] Woolley did, however, insist that he himself did not believe the apparently universal rumours: 'The charge was quite unfounded ... he was in no sense a pervert; in fact he had a remarkably clean mind. He was tolerant, thanks to his classical reading, and Greek homosexuality interested him ... he knew quite well what the Arabs said about himself and Dahoum and so far from resenting it was amused.'[11]

In the summer of 1913, Lawrence even took the unprecedented step of bringing Dahoum home to Oxford, along with another dig-site comrade, Hamoudi. Dahoum and Hamoudi had portraits sketched for the collection of the Ashmolean Museum at Oxford; but Lawrence refused to allow them to be exhibited or commercially photographed, in the then-common tradition of the spectacular exhibition of 'exotic' peoples.

Whether he and Dahoum ever had sex, rumours were not quelled by the dedication poem with which Lawrence opened his 1926 book, *Seven Pillars of Wisdom*. The poem, entitled 'to S. A.', opens:

> I loved you, so I drew these tides of men into my hands
> and wrote my will across the sky in stars
> To earn you Freedom, the seven-pillared worthy house,

> that your eyes might be shining for me
> When we came.[12]

One approach is to interpret this poem as being addressed to 'the Arab People'; others can't help thinking of Dahoum, whose full name was, after all, Selim Ahmed. Full of exciting stories of adventure, *Seven Pillars of Wisdom* also includes some additional passages that read as almost flamboyantly queer to the contemporary eye. Consider this:

> In horror of such sordid commerce our youths began indifferently to slake one another's few needs in their own clean bodies – a cold convenience that, by comparison, seemed sexless and even pure. Later, some began to justify this sterile process, and swore that friends quivering together in the yielding sand with intimate hot limbs in supreme embrace, found there hidden in the darkness a sensual co-efficient of the mental passion which was welding our souls and spirits in one flaming effort [to secure Arab independence]. Several, thirsting to punish appetites they could not wholly prevent, took a savage pride in degrading the body, and offered themselves fiercely in any habit which promised physical pain or filth.[13]

Ah yes. We've all been there, haven't we, girls?

Identifying situational male-male homosexuality – especially in the context of nationalist armed service – as more 'pure' than contact with women seen as diseased and dirty is a long tradition in right-wing gay circles. Ernst Röhm, who we will discuss later in our chapter on the Bad Gays of Weimar Berlin, was a Nazi who saw no conflict between his politics and his homosexuality, which he conceived of as *more* masculine (and therefore more heroic and more pure) than heterosexuality. In his influential work of criticism *Male Fantasies*, Klaus Theweleit argues that anti-feminism and the association of women with impurity and failure in battle was a crucial part of the development of fascist masculinity in the twentieth century.[14] But Lawrence was far from a fascist, and similar ideas about masculinist gay purity also circulated in journals like *Der Eigene* and the anarchist and anti-feminist poetry cult that arose in the early twentieth century around Stefan George. In England, the certified Good Gay and ardent socialist Edward Carpenter, inspired by Walt Whitman, wrote of the 'manly love of comrades', a strain of homosexual identification in which the worship of ancient Greek forms of masculinity and the relationship between homosexual masculinity and democracy emphasized sex as a path towards emotional bonding and political transformation. This was connected to his attempt to combat the idea that gay men were effeminate and unhealthy by stressing the 'health, vitality, and manliness' of men who had sex with men and the ways in which homosexual contact supposedly erased class difference in ancient Greece.[15]

Ancient Greece, the Orient, and the supposed 'primitive' were, for many of these writers, roughly equivalent sources of mythic pasts with which to justify and construct their contemporary identities. 'In these authors', writes the critic Parminder Kaur Bakshi, 'Orientalism is continuous with and culminates the process of affiliation begun with classical scholarship.'[16] The translation of *The Arabian Nights* by Sir Richard Burton, along with the 1859 translation of the *Rubaiyat of Omar Khayyam* by Edward FitzGerald, was seized upon by writers and activists seeking exaltations of sensual love among the stiff and cold world of late Victorian Britain. While these visions were rooted in and limited by their orientalism, they often led to what Joy Dixon calls 'radically inclusive' visions of the way forward for human society.[17]

The 1913 Constantinople coup seemed to open up new political possibilities for Arabs: in Beirut, a council formed to elect a committee demanding the use of Arabic as a state language and local control over revenue.[18] In 1913, in Paris, the first Arab National Congress met to discuss the possibility of revolution and reform; this event, led by Arab students studying in France, was one of the origins of Arab nationalism. Various groups in the Arab-speaking world began to arm themselves for a conflict that seemed increasingly inevitable. Lawrence ended up running guns from Aleppo to Beirut in the spring of 1913, travelling the whole while with Dahoum and visiting various markets where he bought antiquities to decorate the house he had built himself at Carchemish, though first he had to smuggle them past Turkish customs officials.

Biographers disagree as to whether Lawrence was already working for British intelligence at this time. In 1909, the same year that the British Museum began its digs at Carchemish, the Secret Service Bureau, a department of British intelligence that would come to be known as MI6, began operations. Lawrence was working with the Royal Navy and British diplomats, both institutions already deeply tied to the British Museum. The dig was located on the Berlin-to-Baghdad railway, a line under construction intended to link Berlin with the Arab and Ottoman worlds that deeply concerned the British, who saw potential German control over the Arab lands as a threat to their domination of the Indian subcontinent. The sources of funding for the Carchemish dig have also always been somewhat ambiguous. It is certainly not impossible to imagine that intelligence was somehow involved.

By the time that the First World War broke out in July of 1914, Lawrence and his colleagues, whether already spies or not, found themselves co-opted by the British military. Lawrence enthusiastically greeted the war, and the probability that war would dislodge the already tenuous Turkish control over the Arab world. Funded to search for biblical ruins in the Negev Desert, they were sending their survey maps of that strategically important desert back to military intelligence. This trip was conducted under the auspices of the Palestine Exploration Fund and was Lawrence's first confirmed piece of work for the British national security state.

In addition to possible military uses, the exact border between British territory in Egypt and Ottoman territory in Palestine had long been a sore point in British-Ottoman relations. Under the guise of an archaeological dig for evidence of biblical stories about the movement of Moses and the Jews, the expedition began, with Dahoum joining as assistant on the expedition. This was where Lawrence would learn how to travel in the desert and to read a landscape for its potential use in military campaigns. He visited Aqaba, a coastal city in present-day Jordan where he would later lead a spectacular attack on the Turks, and Petra, a historical city in southern Jordan inhabited since 7000 BCE and famous for its rock-carved architecture, many of whose buildings are carved into the rose-stone cliffs.

By December of 1914, Lawrence had been co-opted into the Arab Bureau intelligence unit in Cairo, leaving Dahoum behind to guard the archaeological dig. In 1916, while on an intelligence mission, he was sent to the Arabian peninsula and involved himself in the Arab Revolt, a military uprising against the Ottoman Empire aiming to create a single independent Arab state from Syria to Yemen. The Arab lands had long been considered by European colonial administrators to be somewhat of a backwater, of interest only for their geographic importance in defending and administering colonies in India and Africa. The second Industrial Revolution and the increasing global demand for oil, and its discovery aplenty in the Middle East, sent European powers scrambling to control this newly crucial resource.

The Ottomans had formed a military alliance with Germany, so the Allies, Britain and France, were determined to share the spoils of the oil-rich region. The revolt was declared by Sharif Husayn, the ruler of Mecca, in June of 1916, on the basis of a British promise to recognize an independent Arab state after the First World War. Unbeknownst to Husayn, or to Lawrence himself, the British and French had already drawn up plans that May for how the land would be divided between themselves once the Arabs had helped them defeat the Ottomans. Husayn was the only one of the six leaders of Arabian tribes who was not an Ottoman loyalist: deeply religious and conservative, even reactionary, he was bitterly opposed by liberal Arab nationalists.[19]

Distracted by the other fronts in the war – not least of which, the deadlock on the front in France and Belgium – the imperial powers preferred to let the Arabs do their work for them. If the First World War seems utterly pointless in hindsight, its motivations are utterly clear: if the war was terrible, as Lenin once quipped, it was terribly profitable.

Lawrence became involved in this revolt as one of its leaders, later claiming that he had four motives for doing so: to win the war, to be part of a movement of national self-determination, to see the Arab lands united under a benighted British sovereignty he presumed would lead to independence, and, most importantly, that he 'liked a certain Arab very much, and ... thought that freedom for the race would be an acceptable present'.[20] This certain Arab could only be Dahoum. These drives, and their entanglement with the brute world-historical forces of profit and exploitation, left legacies of violence and broken promises that would shape the making of the contemporary Middle East. If, as Neil Faulkner argues, Lawrence experienced the complexities and contradictions of this conflict as 'inner torment', this led him to participate in and even lead some of the Arab Revolt.[21] The revolt itself began with a gunshot fired by Sharif Husayn from the minaret of the Great Mosque in Mecca. Lawrence enthusiastically wrote, 'I hate the Turks so much that to see their own people turning on them is very grateful,' while other English officers worried that the seemingly disorganized and poorly armed Arab armies would have difficulty countering Ottoman forces.[22]

Despite these fears, the Arabian Peninsula quickly began to fall under Arab control. In October of 1916, Lawrence was formally transferred to the Arab Bureau. 'He entered Arabia', Neil Faulkner writes, 'full of ambition, enthusiasm, and zest for life; he left ... with his mind darkened and destabilized'[23] by his growing awareness that he was participating in a play-acted revolution for the benefit of another imperial power. When Lawrence returned to Cairo and his desk intelligence job a few days later, he was greeted with the news that Ottoman troops were rapidly approaching the Arab front and that the Arab Revolt desperately needed support. Lawrence argued against sending in British troops, arguing that they would be perceived as invaders. Instead, he argued, the seemingly weaker and less-organized Arab armies were best used as defensive guerrilla fighters, whose superior knowledge of the terrain could enable them to defeat much larger armies.

Despite an early setback at the Battle of Nakhl Mubarak in

December of that year, by early 1917 regular guerrilla attacks across the Arabian Peninsula were damaging the Ottoman army's ability to take back the Arab lands. Feuding with British officers who saw the Arabs as uneducated and unsophisticated, Lawrence began to lead a series of daring explosive attacks on rail lines and other Ottoman infrastructure, leading to enormous damage without significant Arab casualties. In the spring of 1917, with the Western Front bogged down in immobile trench warfare and British politicians eager to deliver a splashy victory to their people, the empire began paying more attention to the ongoing conflict in the Middle East.

By now Lawrence was concerned about the imperial horse-trading that continued in Europe. The British seemed amenable to a French proposal to invade Syria with a joint Anglo-French ground force. Lawrence was additionally concerned with the successful political campaign waged by Zionists, who seized upon Britain's aims on Palestine and lobbied for the region to be turned into a homeland for the Jews. And so, in the spring of 1917, Lawrence went rogue, promoting to Arab leaders the idea of taking Damascus with Arab troops. Disobeying British orders, he assuaged his guilt at the betrayal of the Arabs by seeking to assist their troops in Syria. At the Battle of Aqaba, fought over the Red Sea port he had visited as an archaeologist years before, he led the Arab forces to a resounding victory.

It was that November, during the revolt, that Lawrence experienced one of his only confirmable sexual experiences – an experience of such violence that it is difficult to know whether 'sexual' is even an appropriate adjective for it. He was captured in Syria and turned over by Hajim Bey, the Ottoman governor, to be gang-raped by a group of soldiers. Lawrence himself, in a version of *Seven Pillars* thought destroyed and later rediscovered, described a desire 'that had been awakened by the experience and journeyed with me since, fascination and terror and morbid desire, lascivious and vicious perhaps, but like the striving of a moth towards its flame'[24].

It is difficult to make sense of the truth of this encounter. Some historians, like James Barr, have claimed that the episode was exaggerated or even invented out of whole cloth; one might read Lawrence's description of his sexual awakening as a kind of porn story, a narrative of self-awakening. Other biographers believe that the event likely took place, at least in some form. In exchanges with the gay novelist E. M. Forster, he called himself 'funnily made up, sexually', and in a later letter to Forster, claimed 'the Turks, as you probably know ... did it to me, by force ... I couldn't ever do it, I believe: the impulse strong enough to make me touch another creature has not yet been born in me'. Writing to Robert Graves, he reported that, as regarded 'fucking', he 'hadn't ever and didn't much want to'.[25]

The ethics of believing survivors compel us to believe Lawrence, and to assume that his dabbling in BDSM (stay tuned for more on this) represented an erotic processing or reclamation of this experience. Graves provides another fascinating point of entry into understanding Lawrence and his connections to a strain of homosexual identity influenced by primitivism. A mythologist, Graves's most famous work, *The White Goddess: A Historical Grammar of Poetic Myth*, proposes a universal-to-Europe ancient mother goddess whose worship generated 'pure' poetry and who had been violently replaced by patriarchal Christianity.

Graves was in regular correspondence with the American gay liberation activist Harry Hay, whose 1950s research attempted to match Graves's mythologic reflections with the primitivist matriarchal communism hypothesized by Friedrich Engels, and find roles for proto-gay figures in both. While Hay (and, presumably, Graves) did not share the misogyny of Lawrence's descriptions of 'sordid' women, their primitivism was often shared by people who did. Many early illustrations in *Der Eigene*, the anarchist-masculinist gay journal, were by the artist Sascha Schneider, whose illustrations included Winnetou, a Native American character invented by the German author Karl May who popularized European notions of Native peoples as noble savages uncorrupted by civilization.

That December, with Lawrence still recovering from the attack and increasingly doubting that the British would ever make good on their promises to the Arabs, Field Marshal Edmund Allenby, the leader of the British Empire's Egyptian Expeditionary Force, dismounted his Rolls-Royce and strode through the gate of Jerusalem, in a carefully stage-managed event meant to impress upon the locals the supposedly sensitive and enlightened imperialism of the British and upon the British public the success of the empire where previous crusader kings had failed.

Lawrence, who by this time surrounded himself with personal bodyguards commanded by Abdullah al-Nahabi, returned to Aqaba determined to lead an Arab force into Damascus capable of resisting the division of the territory between France and Britain. British leaders, fearful that stalemate would lead to revolution as had begun in Russia, redoubled their efforts to defeat the Ottomans in the Holy Land. A series of unsuccessful military raids in early 1918 lowered morale, but as the year pressed on, just as the tide on the Western Front began to turn, the Ottomans began to fall. Yet another series of spectacular raids reassured Lawrence of the success of his guerrilla tactics.

By this time, far from riding camels like Peter O'Toole in the filmed epic, Lawrence was fighting from a mechanized and armoured Rolls-Royce. At the Battle of Megiddo in September, the Ottoman army began to crumble and retreat, losing its will to fight. The troops under King Faisal, son of Sharif Husayn, prepared to take Damascus. By the end of September, only 17,000 Ottoman troops remained of the 100,000-strong army from the beginning of that month. The Germans destroyed their ammunition in Damascus on the night of 30 September. The British allowed Faisal and his troops to enter first, knowing that such a gesture would make the people more prone to accept what they understood as a kind of pan-Arab liberation. People celebrated in the streets of the city. But the celebrations did not last long: only a few days later, Faisal was informed that the French would serve as 'protecting power' in Syria and rule Lebanon directly.[26] Lawrence claimed that he had no knowledge that this might happen.

Simultaneously, trying to re-establish contact with Dahoum after the tumult of the war, he learned that Dahoum had died in one of the waves of famine and disease that had stricken the war-torn region. 'Men prayed me that I set our work, the inviolate house, as a memory of you,' he wrote of Dahoum, in *Seven Pillars of Wisdom*. 'But for fit monument, I shattered it, unfinished. And now the little things creep out to patch themselves hovels in the marred shadow of your gift.'[27] Later, he would write, 'I went to the very bottom of Arab life – and came back with the news that the seven pillars were fallen down.'[28]

World War I left a tangled and bloody legacy, not least in the Middle East. The Ottoman Empire collapsed but was replaced by the British and French empires. The British takeover of the Holy Land paved the way for the partition of Palestine and the creation of the State of Israel. As Neil Faulkner points out in his excellent history of Lawrence's involvement in the war as it took place in the Middle East, we are still living with the consequences of the fragile, unstable, unjust, and violent 'peace' and partition in the early 1920s.

Lawrence, whose romanticism blinkered him not only to Arab humanity but to political reality, saw in the camels and robes of his Hashemite comrades a savage nobility that contained some essential truth of human existence. There might have been room for a metropolitan anti-colonial fighter on the ground in the Arab world during the revolt. Only a few years before this book was written, many bright young leftists from the United States and Europe went to Syria to support the libertarian-socialist-feminist Rojava, fighting in a war whose contours were shaped by the fighting and borders of the First World War a hundred years before. But Lawrence was not that kind of man. Instead, he sought medieval nobility and a racist vision of ethnic purity – and was condemned to be disappointed by the venal realities of realpolitik.

Upon his return to the UK, Lawrence became involved in a travelling photo show called 'With Allenby in Palestine' bringing orientalism to the masses. This was part of a broader tradition of human zoos and exotic spectacles that the young Lawrence had, by insisting that Dahoum not be photographed or exhibited, once rebuked. When Lawrence's photo dressed as a Bedouin proved the most popular, the show changed its title to 'With Allenby in Palestine and Lawrence in Arabia.' Lawrence was suddenly a celebrity.

In addition to being a celebrity, he advised Winston Churchill, then secretary of state for the colonies. While Lawrence worked there, this office, far from caring for the Arab people Lawrence claimed to love, oversaw the bombing of villages across present-day Iraq; one village was destroyed in only forty-five minutes. Churchill urged the use of chemical weapons against some of Iraq's native populations, whom he described as 'uncivilized tribes'. When others in the Colonial Office opposed this move, Churchill argued that gassing them was more humane than the alternative: methodical genocide. Lawrence, to his credit, seems to have disliked this work, both for its bureaucratic nature and its anti-Arab sentiments; he even wrote a Swiftian satire 'encouraging' the gassing of Arabs in the London *Times*.[29]

He began instead to contemplate writing a biography of the (also gay) diplomat, anti-colonial activist, and Irish nationalist Roger Casement, but was blocked from seeing Casement's unexpurgated diaries (full of scandalous gay content) and decided against the project. Neither fame nor work at the Colonial Office much suited Lawrence, who in 1923 re-enlisted, this time in the Royal Air Force, as an airman. From 1919 to 1926, he wrote *Seven Pillars of Wisdom*, which until his death was only available in a first edition for subscribers. An amended and shortened version, *Revolt in the Desert*, hit the market in 1927 and immediately became a best-seller.

It was at this time that he began living out a particularly kinky sexual fantasy: he invented an uncle, who he referred to as 'R'; and in that persona delivered instructions to John Bruce, a strapping young Scot from the Tank Corps, for the whipping of the naughty 'Ted' – himself. This relationship played out over twelve years, each beating carefully diarized by Lawrence, including the date and the number of lashings. One entry, for example, read '30 from Jock', his nickname for Bruce. The letters were detailed and profoundly kinky. In one letter, he urges the use of birch instead of a belt, claiming that the belt hadn't served its function. In another, which might reveal some of his own psychological contradictions about these experiences and desires, he wrote, 'Please take any chance his friendship for you gives, to impress upon him how wrong it is for him, at his age and standing, to force us to use these schoolboy measures against him. He should be ashamed to hold his head up amongst his fellows, knowing that he had suffered so humiliating and undignified a punishment.'[30] Once again, the allure of heterosexual men within a sexual context, a double-bind allowing desire to be disavowed at the very moment it is enjoyed, was a key ingredient in Lawrence's homosexual desires.

Why did Lawrence's kinky proclivities stay secret for so long? Bruce, upon selling his story to the tabloids in 1969, claimed that he thought that 'Uncle R' actually existed: we'll let you, the reader, decide whether anyone could be quite so thick. If you lived in Great Britain in the late 1960s, when homosexuality was barely decriminalized, and you liked Lawrence, you would have *wanted* to suppress the rumour. His popular revival in the 1960s, timed to the David Lean film, was fuelled by a revisionist history of colonialism that saw British agents as liberatory forces for local populations.

Undeniably an agent of British imperialism, Lawrence was genuinely concerned with the culture and struggle for self-determination of a people he saw himself as becoming part of. That desire to 'go native' was also a colonial act. Even if he wasn't empire's worst agent, he still was one of its agents. And even today, groups like Reddit's 'gaybros', not to mention books like Jane Ward's *Not Gay: Sex between Straight White Men*, prove the lasting appeal of hypermasculine homosexual sex without gay identification.

Two months after leaving military service, in May 1935, Lawrence was killed in an accident near his cottage in Dorset. Trying to avoid hitting some cyclists, he lost control of his motorcycle and was thrown, dying six days later in hospital. He had been appointed a Companion of the Distinguished Service Order, a Knight of the Legion of Honour, and awarded the Croix de

Guerre in his lifetime; after his death, a bust of his likeness was placed in St Paul's Cathedral alongside the tombs of other great British generals. David Lean's 1962 film immortalized him as a tall, daring, dashing, and egotistical hero – when in fact he was short, shy, somewhat nerdy, and deeply conflicted.

8

The Bad Gays of Weimar Berlin

Who are the Bad Gays of Weimar Berlin? Many of us look back on that time and imagine scenes from Bob Fosse's *Cabaret*: maybe the delicate and almost alien beauty of Michael York, or the green-fingernailed and short-bobbed Liza Minnelli embodying the divinely decadent Sally Bowles, a cabaret singer living through the rise of the Nazis in a sleazy, glittery, ambisexual Berlin of nightclubs and fallen aristocrats and cheap flop-houses. The film was a smash, and the vision of Weimar Berlin it helped to cement in the popular imagination was not limited to the United States.

In divided Cold War Berlin, the museum guard and archivist Wolfgang Theis, also active in the *Tunte* or 'sissy' movement of effeminate radical gays, would dress in drag as Sally Bowles as he and other gays organized to create a museum archiving German queer life before, during, and after Weimar, one that still stands today. Theis was part of a movement of post-war radicals who transformed West German society. Post-war West Germany began as a deeply conservative place, governed by Konrad Adenauer's Christian Democrats, who maintained frosty relationships with the Communist East and who depicted the Nazi era as a period of excess brought on by socialist spending and personal immorality.

In this way Weimar Berlin, for growing gay liberation movements in both Germany and around the world, came to embody a rich set of cultural anxieties, hopes, dreams, fears, usable and abusable pasts. Imagine, then, 1970s and 1980s progressive activists' delight at rediscovering the career and prominence of Dr Magnus Hirschfeld: a sexologist who had participated in the 1919 revolution, run for the duration of the Weimar Republic a progressive centre for sexual research and homosexual and pro-trans advocacy, and advocated against racism. Not only that; he was Jewish, and because of his Jewishness had been a particular target of right-wing and Nazi activists. Hirschfeld became the national hero of the new movement for gay liberation, and institutions organizing around the history of Weimar understood him as the protagonist of a movement towards science and justice.

There were, however, darker figures lurking in the background of Weimar-era gay history. Hirschfeld was not, at the time, the movement's undisputed leader: there were multiple strands of the homosexual emancipation movement, with conflicting goals and ideas, vastly different political affiliations and under-standings, and shared blind spots. The alternatingly fascist and left-expressionist 'masculinist' movement emphasized a culture and heroic model of hypermasculine homosexuality; it was cul-turally nationalist, anti-feminist and often anti-Semitic. These were the Weimar gays most influenced by figures like Frederick the Great.

Trashy right-wing books – and even asides in well-respected texts like *The Rise and Fall of the Third Reich*, in which the journalist William Shirer lets loose an astonishing tirade about several homosexual Nazis we will discuss in this chapter as 'notorious homosexual perverts' who 'quarreled and feuded as only men of unnatural sexual inclinations, with their particular jealousies, can' – have made it difficult to talk about associations between homosexuality and European fascism without giving credence to the conspiracy theories of bigots.[1] Nevertheless, as we will discuss in this chapter, one very senior Nazi was in fact homosexual, and his homosexuality became a heated subject of political debate. We will discuss the activist and publisher Friedrich Radszuweit, whose commercial empire formed the only Weimar-era mass gay movement – indeed, the first such movement in the world – but whose late-in-life determination to remain apolitical led him to seek rapprochement with the coming fascist threat. Even Hirschfeld's own Scientific-Humanitarian Committee went through rifts and splits, with new scholarship reassessing the view of Hirschfeld as a hero fighting repression and instead understanding him as embodying a social consensus on sexuality in the Weimar-era combining progress for some with exclusion for others. Having given a speech that helped announce the social democratic German Revolution of 1918–19 – a revolution of compromise and contradiction, in which social democrats who had supported the war now claimed to herald its end and used far-right militias to murder Communists, and in which those far-right militias would never accept the legitimacy of democratic governance – Hirschfeld himself embodied many of the contradictions of the Weimar state.

The Weimar Republic was an unhappy compromise borne of a country humiliated in military defeat; that it lasted as long as it did points to a degree of strength. In retrospect it has been all too tempting for scholars to describe a doomed dance on the lip of the volcano; typically these analyses are accompanied by banal sentences about how the republic was opposed by antidemocratic forces on the right *and* left, as though Rosa Luxemburg's ghost shared responsibility with Hitler and Hindenburg for the collapse of democracy, the invasion of Poland, and the mass murder of Jews, Sinti/Roma, political prisoners, the disabled, homosexuals, and others. Especially given how many of those political prisoners were themselves Communists, this historical analysis is perverse and wilfully ignorant. Instead, we should understand the republic as being buffeted by political and economic forces that were difficult, if not impossible, to control.

The 1918 revolution brought to power Social Democrats whose support for the just-lost First World War had discredited them among portions of their base. Additionally, they were hindered from governing by the near-unified opposition of centre-right parties, many of which preferred increasingly formalized cooperation with the far right to political rapprochement with the centre-left. Until 1929, this system functioned with

Social Democrats, consistently the largest party, mostly agreeing to support centrist politicians to be the chancellor; the pressure of the economic crash of 1929 and the centre-right's decision to enable the Nazis instead of standing with the democratic parties of the left, as we will see, helped bring the whole system down.

Ernst Röhm was born in Munich in 1887 and raised by Protestants in the predominantly Catholic region of Bavaria. A thick-necked man, he injured his nose in the First World War, giving him a pugnacious look. 'It was always my heartfelt desire to be a soldier,' he wrote in the foreword to his 1928 memoirs.[2] For his bravery he was awarded an Iron Cross in June of 1916. The German Revolution of 1918–19 changed everything: for a military man like Röhm, imbued in the authoritarian culture of the protestant Junkers who ran the German military, the sudden influence of socialists, Jews, and other unworthy specimens represented a complete upset of the proper social order. 'In February 1919 in Germany it was not easy to be a Nationalist,' he would write in his memoirs, saying that only one Bavarian newspaper 'had a manly approach'.[3]

Notable here is the collation of 'nationalist' with 'manly'. In a pamphlet written in 1919, he decried the socialist Bavarian leader Kurt Eisner as 'a foreigner' and described him and other revolutionary leaders as having 'contempt' for their country.[4] Along with many other members of the military class, Röhm joined a *Freikorps* militia in the years after the revolution. Early in the Weimar years, these militias were employed by the Social Democratic president of Germany, Friedrich Ebert, to overturn the Communist government in Munich in 1919, and to murder the Spartacist activists Rosa Luxemburg and Karl Liebknecht.[5]

These paramilitaries would eventually agglomerate and transform into the *Sturmabteilung*, or SA; and then, after conservatives and centrists enabled a Nazi assumption of power, they were superseded by the SS. Röhm joined the German Workers' Party (which would become the Nazi Party) before Hitler, and helped devise one of the Nazis' most dangerous political strategies. Despite their complete acquiescence to and service of the

German capitalist class (who helped the Nazis gain power and were richly rewarded with fat, state-funded military contracts, a labour force banned from free association and organization, and eventually forced slave labour), the Nazis adopted a rhetorical strategy focused on the working class. They weren't socialists, but they pretended to be: claiming to represent the 'true' interests of German workers against the evil influence of foreign intellectuals and urban elites.[6] As a military officer and a paramilitary organizer, Röhm could provide both masses of ex-servicemen and the protection of local authorities in Bavaria. Both would prove crucial to the Nazi rise to power.[7]

In November of 1923, Röhm played a key role in the Beer Hall Putsch, the failed Nazi coup. At that time the leader of the *Reichskriegsflagge* militia, he rented and occupied a central Munich beer hall near the beer hall where Hitler staged his attempt to take power. At Hitler's command, he marched a force to the headquarters of the war ministry, which they then occupied for sixteen hours, at which time shots were exchanged, fourteen Nazis and four police officers died, and the putsch came to an end. Röhm and Hitler, along with nine others, were tried for treason the next February. Despite being found guilty, Röhm's sentence was suspended; Hitler served only nine months, and was treated well enough in prison that he was able to dictate his memoirs while serving his sentence.

Only two months after the trial, Röhm was elected to the German parliament as a deputy for the National Socialist Freedom Party, a Nazi front organization formed after the first party was banned. In the following election that December, he lost his seat. He gave only one speech, focusing his time on developing the *Frontbann*, a paramilitary organization rivalling the SA. The *Freikorps* militias were rapidly turning into more coherent stormtrooper forces. In 1925, chafing at what he felt to be overly rule-oriented and moralistic leadership from Hitler, he resigned his party post and moved to Bolivia for two years.

By the mid-1920s, Röhm was describing himself in personal letters as 'same-sex orientated'.[8] He was not the only stormtrooper to be so inclined. Historian Laurie Marhoefer examines one remarkable essay that ran in the academic journal of Hirschfeld's gay rights organization, the 'Scientific-Humanitarian Committee', claiming to represent the viewpoint of an anonymous gay Nazi. Such a thing might seem a contradiction in terms, given the Nazis' vicious homophobia. And yet, as Marhoefer writes, the anonymous stormtrooper 'hated homosexuality', which to him meant 'male femininity, Marxism, and Judaism. Yet in his worldview, there were multiple queer subjectivities.'[9] Public homosexuality and crossdressing were out; 'masculine, discreet, manly Eros' was on the other hand 'wholly compatible' with a Nazi racial consciousness.[10] (Remember that when writing your Grindr profile!) This eroticism was not only something that could be reconciled with his fascism; as Marhoefer argues, it was 'the foundation of it ... Anonymous wrote that the hand of a Nazi militia man "can strike a blow but also caress" ... From the barracks where discreet, manly caresses took place under cover of night, in the morning militia men marched forth to beat anti-fascists to death.' There was, as the historian Andrew Wackerfuss has argued, a powerful collective association between male sexual and male military power.[11] Stormtrooper bands exploited this association by promising and delivering homoerotic and homosocial experiences to their members (collective life, collective battle, collective showers, and so on) even as they violently denounced and murdered queer-identifying people.[12]

Both Marhoefer's and Wackerfuss's arguments are part of a broader scholarly reassessment of the sexual politics of the Weimar Republic. Departing from a historiography emphasizing the radicality of homosexual emancipation and other sexual freedom movements – think of the plot of the film *Cabaret* itself – Marhoefer instead describes a broad 'Weimar consensus' on sexual freedom of 'a particular type ... that liberated a majority of people while curtailing a disorderly minority'.[13] As we will see later, that minority included (as it does today) sex workers and other marginalized people. Rather than being brave outcast voices, activists like Hirschfeld existed at the centre of society and used their influence to fight for a particular vision of sexual liberation.

One of these particular visions was an understanding of masculinist homosexuality that Claudia Bruns argues was a reaction to sexology's description of the homosexual as a 'feminized' and therefore also (not least because many sexologists were Jewish) 'Semitic' man.[14] Reacting against the idea that the homosexual was weak, 'sick … socially useless', these men sought to portray a revolutionary white-Aryan racial homoerotic and hypermasculine bond as the source of purifying political and artistic power.[15] Robert Deam Tobin writes that, with some exceptions, 'most of the masculinists exhibited these anti-Semitic and misogynist inclinations', understanding their heroic cultural model of hypermasculine sexuality in opposition to Jewish sexologist Magnus Hirschfeld's 'sexual steps in-between'.[16] Not all gay masculinists were Nazis: the movement unfolded across a strange spectrum from fascism to a kind of left-expressionist anarchy. Some masculinist figures, like the occultist painter and amateur philosopher Elisar von Kupffer, depicted their male-male utopia as populated by soft-bodied androgynes lounging in trees, a far cry from the kind of hard and impenetrable masculine body politic imagined both by fascism and by the nineteenth-century national liberalism from which it developed.

This worldview was linked to left-expressionism, an anti-liberal cultural movement arising from a young intelligentsia's disappointment and disillusionment with the corrupt elites of early twentieth-century Europe. Angered by those elites' betrayal of liberal ideas for economic advancement and their submission to feudal power, expressionists advocated for and created art that presented extreme and subjective emotional states, viewing themselves as part of a *geistig* (or spiritual) elite that would enact cultural transformation. In this Nietzschean vision, the will of the artist, unconstrained by old codes of law or morality, was a necessary disruptive force.

In any case, the majority of the Nazi Party never got on board with anything close to any of the various forms of masculinist political eros circulating in the Weimar Republic. Röhm, at least, may have seen himself as superior to his hetero clansmen; he was once, perhaps apocryphally, quoted as saying, 'When they stand in the fields and bend down at their work so that you can see their behinds, that's what he likes, especially when they've got big round ones. That's Hitler's sex life.'[17] As for Röhm's own sex life and his understanding of it, and his reconciliation of that sex life with his fascist politics, clues come in his attack, in his memoirs, on the 'literary people' who 'never served in the field' and could thus battle for 'false morality' far from the battlefield.[18] Here he was describing the bourgeois Nazi theorists who, then as now, dream of the battlefield from the safety of their stylish offices.

While Röhm does not specifically mention sexuality here, much of the rhetoric is, as his biographer Eleanor Hancock points out, familiar to anyone who knows much about the homosexual discourses of the time. 'An immoral man who achieves something is far more acceptable to me than a "morally upright" fellow who accomplishes nothing,' he wrote. 'Suicides of the best people speak only too eloquently here.' Note the reference to morality and suicide, a common fate for men who had sex with men and were then blackmailed – common enough that such a story was the plot of *Different from the Others*, the first film about homosexuality to depict it in a neutral-to-positive light, featuring a cameo appearance by Magnus Hirschfeld. Röhm's decrying of a 'social order which replaces healthy recognition of natural processes and understanding with hypocrisy, lies, deceit, prudery, and misplaced indignation' fits in nicely with the rhetoric of at least a certain kind of born-this-way tolerance politics regarding homosexuality. 'If the state thinks it can regulate human instincts or divert them along other channels by force of law', he went on, 'that seems to me so amateurish and inappropriate that it does not surprise me to find that the lawmakers of this state are also the defenders of the social order.'[19] This is strikingly similar to the rhetoric of the homosexual masculinists.

Correspondence between Röhm and the masculinist theorist Dr Karl-Günther Heimsoth confirms that Röhm intended these passages to support the reform of Paragraph 175 and the legalization of homosexuality.[20] 'I pride myself on being homosexual', Röhm wrote in these letters, 'but first really "discovered" this in 1924 ... I am absolutely not unhappy about my inclination, even though it has brought considerable difficulties from time to time.' Before then, he reported sex with women and men; since then, he wrote, 'all women' had become 'an abomination to me, particularly those who pursue me with their love ... On the other hand, I cling to my mother and sister with all my heart.'[21] Eleanor Hancock describes these letters as evidence that Röhm had transformed his same-sex activities into a political sexuality. To paraphrase Foucault, his acts had become an identity; he had become a member, in his own view, of a species. Perhaps even more surprisingly, he named himself in the letters as a member of an organization called the League for Human Rights, a mass-movement homosexual rights organization run by a certain Friedrich Radszuweit.

Radszuweit was born in Königsberg, Germany, in 1876. After moving to Berlin in 1901, marrying Johanna Schneider and opening a women's clothing shop (the more things change ...), he became active in a movement called the Friendship League.[22] While both Hirschfeld's Scientific-Humanitarian Committee and masculinist publications like *Der Eigene* had existed before the 1918–19 revolution and the First World War, these movements were tiny and vanguardist. The Friendship League and its successors, peaking at nearly fifty thousand members, were the first mass-movement organizations towards homosexual emancipation.

Seeing commercial opportunity, Radszuweit split the Friendship League in 1923 and named his section the League for Human Rights. Through this League, he produced magazines for gay men, lesbians, and trans women that claimed high circulation numbers and were sold at newsstands. Unlike the masculinist magazines, which typically featured mystic cultists writing about Spirits and Eros, or Hirschfeld's doctors droning on about scientific facts, his magazines contained frank, person-to-person discussion of sexuality and gender.[23]

One such magazine was called *Das dritte Geschlecht* (The Third Sex). Magnus Hirschfeld himself was, as the historian Susan Stryker argues, 'a pioneering advocate for transgender people' who worked with the police to develop certificates that trans people could use to avoid arrest for wearing clothing 'incorrect' for their sex. He also hired trans people to work at his Institute for Sexual Science, although often in menial roles.[24] But in Hirschfeld's scientific publications, trans people were spoken for and about: mostly described by cisgender male doctors, evaluated and photographed like scientific specimens. On at least some of the pages of *The Third Sex*, trans people regularly wrote about their own trans lives. Alongside scientific articles, short fiction and essays about daily life, by and for trans people, filled its pages. Various entities catering to trans people – parties and associations, and businesses including bars and restaurants – advertised in its pages. The magazine was available on newsstands and had a high subscriber base. Radszuweit's magazines focusing on lesbian-identifying women were similarly written at least in part by the people whom they were about.[25]

Despite this potentially revolutionary aspect of Radszuweit's organization and publishing empire, many of his magazines were still filled with reprinted and shared content, mostly written by men. In between advertisements for lesbian bars and books and personal ads for lonely ladies, one such article appeared in January of 1931 and inaugurated a much darker political stance on Radszuweit's part.

The reasons why Radszuweit took such a turn after 1929 are best explained by the historian Laurie Marhoefer in their argument about the 'Weimar Consensus' on the regulation of sexuality. Again, the thesis is this: rather than understanding the Nazi rise to power as a mass public backlash against a permissive society gone mad, there was instead a broad consensus about sexuality in Weimar political life shared by a coalition of sexologists and politicians from left to centre, one which believed that 'the state's relationship to sexuality ought to be scientific and rational. In a new and democratic era, religious morality ought not to have a major influence on law and public policy.'[26] Opposition to this consensus came from a coalition of conservative women's movements, some moderate politicians, and right-wing conservatives and nationalists. The result of the battle between these factions was, in the functioning democracy of pre-1929 Weimar, 'one of compromise ... resulting in sexual liberation for some at the expense of others'.[27]

In 1925, a coalition of conservative parties attempted to add harsh prison sentences for male sex workers, as well as increasing penalties against abortion. The 1928 elections, however, brought in a Social Democratic prime minister for the first time in many years. By the fall of 1929, just before the crash and the beginning of the Great Depression, a Reichstag committee voted to repeal Paragraph 175, as part of a broader project to reform the penal code.[28] The committee decided to replace it with a new provision, Paragraph 297, which stated that sex between two men was permitted, so long as both were over twenty-one, no one was pressured or influenced, and no money changed hands. Hirschfeld was ready to accept this compromise, which would have been among the most far-reaching reforms to date of sodomy laws in any country with such laws.

While he would have preferred a law setting homosexual sex on equal legal footing to heterosexual sex, he did often describe male sex workers as possessing 'innate degeneration' and described a 'close relationship of male prostitution to crime'; drawing parallels between 'degenerate' male and 'feebleminded' female sex workers, Hirschfeld understood male sex workers as heterosexuals, outside his coalition of the homosexually inclined, and as blackmailers.[29] This makes sense, given the connection in the mind of many middle- and upper-class homosexual men between sex work and blackmail, even if it is doubtful that it was true.

Given the illegality of same-sex contact, working-class men who engaged in sex work often blackmailed middle- and upper-class clients. For the latter group of men, the proposed legal change would have done a world of good: protecting them from prosecution for anything that wouldn't have made the sex workers equally liable. In addition, the proposed legal change would have drawn a line between more and less respectable iterations of homosexual sex.

This was bitterly opposed by two of Hirschfeld's colleagues in the Scientific-Humanitarian Committee, Kurt Hiller and Richard Linsert. Both committed Communists (Hirschfeld was not a member of a political party but generally aligned himself with the Social Democrats), they also both had intimate histories of entanglement with sex work. Hiller, who like Hirschfeld was Jewish, was a regular patron of sex workers, understanding his love for men as best expressed in sexless bonds of devotion and his animal instincts as best expressed with male sex workers.[30] In a 1928 speech to the World League for Sexual Reform, he denounced the Communist critic Henri Barbusse, who had inaugurated a trend in Communist thinking that regarded homosexuality as a kind of bourgeois decadence and implied links between homosexuality and Fascism.[31]

Linsert, on the other hand, had begun his activist career in the Munich branch of the Friendship League before Radszuweit had taken over; dedicated to mass action, he was an enthusiastic member of the German Communist Party. Since the mid-1920s he had been engaged in campaigns to prevent the further criminalization of sex work between men, going even further than contemporary socialist feminist critics to argue for the legalization of sex work even as he advocated for increased welfare programs and social supports to ensure that no one was forced into sex work.[32] Linsert and Hiller's pro–sex work stance was unusual in the movement and became the foundation of a fast, chaste friendship.

When the 1929 legal reform proposals rolled around, they were supported by a broad range of parties, including the Social Democrats and the chairman of the penal code reform committee, the elderly moderate jurist Wilhelm Kahl.[33] Kahl couched his support in starkly homophobic terms, arguing that homosexuality should remain both morally and legally condemned but that the legal reform enabled a focus on homosexual prostitution, which was its worst manifestation. Laurie Marhoefer understands this coalition as reflecting 'a growing consensus in public policy ... that certain types of immorality were tolerable so long as they remained under the public eye'.[34]

This reformist attitude understood public policy as something that addressed the health of society as a whole, and appeared in Hirschfeld's own work as well (as well as that of other Progressive Era reformers across Europe and the United States). It also often went hand in hand with eugenics. Approximately five weeks after the revised law passed committee, the Scientific-Humanitarian Committee voted to endorse a proposal by Linsert and Hiller regarding the change in the law, a proposal for the Committee to oppose the change. Referring to the proposal as 'one step forward and two steps backward', the Committee noted that the majority of arrests under Paragraph 175 were related to sex work. At this same meeting, Hirschfeld resigned as the Scientific-Humanitarian Committee's leader, although he remained the leader of the Institute for Sexual Science. It was widely understood (by Radszuweit, among others) that Hirschfeld had been forced to resign due to a conflict about expert testimony in front of the penal reform committee.[35] Hirschfeld had, at least, been friendlier to the proposed reform, seeing it as a potential step in the right direction.

All of this ended with the 1930 elections, when the previously marginal Nazis increased their seats from 12 to 107, coming in second behind the Social Democrats and rendering the country even more difficult to govern. In this climate of collapsing democracy, Radszuweit turned far-right. In an article, he wrote, 'We do not believe that even the National Socialists will proceed so rigorously against homosexuals as they announced before the September 1930 elections. Anyone who constantly reads the National Socialist newspapers, especially the "Völkischer Beobachter", will sometimes find some very reasonable articles on homosexuality. These newspapers generally do not condemn homosexuals as social pariahs, but on the whole only want to go after those Jews [*das Judentum*] (especially Dr Magnus Hirschfeld) who wish to, in an ugly way ... drag people's sex lives into the public.'[36] Willing to collaborate with and reproduce anti-Semitic attacks on Hirschfeld, Radszuweit had crossed a dangerous political Rubicon.

In the article, Radszuweit argued that even right-wing parties could be trusted to come around on the homosexual question:

> We do not want to argue here and to justify what morality and so-called custom are, we only want to make the point that everything can be changed over the course of time. Moral concepts are different today than they were a hundred years ago. This is even acknowledged by right-wing circles ... the vast majority of homosexual men of Germany do not intend to publicly display their relations, and would never have thought of creating a homosexual movement if the legislators were not so irrational ... The homosexual men of Germany are of the opinion that one should not talk about these things at all, and that no one is concerned with the way in which two men, by their free will, and by mutual consent, have sexual intercourse in their secret chamber.[37]

This is rhetoric that should be familiar to anyone who has engaged with the mainstream respectability politics of gay rights movements. While a more developed analysis of sexuality (like the one we are proposing in this book) reveals otherwise, this line has always been popular for several reasons. It binds white queers to whiteness and (especially) male queers to maleness. And it feels safe: even if proponents of this rhetoric would rather not be governed by people they fear hate them, they think that declaring themselves non-threatening to far-right forces (or even allying with them) will somehow make them safer. The reality, of course, is that this position fails. Most importantly, it fails in solidarity with the marginalized, and it even fails at keeping its proponents safe.

But Radszuweit continued: later that year, in an article in his *Freundschaftsblatt* newsletter so approving of the Nazis it inspired the mainstream centrist paper *Die Welt* to cover it under the headline 'The Third Gender Welcomes the Third Reich', Radszuweit claimed that the presence of homosexuals such as Röhm proved Nazi leaders were not personally homophobic, and that Hitler fit into a line of great manly leaders, many of whom were homosexual.[38] The article, structured as an open letter, praised 'Herr Hitler's' focus on 'political issues' rather than 'sexual questions', offering to 'inform' him in a 'non-partisan' way about 'the prevalence of homosexuality'.[39]

It presented a list of 'reasonable' requests, including equalizing the age of consent for homo- and heterosexual sex, allowing same-sex sexual contact in private between consenting adults, and strengthening laws against prostitution and intergenerational sex. In defences of the article published in later issues of *Die Freundin*, Radszuweit acknowledged that the 'Hitler camp' created anti-homosexual 'propaganda', but argued that the names of homosexuals in the Nazi Party should be kept secret and that their presence meant the party, if it assumed power, would not seriously prosecute what we might now call 'heteronormative homosexuals'.[40] Radszuweit, as the publisher of widely circulated newsletters of a genuinely mass-movement organization, had the opportunity to mobilize his not-insignificant forces against the rise of fascism, and refused. Instead, he chose to collaborate with anti-Semitic rhetoric, denounce the most outrageous fascist statements in mild terms, and hope for accommodations and concessions once the Nazis took power.

But how did Röhm's sexuality become the subject of public conversation? That it was being discussed through a very thin veil of secrecy in the pages of Radszuweit's mass-market gay magazines is evidence that it was very much a part of gossip circles. Radszuweit did not ever reveal in one of his publications that Röhm was a member of the Friendship League, but Röhm's indiscretions had begun to be a matter of more public record and interest. Eleanor Hancock suggests that Radszuweit's arguments may even have been informed by conversation with Röhm; while we have not seen historical evidence of correspondence between Röhm and Radszuweit, we could potentially read the confidence with which Radszuweit thought he could speak directly to Hitler as part of an effort to use Röhm as a potential connection between the 'third sex' and the 'Third Reich'. In any case, after Röhm's return from Bolivia and his resumption of Nazi activity in 1930 to lead the united paramilitary force known as the SA, he was seen spending time at the Eldorado nightclub, one of those glittery Schöneberg drag bars frequented by Christopher Isherwood and the other famed anglophone chroniclers of Weimar Berlin's queer undergrounds, and even felt so confident as to file a police report when a man he had slept with attempted blackmail.[41]

The Nazis were, at the time, a violently homophobic political party. Answering a questionnaire that the homosexual masculinist Adolf Brand put to various political parties in 1928, the Nazi response read, in part, 'Anyone who even thinks of homosexual love is our enemy. We reject anything which emasculates our people and makes it a plaything for our enemies, for we know that life is a fight and it's madness to think that men will ever embrace fraternally.'[42] While Röhm had claimed in his letters to Karl-Gunther Heimsoth that his Nazi colleagues knew of his sexuality and tolerated it, this seems to have been a more complicated story. Laurie Marhoefer calls this attitude 'self-delusion', pointing out that in Goebbels's diary of 1931, an entry read: 'Severe attack on Röhm because of 175 [a reference to the anti-sodomy statute] ... Is this supposed to be true?'[43] His position in the party relied on Hitler's support and trust – earned through effective management of the often unruly and conflicting SA paramilitaries – connections in the German army, and a loyalty confirmed in the 1923 putsch.

So certain leading Nazis – including Goebbels, in his diary – sharpened their knives when, in the spring of 1932, the *Munich Post*, a newspaper which backed the Social Democrats, began publishing splashy articles about Röhm's sexual proclivities. While the Social Democrats had been among the primary supporters of the reform of Paragraph 175, including a famous 1898 speech by August Bebel in the Bundestag, they were not above using homosexual scandals to target their political opponents. The theory was that exposing the Nazi's double standards – violently opposing reforms to the legal code supported by the Social Democrats while tolerating homosexuality in their highest echelons – would destroy the party's image among socially conservative working-class voters, to whom the SPD targeted newspapers and leaflets claiming that Hitler himself was involved in homosexual affairs, and asking, 'Are such people – they can hardly be called men – renewers of the Reich? Are they the revivers of our youth?'[44]

In May of 1932, Röhm's deputy and rumoured lover Edmund Heines attacked and beat the Social Democratic writer Helmuth Klotz in the Reichstag canteen, accusing him of falsifying excerpts from Röhm's letters that had been published in the *Munich Post* and in various SPD leaflets; after the police broke up the fight they were surrounded by a crowd of Nazi deputies who beat Klotz nearly to death.[45] The ongoing session of Parliament was suspended. Clearly, senior Nazis were extremely worried about the rumours and their potential effect on upcoming elections. Hitler himself ignored the rumours. In March of 1932, before the Reichstag beatings but just as the scandal was breaking, Hitler had won 30 percent of the vote in the first round of the presidential election. In July's parliamentary elections, after months of the scandal and propagandizing about it, the Nazis received just over 37 percent of the vote. Unlike previous gay sex scandals before the First World War, which had galvanized public opinion against the monarchy even as they both reified phobic attitudes about homosexuality *and* gave the evolving homosexual emancipation movement more public visibility, this scandal was unsuccessful.

In April of 1932, Friedrich Radszuweit died of tuberculosis. In the issue of *Blätter für Menschenrecht* that memorialized his death, his lover Martin, whom he adopted as his son so that he could inherit the organization and firm, remembered a survey Friedrich had conducted 'in times of political peace'. He had sent 50,000 questionnaires about politics to his members, of which just over 37,000 were returned. The results showed that of the approximately 31,000 members who stated their affiliation with a political party, just over half belonged to parties of the (at least nominally) Marxist left, with the rest approximately evenly divided between the centre and the right. Nevertheless, Radszuweit used this survey to prove a different point: that homosexuality was essentially apolitical, the movement 'based solely on the grounds of law and human understanding'.[46]

Friedrich had met Martin when he was a member of the Hitler Youth, battling Communists on the street. Perhaps Martin had been drawn into the Youth by the homoerotic masculine love described by the anonymous stormtrooper in his article in the Scientific-Humanitarian Committee's newsletter.

In the November 1932 elections, the Nazis lost seats, this time receiving 33 percent of the vote. Nonetheless, on 19 November, nineteen leaders of industry and banking sent a letter to President Hindenburg urging him to name Hitler as chancellor. Conservatives thought Hitler and the Nazis could be tamed, centrists thought the German state too strong to be overwhelmed by the Nazis, whom they considered thuggish amateurs, albeit thuggish amateurs potentially useful when it came to putting down the Communist threat.

After the Reichstag Fire on 27 February 1933, elections took place that were neither free nor fair. Immediately afterwards, centrist and conservative parliamentarians signed the Enabling Act, making Hitler essentially a dictator by the end of March 1933. On 6 May 1933, members of the SA and the Hitler Youth stormed the library and archives of Hirschfeld's Institute, brought the books and documents to a public square next to the State Opera in the centre of Berlin, and burned them.

It was in the context of having lost control of his own political organization, which in part owed to the radicals' refusal to accept the 'Weimar compromise', as well as the sudden explosion in popularity of the National Socialists after the 1929 economic crash, that Hirschfeld decided to embark on his lecture tour of the United States. He began in New York, lecturing at the Labor Temple, having tea with Langston Hughes and Carl Van Vechten, and meeting with Emma Goldman and Margaret Sanger.[47] He then travelled west, meeting with doctors and researchers who had emigrated to the United States throughout the 1920s, including Harry Benjamin, a researcher and pioneering doctor who, like Hirschfeld, promoted a 'scientific' understanding of trans people and bodies and became by the 1950s the United States' main medical authority on transsexuality.[48] Benjamin had helped organize Hirschfeld's US leg, and ended up collaborating with transgender people to create some of the first standards of medical care for trans people in the United States, methods influenced by Hirschfeld's approach in 1930s Berlin but which had evolved from Hirschfeld's concept of 'sexual steps in between' towards a concept of 'gender dysphoria' that required medical treatment. Some of Benjamin's patients and collaborators considered this model and its attendant standards of care to be sympathetic and helpful in the context of phobic and discriminatory medical systems. They, as well as Hirschfeld's model and standards of care, have also come under sustained criticism from transgender critics as racist, pathologizing, medicalizing, discriminatory, and limited in their scope.[49]

By March of 1931 Hirschfeld had reached San Francisco, where he enthusiastically met with the eugenicist Paul Popenoe. Popenoe was known as the founder of marriage counselling in the United States, a topic that Hirschfeld made the subject of many of his lectures; but he was also an advocate for the compulsory sterilization of mentally ill and disabled people, the editor of a journal focusing on eugenics and social hygiene, an advocate for the segregation of 'waste humanity' to concentration camps, and a firm believer in the racial inferiority of Black people. Hirschfeld himself had sometimes advocated for the sterilization and castration of homo- and transsexual people and enthusiastically corresponded with the Austrian doctor Eugen Steinach, who believed that implanting 'heterosexual' testicles could 'cure' male homosexuality.

After this meeting and these lectures, Hirschfeld decided, based both on his own desire to travel and on the political climate in Germany, to delay his return to Europe by travelling through Asia. He had long been fascinated by the sexual and gender practices of non-Western cultures, as well as being an enthusiastic proponent of international cooperation and exchange between researchers. Ethnological study had always been important to his research: sexual ethnology represented one of the main research departments at his Institute for Sexual Science.[50]

Like many other sexologists who were interested in non-white others, Hirschfeld's fascination was doubled. Sometimes he wrote of the sex-gender systems of other places and cultures as a breath of fresh air, a radically different model of sexual and cultural life that could demonstrate the fragility and constructed nature of European understandings of sexual and cultural life. At other times, he participated in modern ethnographic discourse's construction of the 'primitive' other as a kind of people beyond time, whose practices provided a view into Europeans' own past.[51]

Upon his arrival in Shanghai, the sixty-three-year-old Hirschfeld found not only 'exotic' cultures to marvel at but also picked up a new student and lover, Li Shiu Tong. While Hirschfeld only stayed in Shanghai for a few days, when he left, Tong went with him, and remained by his side for the rest of his life. Together they travelled through Indonesia, where Hirschfeld was fascinated by phallic cults and ancient temples; they met with Jawaharlal Nehru in India and discussed decolonization. While Hirschfeld understood himself to be anti-racist (he would write a book about racism after the Nazis assumed power in Germany), his earlier silences on Germany's colonial crimes and the racial assumptions baked into his work are deeply troubling. Heike Bauer analyses his late-life work on race as a belated response to his experiences with German colonialism: while Hirschfeld did not directly participate in colonial projects, she notes, his archives, funding, the conditions in which he practised, the responses to and uses of his work, and the ideas with which he was working were all profoundly shaped by the context of German colonialism.[52]

Back in Germany in late 1932, Hitler was busy consolidating power. There was significant disagreement within the Nazi movement about the future of National Socialist politics after conservatives had enabled their rise to power. Some – like Röhm and Goebbels – advocated for a 'second revolution' that would overturn the right-wing institutions like the army, the aristocracy, and finance that had enabled the Nazi rise to power and the destruction of labour and the Left.[53] Others in the movement, Hitler included, understood the 'socialism' part of national socialism as having been a ruse: a marketing ploy to get the working class on board with what they understood to be a fundamentally reactionary political program.

Röhm described the 2 million stormtroopers (this was twenty times the number of troops in the official army) as 'the incorruptible guarantors of the fulfillment of the German revolution', and conservative Nazis as 'Philistines' who might themselves need to be opposed.[54] Hitler, meanwhile, relied on economic advice from baronial industrialists like Gustav Krupp, Fritz Thyssen, and Kurt Schmitt, who was the director of Allianz, a major insurance firm.[55]

If Hitler understood the revolution as having been only about political power rather than economic transformation, and saw the stormtrooper armies as a brute force for achieving that mission, Röhm instead understood those armies, in ways that were often startlingly coherent with masculinist homosexual ideology, as a crucible of revolution, a 'people's army' that could overcome the old hierarchies and enact a kind of permanent fascist revolution.[56] While Hitler publicly made Röhm a member of the Cabinet as 1933 drew to a close, and praised him warmly in letters that were published in Nazi newspapers, behind the scenes he was reassuring German army leaders that their place was safe in the nation's rigid hierarchies.

When Röhm proposed to the Cabinet in February of 1934 that the SA be transformed into the core of a newly unified defence branch under his control, the officers – and the ailing Hindenburg – revolted. Tales of homosexuality began once again to swirl around Berlin. General Walter von Brauchitsch later testified that 'German rearmament was too serious and difficult a business to permit the participation of speculators, drunkards, and homosexuals'.[57] Hitler agreed in private meetings with military higher-ups to suppress Röhm, the permanent revolution, and the stormtroopers in exchange for being made head of state when Hindenburg died.

That June, Hitler made one more attempt to talk his old friend Röhm down from his position. As matters escalated and instability threatened to break out, Hitler came close to being removed from power by Hindenburg and the army. This was the final straw, and Hitler, on 30 June, declaring that there had been a seemingly fictitious plot against him and the state, declared war on his own ranks. The resulting purge, known as the Night of the Long Knives, lasted three days, during which the more loyal SS and Gestapo forces executed Röhm, other SA leaders, the more revolutionary Nazi Gregor Strasser, and several prominent conservatives. Röhm was dragged from his bed and taken to Stadelheim Prison. At one point, two days into the purge, he was handed a pistol and offered the chance to kill himself. 'If I am to be killed', he reportedly said, 'let Adolf do it himself.'[58] Two SA officers then stepped into his cell and fired at Röhm point-blank.

Betrayed by his former friend, Röhm's life came to a bloody end. Röhm, Heines, and other leading SA members were publicly accused of moral degeneracy, homosexuality, and treasonous alliance with foreign powers. Suitably impressed, the army and other conservative forces relaxed their objections to the Nazi takeover. When Hindenburg died in August, Hitler was named president as well as Chancellor, and the Nazi takeover was complete.

Martin Radszuweit, Hitler Youth brawler and masculinist homosexual, would be betrayed by the elements of National Socialism with which he more likely identified himself. Historians differ as to whether he died in 1933 or survived into the 1980s. A document from June of 1933, the final document in the file of the League for Human Rights at Berlin's Schwules Museum, reads: 'The liquidation has ended. Heil Hitler!'[59]

The League's cautious refusal to take a stand on the crucial issues of its day, its kind words about Hitler, its collaboration with poisonous anti-Semitism, bought it exactly no protection when the Nazi regime set its murderous sights on LGBT people and institutions. Adolf Brand, leading intellectual light of the masculinist movement, managed to survive the Nazi rise to power. The war, however, he could not survive: he died in an Allied raid in April of 1945, less than a month before it came to an end. If some gay Nazis had tried to reconcile far-right politics and homosexuality, the Nazi movement in power proved to be the most murderously anti-queer state regime in recorded human history.

Hirschfeld, at the end of his world tour, settled in the south of France and sent for Karl Giese, his long-time secretary and archivist, who joined Hirschfeld and Li in a three-way relationship. When Hirschfeld died of a stroke in 1935, Giese and Li Shiu Tong were his heirs. Giese committed suicide before that decade was out, and Li returned to China during the war and dropped off the face of the Earth. Archivists and activists from the post-1968 West German gay liberation movement, led by Hirschfeld scholar and biographer Ralf Dose, began searching for more information about Hirschfeld and his institute and library. They were told that everything was destroyed and burned – but kept searching.

In 1993, Adam Smith, who worked in the garbage room of his building in Vancouver, found there a few old leather suitcases: inside, a death mask from someone he'd never heard of named Magnus Hirschfeld, and some papers. He put the suitcases in his attic. Years later, Dose found a Usenet post by Smith and contacted him, and the mask and documents rejoined the historical record. Li had carried the suitcases with him back to Hong Kong and finally to Canada when his family moved there later in the twentieth century.[60]

So who are the Bad Gays of Weimar Berlin? Were they the ambisexual performance freaks whose audacious and aggressive sexuality and playful confusion of gender norms triggered an entire society into fascism, as though the Nazis were an allergic reaction? Or were they people like Ernst Röhm, whose worship of masculine vitality might remind you of some Grindr profiles you've seen – maybe your own – and who followed that impulse towards lifting fascists to power? Were they people like Friedrich Radszuweit, cautious and apolitical men who decided to stand back and stand by while fascism gained steam? Were they people like Hirschfeld, complicated and ambivalent men with deep reservoirs of idealism, knowledge, and compassion who were limited by their blind spots, shaped by and shaping racist and eugenic discourses, and often willing to accept rights for some at the expense of others?

'Hirschfeld is coming, Hirschfeld is coming,' ran one wry cabaret song gently mocking the good doctor's writings on sexuality. 'Everyone runs away! He can find something hidden in everything.'[61] Weimer Berlin is like that for queers: we can find something to celebrate and ally with, but maybe it's better, in the longer term, to look for the things that are hidden, that cause discomfort and pain, the ghosts of a past that refuses to be past.

9

Margaret Mead

In 1928, a book dedicated 'to the girls of T'au', a small island in the Manu'a Group of the Samoas, was published by William Morrow and Company in New York and became a surprise best-seller across the United States. Reviewed respectfully by many academic peers in fields as diverse as anthropology, psychology, and sociology, it was also greeted by sensational headlines in the popular press, egged on by its canny author. 'Samoa Is the Place for Women', one headline read; another called it 'Where Neuroses Cease'.[1]

If its success was rare for a book of academic science, so too was its evocative writing, three hundred–odd small and well-spaced pages of vivid descriptions of T'au, of 'soft, barbaric singing' and 'lovers slipping home from trysts beneath the palm trees or in the shadow of beached canoes', of 'fishing by torch-light' with 'the curving reef [gleaming] with wavering lights' and 'the mellow thunder of the reef and the whisper of lovers'.[2] Although the whole book is written in this lively and accessi-ble prose, its main subject is education: not formal systems of schooling, but instead 'the process by which the baby, arrived cultureless upon the human scene, becomes a full-fledged adult member of his or her society'.[3]

One might imagine beginning such a book by reflecting on the differences between labour and social reproduction in these two worlds: who cooks, who hunts, and the like. This text begins instead with a broad denunciation of the 'unsettled, disturbed status of youth' in the United States, a state of affairs that the text blames on the various neuroses of modern life. In order to understand this 'problem of youth', the author wrote, it was necessary to find a subject whose strangeness made her habits and mores more visible, who spoke 'a language the very sounds of which were strange, a language in which nouns became verbs and verbs nouns in the most sleight-of-hand fashion', who 'slept upon the floor', whose 'house was a mere circle of pillars, roofed by a cone of thatch', and who could be studied by a dedicated ethnographer willing to spend several months 'speaking their language, eating their food, sitting barefoot and crosslegged', doing her best 'to minimize the differences between us and learn to know and understand'.[4]

This author was not the first or the last Western anthropologist to reflect on the cultures and sexualities of exotic women without spending much time contemplating the political and economic forces shaping the lives of, and separating her from, her subjects.[5] Instead of this detailed reflection on the causes and expressions of difference, this book's focus on the fact of difference itself had lofty aims and high hopes: to learn from 'the diverse and gracious patterns' of supposedly primitive people to understand that people's 'one set of human gifts, one set of human values ... an art, a social organization, a religion, which is their unique contribution to the history of the human spirit'.[6]

Samoa's cultural contribution to the human spirit included, according to this text, a great deal of frankness about sex and sexuality. Its author did not mention her own sex or sexual education. 'The seventeen-year-old girl' in Samoa, she wrote, 'does not wish to marry ... It is better to live as a girl with no responsibility, and a rich variety of experience'.[7] Promiscuity and premarital sex, she wrote, were rampant: and this led to fewer sexual neuroses, fewer conflicts, and more openness about natural processes like menstruation and childbirth.

Conservatives were horrified at the book's un-moralistic, breezy endorsement of what it described as a kind of utopia of casual premarital sex. How could an anthropological tome on a tiny and faraway land become such a cultural sensation? Its subtitle holds the clue: 'A Psychological Study of Primitive Youth for Western Civilisation' clearly states the transaction being performed here. While the book was dedicated to the girls of T'au, these girls, and their cultural habits related to their coming of age as women, were its subjects, and not the people to whom it was addressed. The girls of T'au were a measuring stick against which Western Civilization could come to know itself, a rosy savage alternative to the conflicted and impossible Modern.

This anthropological and ethnographic balancing act was, as we have already seen in the Weimar sexologist Magnus Hirschfeld's world journeys and studies of ethnographic sexology, and Roger Casement's anti-colonial cruising, central to the formation of modern homosexual identities in the West. Domestic rebels against bourgeois European sex-gender systems looked to colonial subjects, whose sex-gender systems were being burlesqued and misrepresented by Western ethnographers as part of the project of colonization, for examples of how same-sex desire and eroticism had been integrated into community life.

Nineteenth-century anthropologies and ethnographies typically were explicitly racist and derogatory, producing categories of 'savages' to justify and extend colonial rule. The homosexualities inspired by such ethnographies tended to see 'savages' as being stuck in the past, and therefore understood 'savage' homosexuality as a present-day echo of the past, a kind of living version of Europe's own Greek ancestors. This slim book about Samoa belonged to a different school: one which thought it could apprehend differences between and patterns of culture essentially on their own terms.

These anthropologists operated in a world system dominated by white colonial powers, in which their position at the core allowed them to travel the world searching for subjects they could render legible to domestic audiences. While reaping the spoils of colonization they also found themselves transformed by the people they interacted with. Some worked in state institutions developing neocolonial policy, others advocated for transformative social change. Some of them understood the Western 'us' and the Other as coexisting in time, some reproduced a categorical difference between the 'us' and the Other, and some did both at the same time.

Many of these thinkers were pioneering women, queers, Jews, and people of colour in the academy, yet as a group they regularly reproduced and enacted racist, misogynistic, and homophobic violence. Their ideas and influence shaped virtually every progressive twentieth-century social movement in the Global North, and were, not least because several of them were queer, enormously influential in the development of gay liberation movements. Emerging as a group of radical and often socialist critics of mainstream American and European culture and then disciplined by the mid-century Red and Lavender scares purging communists and queers, they became some of the most influential intellectuals of the post–World War II liberal-internationalist national security state.

Perhaps no single person better exemplifies these contradictions than Margaret Mead, the author of that book dedicated to the girls of T'au, *Coming of Age in Samoa*: a queer woman who hid her queerness from a phobic public. She pursued enthusiastic and passionate relationships with both men and women, was a pioneering woman in academia, and was a scholar who in that career-launching text combated scientistic racism by praising Samoan sexual and social mores as superior to American ones. Yet she also wrote, in the book's introduction, that she had chosen to travel to Samoa because 'in complicated civilizations like those of Europe ... years of study are necessary before the student can begin to understand the forces at work within them ... A primitive people without a written language present a much less elaborate problem, and a trained student can master the fundamental structure of a primitive society in a few months.'[8]

Born in 1901 and dying in 1978, Mead's life spanned the emergence of the United States as a dominant imperial force in world politics.[9] Shaped by her own sense of difference and outsider status as a queer woman, Mead focused her scientific research and advocacy on the description of cultural difference and the use of cultural relativism to combat the rigid hierarchies of scientific racism, and to question the sex-gender system that othered her in her home culture. Blind to the meaning of the enormous economic and racial privilege of her upbringing, she helped to construct post-war American racial liberalism: a political world-view that understands anti-racism in terms of 'color-blindness' rather than resistance to structural racial capitalism, is deeply invested in the exceptionalism of the United States, and collabo-rated with the US national security state's destructions of and incursions into the self-determination and liberation struggles of colonized peoples.[10] This racial liberalism was also, as Lee Baker and others have argued, a key part of 'color-blind' discourses in the United States that minimize racial inequality and disconnect understandings of capitalism from understandings of the origins of race and racism.

In a photograph taken during her Samoan fieldwork in the early 1920s but not published until her career-retrospective memoirs were released in the 1970s, Mead stands in Samoan dress facing a camera, holding hands with a Samoan woman named Fa'amotu. Fa'amotu was older than Mead's target age of study, and of an elite social class that is not the principal subject of Mead's book (indeed, Mead seems uninterested in class in both her descriptions of Samoa and of America). As Mead's 'sister, companion, and friend', Fa'amotu can be, as Joyce Hammond and others have argued, considered a co-creator of Mead's images and ideas. In this photograph, the two of them stare into one another's eyes and appear to flash one another a conspiratorial grin. To the contemporary viewer the queer implications are startling and immediate. Perhaps not entirely coincidentally, the photographs of Fa'amotu that Mead had published in Coming of Age in Samoa, as well as in newspaper articles placed to promote the book, were far less intimate in their posing and framing.[11]

In one image, and in the history of its circulation and recep-tion, we see Mead's queerness and its relationship to her research interests, her dressing herself in the clothing and cultures of others, her posing those cultures as though they loved and wel-comed her, her desire to manage the public's understanding of her by showing and revealing herself differently over time, her willingness to play fast and loose with scientific description, and her genuine tenderness for some of the people she interacted with and wrote about. This photograph is a metonym for Mead's complex life and legacy as the 'matriarch of liberal consciousness' in 1950s and 1960s America.[12]

When Mead was born on December 16, 1901, she had, astonishingly for the time, both a mother and a grandmother who had been college-educated.[13] Her mother, Emily Fogg Mead, had attended Wellesley College for Women and the University of Chicago and did graduate work at Bryn Mawr College; her father Edward had studied economics at Chicago before becoming a professor of finance at the Wharton Business School at the University of Pennsylvania. From birth, in other words, she was steeped in an unusual degree of wealth, an unusual degree of intellectualism, and an unusual degree of educated women. In a late-in-life published dialogue with James Baldwin bearing the almost painfully 1970s title *A Rap on Race*, Mead insisted that she had been raised without any racial prejudice whatsoever: 'I have never been in the position of believing that I had any right because I was white ... I have neither been scarred nor specially benefited by being white.'[14]

She had learned about race as a child, she recalled. 'We had two old Negro men in the neighborhood' who had been slaves, one of whom had 'a very fat, very black wife' who had been raped by a white man, as Mead recalled her mother telling her as a child, careful to recall that her mother 'insisted on calling [the Black neighbour] *Mrs*'.[15] Mead used this story to claim that her experience had been 'a straight reversal' of ordinary American experience. In fact, claiming this kind of born immunity from racism, as though her mother calling the descendants of slaves 'Mrs.' and not immediately assuming that all Black men were out to assault white women erased the difference between herself, descended directly from the Mayflower, and her neighbours, who were one generation away from chattel slavery.[16]

Mead's father studied and promoted corporate growth and consolidation.[17] When Margaret was born, her mother had just published an article on the role of advertising in business which argued that advertising enlightened and educated the masses.[18] Emily Mead also wrote a dissertation on Italian immigrants in New Jersey when Margaret was a small girl, a decision Margaret praised throughout her life as having shown her that women could work and raise a family, but also a decision – which Margaret did not spend much time reflecting on – that was dependent on the Meads having the means to employ cooks, nurses, and other domestic servants.[19]

The family was a progressive one, and so Margaret was educated under the new 'scientific' child-rearing of L. E. Holt, who, as Nancy Lutkehaus writes in her biography of Mead, urged restraint in emotion to protect small children from being stunted or smothered 'by an overabundance of motherly love'.[20] Mead remembered her childhood differently in different memoirs and notes: sometimes recalling a positive childhood that had shaped her into a crack fieldworker and sensitive and introspective person, at other times remembering her father as a bully and unpredictable disciplinarian who cheated on her somewhat frigid mother.[21]

At the age of eleven, Mead was enrolled at the Buckingham Friends School, an independent Quaker school founded in 1794. At this time, deep and even romantic friendships were often encouraged between girls. Such friendships, writes the historian Lois Banner, 'were viewed as an innocent outgrowth of the emotionality of adolescence ... Girls were expected to have a "best" friend or a "bosom" friend; such relationships were often called "smashes" or "crushes"'.[22] It was not generally assumed that such bonding could ever lead to genital contact or interfere with apparently normal heterosexual development.

As a girl, Mead preferred stereotypically feminine clothing, and in her memoir would write of her horror at 'the thought of having one of those vague masculinizing diseases'.[23] At the same time, she had on the wall of her childhood bedroom a reproduction of the painting *Aurora* by Guido Reni, in which a confident goddess urges her blushing male lover forward in a chariot.[24] (Reni's portrait of St Sebastian would be crucial in the life of the young Yukio Mishima, discussed later in this book.) From a young age, she viewed herself as one of two twins, one of whom had disappeared, and that she was seeking this lost twin of the mind and soul in many of her interpersonal relationships.[25]

As the third generation in her family of college-educated women, Mead began her studies at DePauw University in Indiana in 1919 before transferring to Barnard College to complete the remainder of her degree. A childhood interest in writing fiction and poetry drew her towards studying English, but she double-majored in psychology as well, driven to achieving a self-made success apart from a future identity as a wife or a mother.

At college, as the 1920s dawned, Mead bobbed her hair and joined a circle of friends called the Ash Can Cats who idolized Edna St Vincent Millay – especially her famous poem about a candle that burns at both ends.[26] Sexual experimentation was rife among this group. Mead was, at this time, already engaged to Luther Cressman, whom she would marry after her graduation in 1923, but Mead was a supporter of the new free love that sexologists were promoting.

It was in her senior year at Barnard that she made the fateful decision to take a class in anthropology. While women were still not being admitted to Ivy League universities, Barnard College was then, as it is now, affiliated with Columbia University. The Barnard anthropology class was taught by an anthropologist at Columbia named Franz Boas, who was in the middle of instigating a revolution in anthropological and ethnographic thought.

Boas was born in Prussia in 1858 to a secular Jewish family that was friendly with Karl Marx and steeped in mid-nineteenth-century liberalism. After studying geography and philosophy, Boas began travelling to remote corners of Canada to study Inuit adaptations to their harsh physical environment. At that time, German anthropology was dominated by physical anthropologists, who understood differences between peoples as being related to a rigid evolutionary hierarchy of races in which white Europeans were the most developed. Boas, instead influenced by an older strain of German ethnology that approached difference outside of questions of evolution and determinism, began to develop an interest in the cultural patterns of the supposedly 'savage' people he was studying. Alienated by increasing anti-Semitism in Germany, Boas travelled to the United States and began teaching at Clark University and taking annual expeditions to the Pacific Northwest, where he studied the Kwakwaka'wakw, a First Nation of present-day British Columbia.

Boas, write the historians Ned Blackhawk and Isaiah Wilner, 'drew upon what he ... learned among Native peoples to present an alternative approach to modernity'.[27] In a flurry of books published just after the turn of the twentieth century, when Boas had moved to New York and begun teaching at Columbia University, he began to deconstruct and disprove dominant ideologies of scientific racism and the inherent superiority of white and Western peoples. This approach, known as cultural relativism, was founded on fundamentally unequal and racist systems of knowledge production – Boas, the white expert, constructing Indigenous subjects and extracting knowledge from and about them. But it also provided, as Blackhawk and Wilner have argued, opportunities for those Indigenous people to participate actively in dialogues with anthropologists. The ideas that Boas developed – which helped found the discipline of cultural studies and deeply influenced virtually every strain of twentieth-century progressive thought – were accompanied by a radical shift in his academic practice. Boas's graduate students included women and men and Native and Black scholars – scholars who were also subject to racist and misogynistic treatment from both within and outside his circle – at a time when this was quite rare.

One of these pioneering women was Mead's teaching assistant when she took her fateful first class with Boas: Ruth Benedict. Benedict had had a similar progressive and proto-feminist upbringing to Mead, and was at this time already finishing her PhD. While Mead at first resisted Benedict and the discipline of anthropology itself, she became more and more fascinated by the older woman's strange anti-style and her confident intelligence. The two became closer and closer, and as Margaret's undergraduate years came to a close in March of 1923, Benedict encouraged her to enter the PhD program at Columbia.

Although Benedict was married with a home in the suburbs at that time, she only spent weekends with her husband, and wrote in her diary that she desired women 'to lie once with beauty, breast to breast'.[28] Margaret, too, was recently married, and the two of them entered into a relationship with one another that their respective marriages only made seem more secure and more possible.[29] The sexual cross-pollination that had characterized the Ash Can Cats also characterized the anthropology department at Columbia: like the Bloomsbury Group or the Lebensreformers in 1920s Germany, this was a group of liberated, privileged, and well-educated bohemians for whom traditional notions of morality and propriety were passé.

Both Mead and Benedict had, during their affair with one another, affairs with Edward Sapir, who, like Benedict, was seventeen years Mead's senior. Sapir was one of Boas's first graduate students, who extended Boas's cultural approach into the study of linguistics and the relationship between languages and cultures. While Sapir and the other men who surrounded Boas considered themselves welcoming of their women colleagues, Mead later recalled that the welcome was equivocal and tainted with misogyny.[30]

Boas structured the department in the German style, with himself as the only full professor and all others working on contracts underneath him. One of these new contract professors was Benedict, who had finished her PhD and who became, Mead would remember, Boas's 'Left Hand', his 'second self'.[31] While this involved a significant amount of administrative and other gendered labour, it also involved mentoring undergraduate and graduate students, including the Black novelist and anthropologist Zora Neale Hurston. Hurston spent six years between Barnard and Columbia studying with Boas and Benedict in various capacities. That a queer Black woman studying Black folklore and religious practices found space and encouragement in the profoundly white-supremacist 1920s at a white-supremacist institution like Columbia University demonstrates how remarkable Boas's circle was. That she experienced significant racism and misogyny while there, including from her white female colleagues and advisers, demonstrates the limits of the politics and practice of this circle.

Mead enjoyed her graduate studies rather more than her new marriage. She had married Luther Cressman in 1923 but insisted on sleeping in separate bedrooms, even during their honeymoon. Luther was studying for a PhD in sociology, and the marriage settled down but remained uninspiring. Both Margaret and Luther had regular affairs with other women, and Mead and Benedict's relationship in particular began to deepen. Benedict, in their biographer Lois Banner's words, characterized Mead as 'her daughter and protégée in anthropology, her partner, lover, and best friend ... her blithe spirit, who could lift her moods'.[32] 'When I'm happy', Benedict wrote, 'your love makes me sing tera-lira, and when I'm blue it holds a livable world before my eyes.'[33]

As Mead approached the time when she would travel some-where to do the ethnographic fieldwork for her thesis, she resisted the idea of studying Native Americans, as most of Boas's women graduate students had done, influenced both by the relative ease of travel and by Boas's own work among North American Indig-enous societies. Amelia Earhart was exploring the world; Mead, too, wanted to go farther than Arizona or New Mexico. Boas recommended Samoa, as he was seeking a student or acolyte to disprove a competing anthropologist's claim that a period of adolescent angst was a universal and biologically rooted part of human lives.[34] Torn between her affairs with Sapir and Benedict, not to mention her husband, Mead welcomed the opportunity to travel alone – she specifically insisted that Luther not accompany her on her trip. Before departing, she took long duo trips with both her husband and with Benedict, who encouraged her to abandon her affair with the possessive and jealous Sapir.

Clark Wissler, a Boasian who ran the anthropology depart-ment at the Museum of Natural History in New York City, joined Boas in urging her to study sexuality and especially the sexuality of young women in Samoa. This was, after all, only thirty-odd years after Gauguin had travelled to Tahiti and helped construct the South Seas as a primitive, erotic, louche Paradise in the eyes of Western art-viewers and readers. In the intervening years, the United States had begun staking out ever-greater land claims in the Pacific. White businessmen with United States backing overthrew the Hawaiian constitutional monarchy in 1893, and by 1898 the territory had been colonized by the US. The Spanish-American War led to the cessation of Guam and the Philippines (along with Puerto Rico in the Caribbean Sea) to the United States; when an independent and democratic republic claimed power in the Philippines, the United States invaded to quash the insurrection in a war that led to over two hundred thousand Filipino civilian casualties. The island chain of Samoa had been colonized by the United States and Germany, with New Zealand taking over Germany's holdings after the First World War; it was used primarily as a naval base for the expanding global American armed forces. Mead arrived, therefore, not on a dreamy desert island cut off from the rest of the world, but at a node of US imperial power already visited regularly by soldiers and missionaries.

If the prominence of the primitive idyll as radical utopia had much to do with Boas and his circle's work, then Mead's trip to Samoa was the perfect Boasian project: a trip to the idyll to dissolve American sex norms against the free love of supposed savages. In other words, the success of Mead's book on Samoa was not an accident: Mead and her mentors carefully selected the location in order to maximize the possible domestic cultural and political impact of her research.

Upon arriving in Samoa, first spending several weeks in a language and customs crash course, and then transferring to the small village on T'au, Mead considered having an affair with a young Samoan in order to better understand youth sexuality. Her notes and letters reveal that she spent at least one night with a young man from the village who was, as Lois Banner writes, 'the most experienced man in matters of the heart', who 'had told her about the amours of his friends with complete candor'.[35]

In any case, Mead based the majority of her fieldwork on conversations with young Samoan women, with whom, as a woman, she was able to spend what was then an unprecedented amount of time in intense and intimate fieldwork. Midway through her stay she wrote to Boas complaining that she was not getting any good or interesting material, but by the end she had gathered a great deal of data, including charts discussing menstruation and sexual experiences, both homo- and heterosexual.

While in Samoa she had continued to keep up an intense exchange of letters with Benedict. Complaining to her about Sapir and her husband, Mead wrote that she felt 'ecstasy' when thinking of Ruth, fantasized about kissing her, and wrote, 'Knowing you ... has been the same blessed peace-giving effect as knowing there is a god'.[36] In return, Benedict described her feelings for Margaret, advised her to give up Sapir, and described her own free love practice, which involved romantic encounters with several other women, including PhD students she met at conferences.

Over time, however, as Margaret's confidence in the work she was doing in Samoa grew, she seemed to need Benedict and her support less and less, and to become somewhat more conflicted about homosexual relationships in general. It was on the Australia-to-Europe leg of the boat back from Samoa that she met, and fell head over heels for, the strapping young scholar Reo Fortune, who was travelling from his native New Zealand to London to study. Upon her return to New York, Mead set herself to divorcing her husband and pursuing Fortune.

Lois Banner understands Mead's observations about Samoan sexuality in *Coming of Age in Samoa* – especially her observations about homosexual behaviour between young Samoan girls, which she describes as an accepted peripheral practice for heterosexual unions – as being influenced both by her desire to promote free love and her desire to convince Fortune to marry her despite her ongoing relationship with Benedict. 'The whole business', she later wrote about in a dream journal she had been keeping, 'is an expression of a suppressed fear that after all I am primarily a homosexual person.' In the diary, Banner writes, 'she crossed out homosexual and wrote heterosexual above it': further evidence for her confusion.[37]

The book, when published, made Mead a star. This, as historians such as Micaela di Leonardo have written, was the result of a variety of important trends in 1920s American mass culture, all of which the book seemed to embody: panic about youth and the creation of the category of the adolescent as a figure of the popular imagination, an increase in discussions of psychology, shifting roles for women, and the use of the primitive as a utopic figure.[38] Mead's America was in some ways as simplistic as her Samoa: she assumed that upper-class American mores could stand in for all people's way of life. Decolonial political movements and the schools of anthropology that they influenced would later come to criticize Mead and the Boasians for their assumptions that so-called simple cultures like those in Samoa could be best apprehended by a foreign white graduate student with only several months of training. Postcolonial anthropology also emphasizes that it, too, is specific to its time and place: any given anthropology is nothing more or less than one particular group of people's way of understanding another part of the world at a given time.

After her study of teen girls in Samoa was greeted warmly (with the notable exception of her former lover Edward Sapir, who came to detest both the book and Mead and denounce both in profoundly misogynistic terms), Mead next set herself to studying the coming of age of Indigenous people in islands north of Papua New Guinea. Mead travelled to New Guinea with her new husband Reo, who had switched from psychology to anthropology under the force of her personality.

Once again, she set herself to analyse a population before they had been contacted by too many Westerners. Mead's aim this time was even broader: to analyse the question of nature versus nurture, to understand the limits of human nature itself through an analysis of, in Mead's words, 'the brown sea-dwelling Manus'. She wrote, 'In their vaulted, thatched houses set on stilts in the olive-green waters of the wide lagoon, their lives are lived very much as they have been lived for unknown centuries. No missionary has come to teach them ... no trader has torn their lands from them.'[39]

Here, Mead is careful to denounce 'the white man's diseases' and the practices of colonization, and to emphasize that she chose this culture to study because it was 'without economic dependence on white culture'.[40] Focusing on the coming of age of the sea-dwelling Manus people, she contrasts them with the inland Usiai, with whom the Manus traded fish for inland-grown goods. Once again, her account is thick with poetic descriptions: 'To the Manus native', she writes, 'the world is a great platter, curving upwards on all sides from his flat lagoon village where the pile houses stand like long-legged birds, placid and unstirred by the changing tides.'[41] Contrary to her portrayal of Samoan society, which she praised in contrast to the United States, she found Manusian society to mirror the conflicts, double standards, and materialism of the US; fascinated by these similarities, she would return several times in the 1950s, 1960s, and 1970s.[42]

Like many progressive intellectuals in the 1930s, Mead (and Benedict, and other Boasians) fell into doing a significant amount of government and government-supported work in the 1930s and 1940s. The anti-fascist Popular Front in the United States brought together liberals and radicals, and the fight against Naziism legitimized participation in American military efforts for a generation who might otherwise have been more critical of the US national security state.

Mead and the other Boasians, battling dominant narratives of scientific racism, understood themselves as anti-racist. Communism became associated with fights for racial equality in the United States, fights in which many anthropologists found themselves pursuing common goals with Communists or fellow travellers. But in the 1930s, Mead busied herself with a return to New Guinea, where she wanted to study the 'natural sex-temperament' of people who had been reported by earlier generations of anthropological explorers to combine strict sex roles with the possibility of third-sex and transgender ways of being. Once again, she travelled with Reo; first meeting and staying with the Arapesh, who had a way of understanding sex difference that was so incompatible with the Western one that Mead at first rejected the possibility of researching them, once again demonstrating her practice of adapting her fieldwork to fit her research concepts and design.[43]

After crossing to another river valley, Mead and Fortune met another anthropologist, the English researcher Gregory Bateson, who was studying another group of people in the same region. At the same time, the relationship between Fortune and Mead was beginning to strain: Mead began to distrust his anger and he to resent her prominence and success. Lois Banner describes Mead as going through a 'midlife crisis' at the tender age of thirty-one, finally concluding that 'she didn't have to be responsible to anyone or anything, she could now do what she wanted'.[44] She dropped Reo like a hot potato and fell for Gregory Bateson.

Bateson came from a progressive upper-class background like Mead, and shared her commitment to free love; he had fallen in, while studying at Cambridge, with a male-only society that met at an inn called the Half Moon run by an eccentric, sandal-wearing prophet, Noel Porter, who was friends with Havelock Ellis, Edward Carpenter, and Magnus Hirschfeld. Bateson had seemingly had an affair with Porter, and unlike Fortune seemed relatively unfazed by Mead's active bisexuality.

While she was wooing Bateson, she was still in regular contact with Ruth, signing her letters 'I love you, love you' and repeatedly characterizing Bateson and Benedict as similar kinds of intellectual partners, whereas Fortune had been an unfortunate aberration.[45] 'I feel now that when I violated every dictate of my own temperament ... and went away with him and left you,' she wrote Benedict. 'I started on a course which had nothing in the world to do with me, really.'[46] As her relationship with Bateson developed, so too did a new understanding of the sex-gender systems she had come to New Guinea to study.

The book she ended up writing on this trip characterized the three New Guinean peoples with whom she had stayed according to a three-part theory of sex and gender there. The Arapesh and Mundugumor, Mead reported, did not distinguish between men and women, whereas the Tchambuli did – but the Tchambuli reversed Western sex roles.[47] Separate from this finding was the argument that sex and gender systems themselves should be understood as entirely culturally relative, a major departure from then-dominant assumptions about the biological nature of sex and gender roles.

With Bateson, she developed a system of understanding sex and gender called 'the squares', a chart with one male-female axis (defined according to traditional Western sex roles) and one axis of 'temperaments', from rational and calculating to oceanic, mystic, spiritual.[48] Like Magnus Hirschfeld's 'sexual steps in between' and other sexological characterizations of the early twentieth century (and via Bateson, it may have been directly influenced by those ideas), this scheme was an attempt to make space for homosexual and gender non-conforming peoples and desires.

Nonetheless, it used, as Hirschfeld and the sexologists did, a so-called 'primitive' Other as a solvent for conventional Western thinking about sex-gender roles. It also often mischaracterized and misunderstood the societies against which it measured Western concepts of sex and gender, and like much Boasian anthropology could produce an understanding of cultures as flat, fixed, and singular. Even the 'Western gender roles' with which our readers are more likely to be familiar are far less fixed than Mead assumed. Gender roles vary between 'Western' societies, they vary within them by region, race, and especially class, and they have varied over time. Mead was content to assume that she could understand a 'primitive' society in only several months, content to treat her non-state interlocutors as passive material for her research to exploit, and content to substitute the gender roles and cultural traits of the anglophone bourgeoisie for how people live in 'the West', writ large.

At the time of their publication, these works were influential on a generation of more openly queer scholars and thinkers. The anthropologist Esther Newton, whose 1968 study of drag queens helped inaugurate gay and lesbian studies in the American academy, went so far as to claim that Margaret Mead made her gay. She was, she recalls, 'a red diaper baby', tomboyish and unhappy amongst the rigid confines of suburban American gender roles in the 1950s, but Mead's texts helped her 'grasp that my adolescent torments over sex, gender, and the life of the mind could have been avoided by different social arrangements'.[49] It was not that she had dreamed herself into Mead's primitive idyll, but instead that Mead's work, while 'not an overt defense of homosexuality', presented 'a defense of cultural and temperamental difference', and one written by a woman, to boot.[50]

Alongside Ruth Benedict's *Patterns of Culture*, Newton wrote, Mead's anthropology and her status as a female scholar who had also been an 'activist intellectual, dedicated to education and reform', and who had done fieldwork outside the confines of the library and archive, influenced her life and study.[51] Boasian anthropology, especially the work of Benedict, was also a crucial influence on Harry Hay, who co-founded the Mattachine Society, America's first lasting gay rights organization, in 1950.[52] The Boasians' relativism, and their circulation of Native knowledge, influenced many gay activists and thinkers' understanding of the meaning of sexuality.

This of course fits into a larger pattern we have been examining in this book of ethnographic and colonial influences on Western gay and lesbian identity formation. But this circulation was also deeply problematic. Neil Whitehead describes the Western gaze on ethnographic archives as 'an intellectual BDSM, through which the pleasures of classification and analysis' tie up the subject like a dominant binding a submissive to a St Andrews's cross.[53] In these encounters, the reader can imagine direct contact with the observed Other but in fact maintains a safe distance, all while the anthropological or ethnographic text imagines that the reader 'has direct access to the erotics of the Other, as defined by colonial encounters and unequal relations of power'.[54] (Remember again how Mead's very presence in the South Pacific was thanks to US naval expansion and colonization.) This process was fundamental to the development of Western sexuality. Thinkers like Ann Stoler have shown that colonial power affected not only subjects in the colonies but also the politics and social arrangements back home in the metropolis, as classes of people (the urban poor, prostitutes, homosexuals) were classified according to categories developed in the colonies and policed with technologies developed there.[55]

Mead worked as several major global systems were shifting: high imperialist economies moving towards the Fordist consensus of the mid-twentieth century, scientific racism shifting towards racial liberalism, and, as the historian Peter Drucker has pointed out, an associated shift in forms of homosexuality, in which the dominance of the 'invert', a homosexualized figure almost exclusively penetrated who emerged alongside sexological discourses and high imperialism, was replaced with the dominance of a 'gay' man or woman who partnered with like people.[56] The homosexual emancipation discourses of the early twentieth century were an early forerunner of this, and the work of Mead and Benedict influenced its development and directly linked colonization, racial regimes, and sexuality.

The government work Mead was doing as the winds of war began to blow in the late 1930s were not on behalf of European empires, but instead on behalf of an empire whose refusal to acknowledge itself as such is a central part of its myth: the United States. In 1939, Mead, now married to Bateson, discovered that she was pregnant, and their daughter Mary was born in New York in December of that year. Having a young child was hardly conducive to far-flung travels in the South Seas, and indeed the growing threat of war between the United States and Japan made travel in the Pacific far more difficult. Mead had been cut off, ironically, by the very navy that had first enabled her journeys.

The historian Peter Mandler analyses several major changes in Mead's work as the war began: she was cut off from her fieldwork, and thus from her area of expertise, against which she had grounded a series of texts that were fundamentally less about the people they supposedly studied and more about the kind of society she wanted to see created in the United States. Her move was thus to 'return from the natives' – to write about the American national character, and to work with and within the US national security state.[57]

Mead and her colleagues began to turn from imagining their role as offering educative deconstructions of American society towards more explicit social engineering and direct interventions into public policy. With many other activist intellectuals, Mead and Bateson joined the Committee for National Morale, which aimed to draw public support from an isolationist and war-weary public to join in the European war effort. Increasingly in their publishing and writing, they began to focus on what they called 'national character', a subtle shift and evolution from the analysis of specific cultural traits they had pioneered in the 1930s.

How, Mead wondered, could anthropologists and other social scientists help build public morale in the service of a war effort? She passionately believed that social scientists had a political responsibility to engage with questions of public policy, but insisted, especially in contrast to the looming threat of Nazism, where scientific racism was being applied to murderous ends, that they could, as Peter Mandler writes, 'propose means' to social ends and also engage democratically with their beliefs, but that they should not 'impose blueprints of their own'.[58]

To this end, Mead began to do government-funded work about diversity and America's national character, in an effort to see the plurality of the American population as a model for future world cooperation. She took a job working for the Department of Agriculture and set out to use this limited post to help infuse federal policymaking with anthropological insight. Her 1942 book *And Keep Your Powder Dry* presented her view of the American national character: one which had been positively influenced by immigration and diversity.[59]

This book led to yet further growth of her public profile: she began to meet with Eleanor Roosevelt and published regularly in mass-market magazines like *Vogue* and *Harper's*. After the United States formally joined the war after the attacks on Pearl Harbor, she travelled to the United Kingdom to apply herself to the question of how the differing national characters of the United States and the United Kingdom could be resolved into a singular fighting force for the war effort.

Mead later noted with pride that the Second World War was 'a curious and unique war' in which a broad spectrum of 'liberals and conservatives, middle-of-the-roaders and extremists all believed that the war had to be won.'⁶⁰ But the new national security state that was being built rapidly began setting its sights on domestic foes. Anthropologists – not Mead, but some of her colleagues – went to work for the War Relocation Authority and helped to run the Japanese internment camps in the western part of the country.

Mead herself delivered secret lectures at the National War College.⁶¹ New security clearances allowed the FBI, run by the fanatical J. Edgar Hoover (discussed in the next chapter), to collect dossiers on Americans who had been part of the Communist movement or were fellow travellers, including many anthropologists who had been engaged in fights for racial equality. The historian David H. Price has written extensively on the pressures this campaign of political persecution against suspected Communists and queers (the twinned Lavender and Red Scares) placed on anthropologists, especially those who had participated in anti-racist organizing.

State repression not only harmed the livelihoods of the people it directly touched, but also shaped the entire profession's approach to newly sensitive political questions. Even anthropologists like Mead who had jumped at the chance to work with the national security state in the Second World War were subject to FBI surveillance and investigations. And even liberals like Mead could be mistaken for Communists by overzealous investigators.

As the Cold War began, Mead continued her service on the Committee on Food Habits, and worked on a RAND Corporation study of Soviet personality types (later published as a book of anti-Communist caricature called *Soviet Attitudes towards Authority*); she corresponded with Richard Nixon to suggest ways he might account for Soviet personality types in his encounters with Nikita Khrushchev and even advised the State Department on various issues, including taking a hard stance on the developing anti-colonial rebellion in Vietnam.⁶²

Despite all of this, the FBI still compiled a 992-page file on her, primarily because of her advocacy for and belief in racial equality. While Price was only able to analyse approximately half of the files due to ongoing state suppression of research into the FBI's history of domestic repression, he does report that the FBI considered Mead a potential Communist security risk, that she had belonged to various liberal organizations that the FBI characterized as Communist fronts, that the FBI wiretapped Mead at her office in the American Museum of Natural History, that it investigated her based on her daughter's attendance at a progressive pre-school, and that it continued keeping track of her work and her public statements until her death in 1978.

If this repression shaped the discipline of anthropology and helped move the cultural school away from its potentially most radical critiques of Western ways of knowing, it also seems to have been treated, by Mead, as part of the reality of life in post-war America.

In 1950, Bateson filed for divorce, although the two remained friends for the rest of her life. Their daughter Mary was raised, as Mead had been raised, according to the newest and most progressive methods: Dr Benjamin Spock was Mary's paediatrician and friends with Mead; his famous psychoanalytically influenced books on child-rearing, a sensation in 1950s America, especially in progressive circles, were influenced by his medical care of Mary and by conversations with Mead about her ethnographic research.

As the 1950s and 1960s moved on, Mead increasingly moved more and more into the role of America's 'liberal godmother', appearing as an expert on TV talk shows and evincing a kind of strange double response to the post-war crisis over the role of working women. During the war women had joined the workforce en masse, and afterwards, a crisis threatened. In her book *Male and Female*, she advocated, on the basis of research notes about tribal societies in the South Seas she had visited in the 1930s, for relatively conservative gender relations, positions that led Betty Friedan to consider Mead 'the architect of the back-to-the-home movement of the 1950s'.[63]

In other public articles, however, she argued for housework to be replaced by technology and for communal family rearing. As always, her positions on public policy were doubled: radical but not too radical. Radical feminists like Kate Millett and Ti-Grace Atkinson abandoned Mead, but a later generation of feminists in the 1970s and 1980s returned to her example, referring to her as 'super sister' and 'first of the Libbies'.[64]

Benedict had died two years before Mead's divorce, and Mead immediately took up with her assistant on the Committee on Food Habits, a young anthropologist named Rhoda Métraux. Her early letters to Métraux reveal yet again how she understood her relationships as cyclical; she referenced Bateson and even Sapir in early letters, and in one, a Valentine's Day letter in 1949, wrote:

> It's really very odd how little guilt over special symmetries I have. I suppose partly because I never chose asymmetrical relationships on purpose ... but simply chose people who couldn't pay attention, and then accepted their not paying attention as part of the world. Now when you write me long letters to my short ones, or poems where I have only prose – I simply feel touched and delighted – a little strange, but with a pleasant kind of surprise ... as if somehow Ruth had bequeathed me a little of her beauty – by giving some sort of care into her hands – for me ... I have such a firm belief that nothing in the world is too complicated – nothing that I can think up – but that you will but understand and add to it.[65]

The two of them remained primary partners for the rest of their lives, with Métraux's marriage only a minor inconvenience; by 1955 they were sharing a house in Greenwich Village with their two children and collaborating on a project called Research in Contemporary Cultures. Métraux would edit much of Mead's late-life work, and perhaps contributed to what Mead, when a 1960s interviewer commented on how much energy she had for her age, called her 'postmenopausal zest'.[66] Certainly, their love for one another did not decrease. In 1974, from Honolulu, Mead wrote to Métraux, 'I've just pressed the violets and 2 little violet leaves within the unread pages of a new book. Be better, my love. Life does not make sense – you make it make sense for me – I love you.'[67]

During these years Mead served for a time as president of the American Anthropological Association, vice president of the New York Academy of Sciences, and was both president and board chair of the American Association for the Advancement of the Sciences. It was in 1971, while serving as the president of the AAA, that Mead fought to make sure a report on anthropologists' collaboration with the CIA and US Army found that they had not done anything wrong by using their skills in support of murderous counterinsurgency programmes in Latin America.[68] She worked to develop a graphic symbol language, supported UN projects on development, and founded the Department of Anthropology at the Lincoln Center campus of Fordham University in 1968. She also joined in with others of her Anglican faith to draft the 1979 American Episcopal Book of Common Prayer. She was inducted into the National Women's Hall of Fame in 1976, and regularly appeared on talk shows and continued her writing in both academic and popular forms, including a late book of essays with Métraux called *A Way of Seeing* and her 1972 memoir, *Blackberry Winter*.

A representative article in a 1972 issue of *Stars and Stripes*, the magazine of the US armed forces, described her as 'the peppery grand old lady of American anthropology' in a write-up of a press conference she gave in Heidelberg, Germany, advocating for the abolition of laws against marijuana, discussing 'the problem of black and white relations in America', and the need for 'fewer and better parents'.[69] In the article (as in her dialogue with Baldwin from a year earlier, *A Rap on Race*), Mead is careful to indicate her support for racial integration and even the Black Power movement as she understood it ('the growing sense of Black identity', the article calls it). Her support for population control and work with UN and other Cold War–era bodies on contraception and population control, however, indicates the ongoing relationship between liberal anthropology and sexology and eugenics, as active in the 1970s as in the time of Magnus Hirschfeld.

In the last year of her life, 1978, Mead developed pancreatic cancer. She employed a faith healer, a decision with which

Métraux disagreed, and the two became estranged. Her last letter to Métraux was written only a few months before the end of her life, in August of 1978. 'I am much better,' she wrote. 'At present I expect to come back before the end of the month. I hope you are having a good time. I love you.'[70] That November, Mead died, and was buried at an Episcopal cemetery where she grew up, in Buckingham, Pennsylvania.

After her death, Mead's work came in for a sudden flurry of criticism from all sides. Her enormous prominence in the field had previously made criticizing her or her work difficult. The first and most prominent attack on her conclusions came from Derek Freeman, a conservative evolutionary biologist whose attack on Mead's work in Samoa was published by Harvard University Press five years after her death in 1983. His book, *Margaret Mead and Samoa: The Making and Unmaking of an Anthropological Myth*, accused Mead of having used only one source in Samoa and of having twisted what he characterized as conservative, prim, and proper sexual customs into an unscientific advocacy for her own views on free love.

Paul Shankman's history of this anthropological controversy describes the stakes: Freeman believed in nature over nurture, and his attack seemed to 'damage Mead ... not merely as an anthropologist but as a public figure, a feminist, and a liberal'.[71] His book claimed that Mead had been 'grossly hoaxed' by her preconceptions and that she had 'completely misinformed and misled the entire anthropological establishment'. He wrote in a later book that this was 'one of the most spectacular events of the intellectual history of the twentieth century' and characterized Mead, and by extension her credulous liberal audience, as the victims of 'a Polynesian prank' in which 'giggly fibs' came to overrule sober-minded science.[72]

Anthropological critics replied by attacking Freeman's own book as a poorly researched hit job, and pointed out his critiques' less-than-subtle misogyny. This led to an enormous public squabble between Freeman and his conservative supporters, and anthropologists intent on defending Mead, a spat that generated rather more heat than light. Shankman, for his part, describes

Freeman's argument as 'misleading and often inaccurate' in its characterization of Mead's life and work.[73]

Far more interesting and compelling is the tradition of decolonial and postcolonial critiques of anthropology – a tradition that in Western scholarship was pioneered by a 1973 book by Talal Asad called *Anthropology and the Colonial Encounter*, which critiqued anthropological knowledge production in the Boasian style as itself a tool of colonial domination.

Ten years later, a documentary film directed by Barbara Gullahorn-Holecek revisited Manus, that 'flat lagoon village where the pile houses stand like long-legged birds, placid and unstirred by the changing tides' where Mead had produced much of her work on New Guinea. The majority of the film's interviews are devoted to the people who Mead had studied and worked with, as well as their children, many of whom were attending university, learning to read English, and could suddenly read – and react in horror to – Mead's descriptions of their lives and customs. 'Sometimes they tell us you go to the library and look up this book and read something about ourselves, and we ask the lecturers, "Can we do it from our background knowledge?" and they say, oh no, you have to read the book in the library,' a woman from Manus says near the beginning of the film. 'That's why we get upset.'

The inland Usai and their descendants reveal that Mead's descriptions of them were solely based on her interactions with the seagoing Manus – leading to what they understood to be a grossly inaccurate and even insulting depiction of their society. Seleao Yowat, one of the people living in the village of Bunai, says, 'She didn't understand our customs … At that time the customs of the two groups were very different. She never properly examined our customs.'[74]

In 1976, Michel Foucault wrote the following in the opening pages of the first volume of his *History of Sexuality*:

> Something that smacks of revolt, of promised freedom, of the coming age of a different law, slips easily into this discourse on sexual oppression. Some of the ancient functions of prophecy are

reactivated therein. Tomorrow sex will be good again. Because this repression is affirmed, one can discreetly bring into coexistence concepts which the fear of ridicule or the bitterness of history prevents most of us from putting side by side: revolution and happiness; or revolution and a different body, one that is newer and more beautiful; or indeed, revolution and pleasure. What sustains our eagerness to speak of sex in terms of repression is doubtless this opportunity to speak out against the powers that be, to utter truths and promise bliss, to link together enlightenment, liberation, and manifold pleasures; to pronounce a discourse that combines the fervor of knowledge, the determination to change the laws, and the longing for the garden of earthly delights.[75]

Tomorrow, sex will be good again. Here, Foucault writes of the powerful appeal of the 'repressive hypothesis', an idea embedded in the gay liberation discourses that Mead and Benedict's work did so much to inform: an idea that arose from the longing for a mythic (even a primitive) past of earthly delights and simpler pleasures, the desire for bliss and enlightenment and liberation all wrapped up into one.

Mead herself is perhaps most famously quoted as saying, 'Never doubt that a small group of thoughtful and committed citizens can change the world. Indeed, it is the only thing that ever has.'[76] Near the end of Gullahorn-Holecek's film documenting those thoughtful and committed people, the regional New Guinean political figure Utula Samana proposes that any future white anthropologist studying New Guinea be offset by a New Guinean anthropologist studying social behaviours in the West. The film then cuts to a New Guinean anthropological student at the University of California who is studying American society. He is shown in happy conversation with his thesis adviser and discusses his fieldwork on tenants living in a transient hotel in East Oakland, to which he reacts in horror – homelessness would never be allowed in his supposedly primitive country.

The film, like Mead's own work, understands education and exchange as the foundations of a future in which all the world's cultural diversity might be preserved, explored, and shared. Nearly forty years later, in an even more cynical age, with more understanding from postcolonial scholarship about the fraught and violent nature of that exchange and production, even that seems nearly as haunted a fantasy as the idea that the forever-in-the-past girls of T'au are somewhere out there on the horizon of the known world, among the dusky marshes, dancing not for themselves but for us; so that tomorrow, we might return to nature and overcome repression; so that tomorrow, sex will be good again.

10

J. Edgar Hoover and Roy Cohn

It probably will not strike people as shocking, even if they only know a little about the life of J. Edgar Hoover, to discover that the man who founded the Federal Bureau of Investigation, the domestic security and intelligence agency of the United States, and who ran it as his own personal fiefdom for nearly five decades, was something of a maverick. He possessed a force of personality and will that stopped at nothing to ensure his power was secure. It might strike you as shocking, however – even if you *do* know a good deal about his professional life – that he was also a deeply *weird* man.

He was a born cop – as a child, he kept a dossier on *himself*, which included a full formal report on his own birth.[1] A born authoritarian – as an avid member of his high school debate team, he argued that America should annex Cuba, women should be denied the vote, and that 'all Christian nations' should uphold the death penalty.[2] And a born perve, with one FBI official claiming the agency had 'the largest and most comprehensive' collections of pornography in history, for the purposes of suppression, blackmail, and Hoover's personal enjoyment.[3] Throughout his life, he was obsessed with two great, threatening horrors: communism, and fucking.

He was joined in the first of these horrors by another mummy's boy and child of privilege, although of a different sort – another lawyer, another homosexual hellbent on destroying the lives of other queers, and of leftists, Roy Cohn. Unlike Hoover, Cohn held no fear of fucking – quite the opposite – although the idea he might be identified as gay was anathema to him.

Hoover came first, and set the standard for red-baiting that Cohn followed. The America the former was born into, on New Year's Day 1895, was not yet the world superpower he would grow to see, and to control. Edgar, as he was known, was the youngest of four children of a well-to-do family, and throughout his upbringing was extremely close to his mother, who was still mourning the loss of a daughter when he was born. Despite his early success in life, he lived with his mother until she died, when he was forty-three years old. At school he was smart, and though he wanted to be a sportsman (he admired sporty boys greatly), he was small and too light to join the football team.[4] (Even as director of the FBI, he had a small platform installed behind his desk for his chair to sit on, and generally avoided the promotion of tall agents, lest he have to stand next to them.)[5] He studied law at George Washington University. When he was eighteen, he worked as a messenger at the Library of Congress. There, he learnt the usefulness of the Dewey Decimal System, and the importance and power of controlling communication and information.[6]

Hoover graduated in 1916, just as the United States was preparing to enter World War I in 1917. Despite his fervent patriotism, Hoover delayed enlisting straight away, and three months later, just a day after passing the bar exams, took a job at the Department of Justice – a job that included exemption from military service.[7]

Despite joining the department as a mailroom boy, his rise was meteoric, and he quickly took charge of the Alien Enemy Registration Section at the War Emergency Division, rounding up suspect foreign nationals.[8] He tried, unsuccessfully, dating women at this time, but was deeply wounded when a secretary called Alice who he had been seeing got engaged to a returning soldier she had been romancing via mail. He was never to date again, although his niece, Margaret, suggested that even had it worked out, his mother would have prevented any marriage, saying she 'was truly the matriarch ... She would have stopped anything rumoured.'[9]

Hoover threw his energy into work, and there was plenty of work to be done. In the wake of the war, with much of Europe in ruins, debt, and political turmoil, America was in the ascendancy. But, as with Hoover's personal life, the more power the US attained, the more insecure and fearful it became. In the immediate aftermath of World War I, the workers' movement in the US, after decades of organising, was engaged in a series of strikes that had gripped the country. Anarchist, socialist, and communist organisations gained support from many workers, and the Russian Revolution offered a then-hopeful alternative to the US capitalist system. This situation deeply concerned the US government, and bosses, fearful that industrial action could escalate into revolution, fomented another resurgence in the nativist, anti-immigration politics which had always been present in US society.

The state decided to crack down on organisations like the Communist Party and the Industrial Workers of the World, and on dissidents like Emma Goldman and Sacco and Vanzetti, who they regarded as 'importing' radical ideas from the East. Congress approved funds for the Justice Department to establish a 'General Investigation Division' to monitor the activities of radicals. Despite being just twenty-four years old, J. Edgar Hoover was seen as the promising young talent who could make the unit work, and he did.[10] With astonishing zeal, he collected huge amounts of data on radicals, established local squads, and organised agents to surveil suspects, effectively crushing the power of organised labour. By 1921 the supposed threat, known later as the 'First Red Scare', had been largely suppressed, with thousands of socialists, communists, or anarchist either jailed, deported, or killed. For the rest of his life, the fear of communism, something he called 'the most evil, monstrous conspiracy against man since time began', not only obsessed Hoover, but his inculcation of that fear into American society allowed him to accrue a vast amount of personal power.[11]

In 1921 Hoover was named deputy head of the Bureau of Investigation, and in 1924, after less than a decade in the organisation and aged just twenty-nine, he had gone from mailroom boy to the boss. He set about reforming the image of the organisation into a tough, ruthless, and masculine investigating machine, implementing a ban on women agents that lasted until his death.[12]

If the 'red scare' had subsided, there was still plenty to occupy him, as in January 1920 the Eighteenth Amendment came into force, and the Prohibition Era began. Alcohol was effectively illegal across the United States. Unfortunately, prohibition did not work, and a whole new market opened up for organised crime, alongside racketeering, gambling, and prostitution. Hoover, however, recognised the limitations of the agency and focused its work only on achievable, high-profile cases, often piggybacking off the fame of criminals like John Dillinger, the handsome and charismatic bank robber who achieved some popular support after destroying mortgage records during his raids.[13] Bureau of Investigation agents finally cornered and killed Dillinger in 1934; in the wake of the case, Hoover approved a new name for the organisation, the Federal Bureau of Investigation. This combined process of marketing, high-profile law enforcement, and gradual accrual of powers made Hoover a popular public figure, and therefore almost untouchable by the judiciary, who struggled, and ultimately failed, to rein in his powers.

As well as cracking down on leftists more generally while leaving organised crime to develop largely without interference, in the 1920s and 1930s Hoover also focused on the new generation of Black writers, artists, and intellectuals who were emerging in what became known as the Harlem Renaissance. The Harlem Renaissance was a period of intense cultural creativity by Black Americans and Caribbean people in New York from the end of the First World War until the mid-'30s, stimulated, in part, by the arrival of thousands of migrants bringing different Black American cultures from the South. They came to the city as part of the First Great Migration, attempting to escape Jim Crow laws and find work in the industrialising northern cities. They brought with them not just musical, literary, and fashion cultures, but also different attitudes towards sexuality, emerging partly from the dislocation of the migration, creating a Black queer culture and nightlife within the wider cultural explosion. Black women were at the forefront of Harlem's queer culture, but often that queer culture found itself opposed not just by white bourgeois moral guardians but also by Black Nationalist leaders; in the words of historian Cookie Woolner, 'there was no room for women's sexual deviance in an increasingly masculinized struggle for racial equality and full citizenship'.[14] As discussed in our chapter on Margaret Mead, anthropologists, too, were among those policed by this strict regime of political repression, even though their politics did not challenge but in fact actively collaborated with the US security state.

Hoover's 'observation list' on Black American writers is not so much a surveillance file as a syllabus of the country's greatest literary talents, with Hoover setting his goons on everyone from Claude McKay and Alain Locke to Langston Hughes and Georgia Douglas Johnson. According to the academic William J. Maxwell, Hoover surveilled 'nearly half – 23 out of a total of 48 – of the historically relevant writers featured in the classroom staple *The Norton Anthology of African American Literature*'.[15]

The cultural 'revival' of the Harlem Renaissance – actually the fruition of generations of Black American cultural and political life – was in Hoover's view a threat to the white-supremacist system over which he presided, and such a potent source of socialist thinking, that, as with the wider labour movement, it came into his sights as the site of the political sedition that, in reality, was always the FBI's main concern. This became evident again much later in his career, as he attempted to suppress the civil rights movement that emerged in the 1950s. Not only were writers again in his focus – James Baldwin, a Black, gay New York writer whose powerful prose and oratory made him a moral backbone for the movement, had a file almost half the size of that of Malcolm X – but also the leadership of the nonviolent civil rights movement itself.[16]

Here, Hoover's racism was bolstered by his sexual obsessions; the Bureau went to extraordinary lengths to uncover evidence of the extramarital affairs of Dr Martin Luther King, using the evidence to compile a 'sex tape' of his sexual liaisons and sending it to King's house in November 1964, complete with a letter accusing him of 'countless acts of adultery and moral conduct lower than that of a beast', before going on to demand King kill himself, or, presumably, the evidence will be made public. 'You are finished,' it continued. 'You will find on the record for all time your filthy, dirty, evil companions, males and females giving expression with you to your hideous abnormalities.'[17] The accusation that King was having sex with men was totally unsubstantiated, but it must have been concerning, for he was in the public eye and receiving much attention following the March on Washington for Jobs and Freedom, which had taken place the year before, and at which he had given his famous 'I Have a Dream' speech.

One of the key organisers of that march was the conscientious objector, Quaker, and former Communist Bayard Rustin, whose considerable skills acquired as a labour organiser made him the formidable logistical brain who pulled off the extraordinary event. Rustin, however, was also homosexual, and an earlier march planned for the 1960 Democratic National Convention had been dropped when Democratic politician Adam Clayton Powell Jr told King he would release a fake rumour that King and Rustin were lovers were the march to go ahead and embarrass the Democratic Party. Just weeks before the actual March on Washington, South Carolina Democratic senator Strom Thurmond, a racist bigot and segregationist, produced a photograph of King in a bathtub while talking to Rustin, with the implication, again, that they were lovers. The photo had been given to Thurmond by the FBI.

Focused on Black people and leftists, the FBI fundamentally failed to suppress the organised crime cartels that profited so much from prohibition. Why did a man as ruthless and powerful as Hoover fail to ever really crack the power of the Mafia? According to mobsters, the reason was that Meyer Lansky, the mob financier who was one of the key players in mid-century organised crime in the US, held a cache of compromising photos of Hoover 'in some sort of gay situation with Clyde Tolson [Hoover's long-time deputy]'.[18] Hoover refused to acknowledge that the Mafia even existed, stating 'no single individual or coalition of racketeers dominates organized crime across the nation',[19] despite the fact that hidden FBI microphones had just caught Sam Giancana, Chicago's mob boss, repeatedly refer to 'the Commission', the Mafia's governing organisation in the US. John Weitz, an intelligence agent with the OSS (Office of Strategic Services, the World War II precursor to the CIA), also attested to having seen the photos, suggesting a similar dynamic kept Hoover from really claiming ground from his rivals, the CIA.[20]

It is Clyde Tolson's relationship with Hoover that offers the most convincing case that Hoover was homosexual. Tolson had been made assistant director of the FBI in 1930, aged just thirty, and rumours about the nature of their relationship began almost immediately. The two quickly became inseparable, dining together five nights a week for four decades, spending their holidays and even Christmases together.[21] One Democratic congressman complained that Hoover and Tolson 'have been living as man and wife for some twenty-eight years at the public's expense'.[22] By the 1960s FBI agents had begun referring to the pair as 'J. Edna' and 'Mother Tolson'.[23]

Hoover died in 1972, still in his role as director of the FBI, a job he'd held for nearly half a century. His body lay in state in the US Capitol, the only civil servant to receive such an honour, and, 'in the absence of a widow' it was Tolson who received the flag that was draped over his coffin, as well as inheriting Hoover's estate, home, and dogs.[24] Tolson soon slumped into a depression, essentially only leaving the house to visit Hoover's grave. He had the dogs put to sleep. Three years later, Tolson died, and was buried a few yards from Hoover, as per both men's request.[25]

A few years after their death, Hoover was outed by a surprising friend, the Broadway legend and gay icon Ethel Merman. She had been close friends with Hoover and Tolson. Asked her opinions on homosexuals, she replied, 'Some of my best friends are homosexual,' which must have surprised nobody. Then she followed it up with, 'Everybody knew about J. Edgar Hoover, but he was the best chief the FBI ever had.'[26]

There are other, more outlandish allegations about Hoover's sex life, including one, provided with a sworn affidavit, by Susan Rosenstiel, that she attended an orgy with her husband at the Plaza Hotel, New York, in which Hoover was in attendance, dressed in full drag, and watched as he had two boys in leather read Bible verses to him, before he seized the Bible, threw it to the floor, and proceeded to have sex with them.[27] The accusation might sound outlandish, but she was not the only one to have made it. One FBI agent, Guy Hottel, who had been Clyde Tolson's flatmate for years before joining the agency and becoming Tolson and Hoover's 'constant companion' for a decade, also made similar claims after becoming a problem drinker in the 1940s. Despite his indiscretions and alcoholism, he was not fired.[28]

Susan's husband, Lewis Rosenstiel, was a powerful bisexual businessman who was an associate of Meyer Lansky's, and who had leant on Hoover to ensure the passing of the Forand Act, saving him a huge amount in potential taxes on hoarded whiskey.[29] The orgy was, Susan alleged, organised by Roy Cohn, a lawyer whose clients included Rosenstiel as well as various crooks from mobster 'Fat Tony' Salerno to Roger Stone, Rupert Murdoch, and Donald Trump, and whose career had received a major boost thanks to a recommendation provided by J. Edgar Hoover.

Should we believe these allegations? On the one hand, the allegations are multiple, and spread across his career. However, as the historian David K. Johnson points out, 'this account is more of a reflection of Cold War political culture than an analysis of it. It utilizes the kind of tactics Hoover and the security program he oversaw perfected – guilt by association, rumor, and unverified gossip.'[30] It's true that this account of Hoover's sex life is salacious and at the very least embellished, while also perpetuating many homophobic Cold War tropes. Yet, without guilt, rumour, and gossip, most of history's homosexuals would go unnoticed in the torrent of assumed heterosexuality that culture imposes.

Conversely, there is very little gossip or rumour about Hoover's hypothetical girlfriends.

Is it not hard to see what Hoover saw in Cohn? Both men were driven by a hatred of communism, both were ruthlessly cruel, and both lived with their mothers until their forties. Sure, Cohn was a Jew – and Hoover had no time for Jews – but he might not hold that against him ... much. Roy was born in the Bronx in 1927, the product of an unhappy marriage and an unhappy home.[31] His father, Al Cohn, came from a family of Polish Jews who had migrated to the US in the nineteenth century, and his mother, Dora Marcus, from German Jews who migrated at the same time. The Marcus' had done well by providing banking services, while Al Cohn grew up in poverty on the Lower East Side, but was ambitious and had studied hard in law. The dowry from the marriage provided enough money for Al to become a judge, but that was probably the only upside of the nuptials.[32]

Roy's father was aloof and cold, Dora obsessive over her son, doting but also cruel. She employed her poor in-laws as servants and kitchen staff, and cultivated in Roy, her only child, a sense of superiority and disdain that he seemed to be able to turn on and off at will.[33] School friends remembered a teenage Cohn calling the local police precinct to have his teacher's traffic ticket cancelled;[34] relatives remembered him at age eleven sending food back at restaurants.[35]

Al was deeply involved in the Democratic Tammany Hall 'machine politics' that had dominated New York for over a century, a political system built for reproducing power, wealth, and corruption. Thus from a young age Roy understood that law, money, and politics were interconnected tools for wielding power, something he learnt not just from Al, but also from Dora, who built a personal fiefdom amongst Democrat socialites. Even senators' wives were warned, 'Be nice to Dora because if you're not nice to Dora she's gonna make life miserable'.[36]

Roy did not play ball out in the street; he collected political campaign pin badges, and he attended his parents' dinner parties, something unheard of at the time.[37] He studied law at Columbia, and, like Hoover, managed to avoid being drafted in the final days of a war by getting himself sent to West Point military academy, on the recommendation of a New York politician. There was no chance that Cohn, only marginally taller than Hoover but without his mass, would have passed the physical entry requirements, yet he was recommended on three occasions, with the surely coincidental effect that the boy was repeatedly pushed down the draft. He received his lawyer's diploma when he was only twenty, and had to wait almost a year before being sworn into the bar on his twenty-first birthday.[38]

Within a year, Cohn was an assistant US attorney, and began what became a lifelong passion he shared with Hoover: hunting Reds. As after the First World War, the period following World War II, as the Cold War started to crystallize, led to a concerted suppression of not just members of the Communist Party USA, but also of labour organisers and socialists more generally.

Politicians were already taking advantage of these new anxieties. In 1947 Truman passed Executive Order 9835, giving the FBI sweeping powers to investigate state employees for potential allegiance to 'subversive' organisations – largely speaking, communist ones. It also facilitated the creation of the 'Attorney General's List of Subversive Organizations', detailing suspicious organisations to help facilitate the outing of 'subversives'.

Stoking public fears of communist subversion of the US government and institutions, it gave the state increased opportunities to crack down on political undesirables, especially trade unionists and racial justice organisers. Cohn relished the chance to persecute any he could find, including the economist William Remington. Remington worked for the Council of Economic Advisers, a federal agency that advises the executive, and was accused by Elizabeth Bentley, a KGB agent turned informant, of having passed her government information during the war. On top of this, his former wife alleged that he had been a member of the Communist Party, something he denied. In the end they did not get him for espionage, but for perjury. When the first sentence was overturned, he was tried again, for lying in the first.[39]

Sentenced to three years in prison, he was beaten to death a year later by anti-Communist fellow prisoners.

The victory must have given Cohn a taste for blood. In 1951 he took a central role in one of the most notorious espionage trials of the century, that of Julius and Ethel Rosenberg. The Rosenbergs were a young Jewish couple from New York who were accused of having passed nuclear secrets to the Soviet Union during the war. Cohn's role included the high-profile interrogation of Ethel Rosenberg's brother, David Greenglass, on the witness stand. Greenglass, a Communist machinist who had worked on the US Manhattan Project to build a nuclear weapon before being recruited by Julius Greenberg, had struck a plea bargain with the state in order that his wife could stay with their children. His testimony, extracted by Cohn, was crucial to the conviction of the Rosenbergs, who were sentenced to death.[40]

The case caused an international furore, as public figures from Bertholt Brecht to Pope Pius XII appealed for clemency. Many doubted the couple's guilt, or they regarded the harsh sentence, particularly Ethel's, to be motivated by anti-Semitism.[41] Writing in the French newspaper *Libération* the day after the execution, Jean-Paul Sartre astutely diagnosed America as being 'sick with fear … afraid of the shadow of your own bomb'.[42] While the Rosenbergs almost certainly were guilty of the crime of which they were accused, the case was also a miscarriage of justice. In his co-written autobiography Cohn bragged of his discussions with the judge outside of court, via a secret telephone protocol they had established, during which he agitated for Ethel to receive the death penalty too. The judge 'had already decided *before* the trial that he was going to sentence Julius Rosenberg to death', but was reticent about also executing Ethel, a mother of two young sons. 'What was plainly at work here', recalled Cohn, 'was a kind of reverse sexism.'[43] Two years later, both were dead.

Roy Cohn's star, as anti-Communist witch hunter, was on the rise. Hoover had noticed his outstanding role in the Rosenbergs' trial, and saw his potential, recommending him to Senator Joe McCarthy. McCarthy had been an unremarkable Republican senator, elected to the state of Wisconsin in 1946, who, like Cohn and Hoover, had trained in law. He had propelled himself into the headlines, and into the centre of American public life, when in early 1950 he made an explosive speech claiming he had the names of over two hundred people who were 'known to the Secretary of State as being members of the Communist Party and who nevertheless are still working and shaping the policy of the State Department'.[44]

It's important to note that McCarthy wasn't the first to warn of Communist subversion in America: three years previously the House Un-American Activities Committee (HUAC) had already, to take one example, run a series of hearing on supposed Communist influence in Hollywood, leading to the persecution and blacklisting of scores of writers, directors, and actors. Nor was it the first time paranoid accusations were levelled against members of the State Department: it was Democrat President Truman who had implemented the loyalty programme, and in fact McCarthy's speech was riding off the back of the conviction of a senior government official, Alger Hiss, for perjury relating to espionage charges. But McCarthy brought a vituperative, unhinged attitude to red-baiting that thrilled Hoover, made headlines, and both rode, and fuelled, popular paranoia.

It is wrong to characterise McCarthy's brand of anticommunism as hegemonic in the America of the 1950s. While he held a certain degree of power on account of his rhetoric, he faced some pushback from both Republicans and Democrats, and notably lost a large share of his vote in the 1952 election, when in general Republicans fared well across the board, and Dwight D. Eisenhower became the first successful Republican presidential candidate since Herbert Hoover in 1928.

While there may not have been much love lost between McCarthy and Eisenhower, the president was undoubtably helped by an official memorandum, produced by the FBI on J. Edgar Hoover's order, on Eisenhower's opponent, Adlai Stevenson, which smeared him as a homosexual who had 'once harbored communist sympathies'.[45] The rumours that resulted from the memorandum were made concrete in the mind of the electorate in October, when McCarthy appeared on TV clutching papers that reported the accusations, charging Stevenson of being a 'wartime Communist collaborator'.[46]

With Eisenhower in power, his fellow Republicans made efforts to sideline McCarthy, refusing to appoint him to the Internal Security Subcommittee, which was in charge of rooting out communism. The Senate majority leader, Robert A. Taft, was very pleased with himself, saying, 'We've got McCarthy where he can't do any harm,' on the Senate Committee on Government Operations.[47] They underestimated the man, who after his appointment made himself the chairman of the Permanent Subcommittee on Investigations, a role with a wide enough remit that he could relaunch his aggressive investigations into Communist subversion (it was on this subcommittee where McCarthy conducted his investigations; he never appeared on the HUAC).

It was at this point that Hoover recommended the young lawyer Roy Cohn, who would serve as McCarthy's chief counsel. Cohn bought with him a 'friend', David Schine, a Harvard graduate and son of a wealthy hotel magnate; this nepotism, perhaps motivated either by Cohn's lust for the tall, handsome Schine or even on the basis of a sexual relationship, would have disastrous consequences for McCarthy.

There had been a sense of growing anxiety about the prevalence of homosexuals within the US army and within the State Department for years. Attempts to weed them out during the draft in World War II eventually resulted in the codification of a myriad of different prohibitions on gay men and women in 1943, when any 'persons occasionally or habitually engaged in homosexual or other perverse sexual practices' were prohibited from serving in any branch of the armed services.[48] In 1947 the Senate Appropriations Committee had, in a more general warning about potential Communist subversion, also warned of 'the extensive appointment in highly classified positions of admitted homosexuals, who are historically known to be security risks'.[49]

Their reasoning was twofold: they believed that one, 'sexual perversion' was a character weakness, and two, the blackmail of those engaged in illegal and socially taboo behaviour was a risk. However, the deluge of press coverage in the late '40s and early '50s helped link homosexuality and communism in the minds of many people, until both became inseparable, confusing 'security risks' with 'disloyalty'.[50] This fear manifested in many forms, such as the assumption (probably reasonably well founded) that homosexuals tended to congregate and socialise together, and, like Communists, had their own codes of behaviour and language with which they recognised each other, thus increasing the sense of collusion or conspiracy. According to one 1952 article on the subject, homosexuals 'belong to a sinister, mysterious and efficient international', clearly alluding to the Comintern (Communist International): the 'Homintern', as it was sometimes known.[51]

Were these fears unfounded? Not entirely. After all, the blackmail of gay men was, and remained, a security risk. In the UK the combination of communist ideology, homosexual fraternity, and Oxbridge networks underpinned the Cambridge Five spy ring, while the effective use of a KGB gang-bang honeytrap to blackmail civil servant John Vassall in 1954 led to almost a decade of using him as a spy, sourcing huge amounts of information with which to upgrade the Soviet Navy. Meanwhile, on the left, there were, quite understandably, a good deal of homosexuals for whom the promise of overthrowing the bourgeois order made communism an attractive prospect, and who were equipped with a huge range of organising skills provided by the Communist Party.

One such activist, Harry Hay, went on to become a founding member of one of the United States' first gay activist groups that emerged at this time, the Mattachine Society, and adopted the Popular Front model of a minority group agitating for social and political recognition as a social group with a distinct culture, whose legacy endures today in the idea of the 'LGBTQ community'.[52]

This wider conflation of homosexuality and communism in the American popular imagination was ideal for McCarthy, however, giving him a two-way smear tactic. He played up to it, depicting communism as a movement of underhanded, subversive queers, and himself as the tough, macho defender of America and her values. 'McCarthyism', he would rail, 'is Americanism with its sleeves rolled up.'[53] Yet the groundwork was already laid. Even before McCarthy took over as chair, the Permanent Subcommittee on Investigations had released a report, based upon two years of investigations into government employment of homosexuals that were conducted under its previous chair, the segregationist Dixie Democrat senator Clyde Hoey. Just a few months into his presidency, in April 1953, President Eisenhower introduced Executive Order 10450, prohibiting homosexuals from federal employment. Hoover had already authorised the FBI to begin passing all information collected under his Sex Deviates Program, instigated in 1950, to the Civil Service Commission, which oversaw federal recruitment and employment.

Between these organs and laws, Washington now had a comprehensive system for the surveillance and purging of homosexuals from the State Department. All homosexual activity caught by the DC was referred to the FBI as a matter of course, who stored it for future 'leverage' or passed it straight to the Civil Service Commission. Mere weeks passed between arrest and dismissal, and you would never work in the civil service again. Anyone applying to work for the federal government had their details cross-checked with the State Department's list of known *or alleged* homosexuals. Special investigators in the State Department devoted to uncovering homosexuals dug into employees' lives, checking credit records and references and even investigating whether the employees knew other potential homosexuals, as even association suggested guilt.[54]

It is difficult to know how many homosexuals were purged; David K Johnson notes that the undersecretary of state, Donald B Lourie, testified that at the height of the purges his department alone was losing an employee a day. Johnson estimates that five thousand federal government employees lost their jobs over the course of the purges, not including those who, seeing which way the wind was blowing, resigned, nor those who were never employed on the basis of their sexuality.[55]

McCarthy, with his bully pulpit, was neither the first nor the last of the purgers, but rather the public face of a much wider purge of both homosexuals and leftists. Still, the fear, hatred, and malevolence he managed to sow in the public imagination was unparalleled. As he told two journalists visiting his office, 'If you want to be against McCarthy, boys, you've got to be a Communist or a cocksucker.'[56] He would prove a powerful influence on Cohn's life.

Yet, for Cohn, serving McCarthy was the highlight of his life, as he commented later: 'I never worked for a better man or a greater cause.'[57] Meanwhile, the thousands purged often struggled to find work, or were outed to their families and communities. Inadvertently, this had an effect on the nascent gay rights movement that was starting to emerge in tentative, closed circles in cities around the country. The influx of many talented minds, who understood the politics of state, into an ostracised community gave new recruits to what was called the 'homophile movement', including Frank Kameny.

After Kameny was fired as an astronomer in the Army Map Service, he unsuccessfully appealed his dismissal. He had little to lose in throwing his hand in with the gay rights movement, and went on to help found the Washington, DC, branch of the Mattachine Society, and was influential in overturning the Diagnostic and Statistical Manual of Mental Disorders' classification of homosexuality as a mental disorder.

McCarthy put Cohn and Schine to work, alongside assistant counsel Bobby Kennedy. (Yes, that Bobby Kennedy – the Kennedys are too flagrantly heterosexual to fit into our narrative, though they were certainly bad enough.) They turned their fire first on Voice of America, a publicly funded shortwave radio station broadcasting internationally, established in 1942 to help counter Nazi propaganda abroad. Then, having repeatedly purged it of its leaders, McCarthy had Cohn and Schine dispatched to Europe to purge the International Information Administration, a State Department agency that helped run pro-US libraries in Europe, of literature McCarthy had deemed subversive.[58]

Their trip was a farce, a sort of 'National Lampoon's European Suppression', as the two men gallivanted between US embassies; besides, having heard that McCarthy was looking to purge them, many libraries had already removed most offending books.[59] Just the fear of McCarthy's boys saw bonfires of leftist and degenerate books relit across the continent, two decades after Hirschfeld's archives had been destroyed in the pyres and barely a decade after the Battle of Berlin. Nonetheless, the two men had plenty to do: shopping for expensive cigars, paying European officials for dirt on American staff, and, as McCarthy would have wanted, holding press conferences.[60]

In the end, Cohn proved McCarthy's downfall. His attachment to Schine – possibly not platonic, although also possibly not reciprocated – led Cohn to attempt to secure him favourable treatment when he was drafted into the army as a private. When the corruption was discovered, there was a series of hearings into the affair in 1954. In reality, it was a proxy war for a bigger issue: McCarthy had been intending to purge the army, while McCarthy's enemies, from Eisenhower down, wanted to put an end to his reckless publicity shenanigans. The entire proceedings were broadcast live, bringing in over 20 million viewers.[61] McCarthy attempted his old tricks, including suggestions the US Army had been subverted by Communists, but ultimately his showboating had run its course. Although he was acquitted by the hearings, he was censured later that same year by the Senate, spelling an effective end to both his public support and his political career as an influential player.

Cohn, meanwhile, had ostracised most of his support in Washington, and returned to New York, where he returned to practise as a private attorney. He spent the next three decades in the city, living a strange, closeted life of wealth, power, and abuse in which he was, to some extent, the victim of the homophobia he helped stoke in the 1950s.

His record in private practice was as reprehensible as his record as a public prosecutor. His list of clients and friends represents a 'Who's Who' of the most exploitative, greedy, amoral, corrupt, violent, and racist shits in US history, from Donald Trump to Richard Nixon, Roger Stone, and Rupert Murdoch. However, during the whole time he was providing legal and strategic support to the American Right, he was conducting a private sex life that was anathema to their values.

Some later claimed he was straight, or perhaps bisexual, up to his mother's death, and then 'turned'. This seems unlikely, as his biographer Sidney Zion claimed that his homosexual career, like his legal one, started early, at age fifteen, while Cohn was a precocious freshman at Columbia. Also, during the Army–McCarthy hearings there were barely veiled references to him being a 'pixie': a close friend of a fairy.[62] He denied it, of course, as he did throughout his life, but he played a strange game of public and private identities, probably one that would only be viable during the interval between the birth of gay liberation and the eventual acceptance of a certain type of respectable, Mayor Pete–style homosexuality.

One could not really say he was 'closeted': anyone who was anyone in the New York gay nightlife knew he was gay. He partied at Studio 54; his townhouse and country pile were always well-stocked with young, blonde men draped over the furniture or in the pool;[63] he holidayed in his own beach house in Provincetown.[64] To not see that Roy was gay, you had to *choose* not to see it – which is what his network of conservative clients, politicians, and businessmen chose to do. Keeping his side of the bargain, Cohn simply refused to acknowledge what was clear to everyone, and went to great lengths to maintain the fiction.

In the late 1970s, Cohn refused to represent a teacher fired on account of his homosexuality, stating that 'the school system is a hundred percent right ... I believe homosexual teachers are a grave threat to our children, they have no business polluting the schools of America.'[65] Cohn additionally engaged in the most brutal tactics to avoid being outed. For example, a former lover undertook a campaign of harassment against him in the early 1980s, including publishing not one but two magazines dedicated solely to pornographic cartoons that outed Roy Cohn as an 'Attorney. Lecturer. Statesman. Fairy', as well as a size queen and bottom whose butler woke him in the morning with a ready-prepared anal douche.[66] In response, Roy went as far as to bury the hatchet with one of his lifelong enemies, district attorney of

New York County Robert Morgenthau, to ensure his former lover was silenced and jailed.[67]

He railed constantly against 'fags', refusing to identify with them – and why would he? He had spent half his career succeeding in using allegations of homosexuality as weapons to discredit and destroy his enemies. He had been instrumental in securing in the mind of the American public the idea that homosexuals were subversive, corrupt, weak, and treacherous: the *concept* of the homosexual was everything he pretended to hate.

When Tony Kushner wrote Cohn into his landmark play depicting the AIDS crisis in New York, portraying the character as 'the polestar of human evil', he nailed Cohn's attitude. 'To someone who doesn't understand this,' the play's Cohn says, 'homosexual is what I am because I sleep with men, but this is wrong. Homosexuals are not men who sleep with other men. Homosexuals are men who, in fifteen years of trying, can't get a pissant anti-discrimination bill through City Council. They are men who know nobody, and who nobody knows. Now, Henry, does that sound like me?'[68]

Like Hoover, Cohn was driven more by a thirst for power than greed for wealth. He had few actual assets, having used complex accounting mechanisms throughout his life to avoid paying taxes. He had been subject to investigation throughout his life, from the Army–McCarthy hearings on, yet always seemed to evade the law, counting on his powerful contacts and networks of people who owed him favours. Yet the net was always getting tighter, and in 1986 it was money that finally trapped him, and saw him disbarred.

Cohn had been a close friend with his fellow red-baiter Lewis Rosenstiel; it had been Rosenstiel's ex-wife who had dubiously claimed to have visited Cohn's orgies at which Hoover appeared in drag. In 1975, as Rosenstiel lay dying, Cohn had misrepresented a document to him that resulted in a semi-comatose and insensate Rosenstiel signing over Cohn as co-executor of his will. This, combined with a charge that a loan Cohn had received for a divorce case in the 1960s was not in fact a loan, but rather a fee, led to him being stripped of the right to practice law.[69] Asked for comment, he declared 'I could care less,' but in reality, losing his status as a lawyer was a body blow, and he cried following the ruling.[70]

For the courts, the prosecutors, and the myriad enemies he accumulated throughout his life, it was something of a pyrrhic victory, for two years earlier, he had been diagnosed with AIDS, another victim of an epidemic that had swept through the population of homosexual men and intravenous drug users in New York. He had always denied he had it – it was, after all, seen as a 'gay plague' at the time – and when the physical manifestations of the illness became undisguisable, he claimed he had liver cancer. Many people involved in the fight against AIDS at the time were furious that, despite being a person with AIDS, his refusal to acknowledge it meant he could not lend his considerable influence to help increase funding into research to tackle the disease. Their anger only increased when it became known that Cohn, publicly refusing to be identified with the disease, had privately used his influence to jump the queue for access to the experimental treatment for the disease, AZT.[71]

Suffering from dementia, he proved a difficult and unruly patient, especially when told that, as part of the drug trials, he was required to stay celibate.[72] Although the drug trial gave him a short period of recovery, as with many of the participants, it was still only temporary; by the time he was disbarred, he had entered the hospital for the final time. At 5 a.m. on 2 August 1986, he died. His only companion by the bedside was his boyfriend, Peter Fraser, loyal to a relationship that Cohn had publicly denied right to the end.

A year after Roy's death, a group of AIDS activists began the NAMES Project AIDS Memorial Quilt, a public monument to the personal grief experienced by millions of lovers, friends, and families of people who died with AIDS. Each panel, normally produced by someone who knew the deceased, remembers that person's life. The quilt continues to grow to this day, a testament to the fact that the AIDS crisis is not over. It is an almost unbearably beautiful and painful act of remembrance, at times touching and even funny, that recalls the human cost of the AIDS crisis.

One of its founders, Cleve Jones, recalls talking to someone who arrived with a panel remembering the life of Roy Cohn. 'Did you actually know Roy Cohn?' asked Jones. 'I knew him very well,' the man responded. The panel remains part of the quilt to this day – its simple design reads 'Roy Cohn. Bully. Coward. Victim.'[73]

11

Yukio Mishima

In a crowded field, Yukio Mishima must be one the most fascinating, enigmatic, and seemingly contradictory authors of the twentieth century. For his prose – at turns delicate, powerful, and ruthlessly self-critical – he very nearly won the Nobel Prize for Literature. He was an actor, a model, a weightlifter. He was deeply concerned with questions of beauty, while also being deeply patriotic. His depictions of same-sex desire are some of the most thoughtful and sensitive of his time, while he was driven by a sense of personal will that in other hands might seem positively brutish and self-deluded.

A Japanese patriot, he was deeply influenced by European intellectual currents, while vociferously opposing the effect they were having upon Japanese society. He was a martial artist, a bisexual, a militia leader, a dramatist, a fascist. To read his work sometimes feels like you are encountering not a man, but a phenomenon of the will. But then, perhaps this is what he wished anglophones to think. Shortly before his death he told his friend Nobuko Albery, 'The Japanese will never forgive me; I embarrass them. The Westerners won't be able to understand me and as a consequence will make a fuss of me. What fun.'[1]

Many of the themes of Mishima's work – of cultural clash, a modernising Japan, of doing things *properly* – were epitomised in his family life and his childhood. On his father's side of the family, he is descended from peasants married to nobility; on his mother's, from intellectuals. His paternal great-grandfather had accrued enough wealth to send his sons to university, and through this rare honour his youngest son, Jotaro Hiraoka, had found a place in the elite, marrying Natsuko Nagai, the grand-daughter of a powerful *daimyo*, or feudal lord. Their son, Azusa Hiraoka, was a straight-laced, hard-working, and unsentimental man, a lawyer,[2] who, in 1924, married Shizue Hashi, the bookish and sensitive descendant of Confucian scholars, whose father was a school principal.[3]

In 1925, they had their first child, Kimitake, who adopted the pen name Yukio Mishima as a teenager, which for clarity we will use for him throughout the chapter. The Hiraoka home was deeply unhappy: His mother, Shizue, was pulled between two terrible forces. Her husband was cold and unaffectionate, ignoring her when he returned from work late at night. But more terrible still was her mother-in-law, Natsuko. Natsuko had moved into the Hiraoka family home and dominated life there, her attitude toward Shizue switching between affection and total disregard, seemingly on a whim.

Natsuko's moods were inflamed by the debilitating illnesses she suffered from: gout, cranial neuralgia (a painful neurological condition affecting the head), and, according to Mishima's biographer Takeo Okuno, syphilis contracted by her unfaithful, womanizing husband, Jotaro.[4] Mishima would later describe her death, in his autobiographical novel *Confessions of a Mask*, as 'a memento of vices in which my grandfather had indulged in his prime'.[5] For the twenty-year-old girl raised in a quiet scholarly home, it must have been terribly alienating.

Worse was to come when, on the forty-ninth day of his life, Natsuko took the boy from Shizue and kept him for the next twelve years in her dark sickroom on the ground floor. He was raised surrounded by her sicknesses, her jealousy, her neuroses, and her fervent belief in the child's nobility. Mishima's younger siblings were spared this claustrophobic, nightmarish childhood, but he had to endure. In his early years, while still feeding the boy, Shizue was woken by an alarm every four hours. 'Mother would stand over me while Kimitake nursed, timing him on a pocket watch she always carried,' Shizue remembered. 'When the time was up she would snatch him away and take him back downstairs to her room. I would lie in bed wishing I could hold Kimitake and feed him to his heart's content.'[6]

Natsuko became terrified that her grandson might suffer an awful calamity, and as a result he was forced to stay with her, or her maid, constantly. He slept by his grandmother's bed, accompanied her to the toilet, and even changed the dressing on her sores.[7] He was rarely allowed to leave the house, and only in good weather, wrapped up in a coat and facemask. Inside the house, he was to play only with 'girls' games such as dolls, and quietly, to avoid the sensitivity to noise caused by his grandmother's sciatica.[8] The only relief he got from this cloistered, dark existence was in accompanying Natsuko to see Noh and Kabuki theatre.

In such a loaded and portentous childhood, certain experiences struck Mishima for their symbolic and erotic power. *Confessions of a Mask*, his second novel, details many of them. He describes the profound impact of seeing the magician and actor Tenkatsu Shokyokusai on stage, dressed in cheap costume jewellery and gaudy clothing, 'her opulent body veiled in garments like those of the Great Harlot of the Apocalypse'.[9] Enraptured by her performance, he later breaks into his mother's kimonos, and dresses himself up as Madame Tenkatsu, powdering his face, before running into his grandmother's sitting room, where Natsuko and Shizue are taking guests. 'I'm Tenkatsu! I'm Tenkatsu!' he cries, thrilled at his own performance, until he catches his mother's eye, and she lowers her gaze from him.

A maid drags him from the room and strips him of his women's clothes. 'What was it I understood at that moment, or was on the verge of understanding? Did the motif of later years – that of "remorse as a prelude to sin" – show here the first hint of its beginning? Or was the moment teaching me how grotesque my isolation would appear to the eyes of love, and at the same time was I learning, from the reverse side of the lesson, my own incapacity for accepting love?'[10] The anecdote is surely recognisable to all of us who, as a joyful child, unknowingly overstepped the barriers of gender presentation, and were greeted without mercy by the regime that enforces them with its most potent weapon, shame.

As he grew, Mishima experienced other such powerful moments of clarity and recognition about himself and his society, although these he learned to keep to himself, a habit of rigid emotional self-discipline he would practise throughout his life, releasing the experiences as tightly crafted sentences in his later art. He began to become obsessed with the death of men, particularly a violent death, such as a knight devoured by a dragon. He recalled the sense of disgust and betrayal in discovering that a knight in his picture book, a beautiful knight to whom he felt inextricably drawn, was not a young man but rather Joan of Arc: 'If this beautiful knight was a woman and not a man, what was there left? ... This was the first "revenge by reality" that I had met in life, and it seemed a cruel one, particularly upon the sweet fantasies I had cherished concerning *his* death.'[11]

But perhaps his most captivating memory was when a troop of soldiers marched past his garden. He watched with a maid, hopeful they might give him a few used cartridges – contraband forbidden by his grandmother. The cartridges, he would realise later, were a meagre excuse for what he really craved – the odour of their sweat, 'that odor like a sea breeze, like the air, burned to gold, above the seashore'. The smell of the sweaty young men induced in him a lifelong craving 'for such things as the destiny of soldiers, the tragic nature of their calling, the distant countries they would see, the ways they would die'.[12]

It sometimes seems that Mishima's life, and fate, was determined by this brutal, suffocating childhood. For the rest of his life he would be driven by a complicated mix of desire for men and desire for death. Some of his biographers posit that his childhood with his grandmother, obsessed with the traditions and status of the past, pushed Mishima into a world of the past while all around him his peers were embracing, more or less enthusiastically, a changing world. While they were embracing Marxism, and pushing their work towards socially committed themes, his work seemed to revel in the densely poetic, baroque language of metaphor and sensation. His work may have been groundbreaking and daring in his depictions of same-sex desire, of his urge for death, but they were located within a long tradition of confessional literature in Japan, from the courtly diaries of the past twelve hundred years.[13]

Perhaps his closest literary companion, in that sense, was the French writer Jean Genet, who used powerful poetics to raise the most degraded and abject of society – the thief, the queer, the bum – into a position of honour that did not rely upon the acceptance of a society, which was the force of degradation itself. In many ways, the themes on which their literature revolved *remain* taboo *because* of their refusal, in contrast to their social-ist realist colleagues, to simply replicate the old orders of dignity and honour, but this time with the poor and the workers on top.

According to Genet's biographer, Edmund White, Genet turns the main character of his 1948 novel *Funeral Rites*, a traitor and collaborator, into someone to love partly *because* of his dissolute social status, and 'partly because anyone who betrayed France would always be [Genet's]friend'.[14] In Genet, this willingness to affirm and reimagine the dignity of the abject of society as not merely equal to, but superior to, their oppressors, would lead him into a radical anti-imperialism. For Mishima, however, his belief would drive him to an ever more intense belief in rigorous self-transformation in the service of empire.

For someone so fascinated by Japanese history, it's tempting to wonder how far Mishima understood his homosexuality within the legacy of same-sex desire in the country. Japan certainly has a long history of various social forms of same-sex desire and love; the influence of Chinese culture and literature, and particu-larly stories such as the story of the 'shared peach', and later the 'passion of the cut sleeve', both of which feature love between men, helped legitimise homosexuality within Japanese culture in the era of the Tokugawa shogunate, from the seventeenth to the mid-nineteenth century.[15] These stories were among the anthropological and ethnographic references that the Weimar-era Bad Gays relied upon to justify their own sexualities and identities.

However, there are references to same-sex male love reaching much further back, to the eleventh century, in works such as *The Tale of Genji*, and in visual forms throughout the Middle

Ages and early modern period in erotic artworks known as *shunga*. Models for male same-sex relationships, known as *nanshoku*, took a number of forms, but the norm was usually pederastic and pedagogical, as in classical Greece and Rome.[16] Indeed, the last de facto emperor, Go-Shirakawa, whose effective downfall saw the emergence of the shoguns as the real rulers of Japan, was said to be heartbroken upon the execution of his young male lover who took part in the Heiji rebellion against him. Meanwhile, one of the leaders of the rebellion, Minamoto no Yoritomo, who went on to establish the first shogunate and the domination of the samurai noble warrior caste in his victory, also had a male lover, an officer named Yoshinao.[17] In the centuries that followed, the role of the older male warrior inducting the younger warrior into the martial culture would often involve the opportunity for a sexual bond as well. The older partner was expected to be the penetrative party, and his young charge the receptive partner: to take another role was seen as shameful.

Homosexuality was also closely associated with both Noh and Kabuki theatre. Originally Kabuki was a form of dance drama performed by women, who played both male and female roles. Emerging at the start of the Tokugawa shogunate, it was a hugely popular art form in Japan's burgeoning cities, swelling with a new bourgeois class of traders as well as members of the samurai class arriving from the countryside with the new-found peace.[18] Early Kabuki quickly became associated with prostitution, with the actresses being made available for sex after shows, to the extent that in 1629, less than thirty years after the first Kabuki performance, women were banned from Kabuki.

Instead, teenage boys began to take the roles; this had little effect on solving the problem, however, as where previously men had become obsessed with the actresses, they simply switched their desires to the young men, who were just as available for paid sex. When boys' Kabuki was banned twenty years later, only 'adult' men (over the age of fifteen) could perform, but unsurprisingly, the concept of Kabuki as exciting and erotic had already been fixed.[19] Often *onnagata*, men who played exclusively female roles, carried that 'performance' into everyday life, and became highly desirable for both male and female lovers.

As a result of this increasing urbanisation, changing trends in Kabuki, and the desire of the nascent middle class to emulate the noble 'brotherhood bonds' of samurai-class homosexual relationships, male prostitution boomed in eighteenth-century Japan. Unlike in early modern Europe, there were few religious strictures in Japanese Buddhism that suppressed homosexuality per se, while Shintoism, a Japanese polytheistic religion, was more concerned with fostering a religious nationalism than moral surveillance. This meant that the suppression of homosexuality in much of Protestant and Catholic Europe at that time had no complementary force in Japanese society, not least because, starting at the beginning of the seventeenth century, Japan's shoguns implemented Sakoku, an absolutist isolationist foreign policy which prohibited virtually all trade with outside nations, especially European ones, forbade most travel to and from the country, and limited severely the cultural reach of external cultures into Japan.

This period lasted almost 250 years, until in 1853 the US sailed a fleet of gunships into Edo harbour and demanded the country open up its trade routes. The following year the shogun signed a treaty establishing diplomatic relations with the US. These unequal treaties sounded the death knell for the shogunate system that had ruled Japan since the twelfth century. Feeling humiliated by the American success and ensuing treaties, many of the samurai class began to rally around the figure of the emperor, a largely tokenistic, symbolic position that had been politically impotent during the rule of the shoguns. A nationalist cultural and political movement emerged called Sonnō jōi, meaning 'Revere the emperor and expel the barbarians'. In 1867 the Emperor Kōmei died, and his teenage son ascended to the throne as Emperor Meiji. Realising his attempts at reform were futile, the shogun Tokugawa Yoshinobu handed his actual authority back to the emperor. The period of the emperors as puppets, with the shogun as actual dictators, was drawing to a close; after a short period of conflict in which the emperor's rule was consolidated, Japan entered an entirely new political, social, and cultural period, named after a now supreme emperor: the Meiji era. The Empire of Japan had dawned.

During the Meiji Restoration, social and cultural attitudes changed quickly. 'Meiji' itself means 'enlightened rule': the new government started to implement drastic reforms across society, aiming to combine some forms of traditional values with technological innovation, industrialization, and military and market reforms. The government looked increasingly to Europe and the United States for inspiration. The feudal system was abolished, with the old *daimyo* system of feudal magnates and landowners being swept away and private property introduced through a market-based system. Also introduced were a new system of nobility based on the European model and a parliamentary constitutional monarchy based on a new constitution.

As in Germany and Italy, the government viewed a single, standardized language as vital for nation-building, and it reformed education, with a new system of public schools. Japan experienced an industrial revolution, with railways, modern communication systems, and new manufacturing industries taking root. Inevitably, with this changing socioeconomic system and this forcible reorientation towards the West, attitudes towards sexuality also shifted.

While the concept of *nanshoku*, the culture of male love, still held sway within the military and education, it was in the process of being suppressed. In 1873 Japan introduced its first anti-sodomy law as part of the penal code, forbidding *keikan*, or anal sex, directly influenced by Paragraph 175 of the Prussian penal code.[20] The statute remained on the books for just a decade, before the influence of French legal systems led to it being rescinded.

With the general upsurge in interest in scientific and industrial developments from Europe also came, more specifically, a rise in sexology. Increasingly, the Japanese understood homosexuality not within the context of the country's rich erotic and cultural background, but within a medical and legal framework that saw it as an aberration or perversion. Research from European sociologists like Krafft-Ebing and Ulrichs began to influence some Japanese sexologists' thinking; for the first time, the idea of homosexuality being a form of gender inversion began to permeate thought on the subject, where previously homosexuality related much more closely to discourses on age, relating to the bonds between older and younger male lovers.[21]

By the time Mishima was a young man, homosexuality had not been eradicated from Japanese society, but it was marginalised and suppressed to a level of social ostracization similar to that in Europe. Mishima was at high school during the Second World War when he began to recognise within himself strong homosexual desires towards certain friends, desires that were intrinsically tied up with sadomasochistic drives. These are discussed in *Confessions of a Mask*, which also demonstrates his familiarity not just with European sexologists such as Magnus Hirschfeld, writers such as Marcel Proust, and theories of inversion, but also with the premodern depictions of homosexual desire within Renaissance culture in Europe.[22]

It was also while at school that his precocious talent as a writer began to manifest. School had never been easy for Mishima; his grandmother's behaviour had left him overcoddled, and he was regarded as the 'class runt',[23] yet at the same time hardened, having witnessed her increasingly traumatic behaviour, including holding a knife to her own throat and threatening suicide.[24] However, when he became a teenager, his grandmother allowed him to move back with his immediate family, as she was becoming increasingly sick. Nevertheless, the new family home was also an unhappy place; while he bonded with his mother, his father was still cruel to Mishima and tried to suppress the boy's love of literature, which he regarded as girlish.[25] In 1939 Mishima's grandmother died, but she left with him not just a legacy of an intense and probably traumatic childhood, but a deep interest in and love for traditional Japanese culture, including Noh and Kabuki.

While at high school his literary side flourished, despite his father's best efforts. His writing, like his personality, was supremely self-assured, and at just sixteen he was invited by the literary critic Fumio Shimizu to contribute a serialised story to the prestigious literary magazine he co-edited, *Bungei Bunka* (Art and Culture). The story, 'Forest in Full Flower', is a confident piece that addresses many of the issues of Mishima's later work. The young narrator is impelled by the sense that he has inherited from his ancestors the quest for beauty; told through stories from the narrator's ancestors, the work uses highly lyrical forms to address his longing for destiny, and, most specifically, the urge for death. Describing in one story a young woman who has escaped a cold lover only to find herself caught by the terror of the sea, he writes of her confrontation with the waves, 'She was enfolded in the mysterious ecstasy of the moment just before the murderer strikes, when we are conscious that we are about to be murdered ... It was a beautifully isolated present, a moment disconnected and pure as anything in the world.'[26]

The members of *Bugei Bunka*'s editorial board and its surrounding milieu were intoxicated with their discovery; they bestowed on him his pen name, Yukio Mishima, for he was still fearful of his father finding out he had not abandoned his literary dreams. Yet he had found his audience; the magazine continued to publish his work and he was inducted into its circle, attending events and discovering more of the literary world.

His work was particularly attractive to one board member, Zenmei Hasuda, a fervent nationalist who loved Mishima's invocation of a past Japan untroubled by the reformations and modernity that followed the Meiji Restoration.[27] Hasuda's role as mentor cemented in the teenage boy a deep reverence for a Japanese nationalism rooted in its literary history; Hasuda was the author of a study on a seventh-century prince, Otsu no Miko, in which he concluded, 'To die young, I am sure, is the culture of my country.'[28]

Mishima might soon have had the chance; in 1944 he was drafted into the Japanese military. When it was finally time for him to be called up in February 1945, he wrote a farewell note to his family, certain that his awaited death was near, imploring his brother to follow his example and ending it with a traditional salute to the emperor: 'Serve the Emperor! Tennōheika Banzai'

(Long Live His Majesty the Emperor) However, Mishima's health failed him, and he was incorrectly diagnosed first with tuberculosis, and then severe bronchitis, and released from service.

One could only imagine how conflicted a young man so committed to his own death as he was must have felt on this temporary reprieve from annihilation. He later remarked that he had would never 'attain heights of glory sufficient to justify my having escaped death in the army'.[29] Yet he also recalled that he ran from the recruitment barracks, fearful that a soldier might follow him and tell him a mistake had been made, and that he was enrolled after all.[30] In the end, he felt he had been forsaken even by death: 'I delighted in picturing the curious agonies of a person who wanted to die but had been refused by Death.'[31]

Despite being feted by this group of older nationalist writers throughout the war, he had published little; other than his work in magazines, he had privately published just one edition of 'Forest in Full Flower' in 1941, a small run due to paper shortages, and more a memento of what he assumed would be his short life than an actual commercial proposition. At the end of the war, he began writing in earnest, abandoning his career in the civil service to write novels. He was astonishingly prolific, publishing fifteen novels from 1948 to 1958, including the autobiographical *Confessions of a Mask*, about his upbringing and realisation of his sadomasochistic homosexual desires, and *Forbidden Colors*, which tells the story of an older man using his younger male lover to enact revenge upon women, which addressed many of Japan's historical tropes related to homosexuality, especially the idea of the misogynistic boy-lover. In 1956 he published *The Temple of the Golden Pavilion*, which took as its inspiration the real-life arson attack on the Kinkaku-ji, a Zen Buddhist temple in Kyoto, by a Buddhist acolyte.[32] Like many of Mishima's works, the book is a reflection on the intoxicating power of beauty, and the tendency for people to destroy the things that they feel most strongly for. He also wrote dozens of scripts for plays, as well as a number of Kabuki and Noh plays.

Japan was a completely changed country in the aftermath of the war and the atomic bombs dropped on Hiroshima and

Nagasaki. Significantly, the emperor was forced to publicly rescind the idea that he was divine, paving the way for a new constitution in which the emperor was not the head of state, but rather a 'symbol of the state'. This declaration had significant consequences for the far right in Japan, as it represented a betrayal of those who had willingly sacrificed their lives for the emperor on the basis that he was God.

The influx of foreigners into the nation, and the US-driven economic recovery, also changed Japanese society. One new development that arose from people catering to these new arrivals was the emergence of commercial gay establishments such as bars and cafés. In the early fifties, around the time he was writing *Forbidden Colors*, Mishima began to frequent gay bars, especially the 'Brunswick' in Ginza, central Tokyo. It is notable that the figure of the isolated homosexual in *Confessions of a Mask*, alone in his lonely desire and merely an observer of bodies that he desires, had shifted by the time of *Forbidden Colors*, where the relationship *between* homosexuals drives the story. Mishima developed a lively social life between the homosexual world and the literary world, a life that presumably had a few crossovers, and he made few attempts to hide his patronage of gay bars. Indeed, on a trip to the Americas and Europe his companions noted his desire to hit up gay bars in Paris, while in Brazil his guide was surprised by his 'unabashed homosexuality'.[33] Good for you, girl.

Yet he was clearly romantically interested in women, even if not sexually; according to one biographer he was considering marriage to Michiko Shōda, a literature student who went on to marry the crown prince and eventually become the empress. In the end, he married Yōko Sugiyama, with whom he had a son and a daughter; he would claim one of the reasons he married her was because she was unaware of his writing career (by the time of their marriage in 1958, he was already famous in Japan). There is a touch of irony to his claim that Yōko was 'uninterested' in his writing, as after his death she denied what is not just clear in his work, but one of its driving motivations and highest qualities: his intuitive, honest, and direct discussion of homosexual desire. Then again, it's not clear that, even if blackmailers and gossips had told her about his homosexuality, he had ever really broached the subject: 'I believe that a writer is a person never understood by his wife', he wrote, 'and that is fine with me.'[34]

Mishima's sexuality was not just homosexual but was combined with very complex feelings towards his body, a body that, at least as a younger man, both repelled and betrayed him. A close friend from the Tokyo gay bars days was Akihiro Maruyama, a cabaret singer and drag queen who later starred in the film *Black Lizard*, based on one of Mishima's plays. He remembers Mishima as a narcissist with a 'true eye for beauty', yet 'when he looked at himself with those eyes that could really perceive beauty, and he was looking at himself constantly, he was filled with disgust at what he saw'.[35] A persistent allegorical figure in Mishima's writing, and also his photography (did we mention that he was also a photographer, an actor, a model, and a film director?), was the figure of St Sebastian, an early Christian martyr who for centuries has been a model for homosexual artists and writers.

St Sebastian was a Roman soldier martyred by being beaten to death, but only after having survived an attempted execution by being shot full of arrows; some suggest his role as a homosexual icon relates to his having symbolically survived repeated penetration, but what is clear is that his figure, usually represented by a beautiful young man bound to a tree, his flesh penetrated although rarely bleeding, has fascinated queer artists from Il Sodoma to Derek Jarman. In *Confessions of a Mask*, he describes how his first experience of masturbation and ejaculation was over the 'tense, fragrant, youthful flesh' of St Sebastian in a reproduction of Guido Reni's 1625 painting of the saint.[36] It is not just the supple, smooth skin of the young saint that turned Mishima on, but the eroticisation of violence, and particularly *by the victim*. Mishima would, towards the end of his life, depict himself in exactly the position of Reni's paintings for a series of self-portraits as St Sebastian.

This complex relationship with the body, the elevation of pain and brutality into a higher form of erotic experience, is extremely difficult for those who are not themselves masochists to understand; in fact, if one *were* curious to comprehend, it's in Mishima's lifetime of work that they could find some of the most thoughtful, tender, painful, and erotic portrayals of the masochistic impulse. In his 1959 book *Kyoko's House*, Mishima touches upon the potent combination of drives and forces that marked the final stage of his life. It uses four characters to depict different aspects of Mishima's own personality: a businessman, an actor, a boxer, and a painter. The boxer, his identity diminished by an injury that leaves him unable to fight, finds new solace in a new body, taking up weightlifting, and a new ideology, drifting into far-right extremism, finding that the slogans and visions of a Japan reborn along old values 'are closer to anything than death'.[37] Eventually, the boxer signs a blood oath to his beliefs and, with his lover, commits suicide. In a disturbing prelude scene, in which his lover has cut him with a razor, Mishima writes:

> Here the drama of existence materialized for the first time, blood and pain utterly guaranteed his existence, and with his existence at its centre an entire panorama unfolded ... For his beautiful body truly to exist it was not enough that it be merely enrounded by a wall of muscle. What had been lacking, in a word, was blood.[38]

The potency of his prose surely emerges from the fact that these are Mishima's words ventriloquized. Since the mid-1950s, and following a failed attempt at learning boxing, Mishima had been subjecting himself to an intense and highly disciplined weight training regime, revolutionizing his own weedy body in an exercise of self-control and self-transformation. To call this obsession with physical transformation 'narcissism' might be accurate, but it is not the whole truth, or barely even part of it, nor is it entirely correct to see it as an attempt to improve his physical health, something that had hampered him since his homebound childhood. Those things are mixed up in it, but there remains a different motive at the core of his drive.

His weightlifting companion Kubo recalled that when Mishima was asked in the early 1960s to be photographed posing topless to illustrate a new encyclopaedia entry on 'body-build', it was one of the crowning achievements of his life.[39] Astonishingly, however, Mishima always skipped legs day: he never built any mass on his legs, and he would later insist that all his weightlifting photos were taken from the waist up only. But in *Kyoko's House*, and later in *Sun and Steel*, an autobiographical essay on his martial arts and weightlifting practice, it is clear that the discipline is, quite literally, about the body as his own creation. He *makes* his own body, something otherwise weak and vulnerable, through the process of will. The mind can enact change upon the body, and to ignore the body, something poets and intellectuals have a habit of doing, is to ignore the full potential of the mind as well. In his writing on weightlifting, he returned to similar themes he tackled in his writing on sadomasochism – always finding proof of his existence through sensation.

Yet muscles were not enough: death was the real proof of existence. In *Sun and Steel* Mishima described his thoughts on this using the example of an apple. The apple was not created by words, so though words might capture the fact that a core lies at the heart of the apple, one must see the core to believe it really exists. The existence of the core, of the nature of the apple itself, can only be determined once a knife cleaves it. Mishima knew that his own muscles, the flesh of his apple, could be seen in the mirror, but felt that real proof of his existence only comes about in it being extinguished. 'That, precisely, is when the knife of the foe must come cutting into the flesh of the apple – or rather, my own flesh. Blood flows, existence is destroyed, and the shattered senses give existence as a whole its first endorsement, closing the logical gap between seeing and existing. And this is death.'[40]

It is not hard to see that the trajectory of self-sacrifice that had begun in Mishima's childhood was developing both a deeper intellectual justification and a more insistent drive towards extinction. This too was accompanied by an entrenchment of the political ideologies that he had inherited from the Japanese romantics and nationalists with whom he had surrounded himself as a teenager. Many of those writers had been Marxists who had renounced their Marxism for the rising power of Japanese fascism and romantic nationalism. Their devotion towards the divinity of the emperor provided a made-to-measure hook on which Mishima could hang his death wish, giving it a valorizing ideological and moral framework. As the pain of death honours and endorses existence, so too does it endorse the cause for which one dies.

After the war Mishima was not hugely politically involved, although he oriented himself against both the materialism of the Left and the dry, worthy literature of socialist realism that seemed to run contrary to his own literary imagination soaked in myth, metaphor, and historical drama. But in the 1960s, he became increasingly active and wrote more political essays. While his own writing was soaked in the influences of European literary culture, he became increasingly vocal about foreign influences on Japanese culture as a whole. His passion for militarism and *bushido*, a set of codes defining the way of the Samurai warriors, put him at odds with leftists as well. Article 9 of the 1947 constitution of Japan had prohibited both an army for the Japanese and their right to declare war, stating that 'Japanese people forever renounce war as a sovereign right of the nation and the threat or use of force as means of settling international disputes'. For the Japanese far right, this was an unforgivable hobbling of the national spirit, a humiliating emasculation of Japan's honour as a nation. This imposition by the Americans, however, soon looked untenable and expensive, and in the 1950s, under the conceit that Japan was entitled to self-defence, the government built a de facto army called the Japan Self-Defence Forces.

In 1967 Mishima, under his birth name, joined the Self-Defence Forces, taking part in a short basic training course. After the training, he grew concerned about the rise of the Japanese New Left, particularly in the education system, and advocated the creation of a new National Guard for Japan, a civilian force that could help suppress the communist insurrection or revolution he feared. When this campaign was unsuccessful, he instead began to recruit right-wing students to form a new far-right militia. He called this group the Tatenokai, or the 'Shield Society'.

Mishima succeeded in recruiting a force of about fifty new cadets each year, after personally interviewing them. The cadets trained alongside the Self-Defence Forces, but were also expected to attend political lectures, where there was debate (a single political ideology was not enforced) and drills.[41] The basic creed of the organisation was the defence of the honour and divine nature of the emperor, and the belief that the emperor was the 'source and guarantor' of Japanese culture, the thing that made Japan unique.

While he was forming and leading the Tatenokai, Mishima was also working on his most ambitious literary project to date, *The Sea of Fertility*, an ambitious tetralogy of novels that attempted to synthesize his wider thoughts on life, Japanese culture, and the nature of belief through a series of characters as reincarnations. His strengthening belief in nationalism was manifesting in his interest in ultranationalist groups who, in the first half of the twentieth century, had engaged in sometimes spectacular violence in defence of the same beliefs in the emperor's divinity and Japanese tradition, such as the 'League of Blood' campaign to assassinate liberal and pro-Western politicians and businessmen in 1932, or the 'February 26 Incident', an attempted coup d'état by young army officers who were aiming to repeat something akin to the Meiji Restoration, hoping to hand more power to the emperor and purge the government of what they felt were treacherous advisers. In late 1970, Mishima drafted a manifesto which echoed many of these aims, attempting to deliver the Japanese Self-Defence Forces from their limited role under the Constitution and restore them to their rightful role as inheritors of the samurai traditions. The manifesto ended with a call to action:

We will restore Japan to her true form, and in the restoration, die. Will you abide a world in which the spirit is dead and there is only a reverence for life? In a few minutes we will show you where to find a greater value. It is not liberalism or democracy. It is Japan. The land of the history and the tradition we love, Japan.

Are none of you willing to die by hurling yourself against the constitution that has torn the bones and heart from that which we love? If you are there, let us stand and die together. We know your souls are pure; it is our fierce desire that you revive as true men, as true samurai, that has driven us to this action.[42]

Mishima's final act, his final endorsement of existence, was underway. For a year he had been planning, with a small cadre of young officers from the Tatenokai, a spectacular demonstration of his moral and political beliefs, and the denouement of his lifelong drive towards physical self-obliteration. At the end of November 1970, he arranged to meet General Masuda, the commandant at the Ichigaya Barracks, a former military academy for the Imperial Japanese Army. The location for his final showdown was highly symbolic: the building in which he would meet the commandant had housed the courtroom of the International Military Tribunal for the Far East, the post-war trial that had tried Japan's leaders for war crimes.

On the night of 24 November he made his final preparations, writing to a Tatenokai cadet to disband the organisation, and to another officer that he be buried in his uniform with his sword in hand, saying, 'I want evidence I died not as a literary man but as a warrior.' In a letter to his father, he asked that his posthumous Buddhist name include the character *bu*, meaning 'sword', and not *bun*, meaning 'pen'.[43]

The following morning, he dressed in his Tatenokai uniform, took his prized samurai sword, and, with four young cadets, drove to the military base. Inside the general's office, conversation was cordial, and the commandant complimented them on their dress and demeanour. Then, acting on a pre-arranged signal, one of his accomplices, Chibi-Yoga, gagged and bound the commandant while Mishima and the others barricaded themselves into the office. Mishima's demands were simple: he wanted the entire Eastern Division of the Self-Defence Forces to be assembled outside the office at midday, and he would deliver a speech. Any interference, or hiccups, and the commandant would be killed. Mishima's stage-management was impeccable, as you might expect from an artist with his eye for aesthetic detail; he had provided journalists whom he had invited in advance with an envelope containing publicity shots for the attempted coup, a copy of the manifesto, and a letter detailing his itinerary for the day, including his requests for how to handle the written and photographic material.

By noon, eight hundred soldiers had been assembled before the building, and Mishima left the office for the balcony overlooking the troops. Another cadet, his friend Masakatsu Morita, hung from the balcony a banner proclaiming the group's demands. Mishima began his speech to the men; for seven minutes he called for the men to assert themselves, to rise up, for the restoration of the emperor's status as a living god, and a change in the constitution to allow for the return of the full strength and honour of the armed forces. Photographs taken by the invited press are astonishing and striking: with a white band tied around his head, and dressed in his impeccably smart uniform with white gloves, Mishima stands astride the roof, his hands seemingly making a series of sharp, demonstrative movements.

Yet the audience is the one part of the artwork that the writer cannot control; it was always unlikely that they would have joined this attempted coup, and it was clear that for Mishima, there was no expectation that it would 'work'; it was the symbolism of the action, and not its efficacy, that was the point. But it seems unlikely he would have expected them to jeer him. Worse still, the three police helicopters that circled overhead seemed to drown him out, and his voice could not beat the noise. Despite wishing to speak for an hour, he rushed through to his conclusion. Then, he and Morita called out three times their final salute, 'Tennōheika Banzai!'

As the men stepped in from the balcony to the commandant's office, Mishima said, 'I don't think they even heard me.'[44] Then, as planned, he quietly removed his jacket and sat on the floor. He took a short sword and thrust it into his stomach, before drawing it across his body in an act of *seppuku*, a ritual suicide first practised by the samurai as a way to restore honour to one's family. Behind him, Morita had been assigned the role of *kaishakunin*, the one who would decapitate Mishima in a coup de grâce, but after two attempts he had failed to remove Mishima's head. Another cadet, Hiroyasu Koga, stepped in and with a single blow sliced his head from his body.

It was as though the narrative of his life had reached a conclusion that he had written in his first chapter. After his funeral, his mother remarked, 'This was the first time in his life Kimitake did something he always wanted to do. Be happy for him.' He was cremated with his sword, uniform and gloves, as he desired; only at the last moment did his wife, Yōko, place a pen and manuscript paper into his coffin with him.[45]

12

Philip Johnson

Between 1947 and 1949, the architect Philip Johnson built himself a house on Ponus Ridge Road in tony, conservative New Canaan, Connecticut. The house was reduced to its simplest possible state: four walls of clear glass, a brick floor set just ten inches above the ground, with one brick cylinder, containing a bathroom, rising to gently puncture the flat metal roof. A stage set for a life set free of conventional walls. The gesture seemed extraordinarily radical.

The traditional house – a home for a traditionally conceived bourgeois family, in which a strong patriarch brought home a family wage to a mother who controlled the territory of the home and children who knew their place – was conceived of as a domain of zones carefully graded from semi-public to private life. After the front door, perhaps with a large bay window onto the street, you found a living room and dining room for formal entertaining. Further back, facing the rear, a kitchen and perhaps a family room for casual home life. And finally, up a flight of stairs, as if to signal to outsiders, *No further*, the bedrooms, in which the mysteries of sex and sleep, newly linked by the vulgar Freudianism possessing American culture, were lived out in discreet privacy behind curtains and shutters.

In the Glass House, a homosexual architect flipped the script. As the essayist Mark Joseph Stern has written, the Glass House 'represented ... a parodic paradox of closeted homosexual life in the mid-twentieth century'.[1] The living space and sleeping space were melded into one, a raised eyebrow or hand placed on a new friend's knee at cocktail hour could transform into a bedroom romp without even needing to pass through a door. What went on inside – the homosexual buttercream in the social gâteau of the mid-century elite, with strapping young men joining for a cocktail party and discreetly retiring to a bedroom with the host after several drinks and the departure of some of the guests – had usually taken place on the upper floors of country houses or in penthouse apartments higher than the windows of prying neighbours. Here these events were staged with no interior walls, only exterior walls of plate glass, in the middle of a conservative suburb in the heart of a homophobic society, just as the twinned Red and Lavender scares began purging homosexuals and suspected homosexuals from public and civic life.[2] As a final gesture combining the subversion and the architectural expression of the closet, Stern points out, the Guest House, located some distance across the lawn, was entirely made of brick, an inversion of the playful exhibitionism of the main house.

Eve Kosofsky Sedgwick, the fairy godmother of queer theory, named the closet and its attendant epistemology an 'endemic crisis' of male identification. Without a deep understanding of this, any comprehension of modern Western culture was 'not merely incomplete, but damaged in its central substance'.[3] This did not, she emphasized, mean that the binary between homosexual and heterosexual should be assumed to explain everything. Rather, her deceptively simple sentence reads, 'People are different from one another.'[4] Within classes, races, and sexualities there exist multitudes of difference; and the ways in which that difference accumulates, and the relative importance people so grouped give to those kinds of difference, and how outsiders understand those differences as we create narratives about them makes all the difference in how we understand our present and past.

On the one hand, we could end this chapter before it even began and merely understand the Glass House as the architectural enfleshment of the paradox of the closet. Or we could go further, and think about the structural realities, material and racial, needed to hide this Glass House in plain sight on Ponus Ridge Road. If the Glass House was queer space, it was also a wealthy, even aristocratic space. If the Glass House was a glass closet, it was also a 'closet of power', to quote the AIDS activist Michelangelo Signorile.[5] Any untoward or unseeable behaviour between the men that Johnson always referred to as his 'companions' could take place behind the blank walls of the Guest House.

If the Glass House is remembered today as an icon of modernism, in its time it was more a popular success than a critical one, at least at first. The house bears a somewhat striking resemblance to a country house outside Chicago started two years earlier for the progressive and unmarried Dr Edith Farnsworth. This, too, has walls of glass framed in simple steel beams: but in comparison with Johnson's, its corner detailing is more finely resolved and architectural critics praised its simplicity and execution. The architect of this house was Ludwig Mies van der Rohe, then the elderly statesman of international modernism. Mies, as he was known, had cut his teeth working in Europe on the Weissenhof Estate, a modernist social housing project built for the Deutscher Werkbund exhibition in Stuttgart in 1927, a showpiece of the new 'International Style' of architecture bringing simple, clean, modern, light-and-air-filled housing to Europe's urban proletariat.

While the Farnsworth House was a luxury villa for an upper-class client, the news hullabaloo around its design and construction (one which led crowds to storm the villa en masse to see this new provocation for themselves and which led to Farnsworth's suing Mies) included an accusation in the pages of the magazine *House Beautiful*, and supported by the American modernist architect Frank Lloyd Wright, that it was a 'communist-inspired effort' to destroy vernacular American architecture and the American way of life. With this style of architecture, the magazine wrote, Americans would 'set ourselves up for total and authoritarian control', for a replica of European tower blocks; as an antithesis, the magazine promoted the traditional American way of life, in 'homes where the spirit of man can grow and flower, where each can develop in his own peculiar way'.[6] Johnson meant his Glass House as a response to Mies's work, but Mies threw a fit when he first saw the house, which he considered an inferior copy.[7]

But if the conservative grandees of Hearst Publications were worried that the popularity of modernism in elite houses might destroy American capitalism, Johnson's career can be understood as an answer to that charge. Today, we are used to the spectacle of elite architects talking out of the side of their mouths about social change and green development while working with dictators and corporate leaders to help foreclose possible futures for the planet. Modernism began at the turn of the twentieth century as the idea that an entire new way of living could be designed along with a reformation of human nature, as the creation in steel and concrete and glass of the new proletarian whose age had come. By the mid-1950s, it had become an elite bauble, and today its starchitects actively express Marie Antoinette–like disdain for the migrant workers who die en masse while constructing their fantasy forms. Philip Cortelyou Johnson's career in architecture – spanning from his work as a curator at the Museum of Modern Art interpreting the new International Style of architecture and bringing it to the United States, to his postwar reinvention as the architect of choice for several generations of corporate elites – stands as a metonym for the severing of the bonds between modernist aesthetics and progressive politics. That this career was punctuated by dedicated work promoting fascism and racist eugenics at home and abroad demonstrates the extent to which work in the service of American capitalism is also work in the service of racial capitalism.

Born into immense power and privilege, Johnson used his money and connections to whitewash his past (and ongoing) embrace of Hitler in specific and far-right politics in general. As a key curator and preacher of the Modernist gospel in the United States, he was central in divorcing the style from its egalitarian political aspirations. He partnered with architects greater than himself to bring the International Style to the United States, and then helped to explode that style's popularity, ending his career with a parade of glitzy, shiny, corporate office towers perfect for the brash, 'greed is good' era of Reagan and Bush and Clinton. As a curator and mentor, he systematically ignored and suppressed Black and brown architects and designers. Over a remarkably long career – he was building more in his eighties than most people do in their fifties – he was one of America's most successful architects.

The young Philip was born on July 8, 1906, in Cleveland, Ohio, to one of those impeccably pedigreed WASP families whose many-named children helped construct the US empire in the early decades of the twentieth century. He was descended from a family that enjoyed prominence in seventeenth-century Dutch New Amsterdam, the settler colony that became New York. He and his sister Theodate were raised, as was their class's custom, mostly by multilingual governesses. Homer Hosea Johnson, his father, and the former Louisa Osborn Pope, his mother, both believed that fresh air had healing powers, and so they sent their children to sleep outside on screened porches, including in the frigid Cleveland winter months. Even after their younger brother Alfred died, at five, of an infection probably exacerbated by the freezing cold, Philip and Theodate were sent by their parents to sleep outdoors, leading both of them to develop mastoid infections that plagued both for the rest of their lives.

Perhaps not coincidentally, Philip did not remember his parents fondly, thinking of his mother as a 'cold fish' and his father as 'her distracted and seldom-accessible consort'.[8] Starting at five, the young Philip was installed in a series of elite schools: first, the Laurel School, an exclusive local kindergarten at which Philip was the sole exception to the usual girls-only rule; then the University School for Boys, where Philip's academic achievements were hindered by his hatred for athletics and manual labour, until eventually his parents removed him to the elite public schools of Shaker Heights, in a wealthy Cleveland suburb. Because the school was far from the Johnsons' home, their chauffeur drove Philip and Theodate to school every day. By Philip's early teen years, the family was spending winters in North Carolina, meaning that he and Theodate were continually switching schools. By twelve, he was having feelings about his male classmates.

When Philip was thirteen, the family was called to Paris. In the aftermath of the First World War, American munitions were strewn all over European battlefields, and his connected business-man father was named to the Liquidation Committee organized to arrange for their disposal. This was the beginning of the young Philip's solo travels and exploration of the world; he spent the summer doing his best to escape his family and explore the city. After a brief stint in a boarding school in Geneva, Philip returned to the US and completed his primary education at the exclu-sive Hackley School in the Hudson River Valley in New York. Like most elite boarding schools then and now, Hackley existed mainly to reproduce class distinctions. When Philip attended, only white Anglo-Saxon protestants from prominent families were enrolled. Perhaps unsurprisingly for a boy who had con-stantly switched schools, he connected far more with his teachers than his classmates, especially the school's English instructor, a confirmed bachelor known by all the students as 'Daddy'.⁹ All joking aside, it is not clear whether their relationship was ever sexual. Voted 'most likely to succeed' by his classmates and grad-uating near the top of his class, Philip took one of the school's pre-arranged admissions places at Harvard University and went off to Cambridge in the fall of 1923.

Some people are given teddy bears by their parents when they begin university, or a bit of spending money; many people's parents cannot afford to give them anything other than love and support, or even to send them to university at all. Philip's parents gave him a matriculation gift of stock in the aluminium firm Alcoa, which soared along with the stock market, and a specially arranged trip to Europe – after which he used some of his income from the stock to set himself up in a luxurious private apartment and buy himself an expensive sports car.

He had fun in 1920s Boston, a city experiencing a bit of a cultural renaissance. The European emigré conductor Serge Koussevitzky took over the leadership of the Boston Symphony Orchestra in 1924 and began commissioning music by modernist composers including Prokofiev, Copland, Stravinsky, Hindemith, and Ravel; Philip enjoyed these concerts, which expanded buttoned-up Boston's usually rather conservative cultural landscape. Yet the problem of liking boys seemed to come back to him over and again, and his grades dropped.

He felt torn between his sexuality and his responsibilities to his class position. A neurologist told him that his condition was common among people with an artistic temperament and sent him off to a rest cure; his father, on the other hand, told him, 'Boys don't fall in love with boys. Do something to get your mind off it. Forget about it. You'll be all right.'[10] After a brief break, he returned to Harvard but could not find his subject, trying first Greek, then philosophy. In 1928 he took another break from his studies, during which he travelled to Egypt and went through a bit of a T. E. Lawrence phase, dressing like the native Arab population and feeling almost overwhelmingly attracted to them, it seems. His first sexual experience was in a dark corner of an antiquities gallery at the Cairo Museum, with a museum guard.

After returning to the United States and fighting off another bout of depression with a stay at the Battle Creek Sanitarium, a health resort managed by Dr John Harvey Kellogg of cereal fame, who believed that cold baths and cornflakes could combat evils like masturbation and homosexuality, Johnson discovered the philosophy of Friedrich Nietzsche and the burgeoning modernist aesthetic movement. His guide to these two terrors was a bisexual man named Alfred Barr, who was only twenty-seven but already lecturing on modernist art at Wellesley College in Massachusetts, where he had begun teaching long before he finished his PhD at Harvard. At Wellesley, Barr had his students read the society and culture magazine *Vanity Fair* and the Communist weekly the *New Masses* instead of textbooks, and the students toured factories instead of art museums. Barr also founded the Harvard Society for Contemporary Art with three undergraduates, Edward Warburg, John Walker, and Lincoln Kirstein; Kirstein was bisexual and would go on to co-found the New York City Ballet, keep an infamous and gossip-laden diary, and write a wide variety of books on art, dance, and poetry.[11]

Johnson attended a lecture series Barr gave at Harvard and fell under the man's spell, eventually cornering him at the opening of a design exhibition on contemporary typography in the Bauhaus style and at a party after a student performance of *Antony and Cleopatra* at Wellesley College starring Theodate as Cleopatra.[12] Barr had just been appointed the director of a new Museum of Modern Art that was to be built in New York, founded by Abby Aldrich Rockefeller (of the Standard Oil Rockefellers) and two high-society friends.

From the beginning, then, modernist art as institutionalized in the United States was an elitist project, one pursued by the bohemian children of the patrician patrons and patronesses who had built the Beaux Arts temples of figurative art in the centre of most Eastern American cities. Johnson later claimed that Barr had offered him a job on the spot if he could educate himself quickly about contemporary architecture in Europe. Barr, on the other hand, recalled giving no firm job offer but did recall encouraging Johnson to learn German. In either case, Johnson made plans to set off for Europe and Barr gave him a plan for what to see.

'I would rather be connected with that Museum and especially with Barr than anything I could think of,' Johnson wrote his mother. 'I will have to hump myself and learn something in a hurry though.'[13] Johnson's letters to his mother were, his biographer Franz Schulze writes, full of both 'knowledge and sophistication' and also 'an infantile self-indulgence ... He was forever the dutiful Johnson boy child, reporting not only on his lessons but on his ailments.' 'She was my invention,' he would later say. 'I invented her to write my letters to.'[14]

Barr's concept for 'learning something' meant a grand tour through the European continent, with specific instructions as to what Johnson was to look at, whom he was to meet, and what ideas he should expose himself to. Johnson, in his typically grand style, sailed to Europe in August of 1929 travelling first class on the *Bremen*, a brand-new luxury ocean liner on which he had loaded a brand-new sports car purchased for the occasion of the trip. 'My final judgement of the decoration is not so favorable,' he said of the ship, which was modern, but not modern enough for him. Besides, his biographer Mark Lamster writes, 'the food was awful and there were too many Jews'.[15]

After the boat docked in Germany and he set up a home base in Heidelberg, where he toured local cathedrals and modernist housing projects on Barr's list, Philip fell in with a man named John McAndrew, whom he met in a museum in Mannheim. McAndrew was also a Harvard graduate and a Barr disciple, doing fieldwork for a dissertation in architecture. 'He hates the people I hate,' Johnson reported, and that was enough grounds for attraction to send the two off on a lovers' romp through European modernist architecture.[16] Johnson told his mother they were going to report on the new constructions for popular magazines, but no such writing ever appeared.

The men visited the Weissenhof Estate, that showpiece of modernist social housing on which architects like Ludwig Mies van der Rohe, Le Corbusier, and Walter Gropius were proposing radically new and radically egalitarian ways of living. After a brief jaunt to Geneva and London – Johnson's trunks, full of newly purchased British fashions, were heavy enough to almost cause his plane back to Germany to crash – he went to Holland with McAndrew to visit the residential complex at the Hook of Holland, also on Barr's list, designed by J. J. P Oud. Oud's brother Pieter was then mayor of Rotterdam and leader of the left-liberal Free-Thinking Democratic League, and had commissioned Oud to design radically rational and unornamented social housing that Johnson and McAndrew described as 'the Parthenon of modern Europe'.[17]

Like all gays making their way through 1920s Europe, the two eventually wound their way to Berlin, where Johnson soaked himself in architecture, art, opera, cabaret, and gay sex, all things for which Berlin remains world-renowned. He took a late-summer trip to the Bayreuth Festival where, like so many fags before him, he was captivated by the music of Wagner; seated at a dinner next to the composer's gay son Siegfried, a composer who also conducted at the festival, he reported feeling the master's hand stroking his thigh under the table.[18]

Johnson visited the Bauhaus in Dessau near Berlin, also on Barr's list, and greatly admired it. He broke with his anti-ornament orthodoxy to admire the luxurious Baroque palaces of the Prussian monarchs outside Berlin – especially admiring the pink palace at Sanssouci where Frederick the Great had relaxed with Voltaire and played his flute in between wars. In the evenings Johnson drowned these aesthetic contradictions in cocaine and champagne.

On one such evening, he met Jan Ruhtenberg, a descendent of Swedish nobility. Attracted by his connections and striking looks, Johnson dropped McAndrew like a hot potato and began to visit some of the most important modernist artists' ateliers with his new friend. This included Paul Klee, from whom he bought a drawing, alongside works by Picasso and Aristide Maillol. Ruhtenberg also took him to visit the studio of the great Wassily Kandinsky, about whom Johnson wrote dismissively to Barr, 'Kandinsky is a little fool who is completely dominated by his swell Russian Grande Dame of a wife. He has millions of his sometimes painful abstractions sitting around the house and thinks he is still the leader of a new movement. It is sometimes pathetic, sometimes amusing.'[19]

As summer turned to fall, world events began to pick up speed – on 29 October 1929, 'Black Tuesday' hit Wall Street: defying common predictions that the markets would rise forever, billions of dollars of stock were sold off as the mass speculative bubble of the 1920s burst. The seeming economic growth of the previous decade had been driven by speculation and debt, and the gains had concentrated at the very top. When the bottom fell out, banks failed, confidence collapsed, investors were wiped out, people lost their savings and millions their jobs, and the Great Depression began in the United States and Europe. Johnson himself seemed to barely notice, instead busying himself with designs for renovations at his parents' country home. 'I heard something disquieting about a new bottom or something,' he wrote his mother discussing the crash. 'I hope it isn't true.'[20]

The Museum of Modern Art opened in November of 1929, and in January of 1930 Philip returned to the United States to finish school. He received his degree that spring, seven years after starting, and began commuting to New York to work at the museum. The position he was given, at least to start, was as one of a group of young patrons. The chair of this group at the time was Nelson Rockefeller, who would later become governor of New York State. Johnson was given an office and a secretary, but no salary – he hardly needed one. Here, Johnson, Barr, and the architectural historian Henry-Russell Hitchcock, who had written a monograph on modernist architecture in 1929, began collaborating more and more, as Barr worked to convince supporters of the museum that it should exhibit architecture and design alongside painting and sculpture.

Hitchcock was also gay, and for a while he and Johnson were both pursuing another member of the Barr clique, Cary Ross. Johnson and Hitchcock began working together on a new project: the idea was to write an illustrated book about the new modern style of architecture. The two travelled to Europe together in the summer of 1930, and Philip bought yet another new sports car to drive them around Europe visiting architects and sites and planning the book project. There, he became close to Mies van der Rohe, whom he hired to design him a luxurious interior for his apartment in New York.

Upon returning, Johnson proposed to the MoMA board that the book he was working on with Hitchcock also become an exhibition. This was a major move: architecture was, at the time, not typically exhibited alongside fine art. But, inspired by the convergence of various design forms at the Bauhaus, Johnson proposed to present an exhibit on 'a marked activity in architecture' in which 'technical advances, new methods, and fresh thoughts are solving contemporary building problems'.[21] His family wealth was to finance the exhibit, and he offered to curate it himself, with no salary. With the exhibit approved, he set out curating, with an expected opening date in early 1932.

The exhibit was a major success, with visitors seeing in models and photographs works by Le Corbusier, Mies, and other pioneering European modernists. Frank Lloyd Wright was invited to participate; while his style differentiated greatly from the curatorial regime and from the other architects, his domestic fame meant he had to be included.

Most of the projects Johnson had lauded on his European travels had to do with social housing, which seemed to be the great political, social, and architectural question of the time. Mass urbanization led to the creation of enormous and profitable slums in cities across the United States and Europe, where workers lived in cramped, dark, and crowded conditions. The Depression only exacerbated this problem: indeed, as Johnson was planning his exhibit hundreds of thousands of poor Americans were living in self-built urban shanties called Hoovervilles, victims of the spiking unemployment rate and of the doctrinaire laissez-faire economic policies of then president Herbert Hoover.

In this context, one might assume that a major exhibition on the modernist architecture of Europe intending to promote that style in the United States might focus on the question of social housing, and on the potential of architectural modernism to create light-filled, clean, safe, and affordable housing for the masses. Attracted to these architects' work by its aesthetics and not its intellectual roots, Johnson took forceful action to push social housing, possibly the main concern of the founders of architectural modernism, to the sidelines of the show. He turned down an invitation to a national conference on the housing crisis and placed the essay on social housing at the very back of the exhibition catalogue.[22] The exhibition was a major success, and Johnson was named the curator of the museum's department of arts and design.

The summer after, in 1932, Johnson returned to Berlin and began his long, dedicated, and shockingly unrepentant love affair with Nazis and Nazism. He was first encouraged to go see a Nazi rally by his friend Helen Appleton Read, an art critic from a prominent Brooklyn family working for *Vogue* magazine and a private art gallery. Like Johnson, who imagined himself a kind of Übermensch, she was a devotee of Nietzschean philosophy and recommended that Johnson, at that point relatively apolitical, visit a Nazi rally held on a field in Potsdam, outside of Berlin. That July, the Nazis had won 37 percent of the vote and become the largest political party in Germany. On that windy field in October, Johnson was transfixed and transformed. 'You simply could not fail to be caught up in the excitement of it, by the marching songs, by the crescendo and climax of the whole thing, as Hitler came on at last to harangue the crowd,' he told Franz Schulze.[23]

This was, for Johnson, a sexual thrill as well as a political and aesthetic one, with 'all those blond boys in black leather' marching around. Eighty thousand young men and women showed up. Hitler railed against the Jews, echoing Johnson's existing prejudices. While there was a sexual thrill – and Johnson did, apparently, like them blonde and twinkish – his biographer Mark Lamster, who alongside the Johnson Study Group did much to uncover the depth of Johnson's ideological commitment to and material support for fascism and racism, is unconvinced by Johnson's attempt to reduce 'his attraction to the Nazis in sexual terms ... It was easier to whitewash sexual desire', Lamster writes, especially in conversations with biographers in the 1980s and 1990s, 'than the egregious social and political ideas that truly captivated him.'[24]

Johnson travelled to see the Exhibition of the Fascist Revolution, created by modern architects in Italy to commemorate the anniversary of the fascist takeover there, and wrote an approving article for a small magazine in October of 1933 attempting to reconcile his love of the Bauhaus with the school's having been closed, and its teachers scattered into imprisonment and exile by the Nazis: he suggested that the school had been 'irretrievably' damaged by the influence of communism, but hoped that some German architects and artists could unify fascism and Johnson's beloved modernist aesthetics.[25]

Throughout the 1930s, Johnson devotedly advocated for fascism at home and abroad. He wrote once that 'we seem to forget ... we live in a community of people to whom we are bound by the ties of existence, to some of whom we owe allegiance and obedience and to others of whom we owe leadership and instruction'.[26] In his modernist New York apartment, alongside social evenings designed to show, as Lamster writes, that 'the International style ... was not some socialist aesthetic for the working classes, but the new style for a discerning taste-maker of social standing', and where Theodate, who considered herself a singer, would often perform modernist music, Johnson hosted fascist gatherings and shared lists of Nazi sympathizers with German diplomats.[27] Travelling to Germany throughout the 1930s, Johnson toured Hitler Youth camps. He called the Nazis 'daylight into the ever-darkening atmosphere of contemporary America', attended Nazi rallies at Madison Square Garden, and gave financial support to an anti-Semitic street militia called the Christian Mobilizers.[28]

He aimed to create a fascist militia modelled off the Black-shirts, except their shirts would be grey. With the fascist propagandist Lawrence Dennis, he worried about the death of the white race and the threats that Jews posed to society. He plotted a political career, planning to start in the Ohio legis-lature, and then walked away when he realized he'd actually have to spend time campaigning with the unwashed masses. For Charles Coughlin, a fascist radio preacher who sermonized weekly against the dangers of Jews and Bolsheviks, he designed a custom modernist grandstand intended to bring some of the visual spectacle of European fascism to American shores. For Coughlin's fascist newspaper, *Social Justice*, he reported from Jewish Socialist prime minister Léon Blum's France, writing that 'lack of leadership and direction ... has let the one group get control who always gain power in a nation's time of weakness – the Jews'.[29]

When Coughlin's political ambitions were crushed by the defeat of the fascist Union Party in 1936 (its nominee got only 2 percent of the vote to Roosevelt's 60 percent), Johnson kept alight the flame, using his personal wealth to sponsor radio broadcasts in which he argued that Bolsheviks and bankers threatened American patriotism; he started a Young Nation-alist party composed, per Lamster, 'of hard-core reactionaries, pro-Nazi German-American Bundists, and Klansmen', whom he invited to dinners at his country home.[30] He published articles in the fascist journal *The Examiner* arguing that America was committing 'race suicide' through a degenerate lack of national values. In 1938 he took courses in Nazi ideology in schools run by Hitler's government, and helped top Nazi diplomats distribute propaganda to fascist circles in the United States. He published a favourable review of Hitler's *Mein Kampf;* writing that the book was 'an extraordinary document ... Hitler has shown himself to be one of Goethe's "doers".'[31]

When the Germans invaded Poland in September 1939, Johnson embedded himself in a group of friendly journalists and reported that 'the German green uniforms made the place look gay and happy. There were not many Jews to be seen. We saw Warsaw burn and Modlin being bombed. It was a stirring spectacle.'[32] In letters, he called the Poles 'a subhuman Slavic racial type'; the journalist William Shirer reported that Johnson was pretending to be anti-Nazi and gathering information on other American reporters.[33] He did lecture tours in the early 1940s claiming to debunk anti-Nazi propaganda in the United States. As Lamster writes, Johnson 'was the ideal vehicle for the Nazis, a man willing and able to finance their interests out of his own pocket'.[34]

Initially, none of this seemed to impede Johnson's rise in the tiny avant-gardist social circles of 1930s New York. His money and connections helped, as did his charm. Like many elite white New Yorkers, Johnson enjoyed trips to Harlem to experience Black nightlife, where he found a kind of shadow gay life. For a time, he even dated a Black man, Jimmie Daniels, whom he met through an English pimp. Daniels was a sex worker and a struggling actor and singer trying to make it in New York. For Johnson, he was, Mark Lamster writes, 'the ultimate act of transgression ... a love affair and an act of modernity at once'.[35] 'I was naughty,' Johnson reflected later in life when discussing the relationship and reflecting on why it had failed, and claimed he 'didn't realize' how it might have 'galled' Daniels to not be 'included' in Johnson's whites-only circles.[36] Johnson also briefly dated the composer John Cage (in the same year that Cage had a brief affair with Harry Hay, who would go on to co-found the gay rights movement in the United States in 1950).

As politics began to take up more and more of Johnson's life in the early 1940s, he drifted away from the Museum of Modern Art, even as it moved into tony newbuild digs on Fifty-Third Street in Manhattan. He eventually decided to enrol as a student at Harvard University's new graduate school of architecture, setting himself up in a large townhouse with a maid and slowly beginning to cover his political tracks as the public mood shifted against the Nazis. When he attempted to enlist in the US Army, he was rejected by intelligence services because of his Nazi connections. He even formed an anti-fascist committee there, for what we can all presume were entirely honest ideological commitments free from concerns about his career or professional reputation.

When in 1942 he was investigated by the FBI for possible disloyalty, his former secretary reported that Johnson had ambitions to be America's Hitler. His good friends the Rockefellers helped protect him from prosecution, and his new friends and teachers at Harvard, many of whom were Germans who had fled the Nazis, were willing to be bought off by this rich and charming colleague. After all, Philip could afford not only to hire people to do his draughting and model-making for him, but also, as his thesis project, to construct a house on a plot of land next to Harvard.

After graduating and building the Glass House as an attention-seeking way of starting his own practice, Johnson became an enthusiastic, if dilettantish, corporate architect, in addition to continuing his work running the architecture and design department at the Museum of Modern Art. A series of small buildings around the United States cemented his growing reputation, including a synagogue project that some interpreted as an apology for his Nazi collaboration. Describing himself as 'a violent philo-Semite', he refused to take a fee for the project, although, as the critic Joan Ockman points out, he did reuse an existing design for a church building project that had fallen through.[37]

In 1956 Johnson partnered with Mies van der Rohe to design the Seagram Building, an icon of mid-century Manhattan business power. He helped steer the commission to Mies van der Rohe through Phyllis Bronfman Lambert, a MoMA patron and the daughter of Samuel Bronfman, Seagram's CEO. Mies took the broad design lead, changing the fashion for office building construction – instead of walling New York's tight streets and stepping back on upper levels like the pre-war Art Deco sky-scrapers, this skyscraper and its many future imitators would be set back from the street with a wide plaza. The building was clad in glass and steel tinted a luxurious bronze.

Johnson took the lead in designing the Four Seasons restaurant, a swanky power-lunch destination made up of two enormous square dining rooms with twenty-foot ceilings, walnut panelling, marble pools, palm trees, and artworks by Picasso and Richard Lippold. Mark Rothko was initially supposed to create murals for the restaurant, intending to create something that would shock complacent diners out of their martini-fuelled swing, but decided that the space Johnson had designed was so totalizing and resistant to intervention that he withdrew his works.

In the restaurant, metal curtains shimmered in a breeze piped in through special-purpose ducts. The building's structural supports employed a similar kind of artifice: the steel I-beams designed to look as if they were holding the building up were in fact decorative stick-ons hiding the fireproofed load-bearing beams inside. Here was the apotheosis of modernism as orna-ment, as decadent and frivolous as the frippery on the walls of the Prussian palaces at Sanssouci: if Mies van der Rohe had begun his career designing social housing for the proletariat in which form followed function, now, he and Johnson had con-verted this into an applied style for the corporate elite of a new American century.

In 1960, Johnson met David Whitney, who became his life partner. 'He was an eighteen-year-old or something,' Johnson later recalled in an interview. Whitney, a student at the Rhode Island School of Design, came up to Johnson after a lecture and asked why he had purchased a flag painting by Jasper Johns. 'I said, "Because Alfred Barr told me to." I told the truth too soon, as usual. So then we got started.'[38] Johnson had been living a sexual gay life for years now, but as Charles Kaiser writes in his book *The Gay Metropolis*, gay men of his 'class and generation' could attend high-society dinner parties but were not invited to bring a boyfriend along. 'Mrs. Vincent Astor said she always had a homosexual to dinner', Kaiser recalls Johnson saying, 'because they were the only people who could talk.'[39]

Johnson and Whitney, who were primary partners from 1963 until Johnson's death but who maintained active sexual lives of their own, began building a regular gay circle at the Glass House, including artists like Johns, Robert Rauschenberg, Andy Warhol, John Cage, and his partner Merce Cunningham, whose homosexuality was also somewhat of an open secret. Nonetheless, it took years for Johnson to begin bringing Whitney around to see his other friends. It was, Charles Kaiser recalls, the television newscaster Barbara Walters who, at a dinner party in 1975, point-blank asked Johnson why he did not bring his boyfriend to any of the social events at which he was a regular. 'I said, "By God, you're right Barbara,"' Johnson later remembered. 'Got up from the table and went home. She was a very great help. I was so mean and selfish.'[40]

It was not just Barbara Walters's frankness, apparently a hallmark of her social as well as her professional style, that spurred Johnson to begin bringing Whitney around to the straighter parts of high society. By the mid-1970s, things were changing. The 1969 Stonewall Rebellion of drag queens, trans women, and street kids was less the spark of a new movement than the reflection of a growing confidence and political consciousness among some queer people. While it was received with horror by even the more conservative homophile rights groups – never mind the gay elite like Johnson, who lived in closets of power in which their homosexuality could be an open secret, trapped in their privilege like bugs in amber – the effects of this political movement rippled outwards and upwards.

By the mid-1970s, then, it was possible for Johnson to openly dine with corporate executives' wives with his boyfriend by his side. What was not acceptable was the possibility that this might become public knowledge. When critic Calvin Tomkins profiled

Johnson for the *New Yorker* in 1977, Johnson got word that the profile planned to mention Whitney as his boyfriend. He was, at that time, up for a major commission, the design of a new corporate headquarters for AT&T in Manhattan, and reacted to the possible disclosure with horror, calling up the magazine and begging them to refrain from outing him. Whitney appeared in the article as his 'friend'.[41]

Writing in the introduction to a collection of critical responses to Johnson's work, the critic Emmanuel Petit describes him as having a 'nonchalant approach ... at times tainted with brattish and posh cynicism', and as being an architect 'in search of the strong characters in architecture ... mostly to be found in the Greco-German classical tradition', created for 'the judgement of the select few ... an art for the *eyes*'.[42] Setting aside for the moment Petit's decision to minimize Johnson's political beliefs, beliefs that one might associate rather uncomfortably with an aesthetic interest in elite-oriented Greco-Germanism, this emphasis on form, classicism, and richness of material begins to explain Johnson's increasing departure, as the 1960s dawned, from the orthodoxies of the International Style.

Architects were moving on: brutalists were aiming to remake public space and design public housing, a topic Johnson found boring and pointless. Instead, he found himself beginning to experiment with ornamentation, arching, and travertine marble: a series of buildings in Texas, art galleries and private homes for the newly rich oil barons, began evincing a kind of gas-station classicism. He joined the team of architects working on the Lincoln Center for the Performing Arts, a palace of high culture intended to replace several cleared-out slum blocks on New York's Upper West Side.

This was 1960s 'urban renewal' in extremis. Black and Puerto Rican neighbourhoods, designated as slums, were to be cleared of their residents. The resulting land would be used for a temple of high art designed primarily with the car in mind. Ramps led from garages directly to the highway, allowing white patrons to return to their homes in the suburbs without setting foot on a city street. It was as anti-urban as an urban architectural project could be. The team of architects included many of the favoured designers of the mid-century corporate elite.

Johnson contributed two things to the Lincoln Center's design: first, the idea to coat all of the buildings in travertine marble; and second, the design of the New York State Theater for ballet and the City Opera, a thousand-ton bomb of marble, jewelled chandeliers, red velvet, gilding, and everything else expensive and tacky, with horrid acoustics, an Albert Speer building wearing too much jewellery and lipstick. As he participated in urban renewal's expulsion and displacement of the urban poor, his political imagination continued to run wild and far to the right. In lectures at the time, Johnson dreamed of levying national taxes to create dream cities under the control of local dictatorial philosopher-kings. In 1964, he referred, in a private letter, to Hitler as having been 'better than Roosevelt'.[43]

In 1967, Johnson founded a new architectural office, partnering with the architect John Burgee to design a series of buildings that began pushing the boundaries of modernism even further. Petit refers to this as reflecting Johnson's desire to constantly destroy the new forms he had proposed to create. Johnson, he writes, was a media-driven architect: 'The "significance" of his architecture was ultimately defined through the mechanisms of his media appearance and publicity.'[44] Johnson conceived of himself as an intuitive aesthete, for whom architecture was a medium for the promotion of beautiful objects for the elite and for showy spectacles for the masses.

Into the latter category fell his Crystal Cathedral, a vast glass palace of evangelical splendour in the right-wing reactionary hotspot of Orange County, California. Here the pioneering televangelist Robert Schuller, who had first come on the scene preaching from the snack bar at the Orange Drive-In Theater near Disneyland, stripped the dour elements from Calvinism to create a happy, middle-class megachurch. The cathedral, made entirely of glass, seated thousands of people, was outfitted for TV cameras to broadcast Schuller's nationally syndicated religious television program *Hour of Power*, and was surrounded by strip malls and parking lots. In interviews from his New Canaan modernist mansion, Johnson would decry mass culture and car-centred sprawl, but he certainly was instrumental in creating a lot of it. The building was impressive, but its elaborate cooling system often failed when temperatures soared above 26°C (80°F), a problem in southern California. Interior temperatures were sometimes measured at above 44°C (110°F), and sunglasses were needed for early morning or late evening services. When Schuller's church went bankrupt in 2010, the building was extensively modified (including with interior shades) to serve as a Roman Catholic cathedral.

As Reaganism and the 'greed is good' 1980s dawned, Johnson and Burgee began designing a series of skyscrapers that departed even more obviously from the unadorned glass-and-steel aesthetic he had done so much to champion. The AT&T tower in New York rises thirty-seven stories in fairly sober granite and glass, with its windows set back in vertical strips that recall Art Deco, before meeting the sky with an enormous, exuberant broken pediment, as though the whole building were an enormous Chippendale chair. When the design was unveiled it immediately became the symbol of a new 'postmodern' movement in architecture. The *New York Times*'s architecture critic Paul Goldberger referred to the unveiled design as 'postmodernism's major monument', a 'daring – if disconcerting' design that 'suggests a joke may be played with scale that may not be quite so funny when the building, all 660 feet of it, is complete'.[45]

This controversy led Johnson to write an op-ed in the *Times* of his own, laying out the argument for a postmodern aesthetic as seamlessly as he had laid out the argument for a modern one. Suddenly, Johnson was eager to admit that there was an alliance between modernism and progressivism, an alliance he had done so much to deny and destroy: '"Modern" ... taught us that men would live better, cheaper, more moral lives surrounded by such abstract, functional, simple shapes. Today we no longer feel this way.'[46] Appealing to a mass audience that felt threatened by modernism's challenge to traditional forms, exactly the same kind of reactionary position that *House Beautiful* took when it called Mies's Farnsworth House in Illinois a Communist plot,

Johnson suddenly included himself in a 'we' who 'want churches once more to look like churches ... houses once more to look like houses'.[47] Suddenly the 'two great periods' in New York City architecture that he wanted to respect in 'the spirit of Historic New York' were the Beaux Arts period and the Art Deco 1920s, whose architects he had once excluded from MoMA shows on the grounds that their work was too traditional.

The AT&T tower, when completed, was a hit – and was followed by a series of increasingly eye-searing corporate office parks and towers. Johnson and Burgee built skyscrapers that had Gothic points, or leaned in towards one another menacingly over a public plaza; they built skyscrapers like PPG Place in Pittsburgh (mirrored-glass-clad crenellations) and International Place in Boston (pink granite and covered, incongruously, in Palladian windows). In New York City, on Third Avenue, they built a pink granite tower shaped like a stick of lipstick, where they located their new corporate office. This building was also the headquarters of Bernie Madoff's years-long Ponzi scheme. Throughout this entire money-drenched parade of ugliness, Johnson retained his artistic credentials with the same strategy he had used to cover up his Nazism. He used his money and social connections to buy off any potential critics, and his continued association with the Museum of Modern Art, including the design of two additions and a sculpture garden and his remaining a major presence in the architecture department until the mid-1990s, meant he could always influence elite critical opinion.

This focus on *style* as opposed to any social or functional aspect of design separated him from many other modernists, and also enabled him to spin each new style to which he was attracted as a new advance. In a 1973 book of interviews with architects, Johnson told the interviewers, 'What we're talking about is the way a building finally looks ... To talk about architecture as a technical matter, or a social matter, or a participatory democracy matter, is not the point to me.'[48] He illustrated his frustration with the expectation that architects pursue social responsibility with the brilliantly chosen example of 'one of the Negro architects who was here the other day' complaining about going to too many meetings during the design process, as though he and a Black architect had anything in common with one another other than their job title.

This may have been an attempt to insulate himself against charges of open racism or lack of care for others: like Reaganite conservatives, Johnson always couched his attacks on the public sphere and on collective action as concern for the little guy overwhelmed by elite moralists. Later in the interview he laughed off architecture students' organizing against collaboration with the apartheid regime in South Africa: 'Oh, the kids. Very simple: do away with architectural schools.'[49] Hitler, Johnson said in that interview, 'was unfortunately an extremely bad architect ... The only thing I really regret about dictatorships isn't the dictatorship, because I recognize that [in Roman times] they had to have dictators. I mean, I'm not interested in politics *at all*. I don't see any sense to it.'[50] That same year, after a project in Harlem fell through, Johnson said, 'I don't care who builds a monument for blacks. Who cares?'[51] That someone so fundamentally shallow, callous, and racist was praised in his time as an intellectual is a discredit to the profession of architecture.

When Johnson's firm with Burgee went belly-up in the late 1980s, he created a new practice, Philip Johnson / Alan Ritchie Architects. It was also around this time that Johnson began actively promoting a new series of young architects, whom he called 'The Kids' – this group included Frank Gehry, Rem Koolhaas, Richard Meier, Peter Eisenman, Charles Gwathmey, and many other prominent 'deconstructionists'. In 1988 Johnson curated a show at the Museum of Modern Art featuring this generation.

Disenchanted with the redux of historical forms, these architects began to pioneer the concept of building as sculpture, with swooping forms seeming to defy gravity and traditional engineering – think of Frank Gehry's Guggenheim Museum in Bilbao, Spain, for one famous example. Johnson adeptly stepped into this new space, designing some follies for his Glass House estate, including a Gehry-like metal gatehouse he called Da Monsta. In the meantime, he maintained his corporate practice designing increasingly uninspired buildings, including an 'Urban Glass House' in Lower Manhattan that aimed to ape the famous residence but ended up looking pretty much like any other glass-and-metal condominium building, and his final building, a bland suburban performing arts centre in Pennsylvania.

Johnson's promotion of architects like Eisenman meant that they were often willing to defend him both as a designer and as a man. Eisenman, who was eventually commissioned to design the craggy, powerful Memorial to the Murdered Jews of Europe in Berlin, and Gehry, also Jewish, both maintained long associations and friendships with Johnson. When Johnson was finally convinced to allow Franz Schulze to publish his biography in 1995, and the extent of his fascist politics was revealed, it led to some uncomfortable conversations. Johnson deftly connected his fascism to his homosexuality as the two great shames of his life, excusing his fascism as though it had been an inevitable side effect of being gay, as though he were simply transfixed by all those pretty boys in leather pants. 'We forgave, but we didn't forget,' Frank Gehry said in 2005. 'He was so powerful a force for the good in our profession that it overwhelmed all negatives.'[52]

Throughout all this Johnson was a near-daily luncher at the Four Seasons restaurant he had designed; his final office with Ritchie was located upstairs, on the thirty-ninth floor. There, now in his late eighties, trying to re-start his career, he worked on some projects for a brash New York developer named Donald Trump, who wanted some casino projects in Atlantic City to get a little bit of extra class. Johnson was all too happy to oblige. He would also later reskin a 1960s skyscraper in golden glass, a project that became the Trump International Hotel and Tower.

The bookish aesthete and splashy power broker sides of Johnson came together for his ninetieth birthday party, celebrated a year after the publication of his biography, Nazi past on at least partial display and partner by his side (who even made a joke about how Johnson was still 'great in the sack'). Johnson dined at the Museum of Modern Art with a birthday cake

featuring a frosted glass house on top, and the guests, number-
ing about two hundred, wore pairs of his signature glasses.[53] The
museum honoured him by naming its design galleries after him,
and showing works that had been donated to the museum both
by him and in his honour. The *New York Times*'s new architecture critic, Herbert Muschamp, wrote paeans to the master in the
newspaper, including fawning reviews of Johnson's gatehouse,
Da Monsta; in one article, Muschamp wrote, 'No architect alive
is as thrillingly attuned as Philip Johnson to promotion's sordid
glories.'[54] It was the 1990s; time had collapsed on itself, and
history had ended. Gays were now welcome to joke about their
sex lives at receptions at the Museum of Modern Art (as long as
they were white and appropriately dressed), and Philip Johnson
was ninety and still on top of the field.

Since his death, his association with the MoMA has come
under increasing scrutiny. Lamster's biography, from which we
have been quoting extensively here, created a scandal when it
appeared in 2018. Lamster was the first to reveal publicly the
extent and depth of Johnson's fascist collaboration – not merely
the youthful fascination with strapping young soldiers Johnson
had palmed it off as to his official biographer. Lamster's research
also revealed that Johnson's commitment to reactionary and
white-supremacist politics had extended long after the Second
World War. A collective of Black architects and researchers,
the Johnson Study Group, formed and began to agitate for the
removal of plaques and job titles honouring Johnson from the
Museum of Modern Art and the Harvard Graduate School of
Design. 'Johnson's commitment to white supremacy was significant and consequential,' their letter reads; they point out that
'under his leadership, not a single work by any Black architect
or designer was included' in MoMA's collection. 'He not only
acquiesced but added to the persistent practice of racism in the
field of architecture.'[55]

While Harvard reacted only a week after the letter, eventually
removing Johnson's name from its Thesis House, which the university used as an event and program space for the design school,
the Museum of Modern Art has still not removed Johnson's name

from the galleries dedicated to his honour or from the honorary title of its curator of architecture and design. In March of 2021 the Black Reconstruction Collective, a group of architects participating in an exhibit at the museum called 'Reconstructions: Architecture and Blackness in America', temporarily covered the sign titling the Philip Johnson Galleries with a tapestry bearing its manifesto. A spokesperson for the museum told *ARTNews* that 'the Museum currently has underway a rigorous research initiative to explore in full the allegations against Johnson and gather all available information. This work is ongoing.'⁵⁶ The Johnson Study Group continues to organize to address Johnson's legacy of white supremacy and study the ways in which it affected the institutions he helped build.

Just after that splashy ninetieth birthday, Johnson had open heart surgery and disappeared from public life for a year to recover. His return in 1997 was enthusiastically covered by the *Times* and the *New Yorker*, but his public appearances and office works became ever more infrequent. He began to slowly retreat from public life, and his memory began to fail. In August of 2003, he made his last appearance in the office. 'I don't know where I am', he told an assistant, 'and I never want to come back here again.'⁵⁷

Living in his Glass House, his life increasingly restricted to the boundaries of his estate, he ate less and less. Whitney, many years younger, began spending more and more time in California after his own diagnosis with terminal lung cancer. Alone except for his staff, Philip Johnson died early in 2005 at the age of ninety-eight, on a snowy day, lying in bed in the Glass House. Describing the inspirations that produced that house, he had once suggested that the first idea, of an illuminated house glowing at night, came from 'a burnt wooden village I saw once where nothing was left but foundations and chimneys of brick'.⁵⁸ Lamster wonders if this image may have been a burning Jewish village, destroyed by the advancing Wehrmacht, and notes that Johnson used that brick fireplace at the Glass House to try to burn away the evidence, in notes and letters and articles he had written, of the death of his fascist involvements.

Ultimately Johnson died alone in his luxury glass closet, an enactment of queer space but also an enactment of the divorce of American modernism from socialist or even social democratic politics and its ascension to the pinnacle of elite style, and potentially a monument to the aestheticization of genocide. His *New York Times* obituary described him as 'at once the elder statesman and enfant terrible of American architecture', and did not mention the Nazis, fascism, racism, or politics.[59]

13

Ronnie Kray

London in the Swinging Sixties has cultivated an image for itself that still seems to beguile over half a century later: impossibly glamorous models, sexual liberation, new post-war fashions, Princess Margaret and Antony Armstrong-Jones zipping between lovers in high-end, British-made sports cars. It was the era of James Bond, England's only World Cup victory, and of course music, especially the Beatles and the Rolling Stones. The reality, of course, was very different; glamour was limited to a generation of well-off young people who had been born after the war. Normal life, as attested to in the diary of Joe Orton, a young playwright who was part of the movement to reshape British cultural life, was full of milky tea in chipped porcelain, horrible sandwiches filled with egg or prawn, blow jobs in the public lavatories outside tube stations, and damp – constant damp, whether in the bedrooms of guys he picked up, in the libraries where he spent his time, or on the top deck of winter buses.

The gap between the glamorous image of the era and the abject grimness of its everyday life is perhaps best depicted in one of the most famous images of the day. Taken by one of the most fashionable photographers of the time, David Bailey, it shows two thick-set young men, built like wardrobes, coolly staring down the cameraman. One stands behind the other, they are clearly well fed, and with their thick necks, heavy brows, and well-tailored suits they project a new working-class confidence that was seeming to shake up the era. The two are brothers, twins, and their no-nonsense masculinity and power made them icons for a generation, complete with their own mythology of absolution. Yet behind the striking image is a more abject reality of pitiless violence, bullying, and sexual abuse. The man at the front, Ronnie Kray, was a particularly brutal and violent man, yet the course of his life as a gangster, celebrity, and homosexual helps illustrate the complexities and changes within British society at the time.

The story of the Kray twins is, like most British stories, one of class, and it begins in the grinding poverty of 1930s England, still reeling from the effects of the Great Depression. They were born in 1933 in the heart of London's East End, a historically impoverished neighbourhood still suffering from appalling deprivation, despite the best efforts of both patrician Victorian reformers who had tried to improve conditions from above, and the nascent Communist Party advocating revolutionary change from below.

Poverty was accompanied, understandably, by crime, both petty and organised. The year before the boys were born, 60 percent of children in nearby Bethnal Green were malnourished, and tenements and slums, legacies from London's rapid industrialization, made up the vast majority of housing.[1] Men who could find work laboured on the docks, or in the large, foul-smelling industries that filled the area. The poverty and proximity to the Thames meant that, for hundreds of years, the East End was a recurrent site of arrival for immigrants to Britain. Huguenots, Protestant dissidents fleeing persecution in France, had settled in the district in the seventeenth century, establishing a thriving textiles trade using the skills they brought with them. From the Victorian era right up until World War II, Shadwell and Limehouse had a thriving Chinese community sustaining a lively Chinatown, while Lascars, sailors from the Indian subcontinent and Southeast Asia, also formed small communities in the area. Perhaps the most significant demographic change was the arrival of tens of thousands of Jews, starting during the Interregnum, when Oliver Cromwell lifted the ban on Jewish people living in Britain, up to its peak in the late Victorian era when pogroms in Russia and eastern Europe forced millions to leave their homes for the UK and the US. The Jewish community around Brick Lane and Hoxton sustained not just hundreds of synagogues, but also a network of Jewish restaurants, businesses, Yiddish theatres, and even a Russian Jewish Operatic Company. Many continued the busy textile trade in the area.

The Kray family were part of this busy working-class, multi-ethnic culture. Their mother, whom they idolised throughout their lives, was descended from Irish and Jewish migrants, and her father was a local character, a boxer and circus performer who had toured the country before becoming a market porter.[2] When Violet decided to marry Charles Kray when she was just seventeen, her father disowned her, but upon the birth of their first son, Charlie, his attitude towards the marriage softened. The twins were born in Stean Street, Haggerston, but by the time they were five or six she'd moved the family closer to her family in Bethnal Green. Their new home, at 178 Vallance Road,[3] was only half an hour's walk from their old home in Hoxton; it was not only seen as a step towards reconciliation with Violet's family, but also as a symbol of her pre-eminence within her new family. Nonetheless, the area would become the boy's manor, their spiritual territory, for the rest of their lives.

Charles was frequently absent for much of their childhood; working in the 'rag trade', the second-hand clothes industry, he frequently travelled for long stretches buying up goods, and then, when the Second World War began in 1939, he was a deserter.[4] Violet took on most of the responsibility of raising the children and running the home, and by all accounts regarded her sons as angels, despite Reggie later admitting that 'we were wicked little bastards really'.[5]

It is unsurprising that the lads turned to crime, given both the poverty of the area and the example they were set. Life in London, particularly in working-class and immigrant communities, was marked by the presence of organised crime gangs. They operated on various levels of sophistication, taking part in everything from pickpocketing rackets to gambling, extortion, prostitution, and blackmail. The gangs were often arranged around both ethnic identities and local loyalties, and spread across most of the capital in the 1930s and '40s. There were East End Jewish streets gangs like 'The Yiddishers', the Aldgate Mob, the Bessarabian Tigers, who often took part in street fights with fascist organisations. In Clerkenwell there was a mob led by the Italian Charles Sabini that ran lucrative protection rackets at racecourses, a territory they fought for against the McDonald brothers, who ran the Elephant and Castle Gang and who went into alliance with the Brummagems, a Birmingham gang.[6] There were the Titanics in Hoxton, the Hoxton Mob, the Kings Cross Gang, the Odessians, the West End Boys, and the Whitechapel Mob: an endless array of gangland groups that emerged, some surviving longer than others, before being amalgamated, suppressed by police, or broken up by rivals.[7]

Within working-class London in the interwar period, there was also an independent homosexual culture of sorts that was distinct from that of the guardsmen and middle-class johns of Hyde Park and St James's Park, or the various more bourgeois gay scenes of Piccadilly, the Haymarket, and Soho. It would have been a queer geography recognisable, in part, to a young Jack Saul some half century earlier. Pubs that were congregated around the docks and industrial areas often developed a distinct homosexual or queer clientele, including establishments like the Prospect of Whitby in Wapping and Charlie Brown's on West India Dock Road, both little more than half an hour's walk from the Kray's manor. According to the noted historian of queer life in interwar London Matt Houlbrook, 'Dock laborers, sailors from across the world, and families mingled freely with flamboyant local queans and slumming gentlemen in a protean milieu where queer men and casual homosexual encounters were an accepted part of everyday life.'[8]

Given the twin temptations of gang warfare and illicit, criminal sex that existed right on Ronnie Kray's own doorstep, it is perhaps surprising that the Kray twins' first major clash with the law was not a result of either, but rather during their enlistment into the British army. From the end of the war until 1960, nearly all British men between the ages of seventeen and twenty-one were required to serve in the armed forces for eighteen months, and then remain as reservists for a number of years afterwards. In 1952, the twins were called up. Their schooling had already been interrupted by the closure of schools during the Blitz, then by their evacuation with their mum, Violet, to Hadleigh in Suffolk.[9] At fifteen they had left school altogether, trying to find odd jobs working with their grandfather on his rags stall, selling firewood, or working in the market, but their real passion was boxing, which they had taken up in a local club when they were just twelve. Between their fists, pellet guns, and street fighting, they had been in and out of contact with the police, including getting probation for assault, but never any more serious punishments.

When they turned up at the Tower of London, conscription papers in hand, in 1952, they were about to be prepared for a level of discipline they had hitherto never experienced. They did not fancy it much, and were leaving the barracks when a corporal demanded to know where they were going. 'We're off home to see our mum,' they replied, and Ron knocked him out with a punch. After visiting Mum and then going out on the town, they were arrested the next day back at Vallance Road, where they were court-martialled and imprisoned for a week.[10] As soon as they were released from their cells, they went on the run. For the next two years they played a cat-and-mouse game with the army and police, finding support while on the run from friends and well-wishers within a community that had little time for the authorities.

It ran in the family: their brother, father, and uncle had all run away from their service at some point, and Violet's house at 178 Vallance Road was known as 'Deserter's Corner'. After assaulting a police officer who came to nick them, they served a short period in Wormwood Scrubs jail, before being taken back to barracks and escaping again. Their time in the army was marked by an increasing level of violence and aggression. In Ron's words, this was the point at which he 'started to go a bit mad'.[11] He regarded himself as having psychic powers, allowing him to read people's auras to determine their motives. This, combined with his supposed shit list of enemies, must have been concerning to people; when he started to use the nickname 'The Colonel', everyone obliged him.[12]

Upon their release, their criminal career really began. The Regal, a billiard hall on Eric Street in Mile End, had been experiencing a plague of nightly violence and vandalism, and the owner was at his wits' end. The brothers made themselves available to take it over for a fiver a week; the day they took it over, the violence stopped. They turned its fortunes round, and the venue became popular with young people in the area.[13] They began to establish a pattern: Reggie provided the brains, turning around the business, while Ronnie provided the brawn, in this instance fighting off the Maltese gangs attempting to shake the boys down for protection money. Reggie considered going straight, but for Ron, that was never an option.

Their gang began to grow, and with it, both their organisation and firepower became more serious. Ron became obsessed with weapons and firearms: beneath the floorboards of 178 Vallance Road was a veritable arsenal of weaponry, including a Mauser rifle and a Luger automatic, plus revolvers, knives, and even cavalry swords.[14] Their protection racket was organised into two forms of payments. For smaller premises – pubs, shops, and the like – there was the 'Nipping List', whereby the gang was assured that if they ever needed to drop in for some goods, such as a crate or two of champagne, it would be given free of charge. Then there was the 'Pension List', where larger establishments like casinos or restaurants provided a regular fee for their premises to be 'protected' by the gang.[15] If they refused to pay the fee, of course, they soon realised that it was necessary, as their venues were mysteriously visited by thugs, vandals, or arsonists.

Quickly, the gang started to get a serious reputation, demanding respect from all and sundry while 'looking after their own' who were 'away' in prison. Despite the fact they still lived with their mum, they were buying snappy new suits and getting home visits from the barber, a habit they picked up from watching US gangster movies.[16] Ronnie was also gaining a reputation as a 'hard man'. While there were guns in the London underworld, they were usually for threatening rather than firing, but Ronnie was known as a man prepared to use them, after shooting a boxer who threatened one of his protected businesses. The following year, Ronnie was involved in a gang fight with a group of rivals, the 'Watney Streeters', and one of them broke what was known as the 'East End code of silence' and shopped him; it was 1956 and he was back inside, sentenced to three years in Wandsworth Prison.[17]

After two years in Wandsworth, where he continued his criminal activities, Ron was transferred to a lower security prison on the Isle of Wight. Despite its relative comfort, he hated it, and began to suffer again from increasingly severe mental health problems, including paranoid delusions, which he put down to being triggered by the death of his mother's sister, Aunt Rose. He had been particularly close to her, admiring her anti-authoritarian attitude, and her death from leukaemia devastated him. He was transferred to Long Grove, a psychiatric hospital, and contrived with his brothers to escape from the institution, fearing he might be permanently incarcerated. After a few months he handed himself in, and, astonishingly, was allowed to simply serve the short remainder of his sentence before being released in 1959.

It was a fortuitous moment for the boys, to be released just as London was entering a decade in which society and culture would be radically transformed. They were twenty-seven, charming and handsome, feared and respected, rich enough to wear sharp suits and drive fancy cars, and they were looking to make a name for themselves.

While Ronnie was inside, Reggie had begun expanding the business empire with second-hand car dealerships, gambling dens, and a new club, the 'Double R', in tribute to his incarcerated brother.[18] With Ronnie out, they could do more, and in 1962 established the 'Kentucky' club in Mile End.

One regular was a young actress called Barbara Windsor, another East End local who was starting to make a name for herself in film and on the stage. She arranged for the Kentucky to be used as a location for Joan Littlewood's 1963 kitchen sink drama *Sparrows Can't Sing*, in which she starred. The premiere for the film was held across the road in the ABC Cinema (now the

Genesis), with the afterparty at the Kentucky, filled to capacity. The club was garishly decorated with red carpets, large mirrors, and fake gold-leaf furnishings, and attracted wealthy, famous, and aristocratic guests including Antony Armstrong-Jones, then husband of Princess Margaret, and Roger Moore.

Britain was changing: a new generation of young people raised without the memory of war, and with increased ready cash to spend on consumer items, was producing a new working-class culture which was bucking against the rigid class divisions and cultural elitism that preceded the war. Working-class youth cults like the Mods, Rockers, and Teddy Boys had raised fears of degeneracy throughout the early '60s, while playwrights and authors from the 1950s on were producing representations of working-class life that had previously been inaccessible to working-class viewers and readers.

Shelagh Delaney, for example, was a working-class woman from Salford who wrote her first play, *A Taste of Honey*, at nineteen, after seeing what she felt was a negative portrayal of homosexuals in a play by middle-class playwright Terence Rattigan at Manchester Opera House. Before the war it would have been much harder for working-class young people to access such culture, let alone get their own work produced. Yet *A Taste of Honey* was a hit; rather than depicting working-class people as idealised but unintelligent workers, it featured a far more realistic portrayal of life in Manchester, with mixed-race relationships and homosexual characters, and in 1961 it was made into a film.

Other work, like Alan Sillitoe's novel *Saturday Night and Sunday Morning* – also turned into a film – depicted the disaffection of young people with the steady, monotonous way of life they experienced as industrial workers, as well as their desire for the excitement and opportunity they saw on the screen. For working-class people to see their own lives reflected on screen was one thing, but for middle- and upper-class people to see working-class culture as something dangerous, sexy, and exciting also helped propel this new interest in people like the Krays. As they coalesced their power base in the East End, they decided to branch out, and in the process, made themselves into celebrities too.

No sooner was Ronnie out of jail than Reggie was in, for a bungled attempt at extortion on behalf of a friend.[19] While he was locked up in 1960, Ronnie's worst tendencies for mindless violence, self-aggrandisement, big spending, and alienating allies all ran wild. He became aware of the wealth of a notorious slum landlord, Peter Rachman, who had built up a property empire in Notting Hill by overcharging West Indian immigrants for sub-standard housing, enforced by rent collectors and thugs. He wanted a slice of the pie and approach Rachman at a club, driving him back to Vallance Road for a cup of tea and some 'negotiations'. The negotiations were typical Ronnie: give me £5,000 right now (equivalent to over £100,000 today), or else.

Rachman gave him £250 in cash, and cut him a cheque for another £1,000, but the cheque bounced. Fearful for his life, and aware that he didn't want to open up a rolling financial obligation with Ronnie for 'protection', he cut him a deal, arranging for the twins to buy out a gambling club in swanky Knightsbridge in West London. They jumped at the chance, and soon were the proprietors of 'Esmeralda's Barn', their very own West London casino. Although Ronnie proceeded to run the place into the ground, he revelled in the new-found status it bought him: he was no longer just an exotic sight for visitors to the East End, but a player in West End culture. He began hanging around with more and more important people. The film stars were now more famous – even Judy Garland visited the club and got an invite to meet Mum back at Vallance Road – and were joined by artists, especially inveterate gamblers Lucian Freud and Francis Bacon, and politicians and peers. Ron particularly liked the powerful politicians, and the access to dinners at the House of Lords, private members clubs, and sex with young men that accompanied them.

While homosexuality was certainly the subject of public disapproval, if not repulsion, in the early 1960s, it was not *unknown* to the man on the Clapham omnibus. There had been growing public concern over what was perceived as a rise in homosexual behaviour in the decades following the Second World War, as prosecutions increased. To investigate this 'problem', in 1957 the Conservative government commissioned a report from a Departmental Committee on Homosexual Offences and Prostitution: as when the 1885 Criminal Law Amendment Act was introduced, homosexuality was considered as intrinsically linked to prostitution. The report, better known as the Wolfenden Report, after the chair of the commission, educationalist John Wolfenden, suggested that this perceived rise was owed more to changing public conversations around sex, increased newspaper coverage, and increased policing, than a moral contagion overtaking the country.[20] While the report clearly took a dim view of homosexuality, it suggested that the purpose of the law extended to the protection of the vulnerable, but that 'there must remain a realm of private morality and immorality which is, in brief and crude terms, not the law's business', and went on to recommend that 'homosexual behaviour between consenting adults in private should no longer be a criminal offence'.[21]

But earlier in the sixties, the recommendations of the Wolfenden Report, which would surely be unpopular with the general public, had been kicked into the legislative long grass, and the law was not changed until the Labour administration of Harold Wilson, first elected in 1964, engaged in a widespread campaign to liberalise many of Britain's social laws, including not just homosexuality but laws on divorce, censorship, the children of unmarried couples, and the abolition of the death penalty. Before that, the provisions of the Labouchere Amendment in the 1885 Criminal Law Amendment Act, which criminalised the extremely broad (and contingent) spectrum of behaviours that were regarded as 'gross indecency', were still on the books. In the period after the Second World War the growth of homosexual subcultures was accompanied by an enormous growth in the prosecution of gay men. Historian Matt Houlbrook argues that this peak in post-war prosecutions was not so much a 'top down' persecution of homosexual men so much as a campaign that 'worked from the bottom of the criminal justice hierarchy up',[22] driven by the perception of vice squad officers that homosexual behaviours were increasing and hence required a change in operational response to them.

As a result, the persecution of gay men in the period immediately after the war was uneven, and often determined by class, age, or status, as those arrested were, typically, those whose sole recourse for sex was cruising and cottaging. Those who could afford their own flats, rooms in private clubs, or chambers were less likely to suffer exposure, prosecution, or criminalization. That is not to say there were not high-profile people caught up in vice policing. Then, as now, there was a discrete and closeted but very active homosexual subculture within the Houses of Parliament. As in the lives of Hadrian or James VI and I, power was not just an aphrodisiac, but a shield.

In November 1958 Ian Harvey, a Conservative MP, had been cruising in St James's Park when he caught the eye of a nineteen-year-old guardsman, Anthony Plant. They ended up engaging in an act of gross indecency when they were interrupted by a park warden. They were charged with gross indecency and breaking park regulations, although the gross indecency charge was dropped and Harvey, very decently, paid Plant's fine as well as his own. It cost him his job as parliamentary under-secretary of state at the Foreign Office, however, and his seat in Parliament. When told, Winston Churchill supposedly remarked, 'On the coldest night of the year? It makes you proud to be British.'

Others, more charming than Harvey, got away even more easily. When Labour MP Tom Driberg was caught by a policeman in Edinburgh on his knees sucking off a Norwegian sailor in an air raid shelter during the war, he swiftly produced a business card with 'Member of Parliament' on it and was let off, even striking up a friendly correspondence with the arresting officer whereby he would send him book tokens.[23] 'There was a strong and confiding *camaraderie* among some bisexual and homosexual members [of Parliament],' notes Driberg's biographer, Francis Wheen. 'On his first day at Westminster Tom was shown round the Members' lavatories – "the most important rooms" – by the rich and homosexual "Chips" Cannon, Conservative MP for Southend.'[24] Far from exposing the powerful to the risk of potentially scandalous homosexual liaisons, the British class system actually *encouraged* it; in Driberg's words 'if anything, I became more promiscuous after my election to Parliament, relying on my new status to get me out of tight corners'.[25] Ronnie seemed to have realised the same perks of power and status.

Ronnie was owed money by a West End 'character', a friend of the jazz singer George Melly, as well as of Freud and Bacon, called David Litvinoff, who helped Ronnie 'find' young men to fuck. (The original title of Freud's portrait of Litvinoff, now known as *Man in a Headscarf*, was *The Procurer*.) Ronnie agreed to write off the debt in exchange for Litvinoff's flat – and his boyfriend. Ronnie liked young, pretty guys, and the boyfriend, Bobby Buckley, was just his type. It seems he probably fell in love with Buckley, and enjoyed pampering him, taking him to dinner, on holiday in the Canary Islands, and buying him new suits. He called his boyfriend 'son' and referred to himself as 'your old Dad'. Yet Ronnie was never going to be a 'one boy' kind of guy.

His friendships amongst the rich and famous were starting to pay off. In 1963 he was introduced by his friend, the Labour MP Tom Driberg (who, ever the adventurer, had turned up at the Kentucky for a drink), to the powerful bisexual Conservative peer Lord Boothby.[26] Boothby had been dating a young cat burglar from Shoreditch called Leslie Holt, whom he employed as his driver. Holt had a flat in an art deco apartment block in Stoke Newington called Cedra Court; his neighbours were the Kray twins, who each owned a place there.

Boothby wined and dined Ronnie in his West London clubs, such as White's; in return, Ronnie organised 'sex shows' and orgies with young men in East London.[27] Politicians were useful: they were some of the few in society who could put pressure on the police and prosecutors who were increasingly sniffing around the Kray's empire. Driberg, and most likely Boothby too, were invited to parties at Cedra Court where, in the words of Francis Wheen, 'rough but compliant East End lads were served like so many canapés'.[28]

In July of 1964, the friendship hit a crisis. The *Sunday Mirror* published an exclusive, claiming that Scotland Yard had begun an investigation into the relationship between an unnamed peer and an underworld kingpin. Under the headline 'Peer and a Gangster: Yard Inquiry', it claimed to possess photographic evidence of a lord sat with a mobster who was running London's largest protection racket. When a German magazine published Boothby and Kray's names, Boothby called the *Sunday Mirror's* bluff, outing himself in a letter to the *Times* as the subject around whom so many rumours had been flying. What's more, he denied all charges, claiming he'd only met Kray three times on business matters.

With his high-powered lawyers behind him, the *Mirror* capitulated to Boothby, and settled with a huge fee and unreserved apology. The fact was that, although he and Kray were not lovers (they shared tastes in younger men instead), the allegations were largely true. Both Boothby and Driberg had intervened on behalf of the Krays behind the scenes in the past, and what's more, there *was* a police investigation into the twins.[29] The *Sunday Mirror's* reporter had got his lead from his informants in Scotland Yard's criminal investigation department, C11, that Cedra Court was under observation and an investigation into the Krays' protection racketeering, fraud, and blackmail was underway. Even MI5 had been aware of the relationship, with one of their informants claiming that

> Boothby is a kinky fellow and likes to meet odd people, and Ronnie obviously wants to meet people of good social standing, he having the odd background he's got; and, of course, both are queers ... Leslie [Holt] never suggested that there was any villainous association between the two and they are not likely to be linked by a queer attraction for each other: both are hunters (of young men).[30]

Yet Driberg had persuaded the Labour prime minister, Harold Wilson, that Boothby had been libelled, and deserved his support. In reality, the calculation was political: it had barely been a year since the Profumo Affair, another sex scandal, had brought down the Conservative government and brought him to power. But their majority was slim, and another scandal, this time involving Driberg, would have been as damaging to him as the Tories. Driberg was such an inveterate and pro- lific cocksucker that any cub reporter would have been able to dig up a raft of men he had blown. Better for everyone, it was decided, if the papers, and the police, back away. As the Met Commissioner had lied and publicly denied there was any investigation into the twins, evidence gathered up to that point had to be discarded.[31]

It was only ever going to be a temporary reprieve, however. Ronnie was becoming increasingly out of control. The twins were becoming increasingly concerned with the activities of their rivals, the Richardson Gang, who controlled territory in South London. At Christmas 1965, Ronnie heard that one of its members, George Cornell, a nasty piece of work who worked as a torturer for the gang, had called him a 'fat poof'. Trouble was brewing, and in February of 1966 a gang war erupted. There was a series of tit-for-tat attacks, and Ronnie was in his element, co-ordinating his troops as 'The Colonel' he had always dreamed of being. In March, a Kray ally, although not a member of the gang, was killed in a mass shootout at a club in Catford. Major figures in the Richardson Gang had been shot, and the police had swooped down on it. It looked like victory for the twins was on hand as their main rivals went to ground.

The next day, however, Ronnie heard that Cornell was drink- ing in the Blind Beggar pub, on their turf. Ronnie holstered his Mauser pistol and got his driver to take him to the public house opposite Whitechapel Hospital. Entering the bar, Cornell was said to have greeted him by saying, 'Well look who's here.'[32] Ronnie put a bullet straight through his head, and left.

Of course, nobody saw anything, but after his brother Reggie went on to kill Jack 'the Hat' McVitie the following year, the pressure was on. Police detective Leonard 'Nipper' Read had been foiled in his investigations once following the Boothby inci- dent, but now he went after the twins with renewed vigour, and finally managed to track down the barmaid of the Blind Beggar. She was the crack in the East End code of silence; given a new identity, she testified against Ronnie, and alongside his brother he was sentenced to at least thirty years in prison in 1969.

Ronnie was eventually, after ten years in prison, moved to the high-security psychiatric hospital at Broadmoor after being diagnosed with paranoid schizophrenia. He would live there for the rest of his life. He never denied his homosexuality, although sometimes qualified himself as a bisexual. For Ronnie, his homosexuality was a natural part of his personality, something he was born with, and as long as he retained his masculine virtues, he was fine with being seen as a homosexual. What he hated was being regarded as weak; 'I'm a not a poof, I'm homosexual,' he would claim, and loved to identify with icons of British imperialism, such as Lawrence of Arabia, in whom he saw a model of masculinity that accommodated violence and bravado as well as desire.[33] Referring to the imperialist hero Gordon of Khartoum, he said, 'Gordon was like me, homosexual, and he met his death like a man. When it's time for me to go, I hope I do the same.'[34] He died in 1995, his 'reputation' seemingly intact: alongside Reggie, he remains something of a folk hero for many, and an unironic icon of masculinity for many young men.

14

Pim Fortuyn

September 11, 2001, arrived at a strange time for the world, and for the gays, and made that strange time far worse. It was the dawn of a new millennium. In Europe, a Third Way of young and confident social democrats was shredding welfare states with much smiling talk of progressive modernization; in the United States, their spiritual predecessor Bill Clinton had departed the White House popular, but unable to place his successor in office. It did not seem to matter much, anyway. Voter turnout was broadly down; it seemed there was less and less to vote for. The Soviet Union had collapsed and China was just beginning to integrate into the global economy. History, it was confidently believed at the commanding heights of the increasingly interchangeable faces of corporate and state power, had ended. Liberal capitalism had won. Sure, there might be little flare-ups of protest, like the 1999 movement against the WTO meeting in Seattle, but these were confidently dismissed by the people in charge as hangovers from an older era when the future of the world was in serious doubt.

On the ground, for the gays and their friends, things looked a little different. The HIV pandemic had ravaged queer communities for two decades. Murderous and active indifference had turned to passive indifference through the heroic activism of two generations of queer people united in anger and fear for their lives.[1] The HIV virus was likely spreading slowly since the 1920s, and began to spread rapidly in urban gay communities in the 1970s. By 1981, when rare cancers began being identified in gay men in Los Angeles and New York, hundreds of thousands were likely already infected.

From its discovery in 1981 onwards, AIDS was a death sentence for millions, spreading rapidly through urban gay communities to indifference and even active scorn from political leaders. It was not until 1996 that queers were certain that HIV caused AIDS; this discovery was prompted by that year's introduction of HAART antiretroviral therapy, which helped to suppress viral loads and increase T-cell counts in people who before were desperately ill.[2] Almost as soon as these therapies became available, the fragile coalition between white gay men, lesbians, Black women, IV drug users, and queer street kids that Sarah Schulman, among others, identify as having been vital to the political movements in New York (her focus) and across the Western world, movements that helped create the therapies, get drugs into bodies, fight for state support for sick people, and build organizations to care for one another, was severed.

'A trend of white male journalists proclaiming that AIDS is over began on November 10, 1996,' she writes, with the publication of a *New York Times Magazine* cover story by amateur race scientist and professional Bad Gay Andrew Sullivan.[3] Later in her account of AIDS in New York City, she quotes the experimental filmmaker Tom Kalin, a member of both ACT UP and its artistic branch Gran Fury, responding to the article:

> AIDS is over for white fags like me. Andrew Sullivan embodies to me that kind of privilege. Well, bully for you. You got the drugs. You're an upper-middle-class, white, gay man, who has access and is connected in an urban environment and getting your hands on them and take them, and they work for you. Yippee, I'm so happy. Now, what about all the other people who … could not get their hands on the drugs? Why is the narrative of your life and your survival somehow more important or more interesting than all those other people?[4]

Charles King, who co-founded Housing Works, an organization supporting people living with HIV and experiencing homelessness, remembered the article as a watershed. Schulman quotes him as saying,

> ACT UP, at its core, was gay men and their allies fighting for their lives ... I really truly believe that the LGBT community officially abandoned AIDS with Sullivan's article ... and the reason they abandoned it was, for them, it was over. It was now a Black disease, not their disease. You can almost see the mark of that article and sort of the handoff: this is no longer our problem. We're going to move on to gay marriage and other things that pull us in towards the center, with the presumption that everybody wants to be in the center instead of at the margins.[5]

By 1992, the Treatment and Data Committee of ACT UP had already departed to form the Treatment Action Group, a more formalized, more professional, more male, and more white organization that had often disagreed with the more working-class and more radical membership of ACT UP over collaboration with drug companies, the aggressiveness of protest tactics, and the breadth of structural goals.

This kind of split had occurred even earlier in some western European countries. In West Germany, where first a Social Democratic and then a Christian Democratic federal government had funded the AIDS-Hilfe network starting in 1983, this state recognition meant that the reconciliation between gay and lesbian groups that characterized AIDS movements in the anglophone world never occurred, with gay men integrating into state institutions far earlier. In the Netherlands, Amsterdam's local municipal health service already had a relationship with many gay men because of earlier outreach work around hepatitis B, and so already had experience working with gay men in sexual spaces like bars and bathhouses; the Dutch 'polder model' of consensus-based policymaking informed cooperation (although of course there were still struggles, inequalities, and power conflicts) between queer communities and public health officials.[6] In the fall of 2001, five years after Sullivan's article was published, the effects of these splits were becoming more and more visible. For urban gay men and lesbians with access to the new life-saving drugs, life seemed good: a new generation of spokespeople had emerged, replacing many gay liberation and AIDS activists who had either died or burned out, spokespeople neatly embodied by Sullivan himself, whom Benjamin Shepard referred to as 'a free-market loving Tory Thatcherite'. Now that medication was available to keep Sullivan alive, he 'felt privileged to ignore' intersectional politics, the brutal inequalities of the global health system, and the millions of people who did not have access to the drugs, which he estimated cost his insurance company almost $16,000 per year.[7]

This brutal inequality underlay what Shepard called 'the queer/gay assimilationist split', in which those who could afford and have access to AIDS treatment in the Global North developed a different kind of gay politics, one focused on integration into middle- and ruling-class life and the enabling of the seamless generational transfer of property and wealth. If gay liberationists had organized against the draft, 'gay rights' groups petitioned for the right to fight in the military. If lesbian separatists had inveighed against the brutality and misogyny of the institution of marriage, 'gay and lesbian rights' groups suddenly proposed that marriage was the ultimate sanctifying act needed to make their love meaningful.

A series of challenges against these norms continued to be mounted by activist collectives – including, in the United States, Against Equality and Queers for Racial and Economic Justice, and in the Netherlands, the Black migrant and refugee lesbian group Sister Outsider. Meanwhile, AIDS had, in addition to killing and/or burning out large swaths of two generations of queer activists and community leaders, made a powerful argument to many gays and lesbians that normalcy and integration into state institutions might not be such a bad thing, after all.

The Netherlands became a breathlessly discussed model of the brave new world to come for gay rights in the late 1990s, under the rule of a 'purple' coalition government of social democratic and social-liberal parties that made their pro-gay policies a centrepiece of their coalitions.[8] If leftist queers in the Netherlands still laughed off marriage – one gay editor of a communist daily newspaper had written, in 1986, that centrist politicians 'should stop giving presents we haven't asked for: nuclear plants, cruise missiles, gay marriages ... As if we haven't got our hands full with AIDS.' A new movement, pioneered by the glossy gay bar rag *Gay Krant*, ended up bringing around the masses, and converting COC Nederland, the main Dutch gay and lesbian organization, from its previous anti-marriage stance to a pro-marriage one.[9] However, even those queer radicals, as the historian Andrew D. J. Shield has written, were too often 'silent on intersectional issues'.[10]

The Netherlands became a pioneer for countries like the United States and the United Kingdom in regard to this process of the promotion of marriage equality as both the marquee goal of the gay and lesbian movement *and* broadly acceptable to a majority of citizens; Nathaniel Frank's breathless pro-marriage history *Awakening* notes that it was the first country to legalize same-sex marriage.[11] This movement orientation – as Frank approvingly notes in his epilogue, a reorientation of liberation movements towards 'an institution defined by the public recognition of the dignity of a private bond' – carried with it other political implications, both in the Netherlands and elsewhere.[12]

The September 11 attacks restarted history. In the capital cities of the West, it awakened the desires of bloodthirsty neoconservatives who had long sought a new civilizational opponent. These men began a series of criminal and murderous wars in the Middle East, and established a sharpened security regime that targeted refugees and migrants, specifically Muslims – ironically, precisely the reaction that the terrorists had hoped for. With the state itself becoming even more securitized, this new integrationist gay movement began to morph in even more discomforting ways.

In the fall of 2001, a previously marginal populist political party in the Netherlands called Liveable Netherlands named as its leader a charismatic man named Pim Fortuyn. Two months before, as an increasingly popular newspaper columnist, he had called for 'a cold war against Islam', which had 'taken over' the role of communism as the civilizational opponent of the West.[13] When his outrageous public statements became too hot for the party to handle, he split off his own party, the Pim Fortuyn List, and, in the aftermath of September 11, rocketed to the top of polls for the upcoming Dutch elections.

What made this racist different from all the others? Readers of the British liberal newspaper the *Observer* found out in 2002, when they opened the Europe section of their papers to find a headline reading 'Dutch Fall for Gay Mr Right'. 'Under the watchful gaze of his black-clad, dark-skinned bodyguards,' the article read, this 'new dynamic face of the Right in Europe' had just come from nowhere to take over the Rotterdam city council. 'Unconventional, with a penchant for lapdogs and luxury', Fortuyn favoured 'zero immigration because he believes it is undermining the ultra-liberal permissive society he cherishes'.[14]

Fortuyn embodied the compatibility between a pro-homosexual politics, racism, and the far right, the way that a certain kind of 'live and let live' attitude at the heart of liberal gay politics can transform into a wave of immigrant-bashing hatred that can then turn back on queers themselves. His sweeping success in local and national elections before being murdered by an animal rights activist made him an emblem of the global far right. The uncomfortable conclusion of this, the final chapter in our book, is that Pim Fortuyn may be less a dismaying artifact of a specific moment in post-2001 gay politics in the West than a preview of its future.

Little about Fortuyn's youth suggested that he might become such an emblem both of a resurgent far right able to cloak its racism in a supposed defence of liberalism, and of the reconciliation of extremely 'out' gay politics with neoconservative and even fascist anti-immigration politics. He was born in February of 1948, the third child in a Catholic family led by a salesman and a housewife, in the small town of Driehuis on the Atlantic coast north of Haarlem. The country had been liberated by the Allies only three years before, and there had been a famine at the end of the Second World War. The Nazis had levelled many Dutch cities in their invasion but also encountered a population that was, at least in large part, willing to collaborate. Seventy percent of Dutch Jews were murdered in the Holocaust, more than in France or Belgium.

After the war, Holland had to find a new place for itself in the world; the country was forced to divest itself of its colonies in Indonesia. Several hundred thousand Dutch people and Indonesian supporters of Dutch colonial rule were exiled, and many of them moved to the Netherlands, which, because of the post-war economic boom and a shortage of working-age men because of the war, began encouraging immigration from southern Europe and the Middle East, mainly Turkey and Morocco. Like political leaders in Germany, the Dutch assumed that most of these migrants would make their money and return home, but they did not. It was this intense climate of a newly multicultural society and a declining colonial power, in the aftermath of war and fascist collaboration, that shaped the Netherlands in which Fortuyn grew up.

The sexual revolution of the 1960s and 1970s took place in an environment which historian Andrew D. J. Shield calls a 'disavowal of heterogeneity' – an insistence by a white Dutch majority that the Netherlands was a homogeneous state.[15] Nonetheless, as he demonstrates, 'immigrants shared many of the same geographies – and even some experiences – with European activists, communards, artists, musicians, feminists, gays, lesbians, and squatters ... Thriving youth protest cultures' that spurred on sexual freedom movements existed 'in an environment that was already linguistically, culturally, ethnically, and religiously diverse'.[16]

Without denying the often ambivalent and racist relationship between white activists and people of colour and migrant activists, he describes a diverse set of ways in which migrants' movements around sexuality and gender articulated themselves both independently and in coalition with white movements, and formed, occasionally, integrated movements and spaces. Shield interviews one Turkish so-called 'guest worker' who remained in the Netherlands and recalled initially being surprised at seeing gay men on television, but eventually came to see gay liberation as part of a pro-worker and anti-authoritarian politics, aligned with his understandings of his fight for more freedom at work.[17]

Similarly, Gloria Wekker, herself both an academic and an activist in the refugee, migrant, and people of colour lesbian organization Sister Outsider (named after the book by Audre Lorde), describes these movements as taking place in a 'balancing act between various societal groups' – the so-called polder model of Dutch political coalition building – in which a state Directorate of Emancipation Affairs supported the work of various social groups, including Sister Outsider.[18] The women's movement was, she writes, 'more prepared – at least in principle – than the gay movement to reflect on race as a social and symbolic grammar as important as gender', even in an environment where the predominant racism of white feminist movements led to the creation of feminist movements specifically led and organized by people of colour, such as the ones in which she participated.[19]

The young Fortuyn participated enthusiastically in some of these left-wing liberation movements as a PhD student in sociology, studying in Amsterdam and Groningen in the 1970s. After completing his PhD, he taught as an associate professor of sociology at the University of Groningen and then in Rotterdam, working in a broadly social democratic tradition and joining the social democratic Partij van de Arbeid. At that time in opposition, the party transformed itself along the lines of the Clintonite and Blairite Third Way, with former labour leader Wim Kok becoming a junior partner to the centre-right after the 1989 elections and accepting neoliberal reforms. In 1994, Kok's party became the country's largest and, as the driving force in a social-liberal coalition, the party remained in power until 2002.

This was one of the first Dutch governments not to involve a Christian political party; excitement over the possibilities for liberal reform overtook concern that this purple government coalition was essentially accepting and continuing a program of hard austerity. The combination of austerity cutting the kinds of (however imperfect) opportunities for intersectional collective thinking and movement making in the 1970s and 1980s plus a reluctance to discuss colonial-era crimes, the reasons for migration, and racism in the Netherlands led to a rather strange code of silence around race and migration. 'Immigrants … are a taboo subject in the Netherlands, where it is extremely important always to be politically correct on ethnic issues,' read one business manual for foreigners working in the Netherlands.[20]

The austerity of the 1990s eventually cost Fortuyn his job and his professorship: budget cuts meant that Fortuyn was made redundant, and he opened a successful business consulting firm, began writing newspaper columns, and bought himself a large house in downtown Rotterdam with a butler. Single and sexually active in darkrooms and sex clubs, he was in lifelong unrequited love with a photographer.

Fortuyn's first forays into politics occurred in the early 1990s, when he wrote a pamphlet called 'To the People of the Netherlands', a populist, patriotic, and nationalist manifesto (mirroring a similar text from the 1780s) attacking the political elite. The polder model of cooperative decision-making led to a certain cosiness at the top of Dutch politics, which Fortuyn attacked both in the pamphlet and in his newspaper columns. Similarly, he began to 'sound the alarm bell' about migration, as he saw it, tying the government's cosy pursuit of austerity and cooperative decision-making model that seemed to shut out all outside influence to the lack of public conversation about migrants and migration. The substantial influence of the country's tabloid media led to a moral panic about migrant crime, while, as Shield provocatively proposes, the formation of the European Union itself led to a series of debates about and emphases on 'Europeanness' that took on a racialized character.[21]

As unemployment rose and budget cuts continued to hack away at the social welfare state, Fortuyn, despite favouring neoliberal economic policies, saw an opportunity to argue that migrants were the reason why the cuts were being made, and Islamic ethno-religious inferiority the reason for the country's increasing social divisions. As both Shield and Wekker demonstrate, dominant remembrances of the diverse post-'68 liberation movements began by the 1990s to congeal into a narrative in which migrants, a separate category and absent from emancipation struggles, posed a threat to liberation. In this view, liberation and tolerance had already been accomplished until the immigrants showed up to spoil the party.[22]

If tolerance was the Dutch national brand, then Fortuyn could develop a Dutch-branded far-right politics by accusing migrants, and especially Muslims, of lacking that tolerance. It was not Fortuyn, whose proposals came to include the forcible re-education of Muslims living in the Netherlands and a complete ban on immigration, who was intolerant, but the people he sought to deport and lock up. In her 2007 monograph *Terrorist Assemblages*, the queer theorist Jasbir K Puar examines what she calls 'homonationalism', a network of 'connections among sexuality, race, gender, nation, class, and ethnicity in relation to the tactics, strategies, and logistics of war machines'.[23] A new 'benevolence' towards gays and lesbians in the public sphere on issues like marriage, she writes, 'is contingent upon ever narrowing parameters' – of whiteness, of class position, and of adherence to gender norms. The married gay subject can then be defended by the state, and set off against supposedly terrifying terrorists who threaten the liberal freedom these subjects embody. This neat trick of reversal, familiar today as a key part of the far-right playbook in debates about the provision of healthcare to transgender children and the supposed scourge of 'cancel culture' at universities, was pioneered by Fortuyn. In a political landscape constrained by the common sense of neoliberalism and capitalist realism, it plays on the racism inherent in neoliberalism to create a frisson of radicalism regarding standard-issue conservative politics.

Today's conservatives, busy starting money-losing, billionaire-underwritten media empires where they write every day to baying choruses of approval about the ways that teenagers are mean to them on the Internet, have decided that the real prohibitions on speech are not the material risks presented by precarious employment but the fact that someone might exercise their own free speech and disagree with you. Historians whose work fails every possible test of professional standards and who have conveniently decided that critique of those failures is a violation of their right to free expression clap and cheer as governments ban, and threaten to ban, the teaching of critical race theory, gender studies, and anti-capitalist thought. They encourage their students to insult and attack their colleagues and then claim that they are the victims of organized campaigns of persecution. It is an idiocracy of bootlicking elitists doing backflips to evince the radicalism of what is, in fact, a boring set of political beliefs commonly held among people with power that serve to maintain and reproduce that power in the most banal ways imaginable.

It is only the impoverished nature of the debate – in the Netherlands then and in the anglosphere now – that makes such a cheap trick compelling to a terrifyingly broad swath of the population. A memory culture that diminished the colonial crimes of the Dutch combined with a social-liberal government that slashed budgets while celebrating a cosmetic version of diversity and emancipation to form a petri dish for this kind of resentment-based politics. 'The hegemonic Dutch reading', Wekker writes, became that 'the women's and gay movements [had] largely accomplished their aims', leading to these perceived national victories becoming a point of nationalist pride. Fortuyn himself wrote, in 1997, that these movements were 'the greatest mental and cultural achievement after the creation of the welfare state in the modern history of mankind'.[24] Despite research showing that Dutch baby boomers of all ethnic backgrounds were becoming more sexually conservative as they aged, with members of Dutch Christian churches among the most conservative, the narrative that it was specifically immigrants who were threatening the progress of Dutch women and homosexuals, who were cast as uniformly white, became more and more prevalent throughout the 1990s.[25]

Rotterdam, where Fortuyn made his home, was historically a hotbed of the Dutch Labour Party. Rotterdam – one of the largest cities in the Netherlands, and Europe's largest seaport – shrunk significantly from the 1970s to the end of the twentieth century as technologies developed in the distribution and logistics sector, including the introduction in the 1970s of intermodal container shipping, in which goods can be moved from ship to train to truck without ever being taken out of their containers. This advance dramatically reduced the need for union labour by longshoremen, who responded with waves of labour militancy in the 1970s and 1980s but who were largely unable to fight back against the tidal wave of automation. In Rotterdam, unlike in some other cities, there was land available (and land was created) to build the wider and deeper shipping lanes and large, systematized unloading equipment necessary for container shipping.

Nevertheless, less labour was required; additionally, in the 1970s, 1980s, and 1990s, an accelerating process of deindustrialization hit the city as with many other industrial cities in Europe and North America. The guest worker program, which had brought mainly blue-collar industrial workers, made Rotterdam one of the Netherlands' most diverse cities by race and country of origin, with foreign-born citizens making up nearly 50 percent of Rotterdam residents. The Turkish population of Rotterdam increased from 1.5 to 35 percent of labourers between 1961 and 1975, and the share of Moroccans went from 0 to 10.5 percent.[26] Guest workers were initially kept from integrating by official city policy that intended them to continue working as cheap labourers.[27] In the late 1970s, after a series of riots in the Afrikaanderwijk neighbourhood, the Labour Party proposed an integration program. This coincided with federal-level neoliberal policies from the Labour Party, and prompted an extreme-right response: the extreme right went from zero to six council seats between the mid-1980s and the mid-1990s, before being kicked off the council in 1998.[28]

It was in the 1990s that Fortuyn began turning more formally towards politics. While his early books and columns were, according to the historian Merijn Oudenampsen, 'neoliberal tributes to ... the calculating and emancipated citizen who happily entered the globalized marketplace and no longer needed the welfare state', his 1995 book *The Orphaned Society* actually argued against the post-1968 emancipation movements and called for the restoration of the patriarchal family – but in potentially gay or lesbian form.

'Fruit of emancipation', he wrote, 'could be that the care-giving role of the mother, and the law-function of the father, do not have to be linked to the biological position of men and women.'[29] In 1997, he wrote a pamphlet called *Against the Islamisation of Our Culture*, in which he tied the moral relativism of Dutch culture to its cosy political elite and insisted that liberation required aggressive action on moral norms.[30] In the summer of 2001, continuing his program of escalating rhetoric against migrants, he gave an interview to a local newspaper in Rotterdam complaining about the number of immigrants: 'The Netherlands is full. Rotterdam as well. In a couple of years, this city will consist of 56% of people who are not from the Netherlands ... We allow too many foreign people to enter. In that way we get an underclass that consists of too many people who are badly equipped to contribute either economically or culturally.'[31] That same summer, he called for a 'cold war' against Islam in the Netherlands.

His statements were greeted with complacency by members of other political parties, who tended to dismiss him and his popularity; this dismissal was often aided by his colourful public presence, open homosexuality (still a novelty among politicians), and public discussion of his own sexuality. He displayed, as Gloria Wekker writes, 'simultaneous disgust and desire ... towards male Muslims', often bragging of his sexual exploits with young Moroccans and Turks.[32] Fortuyn once joked in an interview that semen tasted like the Dutch liqueur Berenberg.[33]

Whereas the Church had traditionally been the source of authority for right-wing Dutch politics – the Netherlands has a large presence of Catholic and Calvinist churches – Fortuyn was willing to criticize the Church, especially those parts of it that had followed what some of us might consider to be a Christian line on how to treat other people. 'The leftist church, which includes part of the media, the Green Party and the Labour Party, has for years forbade discussions that deal with the multicultural society and the problems it brings forth', Fortuyn wrote, 'by continuously combining those with discrimination, with racism, and not in the last place, with the blackest page of the history of this part of the continent: fascism and Nazism.'[34]

Asked in an interview to discuss the Ten Commandments, he began waxing poetic about clubs' darkrooms:

> It is absolutely not my intention to speak blasphemy, but I have to tell you that I find the atmosphere of the Catholic liturgy back in certain acts in the dark room of such a gentlemen's club. The dark room that I frequent in Rotterdam is not totally blacked out: just like in an old cathedral, the light comes in filtered. In such circumstances, making love has a religious aspect to it. Religiosity and merging–that you sometimes have in sex–can be two sides of the same coin.[35]

In darkrooms, he said, 'you find the whole range of emotions there that also exists within a relationship: from blowing your nose to the most intimate form of being together'.[36]

'I don't hate Arabs', he said, 'I even sleep with them.'[37] Discussing sex with Muslims, he said, 'there is a remarkable extra weight attached to doing homosexuality ... Their suppressed feelings make for a really strange kind of sex: very focused on fucking, without intimacy, a quick climax, no kissing.'[38] Wekker reads the 'political economy of desire' that wraps around Fortuyn's seemingly off-hand sexual comments against the Dutch cultural archive, in which 'men and women perceived as others ... are always already sexualized ... wild and excessive'.[39] His 'verbal transgressions', she argues, served to position him as a sovereign and emancipated sexual subject, revealing something of the shape and scale of the relationship between the development of sexuality and the development of colonial capitalism.[40]

Here the charismatic Fortuyn, through his sexuality, was able to present as the apotheosis of the 1960s emancipation movements what was in fact their opposite: he was the voice of what Oudenampsen calls a broader 'conservative backlash' against permissiveness, relativism, and anti-authoritarianism.[41]

September 11 only lit a fire under Fortuyn and his supporters. While he had already declared his intention to enter national politics, after the attacks, in a wave of islamophobia that was among the attackers' principal intents, he was recruited to lead a political party called Liveable Netherlands. A movement of 'Liveable' independent political parties, organizing around a shared hatred of the establishment political parties, had been forming around the Netherlands from rump local independent groups on municipal councils since the late 1980s.

Liveable Rotterdam, in which Fortuyn also ran, was founded by a fan of his, the former high schoolteacher Ronald Sørensen. The party was at that time mostly ideologically incoherent, but Fortuyn, after being named its chief candidate, began to transform the party in his image in anticipation of the May 2002 national elections. He repeatedly argued that Muslims were an internal threat, did not accept Western values, and that the religion had not yet been reformed. Here, he echoed the words of orientalists like Bernard Lewis, one of the chief academic advisers to the neoconservatives who were then busily planning to murder millions of Iraqis.

The party began to climb in opinion polls. In October of 2001 it still looked like the Labour-led social-liberal coalition was to cruise to a third term under Kok. But it began to falter. In February of 2002, at which point Fortuyn's party had risen in the polls from zero seats to twenty, he gave an interview to the newspaper *Volkskrant*. In it, he combined calls to restrict immigration – 'the borders are closing, we are cancelling the Refugee Convention' – with populist promises to 'eliminate waiting lists in health care', targeting the social-liberal government's cuts. He called for no asylum seekers to be admitted. And with a somewhat regretful tone, he admitted that he could not strip civil rights from Muslims – 'they are our Moroccan bastard boys' – but said that he wished to 'abolish that strange article of the Constitution, you will not discriminate ... I don't hate Islam. I think it's a backward culture,' he said, using a word *achterlijk*, that also means 'retarded'. 'In what country could a party leader of such a big movement as mine be openly gay? How fantastic that this is possible here. You can be proud of that. And I would like to keep it that way.'[42]

The use of the word 'retarded' and the call to abolish the constitutional clause prohibiting discrimination under the law were somehow too much for the other leaders of Liveable Netherlands, who kicked Fortuyn off their list. He remained leader of Liveable Rotterdam as their candidate for the March 2002 local elections, and promptly founded his own national list, the Pim Fortuyn List. The first public opinion poll taken after his *Volkskrant* interview saw his list in fourth place, with the list projected as winning thirteen seats to the governing Labour Party's thirty.[43] If there had been a small setback from the twenty that Liveable Netherlands had polled before his interview, he quickly set himself to making up the gap.

In the March 2002 local elections, Liveable Rotterdam, under Fortuyn's leadership, swept to victory with 36 percent of the vote, and went into governing coalition with the Christian Democrats and a conservative liberal party, knocking Labour out of power in Rotterdam for the first time since the Second World War. This victory lent Fortuyn a great deal of legitimacy. Later that month he released a book in which he presented his politics as a kind of common sense liberalism. 'In Holland', he asked, 'homosexuality is treated the same way as heterosexuality: in what Islamic country does that happen … how can you respect a culture if the woman has to walk several steps behind her man, has to stay in the kitchen and keep her mouth shut?'[44]

Profiling Fortuyn for the *New Yorker*, the journalist Elizabeth Kolbert noted that he 'claimed the Jews … as his allies'. He had written a book worrying 'that the Jewish State', Kolbert writes, 'might not be able to survive the threat posed by its fundamentalist neighbors'.[45] Along with the neoconservative clash-of-civilizations whizz-kids who surrounded Bush and Blair as they prepared to murder millions of Iraqis on behalf of military contractors, Fortuyn was one of the first far-rightists to recruit Jews as a kind of body armour. 'Christianity and Judaism have gone through the process of enlightenment, making them creative and constructive elements in society,' he once said. 'That didn't happen in Islam. There is a tension between the values of modern society and the principles of Islam.'[46]

Mainstream conservatives had pioneered this move, reformatting their paeans to 'Christian values' into 'Judeo-Christian' as, in the words of the historian James Loeffler, 'an ecumenical marketing meme for combating godless communism'.[47] European far-right leaders before Fortuyn (like the French Jean-Marie Le Pen, who led his far-right National Front party into the second round of the French elections at the same time that Fortuyn was on the upswing in the Netherlands) had tended, like Le Pen, to be Holocaust deniers and open fascist sympathizers. Fortuyn used his homosexuality and his apparent sympathy for Jews to distance himself from Le Pen, claiming his policies had nothing to do with Le Pen and that comparisons were 'intolerable'.[48] However, both platforms called for the reduction of migration to zero and enormous expansions of prisons. 'Why is it, in the Netherlands', read Fortuyn's manifesto, 'that we can allow four elderly people to a room in a nursing home, but not four criminals to a cell?'[49]

While Fortuyn publicly decried almost all of the old parties and refused to acknowledge the idea that he would accept being a junior minister in anyone's government – he intended, he claimed, to be the Netherlands' first gay prime minister – he in fact had a privately quite warm relationship with the Christian Democrats, who had been locked out of power since the social-liberal coalition took over in the mid-1990s. His 1995 book *The Orphaned Society* was introduced at its launch by the then-leader of the Christian Democrats; Oudenampsen writes that senior Christian Democrats saw 'important overlaps between the "ideology critique" developed by Fortuyn and that of the Christian Democrat Party. Fortuyn … had taken much of his conservative ideas from the CDA [Christian Democrat Appeal] … In the campaign for the 2002 elections, Fortuyn's party and the Christian Democrat Party agreed not to attack each other. In the autumn of 2001, Fortuyn is said to have privately professed his faith' in Jan-Peter Balkenende, the leader of the Christian Democrats.[50]

This, too, is a common dynamic of interplay between the new far right and the old conservative right. The general cordon sanitaire across Europe that existed between the centre-right and far-right had broken when, in 2000, the Austrian People's Party, a Christian-democratic party, agreed to enter in coalition with Jörg Haider's far-right and partially neo-fascist Freedom Party. (Rumours that Haider was gay and had male lovers may no longer be published after a successful lawsuit by his widow in 2008, after his death in a car accident.)[51]

Once again the question of style was increasingly important here. Openly gay, Fortuyn wore his dandyism and his homosexuality as a carefully selected marketing tool through which even liberal journalists often found themselves being charmed into writing fluffy articles about him, in much the same way as journalists clamoured to cover the sharp suits and sharper hairstyles of alt-right ideologues like Richard Spencer and Milo Yiannopoulos in the wake of Donald Trump's election as US president in 2016. No profile passed by without reference to 'his expensively tailored suits, immaculate shirts, matching silk handkerchiefs and ties', to his shaved head, to his immaculately decorated city palace; 'the dapper, witty rabble-rouser' was compared favourably with Le Pen, who 'has clearly been gone over by the style police ... but the result is a rather unconvincing "cuddly granddad"', and with Italy's Umberto Bossi, who looked 'like he's been dragged through a hedge backwards ... Only Jörg Haider in Austria', this particular article read, 'comes anywhere near Pim in the style stakes – but even here the two men are quite obviously in different leagues.'[52]

If part of Fortuyn's horror at being compared with Le Pen was his reluctance to be seen as a low-class thuggish reactionary, then this was also a key part of his political appeal – he could whitewash and repackage those ideas for an audience that thought of itself as enlightened and progressive. And liberal journalists persisted in enabling him. 'There was nothing the effete, former sociology professor hated more than being cast in the same mould as the burly, former French paratrooper,' Kirsty Lang wrote in the *Guardian*, in 2002, of the comparisons being made between Fortuyn and Le Pen. 'He was a civilized man, and Holland was a civilized country,' she went on. 'His belief was that Muslim immigration undermined the society he cherished.'[53] This mix created a form of xenophobia perfect for a nation whose nationalism is based on tolerance: *they* can't be here because *they* are intolerant, and *we* are tolerant. By May 6, independent surveys were predicting that the Fortuyn List would come in first in the national elections, just more than a week away.

The next day, Fortuyn was leaving a radio studio in the town of Hilversum, having given an interview. He was attacked by a single gunman who shot him, point-blank, in the head.[54] This was the first peacetime political assassination in Holland since the seventeenth century. The fact that Fortuyn was shot outside a radio studio meant that the events – and the quick manhunt for the killer – could all be broadcast live.

Fortuyn's murderer was almost immediately identified as the thirty-two-year-old environmental activist Volkert van der Graaf, an animal rights campaigner with no history of violent crime, and no weapon permit, and no getaway plan; he was rapidly apprehended, and many Dutch people, especially Fortuyn fans, were suspicious that such an event had been perpetrated by someone seemingly so random. 'Pim was too outspoken – they were afraid of that,' one woman told a journalist in the aftermath of the murder.[55]

The Dutch prime minister Wim Kok gave a speech on television, mourning the death of Fortuyn in starkly nationalistic terms. 'What went through my head', he said, 'is "this is the Netherlands, a nation of tolerance".'[56] A more gimlet-eyed view might argue that both Fortuyn's emergence as a national political figure and his murder revealed the limits of the Netherlands' embrace of tolerance and of its adoption of supposedly complete emancipation movements as a national brand.

The murder was experienced, writes the anthropologist Peter Jan Margry, as 'a cultural shock through which The Netherlands lost its innocence as an honest and peace-loving nation', with enormous public shrines being built in front of Fortuyn's home; in front of Rotterdam's City Hall; in the parking lot where he had been shot; at the monument of William of Orange, a Dutch national hero himself rumoured to have had some homosexual inclinations; and at both the National War Monument and the Homomonument in Amsterdam.[57]

Crucial here, recalling both Jasbir Puar and Gloria Wekker's related if different arguments about white homosexuality, colonialism, and the nation, is the simultaneous use of the War Monument and the Homomonument. It marks the symbolic reclamation of a monument to gay liberation as a place of national and nationalist mourning and political signification. After Fortuyn's death, Margry writes, there was a 'sharp increase' in discussions of him as 'a prophet or hero', discussions that gelled with Fortuyn's own comparisons of himself to Moses leading his people to the Promised Land.[58] On the evening of the assassination a protest of Fortuyn acolytes in front of the Dutch parliament demanded that politicians who had called Fortuyn a racist and 'the "leftist" press' pay for their incitement of violence and hatred.[59]

Campaigning was suspended, but it was decided that the elections should go ahead as scheduled, as a demonstration of the ongoing strength of Dutch democracy. With a sharp uptick in turnout, the parties comprising the social-liberal coalition all suffered massive losses. In first place were the Christian Democrats, and in second place the leaderless Pim Fortuyn List, which, along with the Christian Democrats and the more conservative of the two liberal parties, entered government coalition under Prime Minister Jan-Peter Balkenende.

This government declared, in 2003, that emancipation was complete – though Gloria Wekker noted that declaration didn't apply to 'black, migrant, and refugee women'.[60] Massive budget cuts for women's programs and centres followed, examples of what David Roediger once called 'the wages of whiteness' – white women accepting cuts to their movement in exchange for a position atop the racial hierarchy. The new coalition did not even last a year – infighting in the newly leaderless Fortuyn List made the cabinet dramatically unstable, and in the next year's elections the list lost 12 percent of its support and eighteen seats in Parliament. By the following election in 2006, it was no longer represented there.

But the changes in Dutch, and European, politics that Fortuyn inaugurated were far longer lasting. 'What had started as one peculiar "gay" perspective on immigration and integration soon became an acceptable political view for huge swathes of the Dutch population,' Shield writes. Indeed, many new far-right politicians, like Marine Le Pen or Germany's lesbian Alice Weidel, have followed Fortuyn's model of sanitizing far-right anti-immigrant politics by tying them to defences of a kind of national liberalism.[61] The Dutch conservative-liberal party VVD (Volkspartij voor Vrijheid en Democratie, or the People's Party for Freedom and Democracy) began to adopt many of Fortuyn's positions on race and immigration, as did the Christian Democrats, who would remain in office until 2010 (when they were surpassed by the VVD).[62]

Even Wouter Bos, the new leader of the Social Democrats, began to echo some of Fortuyn's points, writing in 2005 that it was 'naive' for social democrats to ignore 'problems with managing migration and diversity', writing that 'unlimited migration and failing integration are a serious threat to solidarity and to the degree of welfare sharing we are proud of as social democrats', and that a 'fear of racism' had prevented leftists from speaking up on this issue.[63] The Netherlands has not had a social democrat–led government since Fortuyn's murder.

In 2006, when the Fortuyn List lost parliamentary representation and no far-right party entered parliament, a *Guardian* article was eager to present the integration of anti-immigration sentiment into the Dutch polder model as a victory: 'The ending of the Fortuyn era', the newspaper opined, 'shows that ... consensus politics is finally asserting itself over the highly sensitive issue of immigration.'[64]

Four years later, under the leadership of its autocratic leader Geert Wilders, a former member of the conservative-liberal VVD, a new party called the Party for Freedom stormed the Dutch parliament, taking twenty-four seats and third place. Wilders, who campaigned on banning the Qur'an, taxing the wearing of hijabs, closing all mosques in the Netherlands, exiting the European Union, and restoring years of cuts to welfare, and who was banned from entering the United Kingdom due to inciting racial hatred, ended up propping up a right-liberal government for two years.

The Party for Freedom was, in that election, the most popular political party among white Dutch gay men; and this party's participation in a coalition government, breaking the cordon sanitaire against the participation of the far right in government, was supported by the formerly radical COC Nederland, the country's largest gay organization, which made a dismissive comment about 'Moroccan boys' being violent to gay men in the streets.[65]

By October of 2013, racial profiling was common enough among Dutch police to become the subject of an Amnesty International report. A district police officer in The Hague gave a television interview in 2010 arguing that Moroccans were genetically more disposed to violence than Dutch people: 'The people responsible for violence in Gouda [a Dutch city] come from the Rif Mountains. They are Berbers. The word Berber derives from the word "barbarian". And that naturally means they are culturally somewhat more tempered. They find it easier to live on the streets. You could say that it is a genetic trait.' In 2015, Gerard Bouman, then the chief of police in the Netherlands, revealed that far-right infiltration in police circles had led to the common occurrence of officers calling to burn mosques and attack Muslims.[66]

By 2015, national media were counting at least thirty-five daily instances of police violence, with estimates that far more were likely going unreported; only 0.7 percent of reports were ever officially investigated.[67] That year Mitch Henriquez, an unarmed Black man, on vacation in the Netherlands from its colony in Aruba, was strangled to death by a police officer. In response to protests, politicians insisted that there was no racism in the police and referred to protestors as 'hooligans' and 'retards'.[68] One NGO estimates that forty-one people, half of them with a migration background, have been murdered by police in the Netherlands since Henriquez's death; in none of these cases have charges been filed against the officer.[69] A 2019 United Nations report on the Netherlands condemned racist policing, redlining, and employment and economic inequality based on race and country of origin.[70]

When Fortuyn was exhumed ten weeks after his burial to be reburied near his summer home in Italy, the exhumation was broadcast on television. Mourners sang the hymn 'Amazing Grace' in Dutch. A white hearse covered in sunflowers transported the corpse. In the ten weeks he'd been buried in Driehuis, 150,000 mourners visited his grave. The rifle with which Fortuyn was murdered is in the permanent collection of the Rijksmuseum in Amsterdam. At his trial, Van der Graaf said that he had murdered Fortuyn to protect vulnerable people. After refusing to give a statement for many months, he confessed to the shooting in court. 'The idea was never concrete until the last moment, the day before the attack. I could see no other option than to do what I did,' he said. 'I saw it as a danger, but what should you do about it? I hoped that I could solve it myself.'[71]

The murder of Fortuyn had, of course, the opposite effect: rather than effectively combating his politics, as nonviolent activism might have done, it instead claimed a human life. In so doing, Van der Graaf cemented the idea that this man had represented the apotheosis of emancipation, and helped to write Fortuyn into the character of the Dutch nation itself. In 2004, Fortuyn was voted, by a state television poll, as the Greatest Dutchman of all time.

Conclusion

Homosexuality is not an ever-fixéd mark; it's a contingent identity, something developed through a slow accrual of meaning over the centuries. Within it are still the remnants of sin, its half-life still slowly poisoning gays millennia on, and sickness, and crime. There are remnants of a heritage of rebellion, of throwing established norms into anarchy, but also of order, of the relentless policing of the self, and of the behaviour of other queers.

The history of homosexuality is a long history of failure – failure to understand ourselves, failure to understand how we relate to society, and the failures of racism and exclusion. It is also a history of dead ends; of movements like the Uranians or the masculinists, trying to find new ways to express same-sex desire. It is not just an issue of shifting language, from 'sodomite' to 'urning', from 'invert' to 'queer': the changing words emerge out of a recognition that what it means to be gay has shifted, and new words are needed to understand it.

Just as it has always changed, it will keep changing, too. If the conflicts within queer cultures sometimes seem to be split along largely intergenerational lines, that is because old understandings of what constitutes the identity are brushing up against new ones.

It might seem counterintuitive, given the title of the book, but we want to be clear that we profile these characters from history not because we want to condemn them – or, at least, not totally. A principle of understanding our status as gay people both within our culture and within wider society is this: we are not just the protagonists, but also the products of history. Not only do our rights come from prior political struggles that were full of faults and fault lines, but everything about what we conceive of gay to mean is also the product of centuries of accretions of meanings, roles, and experiences.

What are the implications of trying to build a sense of political solidarity upon these shifting sands? Well, perhaps it's that the shifting sands make solidarity vital: it's the only thing that has ever worked for queer people. If our history of homosexuality has any consistent lesson, it's that the ability to live as queer people faces challenges that are always fluctuating. Certain narratives within liberal gay circles like to paint the gay rights enjoyed in some Western countries not just as the inevitable product of the Western nation-state, a slow forward march towards rights and justice, but also as permanent, intractable, the end-point of progress. But the history of bad gays complicates that; our history is full of failed attempts at liberation, at new boundaries rolled back in public book burnings, of the ever-present threat of state suppression and social stigma. The value of your liberation may go down as well as up.

Where some might see the wide-ranging acceptance that some forms of homosexuality now enjoy in some places as a result of increased liberalism bringing more people into the social contract of the state, we see, instead, the fruits of hundreds of political, social, and cultural movements making homosexuality visible; making alliances with other political and social identities; and broadening contact between political struggles. As Roderick Ferguson argues in *One-Dimensional Queer*, it was in these alliances that the parts of gay liberation worth saving originated, and it is to these alliances that any queer politics worth its salt must now turn.[1]

It is only through solidarity and alliance that liberation is possible; it is also as part of the same process that we can build towards a better form of being, realising in ourselves new facets of being together, new ways to inhabit what Michel Foucault called the 'slantwise', the 'diagonal lines' cut through the social fabric.[2] For alongside our history of homosexuality, drawn from the malignant homos of our culture, run brilliant counter-histories, experiences of alliance and solidarity that offer us alternative futures, should we wish to dream them forward.

The labour union representing marine cooks and stewards in 1930s California slowly radicalized under pressure from members upset with racism in the union's ranks and its limp resistance to management. Eventually, they formed a Communist, explicitly anti-racist, explicitly pro-queer union. 'No red-baiting, no race-baiting, no queen-baiting' became their slogan, and they stood in solidarity with other radical unions in waves of general strikes across the State of California that transformed labour relations. One member of that union went on to help co-found the Mattachine Society, one of the first gay rights organizations in the United States, and which had, at least at the beginning, a radical, Communist, anti-racist analysis of the contradictions producing homosexuality. You can learn more about this in Allan Bérubé's essays on the Marine Cooks and Stewards Union, brilliant pieces of queer history and labour history full of lessons, tools, and paths forward.[3]

On a June night in 1969, a multiracial group of working-class street kids, drag queens, trans women, sex workers, and sissies, not at all the kinds of people History remembers as its typical heroic subjects, got pissed off and resisted arrest and took to the streets and rioted. Three days of street riots ensued. A few years before, similar riots had taken place at the Compton's Cafeteria in San Francisco; but these riots outside the Stonewall Inn in the West Village marked a sea change in the self-confidence and exterior politicization of queer movements. Sylvia Rivera and Marsha P. Johnson, two crucial participants at Stonewall, trans women of colour who engaged in sex work, created an organization called Street Transvestite Action Revolutionaries, or STAR, demanding that Gay Power include fighting back against police and fighting for gay men and trans women in prisons. They pooled their earnings to create a safe house for street kids, queens, and trans women to live in.[4] Throughout the 1970s, prison outreach and liberation continued to play a major role in radical gay and lesbian organizing.

In the 1970s, gay liberation evolved along the explicit model of alliance with anti-colonial and Third Worldist liberation groups. Immediately, there were fault lines: Third World Gay Revolution, in New York City, split off from the local main gay liberation group and developed analyses of racism and colonization and how those processes intersected with the development of sexuality as we understand it today. They protested single-issue politics and racism among white gay and lesbian movements.

Throughout the 1970s and 1980s, gay liberation continued to exist in meaningful, if complex, alliance with anti-colonial struggles in the imperial core. (Emily Hobson's excellent book *Lavender and Red* covers this well.) A group of Black socialist lesbian feminists, the Combahee River Collective, developed a theory of the relationship between politics and their sexuality, insisting that if they were not free, then no one would be. Audre Lorde brought this theory to Berlin, where a group of Black German women created an anti-racist, lesbian-feminist movement.[5]

With the advent of the 1980s came a new wave of right-wing politics, a backlash to the multiple revolutions of the long 1960s. Brutal austerity was accompanied by attacks on democracy and collective political, cultural, and social expression – first in the neocolonial laboratories of neoliberalism in South America, and then by Reagan in the United States and Thatcher in Great Britain. In Britain, during the miners' strike of 1984–85, a group of gays and lesbians in London created an activist group, Lesbians and Gays Support the Miners, to support the striking miners as they attempted to take Thatcher on, backing the miners' efforts to secure a dignified livelihood for themselves and their communities. When Thatcher, in a shocking attack on democracy, stole control of the union's bank accounts, LGSM held benefits (such as the infamous Pits and Perverts concert, featuring Bronski Beat) to raise funds. In return, the miners opposed Thatcher's Section 28, a brutal attack on queer children and on freedom of speech in public education that effectively forbade any discussion of sexuality in the school system.

This is where the Right wants to take us back to, and there are certain elements of the Left that are astonishingly eager to blame neoliberalism on the vicissitudes of queer French philosophers rather than the crisis of profits of the 1970s and capital's need to generate a backlash against the ghosts of liberation.

When AIDS ravaged queer communities, we organized, creating direct service organizations to help people survive and be cared for in sickness, and direct action organizations to fight the murderous, ignorant indifference shown by state officials; fighting to change official definitions of AIDS to include women in drug trials and social services; fighting for universal health care and free pharmaceutical care; fighting for drug users and people living on the street; fighting for patents to be lifted on life-saving medication so that people in the Global South could survive. In the aftermath of AIDS, as movements in Britain and the United States began to be more and more dominated by a class of people who had never before been so involved in gay and lesbian organizing but who sought to throw away multiple-issue concerns in favour of securing relationship recognition and military service rights for gay and lesbian people, they were challenged by groups like Queers for Racial and Economic Justice.

It is not always so easy, especially when subjects are marked by whiteness and other forms of power and privilege, to neatly separate the good from the bad, the right from the wrong. The answer, though, is not to simply stan our heroes and shush up about their flaws and faults; rather, it's to understand how people have made and been made by history, how and why they have failed, and how and why we might succeed.

In 1977, the mostly good gay Larry Mitchell, from his compound in upstate New York, wrote a fable called *The Faggots and Their Friends between Revolutions*. 'The faggots and their friends', he wrote, 'live the best while empires are falling. Since the men are always building as many empires as they can, there are always one or two falling and so one or two places for the faggots and their friends to go.'[6] He dreamed that faggots were a kind of being other than men, that we inhabited communities of exquisitely liberated homosexuality in which we cultivated the states of beauty and harmony and peace that men do not know about. But near the fable's end, he perceived that this, too, served the system: 'The faggots and their friends and the women who love women', he wrote, 'can keep the men off balance for a long time by subtly, but continually, changing their identities. The men who are in charge of controlling it all find it difficult always to know how many of each kind there are and who they are ... They can play with the men's categories to try to neutralize the men's guns. Yet this will not make them free. They begin to know, from the inside, that they cannot be free until this dance is stopped ... When the faggots and their friends cease being the faggots and their friends, the deathly dance of the men will begin to wane and a new dance will begin to emerge. Then the third revolutions will engulf us all.'[7]

We do not get to choose who we are but we do get to choose how, and with whom, we dance: what queerness, what faggotry, what transness, what gender trouble and abolition will be for us and with us and to us. The past is still with us; the revolutions of the queer future beckon.

Acknowledgements

When we began producing our podcast we thought we were making it for a tiny audience, one made up of mostly our friends. The fact we have been able to reach a much wider audience than that is down entirely to our listeners, and we are enormously grateful to all those who have listened to, shared, and recommended the podcast, and especially those who have supported us through Patreon and sent us their own suggestions for future bad gays, without whom the show and this book would have been impossible. Thank you.

We would like to thank our editor Leo Hollis for his guiding hand in shaping the book, and to Huw's agent, Niki Chang, and Ben's agent, Doug Young, for their help in realising the project from an idea over coffee to the book in your hand. It takes many hands to produce a book, and we're grateful for all those at Verso whose hard work is involved, especially Jennifer Tighe, Maya Osborne, Michelle Betters, Catherine Smiles, Rowan Wilson, Federico Campagna, Brian Baughan, Jordan Taylor-Jones, Mark Martin, and Bob Bhamra.

Many thanks too to our guests over the years, for the insight and energy they have brought to the show: Sholem Krishtalka, Juliet Jacques, the late and much-missed Decorsey Macauleney ('Mac') Folkes, Edna Bonhomme, Jana Funke, Richard Power Sayeed, Diarmuid Hester, David Eichert, Max Fox, and Ari Níelsson.

Acknowledgements

For the researchers, writers, theorists, thinkers, and activists on whose work this book and its arguments are based, we have nothing but awe and respect; we hope that our citations have been generous enough to drive more people to engage more deeply with the rich variety of material available on queer pasts and queer futures.

Thanks to our friends, colleagues, and comrades who are always sharing, discussing, and expanding ideas on sex, identity, gender, and history, and have been such a rich source of knowledge over the years. Thanks are in order to those people, in no particular order: Davey Davis, Sz Huldt, Robin Craig, Joan Escofet, Joan Morera, Jay Owens, James Butler, Jesse Darling, Angelica Sgouros, Felix del Campo, Jack Young, Isabel Waidner, Shon Faye, Mathew Parkin, Claudia Pagès, Jasper Murphy, Jaakko Pallasvuo, Ray Filar, Andrew D. J. Shield, Sarah Shin, Seán McGovern, McKenzie Wark, Mattilda Bernstein Sycamore, Samuel Delany, Jay Springett, Ben Vickers, Fer Boyd, Madeleine Stack, Connor Friesen, Onyeka Igwe, Pete Mills, Nina Wakeford, Richard John Jones, Tamar Shlaim, Michael Harding, Liz Rosenfeld, Connor Spencer, Sawyer Huff, Syd Ramirez, Harry Stopes, AA Bronson and Mark Jan Krayenhoff van de Leur, Dr Isabel Valli, Arash Fayez, Jim Richards, Danilo Rosato, Giovanni Turco and Giacomo Garavelloni, Peter Welz, Ronny Matthes, Khary Polk, Nicholas Courtman, Angela Zimmerman, Ashkan Sepahvand, Birgit Bosold and Heiner Schulze (and the entire team at Berlin's Schwules Museum), Colin Self, Juliana Gleeson, Gabe Rosenberg and Harris Solomon, Sébastien Tremblay, all twelve brilliant Doctoral Fellows of 2020 at the Graduate School of Global Intellectual History at the Free University of Berlin, Barrie Kosky, Kate Davison, Rosa Lee, Michelle Esther O'Brien, Anna Hájková, Jennifer Evans, and Elijah Burgher and Jonathan Carreon. Thanks to the people we surely and shamefully forgot. Thanks also to our teachers, including Sherry Edwards, Sebastian Conrad, Marcelle Clements, Margrit Pernau, Linda Gordon, K Kevyne Baar, Martin Lücke, Greg Drake, and the late and dearly missed Ty Vignone. Finally, acknowledgements are due to the wider queer community that has nurtured us both for most of our lives, offering hope and consolation and bottles of poppers on the dancefloor, chatted with us on Twitter and in chatrooms and darkrooms, people who have held our hands and lived by example. We just love the faggots, and their (our) friends.

Last but certainly not least: thanks to our families and our partners, João and Cory John, for their care, love, and tolerance.

Further Reading

Introduction

Bérubé, Allan. *My Desire for History: Essays in Gay, Community, and Labor History*. Edited by John D'Emilio and Estelle B. Freedman. Chapel Hill, NC: University of North Carolina Press, 2011.

Cohen, Cathy J. 'Punks, Bulldaggers, and Welfare Queens: The Radical Potential of Queer Politics?' *GLQ: A Journal of Lesbian and Gay Studies* 3, no. 4 (January 1, 1997): 437–65.

D'Emilio, John. 'Capitalism and Gay Identity'. In *Powers of Desire: The Politics of Sexuality*, edited by Ann Snitow, Christine Stansell, and Sharan Thompson, 100–13. New York: Monthly Review Press, 1983.

Drucker, Peter. 'Warped: Gay Normality and Queer Anti-Capitalism'. *Historical Materialism* 92. 2016.

Ferguson, Roderick A. *One-Dimensional Queer*. Medford, MA: Polity, 2019.

Herzog, Dagmar. *Sexuality in Europe: A Twentieth-Century History*. Cambridge, UK ; New York: Cambridge University Press, 2011.

Hobson, Emily K. *Lavender and Red: Liberation and Solidarity in the Gay and Lesbian Left*. Berkeley, Calif.: University of California Press, 2016.

Houlbrook, Matt. *Queer London: Perils and Pleasures in the Sexual Metropolis, 1918–1957*. Chicago, IL: University of Chicago Press, 2006.

Schulman, Sarah. *Let the Record Show: A Political History of*

ACT UP New York, 1987–1993. New York: Farrar, Straus and Giroux, 2021.

Stanley, Eric A., and Nat Smith, eds. *Captive Genders: Trans Embodiment and the Prison Industrial Complex*. Oakland, CA: AK Press, 2011.

Stryker, Susan. *Transgender History*. Seal Studies. Berkeley, CA: Seal Press, 2008.

Weeks, Jeffrey. *Making Sexual History*. Cambridge, UK; Malden, Mass.: Polity Press, 2000.

1. Hadrian

Birley, Anthony Richard. *Hadrian: The Restless Emperor*. London: Routledge, 1997.

Lambert, Royston. *Beloved and God: The Story of Hadrian and Antinous*. New York: Viking, 1984.

Richlin, Amy. 'Sexuality in the Roman Empire', in *The Companion to the Roman Empire*, edited by David S. Potter. Oxford: Blackwell Publishing, 2006.

2. Pietro Aretino

Chitty, Christopher. *Sexual Hegemony: Statecraft, Sodomy, and Capital in the Rise of the World System*. Durham: Duke University Press, 2020.

Hutton, Edward. *Pietro Aretino: The Scourge of Princes*. London: Constable and Co., 1922.

Rocke, Michael. *Forbidden Friendships: Homosexuality and Male Culture in Renaissance Florence*. Oxford: Oxford University Press, 1996.

3. James VI and I

Bergeron, David M. *King James and Letters of Homoerotic Desire*. Iowa City: University of Iowa Press, 2002.

Bevan, Bryan. *King James VI of Scotland and I of England*. London: Rubicon Press, 1996.

Croft, Pauline. *King James*. New York: Palgrave MacMillan, 2003.

Fraser, Antonia. *King James, VI of Scotland, I of England*. London: Weidenfeld and Nicolson, 1994.

4. Frederick the Great

Ashton, Bodie A. 'Kingship, Sexuality and Courtly Masculinity: Frederick the Great and Prussia on the Cusp of Modernity'. *ANU Historical Journal II* 1 (May 2019): 109–35.

Blanning, Tim. *Frederick the Great: King of Prussia*. New York: Penguin, 2015.

MacDonogh, Giles. *Frederick the Great: A Life in Deeds and Letters*. New York: St. Martin's Press, 2000.

Tobin, Robert Deam. *Warm Brothers: Queer Theory and the Age of Goethe*. Philadelphia: University of Pennsylvania Press, 2000.

5. Jack Saul

Chandler, Glenn. *The Sins of Jack Saul*. Surbiton, UK: Grosvenor House Publishing, 2016.

Hyde, H Montgomery. *The Cleveland Street Scandal*. New York: Coward, McCann & Geoghegan, 1976.

McKenna, Neil. *Fanny and Stella: The Young Men Who Shocked Victorian England*. London: Faber, 2014.

Saul, Jack. *The Sins of the Cities of the Plain*. London: William Lazenby, 1881.

6. Roger Casement

Casement, Roger. *The Amazon Journal of Roger Casement*. Edited by Angus Mitchell. London: Anaconda Editions, 2000.

Dudgeon, Jeffrey, and Roger Casement. *Roger Casement: The Black Diaries: With a Study of His Background, Sexuality and Irish Political Life*. Belfast, Northern Ireland: Belfast Press, 2002.

Gandhi, Leela. *Affective Communities: Anticolonial Thought, Fin-De-Siècle Radicalism, and the Politics of Friendship.* Durham, NC: Duke University Press, 2006.

Nzongola-Ntalaja, Georges. *The Congo: From Leopold to Kabila: A People's History.* London: Zed Books, 2002.

Uriarte, Javier. 'Splendid Testemunhos: Documenting Atrocities, Bodies, and Desire in Roger Casement's Black Diaries'. In *Intimate Frontiers: A Literary Geography of the Amazon,* edited by Javier Uriarte and Felipe Martinez-Pinzon, 88–112. Liverpool: Liverpool University Press, 2019.

7. Lawrence of Arabia

Aldrich, Robert. *Colonialism and Homosexuality.* London: Routledge, 2003.

Boone, Joseph Allen. *The Homoerotics of Orientalism.* New York: Columbia University Press, 2014.

Faulkner, Neil. *Lawrence of Arabia's War: The Arabs, the British and the Remaking of the Middle East in WWI.* New Haven, CT: Yale University Press, 2017.

Guy, Simon. 'The Use and Abuse of the Arab Revolt'. *Socialist Review,* no. 414 (June 2016).

Lawrence, Thomas E., Jeremy Wilson, and Nicole Wilson. *Seven Pillars of Wisdom: The Complete 1922 'Oxford' Text.* Fordingbridge, Hampshire, UK: Castle Hill Press, 2004.

Sattin, Anthony. *The Young T. E. Lawrence.* New York: W.W. Norton, 2015.

8. Weimar Berlin

Bauer, Heike. *The Hirschfeld Archives: Violence, Death, and Modern Queer Culture.* Philadelphia: Temple University Press, 2017.

Dose, Ralf. *Magnus Hirschfeld: The Origins of the Gay Liberation Movement.* New York: New York University Press, 2014.

Hancock, Eleanor. *Ernst Röhm: Hitler's SA Chief of Staff.* London: Palgrave Macmillan, 2008.

Marhoefer, Laurie. 'Queer Fascism and the End of Gay History'. Notches (blog), 19 June 2018. notchesblog.com.

——.*Sex and the Weimar Republic: German Homosexual Emancipation and the Rise of the Nazis*. Toronto: University of Toronto Press, 2015.

Samper Vendrell, Javier. *The Seduction of Youth: Print Culture and Homosexual Rights in the Weimar Republic*. Toronto: University of Toronto Press, 2020.

Tobin, Robert Deam. *Peripheral Desires: The German Discovery of Sex*. Philadelphia: University of Pennsylvania Press, 2015.

9. Margaret Mead

Anderson, Mark. *From Boas to Black Power*. Stanford, CA: Stanford University Press, 2019.

Asad, Talal. *Anthropology and the Colonial Encounter*. London: Ithaca Books, 1973.

Banner, Lois W. *Intertwined Lives: Margaret Mead, Ruth Benedict, and Their Circle*. New York: Vintage Books, 2004.

Caffrey, Margaret, and Patricia Francis. *To Cherish the Life of the World: The Selected Letters of Margaret Mead*. New York: Basic Books, 2006.

Di Leonardo, Micaela. *Exotics at Home: Anthropologies, Others, and American Modernity*. Chicago, IL: University of Chicago Press, 2000.

Gullahorn-Holecek, Barbara. *Papua New Guinea: Anthropology on Trial*. Ambrose Video Publishing, 1983.

Lutkehaus, Nancy. *Margaret Mead: The Making of an American Icon*. Princeton, NJ: Princeton Univ. Press, 2011.

Shankman, Paul. *The Trashing of Margaret Mead: Anatomy of an Anthropological Controversy*. Madison: University of Wisconsin Press, 2009.

10. J. Edgar Hoover and Roy Cohn

Gentry, Curt. *J. Edgar Hoover: The Man and His Secrets*. New York: Plume, 1992.

Johnson, David K. *The Lavender Scare: The Cold War Persecution of Gays and Lesbians in the Federal Government*. Chicago: University of Chicago Press, 2004.

Summers, Anthony. *Official and Confidential: The Secret Life of J. Edgar Hoover*. New York: Random House, 2012.

Von Hoffman, Nicholas, *Citizen Cohn*. New York: Bantam, 1988.

11. Yukio Mishima

Mishima, Yukio. *Confessions of a Mask*. St. Albans, UK: Panther, 1977.

Nathan, John. *Mishima: A Biography*. Boston: Little, Brown, 1974.

Pflugfelder, Gregory M. *Cartographies of Desire: Male-Male Sexuality in Japanese Discourse 1600–1950*. Berkeley: University of California Press, 1999.

Scott-Stokes, Henry. *The Life and Death of Yukio Mishima*. New York: Farrar, Straus and Giroux, 1974.

12. Philip Johnson

Archives of the Johnson Study Group. instagram.com.

Lamster, Mark. *The Man in the Glass House: Philip Johnson, Architect of the Modern Century*. Boston: Little, Brown, 2018.

Petit, Emmanuel, ed. *Philip Johnson: The Constancy of Change*. New Haven, CT: Yale University Press, 2009.

Schulze, Franz. *Philip Johnson: Life and Work*. Chicago: University of Chicago Press, 1996.

13. Ronnie Kray

Kray, Reg, and Kray, Ron, with Dinenage, Fred. *Our Story*. London: Pan, 1989.

Linnane, Fergus. *London's Underworld: Three Centuries of Vice and Crime*. London: Robson, 2004.

Pearson, John, *The Profession of Violence: The Rise and Fall of the Kray Twins*. London: William Collins, 2015.

14. Pim Fortuyn

Herzog, Dagmar. *Sexuality in Europe: A Twentieth-Century History*. Cambridge: Cambridge University Press, 2011.

Elizabeth Kolbert, 'Beyond Tolerance – What Did the Dutch See in Pim Fortuyn?', *New Yorker*, 1 September 2002.

Oudenampsen, Merijn. *The Rise of the Dutch New Right: An Intellectual History of the Rightward Shift in Dutch Politics*. Abingdon, Oxon, UK: Routledge, 2020.

Puar, Jasbir K. *Terrorist Assemblages: Homonationalism in Queer Times*. Durham, NC: Duke University Press, 2007.

Shield, Andrew DJ. *Immigrants in the Sexual Revolution: Perceptions and Participation in Northwest Europe*. London: Palgrave Macmillan, 2017.

Wekker, Gloria. *White Innocence: Paradoxes of Colonialism and Race*. Durham: Duke University Press, 2016.

Notes

Introduction

1 Oscar Wilde, *De Profundis* (London: Menthuen & Co., 1927), 106.

2 H. Montgomery Hyde, *The Three Trials of Oscar Wilde* (New York: University Books, 1956), 236.

3 See Douglas Murray, *Bosie: A Biography of Lord Alfred Douglas* (New York: Hyperion, 2000).

4 Emily K. Hobson, *Lavender and Red: Liberation and Solidarity in the Gay and Lesbian Left* (Berkeley: University of California Press, 2016); Allan Bérubé, *My Desire for History: Essays in Gay, Community, and Labor History*, ed. John D'Emilio and Estelle B. Freedman (Chapel Hill: University of North Carolina Press, 2011); Aaron Lecklider, *Love's Next Meeting: The Forgotten History of Homosexuality and the Left in American Culture* (Berkeley: University of California Press, 2021); Tiffany N. Florvil, *Mobilizing Black Germany: Afro-German Women and the Making of a Transnational Movement* (Urbana: University of Illinois Press, 2020).

5 Susan Stryker, *Transgender History* (Berkeley, CA: Seal Press, 2008); Susan Stryker, 'Transgender History, Homonormativity, and Disciplinarity', *Radical History Review*, no. 100 (Winter 2008).

6 C Riley Snorton, *Black on Both Sides: A Racial History of Trans Identity* (Minneapolis: University of Minnesota Press, 2017); Jules Gill-Peterson, *Histories of the Transgender Child* (Minneapolis: University of Minnesota Press, 2018); Ann Laura Stoler, *Carnal Knowledge and Imperial Power: Race and the Intimate in Colonial Rule* (Berkeley: University of California Press, 2003); Anne McClintock, *Imperial Leather: Race, Gender, and Sexuality in the Colonial Contest* (London: Routledge, 1995).

7 'Faggots and Class Struggle: A Conference Report', *Morning Due: A Journal of Men Against Sexism*, December 1976.

8 John D'Emilio, 'Capitalism and Gay Identity', in *Powers of Desire: The Politics of Sexuality*, ed. Ann Snitow, Christine Stansell, and Sharon Thompson (New York: Monthly Review Press, 1983), 100–113.

9 Christopher Chitty, *Sexual Hegemony: Statecraft, Sodomy, and Capital in the Rise of the World System* (Durham, NC: Duke University Press, 2020).

10 Susan Stryker, 'Gay American History @ 40: Keynote', Gay American History at 40, The New School, New York, 2016, YouTube.

11 See Jeffrey Weeks, *Making Sexual History* (Cambridge: Polity Press, 2000); Michel Foucault, *The History of Sexuality, Volume 1: An Introduction*, trans. Robert Hurley (New York: Pantheon Books, 1978); Karen E. Fields and Barbara Jeanne Fields, *Racecraft: The Soul of Inequality in American Life* (London: Verso, 2012); Ann Laura Stoler, *Race and the Education of Desire: Foucault's History of Sexuality and the Colonial Order of Things* (Durham: Duke University Press, 1995); Peter Drucker, *Warped: Gay Normality and Queer Anti-capitalism*, Historical Materialism series, vol. 92 (Leiden, Netherlands: Brill, 2016).

12 See Foucault, *The History of Sexuality, Volume 1*; Weeks, *Making Sexual History*, Laurie Marhoefer, *Sex and the Weimar Republic: German Homosexual Emancipation and the Rise of the Nazis* (Toronto: University of Toronto Press, 2015).

13 See Foucault, *The History of Sexuality, Volume 1*; Elizabeth Freeman, *Time Binds: Queer Temporalities, Queer Histories* (Durham, NC: Duke University Press, 2010); Jonathan Martineau, *Time, Capitalism and Alienation: A Socio-Historical Inquiry into the Making of Modern Time*, Historical Materialism series, vol. 96 (Leiden, Netherlands: Brill, 2015); Sebastian Conrad, '"Nothing Is the Way It Should Be": Global Transformation of the Time Regime in the Nineteenth Century', *Modern Intellectual History* 15, no. 3 (November 2018): 821–48. Anjali Arondekar, 'Without a Trace: Sexuality and the Colonial Archive', *Journal of the History of Sexuality* 14, no. 1 (2005): 10–27.

14 For the invention of heterosexuality, see Jonathan Ned Katz, *The Invention of Heterosexuality* (New York: Dutton, 1995).

15 See Marhoefer, *Sex and the Weimar Republic*; Laurie Marhoefer, 'Was the Homosexual Made White? Race, Empire, and Analogy in Gay and Trans Thought in Twentieth-Century Germany', *Gender and History* 31, no. 1 (March 2019): 91–114; McClintock, *Imperial Leather*; Rosemary Hennessy, *Profit and Pleasure:*

Sexual Identities in Late Capitalism, 1st ed. (New York: Rout-ledge, 2000); Gill-Peterson, *Histories of the Transgender Child*.

16 See Drucker, *Warped*, Roderick A. Ferguson, *One-Dimensional Queer* (Medford, MA: Polity, 2019); Hobson, *Lavender and Red*; Lecklider, *Love's Next Meeting*.

17 To cite just one major example, there was the gay elite's reaction to the Stonewall Rebellion: initially horrified at the messy street queens' confrontational tactics, they have since converted the event and its participants into heroines. See Martin B. Duberman, *Stonewall: The Definitive Story of the LGBTQ Rights Upris-ing That Changed America*, rev. ed. (New York: Plume, 2019); Elizabeth A. Armstrong and Suzanna M. Crage, 'Movements and Memory: The Making of the Stonewall Myth', *American Socio-logical Review* 71, no. 5 (October 2006): 724–51.

18 See George Chauncey, *Gay New York: Gender, Urban Culture, and the Making of the Gay Male World, 1890–1940* (New York: Basic Books, 1994).

19 Robert Aldrich, *Colonialism and Homosexuality* (London, UK; New York, NY: Routledge, 2003), 1.

20 See Ralph M. Leck, *Vita Sexualis: Karl Ulrichs and the Origins of Sexual Science* (University of Illinois Press, 2016).

21 See Manfred Herzer, "Kertbeny and the Nameless Love," *Journal of Homosexuality* 12, no. 1 (7 March 1986): 1–26,

1. Hadrian

1 Anthony Richard Birley, *Hadrian: The Restless Emperor* (London: Routledge, 1997), 16.

2 Charles Dudley Warner, *A Library of the World's Best Literature, Ancient and Modern Vol. VIII* (New York: Cosimo, 2008).

3 Plato, *Symposium* (Oxford: Oxford University Press, 1994), 28.

4 Ibid., 11.

5 K. J. Dover, *Greek Homosexuality* (Cambridge, Mass.: Harvard University Press, 1989), 104.

6 Claudia Moser, 'Naked Power: The Phallus as an Apotropaic Symbol in the Images and Texts of Roman Italy', Undergraduate Humanities Forum 2005–6: Word and Image, 2006, p. 11.

7 Amy Richlin, 'Sexuality in the Roman Empire', in *The Compan-ion to the Roman Empire*, ed, David S. Potter (Oxford: Blackwell Publishing, 2006), 353.

8 As cited in Richlin, 'Sexuality in the Roman Empire', 339.

9 Birley, *Hadrian*, 31.

10 Ibid., 32.

11 *Historia Augusta* (London: Heinemann, 1922), 7.

12 Ibid., 68.

13 Ibid., 251.

14 *Historia Augusta*, 37.

15 Birley, *Hadrian*, 68.

16 Ibid., 98.

17 Ibid., 118.

18 Royston Lambert, *Beloved and God: The Story of Hadrian and Antinous* (New York: Viking, 1984), 68.

19 Birley, *Hadrian*, 179.

20 Ibid., 220.

21 Lambert, *Beloved and God*, 112.

22 Ibid., 120.

23 Quoted in *Rome: Echoes of Imperial Glory* (Alexandria, VA: Time-Life Books, 1994), 56.

24 Lambert, *Beloved and God*, 154.

2. Pietro Aretino

1 Gaetana Marrone, ed., *Encyclopedia of Italian Literary Studies: A-J* (New York: Routledge, 2007), 76.

2 Edward Hutton, *Pietro Aretino: The Scourge of Princes* (London: Constable and Co., 1922), 11.

3 Ibid., 16.

4 Christopher Chitty, *Sexual Hegemony: Statecraft, Sodomy, and Capital in the Rise of the World System* (Durham: Duke University Press, 2020), 47.

5 Ibid., 45.

6 Ibid., 60.

7 Ibid., 33.

8 Marrone, *Encyclopedia of Italian Literary Studies*, 74.

9 William Roscoe, *The Life and Pontificate of Leo X* (London: Henry G. Bohn, 1846), 271.

10 Hutton, *Pietro Aretino*, 15.

11 Hutton, *Pietro Aretino*, 26.

12 Martin Luther, *Luther's Works*, vol. 47, *The Christian in Society IV*, ed. Franklin Sherman and Helmut T. Lehmann (Philadelphia: Fortress Press, 1971), 38.

13 Marrone, *Encyclopedia of Italian Literary Studies*, 74.

14 Ibid., 74.

15 Silvio A Badini, *The Pope's Elephant* (Nashville: J.S. Sanders and Company, 1998), 158.

16 Hutton, *Pietro Aretino*, 49.

17 Michael Rocke, *Forbidden Friendships: Homosexuality and Male Culture in Renaissance Florence* (Oxford: Oxford University Press, 1996), 327.

18 Hutton, *Pietro Aretino*, 44.

19 Ibid., 53.

20 Keir Elam, ' "Wanton Pictures": The Baffling of Christopher Sly and the Visual-Verbal Intercourse of Early Modern Erotic Arts', in *Shakespeare and the Italian Renaissance*, ed. Michele Marrapodi (London: Routledge, 2016), 139.

21 Hutton, *Pietro Aretino*, 66.

22 Rictor Norton, *My Dear Boy: Gay Love Letters through the Centuries* (San Francisco: Leyland Publications, 1998), 54.

23 Ibid., 55.

24 Deanna Shemek, 'Aretino's Marescalco: Marriage Woes and the Duke of Mantua', *Renaissance Studies* 16, no. 3 (2002): 366–80.

25 Hutton, *Pietro Aretino*, 94.

26 Jacob Burckhardt, *The Civilization of the Renaissance in Italy* (London: George Allen and Unwin, 1937), 86.

27 Hutton, *Pietro Aretino*, 123.

28 Will Durant, *The Renaissance: A History of Civilization in Italy from 1304–1576 A.D.* (New York: Simon and Schuster, 1953), 656.

29 Ibid., 660.

30 Hutton, *Pietro Aretino*, 123.

31 Marrone, *Encyclopedia of Italian Literary Studies*, 79.

32 Durant, *The Renaissance*, 658.

33 Erik Berkowitz, *Sex and Punishment: Four Thousand Years of Judging Desire* (Berkeley, CA: Counterpoint, 2012), 193.

34 Marrone, *Encyclopedia of Italian Literary Studies*, 79.

35 Hutton, *Pietro Aretino*, 133.

36 Ibid., 159.

37 Ibid., 162.

38 Durant, *The Renaissance*, 657.

39 Ibid., 661.

40 Hutton, *Pietro Aretino*, 159.

41 Roscoe, *The Life and Pontificate of Leo X*, 271.

42 Hutton, *Pietro Aretino*, xi.

43 Samuel Pepys, *The Diary of Samuel Pepys, Volume III* (London and New York: G. Bell and Sons, 1893), 123.

3. James VI and I

1 David M. Bergeron, *King James and Letters of Homoerotic Desire* (Iowa City: University of Iowa Press, 2002), 33.

2 Ibid., 37.

3 A. L. Rowse, *The Expansion of Elizabethan England* (New York: Palgrave MacMillan, 2003), 23.

4 Peter Ackroyd, *Queer London* (London: Chatto and Windus, 2017), 41.

5 Diarmaid MacCulloch, *Reformation: Europe's House Divided 1490–1700* (London: Penguin Books, 2004), 623.

6 John Bale, *The Actes or Unchaste Examples of Englyshe Votaryes*, as cited in: Tom Betteridge, "The Place of Sodomy in the Historical Writings of John Bale and John Foxe," in *Sodomy in Early Modern Europe*, ed. Tom Betteridge (Manchester: Manchester University Press, 2002), 13.

7 MacCulloch, *Reformation*, 626.

8 Louis Crompton, *Homosexuality and Civilization* (Cambridge, MA: Belknap Press of Harvard University Press, 2003), 383.

9 Pauline Croft, *King James* (New York: Palgrave MacMillan, 2003), 23.

10 Ibid., 24.

11 Bryan Bevan, *King James VI of Scotland and I of England* (London: Rubicon Press, 1996), 48.

12 MacCulloch, *Reformation*, 571.

13 Karl Marx, *Capital, Volume 1* (London: Penguin Books, 1990), 874.

14 Silvia Federici, *Caliban and the Witch: Women, the Body, and Primitive Accumulation* (New York: Autonomedia, 2014), 165.

15 King James I, *Daemonologie in Forme of a Dialogue* (London: The Bodley Head, 1924), xii.

16 Ibid., 43.

17 Croft, *King James*, 71.

18 Ibid., 52.

19 Antonia Fraser, *Faith and Treason: The Story of the Gunpowder Plot* (New York: Doubleday, 1996), xxx.

20 Ibid., 178.

21 James VI and I, *The Basilikon Doron of James VI and I* (Edinburgh: William Blackwood and Sons, 1944), 55.

22 Bryan Bevan, *King James VI of Scotland and I of England* (London: Rubicon Press, 1996), 116.

23 Ibid., 90.

24 Ibid., 97.

25 Peter Ackroyd, *Queer London* (London: Chatto and Windus, 2017), 60.

26 Christopher Hill, *Milton and the English Revolution* (London: Penguin Books, 1979), 50.

27 Croft, *King James*, 97.

28 Perry Anderson, *Lineages of the Absolutist State* (London: Verso, 2013), 138.
29 Rictor Norton, *My Dear Boy: Gay Love Letters Through the Centuries* (San Francisco: Leyland Publications, 1998), 67.

4. Frederick the Great

1 Kathryn Hadley, 'Frederick the Great's Erotic Poem', *History Today*, 21 September 2011.
2 Praxiteles of Athens, one of the most acclaimed Attic sculptors, especially of the nude form.
3 As cited in Bodie A. Ashton, 'Kingship, Sexuality and Courtly Masculinity: Frederick the Great and Prussia on the Cusp of Modernity', *ANU Historical Journal II*, no. 1 (May 2019): 112.
4 Christopher Chitty, *Sexual Hegemony: Statecraft, Sodomy, and Capital in the Rise of the World System* (Durham, NC: Duke University Press, 2020).
5 As cited in Tim Blanning, *Frederick the Great: King of Prussia* (New York: Penguin, 2015), chap. 1, iBooks.
6 Peter H. Wilson, 'The Causes of the Thirty Years War 1618–48', *English Historical Review* 123, no. 502 (2008): 554–86.
7 Giles MacDonogh, *Frederick the Great: A Life in Deeds and Letters* (New York: St. Martin's Press, 2000), 17.
8 Blanning, *Frederick the Great*, 34.
9 Ibid., 42.
10 MacDonogh, *Frederick the Great*, 49.
11 Michel Foucault, *The History of Sexuality, Volume 1: An Introduction*, trans. Robert Hurley (New York: Pantheon Books, 1978), 17.
12 Historians diverge on how to deal with such historical figures – they have often been claimed by lesbian historians seeking historical figures to call their own, as well as by trans historians who argue that such figures are better historicized under the gender they lived as opposed to the sex they were assigned at birth. Allying ourselves here with the trans movement's argument that someone who spent their life insisting – even, in the end, being executed for – their status as a man is best spoken of using their chosen name and pronouns, we differ from the author of the academic article containing the translated court records on the case of Rosenstengel, who uses Rosenstengel's birth name and pronouns and considers the case entirely under the framework of lesbian relations. In any case, the transcripts

make fascinating reading: Brigitte Eriksson, 'A Lesbian Execution in Germany, 1721', *Journal of Homosexuality* 6, nos. 1–2 (January 1981): 27–40.

13   MacDonogh, *Frederick the Great*, 67.

14   Blanning, *Frederick the Great*, chap. 2, iBooks.

15   MacDonogh, *Frederick the Great*, 72.

16   Ibid., 73.

17   As cited in Ibid., 86–7.

18   Ibid., 131.

19   Blanning, *Frederick the Great*, chap. 3, iBooks.

20   Ibid.

21   MacDonogh, *Frederick the Great*, 136.

22   Louis Crompton, *Homosexuality and Civilization* (Cambridge: Harvard University Press, 2003), 508.

23   Giles MacDonogh, "Hogarth's Portrait of Frederick the Great," Giles MacDonogh – Blog, 15 December 2015.

24   Blanning, *Frederick the Great*, 230.

25   Ashton, 'Kingship, Sexuality and Courtly Masculinity', 128.

26   This brilliant and evocative analogy comes from the very stylish and beautiful telling of this story in James R. Gaines, *Evening in the Palace of Reason: Bach Meets Frederick the Great in the Age of Enlightenment* (London: New York: Fourth Estate, 2005).

27   Blanning, *Frederick the Great*, chap. 3, iBooks.

28   MacDonogh, *Frederick the Great*, 384.

29   Klaus Büstrin, '"Ich Habe Gemeinet, Du Häst Mihr Lieb": Friedrichs Enge Beziehungen Zu Seinem Kammerdiener Fredersdorf', *Potsdamer Neueste Nachrichten*, 1 September 2012.

30   Blanning, *Frederick the Great*, chap. 15, iBooks.

31   Ibid.

32   See Elizabeth Freeman, *Time Binds: Queer Temporalities, Queer Histories* (Durham, NC: Duke University Press, 2010).

33   Hagen Schulze, *The Course of German Nationalism: from Frederick the Great to Bismarck, 1763–1867* (Cambridge: Cambridge University Press, 1991), 44.

34   Ibid.

35   Ashton, 'Kingship, Sexuality and Courtly Masculinity', 113.

36   Jason Crouthamel, '"Comradeship" and "Friendship": Masculinity and Militarisation in Germany's Homosexual Emancipation Movement after the First World War', *Gender and History* 23, no. 1 (2011): 125.

37   Hilmar Hoffmann, *The Triumph of Propaganda: Film and National Socialism, 1933–1945* (Berghahn Books, 1996).

5. Jack Saul

1   Jack Saul, *The Sins of the Cities of the Plain* (London: William Lazenby, 1881), 8–9.
2   Glenn Chandler, *The Sins of Jack Saul* (Surbiton, UK: Grosvenor House Publishing, 2016), 8.
3   Ibid., 14.
4   Jeffrey Weeks, *Sex, Politics and Society* (London: Longman, 1989), 86.
5   Matt Houlbrook, *Queer London: Perils and Pleasures in the Sexual Metropolis, 1918–1957* (Chicago: University of Chicago Press, 2005), 228.
6   Chandler, *The Sins of Jack Saul*, 26.
7   Ibid., 35.
8   Ibid., 44.
9   Heike Bauer, *The Hirschfeld Archives: Violence, Death, and Modern Queer Culture* (Philadelphia: Temple University Press, 2017), 59.
10 Chandler, *The Sins of Jack Saul*, 81.
11 Ibid., 90.
12 Ibid., 94.
13 Neil McKenna, *Fanny and Stella: The Young Men Who Shocked Victorian England* (London: Faber, 2014), 27.
14 Ibid., 9.
15 Ibid., 39.
16 Ibid, 39.
17 Ibid, 4.
18 Ibid, 51.
19 Weeks, *Sex, Politics and Society*, 101.
20 Oscar Wilde, as quoted in James P. Wilper, *Reconsidering the Emergence of the Gay Novel in English and German* (West Lafayette, IN: Purdue University Press, 2016), 51.
21 Houlbrook, *Queer London*, 196.
22 Jeffrey Weeks, 'Inverts, Perverts and Mary-Annes', in *Hidden from History: Reclaiming the Gay and Lesbian Past*, ed. Martin Duberman, Martha Vicinus, and George Chauncey Jr (New York: Meridian, 1990), 202.
23 Ronald Pearsall, *The Worm in the Bud: The World of Victorian Sexuality* (London, Weidenfeld & Nicolson, 1969), 465.
24 Chandler, *The Sins of Jack Saul*, 107.
25 Ibid., 109.
26 Ibid., 146.
27 H Montgomery Hyde, *The Cleveland Street Scandal* (New York: Coward, McCann & Geoghegan, 1976), 20.

28 Hyde, *The Cleveland Street Scandal*, 25.
29 Colin Simpson, Lewis Chester, and David Leitch, *The Cleveland Street Affair* (Boston: Little, Brown, 1976), 74.
30 Hyde, *The Cleveland Street Scandal*, 122.
31 Ibid., 106.
32 Ibid.,144.
33 Ibid., 147.
34 Chandler, *The Sins of Jack Saul*, 263.
35 Hyde, *The Cleveland Street Scandal*, 160.
36 Ibid., 161.
37 House of Commons Debate, 28 February 1890, vol. 341, 1546.
38 Chandler, *The Sins of Jack Saul*, 269.
39 Ibid., 285.

6. Roger Casement

1 Marx's classic essay on the East India Company was published in 1853: Karl Marx, 'The East India Company – Its History and Results', *New York Herald Tribune*, 24 June 1853, marxists. org. For a comprehensive history of India under company rule, see among others C. A. Bayly, *Indian Society and the Making of the British Empire* (Cambridge: Cambridge University Press, 1988).
2 As cited in Jeffrey Dudgeon and Roger Casement, *Roger Casement: The Black Diaries – with a Study of His Background, Sexuality and Irish Political Life* (Belfast, Northern Ireland: Belfast Press, 2002), 53.
3 For definitions of and debates on imperialism, see Patrick Wolfe, 'History and Imperialism: A Century of Theory, from Marx to Postcolonialism', *American Historical Review* 102, no. 2 (1997): 388–420.
4 The best introduction to this era of imperialist expansion is Eric J. Hobsbawm, *The Age of Empire: 1875–1914* (New York: Vintage Books, 1989).
5 For an overview of the Scramble for Africa, see Muriel Evelyn Chamberlain, *The Scramble for Africa*, 3rd ed. (London: Routledge, 2013).
6 See Chamberlain, *The Scramble for Africa*; Adam Hochschild, *King Leopold's Ghost: A Story of Greed, Terror, and Heroism in Colonial Africa*, (Boston: Houghton Mifflin, 1999).
7 Michael Taussig, *Shamanism, Colonialism, and the Wild Man: A Study in Terror and Healing*, 1st ed. (Chicago: University of Chicago Press, 1991), 11.

8   Chinua Achebe, 'An Image of Africa: Racism in Conrad's Heart of Darkness', *Massachusetts Review* 57, no. 1 (2016): 14–27.

9   See Leela Gandhi, *Affective Communities: Anticolonial Thought, Fin-De-Siècle Radicalism, and the Politics of Friendship* (Durham, NC: Duke University Press, 2006); Priyamvada Gopal, *Insurgent Empire: Anticolonial Resistance and British Dissent* (London: Verso, 2019).

10 This system is discussed at length throughout Hochschild's book and is summarized concisely in Michael A Rutz, *King Leopold's Congo and the 'Scramble for Africa': A Short History with Documents* (Indianapolis, IN: Hackett, 2018), 12–15.

11 Ibid., 13.

12 Georges Nzongola-Ntalaja, *The Congo: From Leopold to Kabila: A People's History* (London: Zed Books, 2002), 22.

13 Ibid., 23.

14 Nzongola-Ntalaja, *The Congo*, 23–4.

15 Ibid. 26.

16 'PRO FO800/106 Consul-General Casement to Tyrrell', in Roger Casement, *The Amazon Journal of Roger Casement*, ed. Angus Mitchell (London: Anaconda Editions, 2000), 'Part Two: The Voyage to Putumayo', iBooks.

17 'NLI MS 13,087 26/I Notes of a talk with Mr Victor Israel, a trader of Iquitos, on board SS *Huayna* when anchored off mouth of Javari, on night of August 24th, 1910 – bound for Iquitos', in Casement, *The Amazon Journal*.

18 'NLI MS 13.087 (24) Notes on the Peruvian Frontier on board the *Huayna* – Friday 26th August 1910', in Casement, *The Amazon Journal*.

19 Alison Garden, *The Literary Afterlives of Roger Casement, 1899–2016* (Oxford: Oxford University Press, 2020), 6.

20 Casement and Dudgeon, *The Black Diaries*, 241.

21 Ibid., 207.

22 Ibid.

23 Ibid., 208.

24 Ibid.

25 WG Sebald, *The Rings of Saturn* (New York: New Directions, 1998), 134; as cited in Brian Lewis, 'The Queer Life and Afterlife of Roger Casement', *Journal of the History of Sexuality* 14, no. 4 (2005): 363–82.

26 Gandhi, *Affective Communities*, 21.

27 Silvia Federici, *Caliban and The Witch: Women, the Body, and Primitive Accumulation* (New York: Autonomedia, 2014), 136–41, 144, 146.

28 Javier Uriarte, 'Splendid *Testemunhos*: Documenting Atrocities,

Bodies, and Desire in Roger Casement's *Black Diaries*', in *Intimate Frontiers: A Literary Geography of the Amazon*, ed. Javier Uriarte and Felipe Martinez-Pinzon (Liverpool: Liverpool University Press, 2019).

29 See among others José Esteban Muñoz, *Cruising Utopia: The Then and There of Queer Futurity* (New York: New York University Press, 2009).

30 Uriarte, 'Splendid *Testemunhos*', 93.

31 The book is still in print. See John Atkinson Hobson, *Imperialism: A Study* (New York: Cosimo Classics, 2005).

32 Ibid., 224–5.

33 Today's more enthusiastic boosters of colonialism include Niall Ferguson, Bruce Gilley, and Nigel Biggar; in the view of the authors, they deserve the same degree of respect and deference as Holocaust deniers.

34 Noel Halifax, 'The Queer and Unusual Life of Roger Casement', *Socialist Review*, February 2016.

35 Lesley Wylie, 'Rare Models: Roger Casement, the Amazon, and the Ethnographic Picturesque', *Irish Studies Review* 18, no. 3 (2010): 316.

36 Brian Inglis, *Roger Casement* (New York: Harcourt Jovanovich, 1974) 281

37 Roger Casement, ed. Angus Mitchell, *The Amazon Journal of Roger Casement* (London: Anaconda Editions, 1997), 18.

38 Casement and Dudgeon, *Black Diaries*, 515.

39 See Angus Mitchell, *Roger Casement: 16 Lives* (Dublin: The O'Brien Press, 2016); Frank McGabhann, 'Roger Casement: 16 Lives by Angus Mitchell Review: An Excellent Effort', *Irish Times*, 15 February 2016.

40 Casement and Dudgeon, *Black Diaries*, 565.

41 Brian Inglis, *Roger Casement*, 370.

42 Hochschild, *King Leopold's Ghost*, chap. 18, iBooks.

43 Casement and Dudgeon, *Black Diaries*, 593.

7. Lawrence of Arabia

1 Gregory Katz, "'Lawrence of Arabia' Star Peter O'Toole Dead at 81', *Associated Press*, 15 December 2013.

2 Robert Aldrich, *Colonialism and Homosexuality* (London, UK; New York, NY: Routledge, 2003), 1.

3 Anthony Sattin, *The Young T. E. Lawrence* (New York: W. W. Norton & Company, 2015), chapter 2: iBooks.

4 Ibid.

5   Elizabeth Freeman, *Time Binds: Queer Temporalities, Queer Histories* (Durham: Duke University Press, 2010), 100.

6   Joseph Allen Boone, *The Homoerotics of Orientalism* (New York: Columbia University Press, 2014), 19.

7   T. E. Lawrence, *Seven Pillars of Wisdom* (London: Penguin, 2000), chap. 1: iBooks.

8   Neil Faulkner, *Lawrence of Arabia's War: The Arabs, the British and the Remaking of the Middle East in WWI* (New Haven, CT: Yale University Press), 195.

9   Sattin, *The Young T. E. Lawrence*, Chapter Five: iBooks.

10 As cited in Malcolm Brown, *T. E. Lawrence* (New York: New York University Press, 2003), 42.

11 Ibid., 42.

12 Lawrence, *Seven Pillars of Wisdom*, dedication: iBooks.

13 Ibid., chap. 1.

14 Klaus Theweleit, *Male Fantasies, Theory and History of Literature*, vol. 22–3 (Minneapolis, Minn.: University of Minnesota Press, 1987).

15 James Patrick Wilper, 'The "Manly Love of Comrades"', in *Reconsidering the Emergence of the Gay Novel in English and German* (West Lafayette, IN: Purdue University Press), 71–88.

16 Parminder Kaur Bakshi, 'Homosexuality and Orientalism: Edward Carpenter's Journey to the East', *Prose Studies* 13, no. 1 (May 1990): 154.

17 Joy Dixon, 'Out of Your Clinging Kisses I Create a New World: Sexuality and Spirituality in the World of Edward Carpenter', in *The Ashgate Research Companion to Nineteenth-Century Spiritualism and the Occult*, eds Tatiana Kontou and Sarah Willburn (Abingdon: Routledge, 2016), 166.

18 Sattin, *The Young T. E. Lawrence*, Chap. 13. iBooks.

19 Faulkner, *Lawrence of Arabia's War*, 158.

20 Sattin, *The Young T. E. Lawrence*, Chapter Nineteen, iBooks.

21 Ibid., xiv.

22 Ibid., 174.

23 Ibid., 191.

24 Thomas J. O'Donnell, 'The Confessions of T. E. Lawrence: The Sadomasochistic Hero', *American Imago* 34, no. 2 (1977): 129.

25 Sattin, *The Young T. E. Lawrence*, chap. 15: iBooks.

26 Faulkner, *Lawrence of Arabia's War*, 453.

27 Lawrence, *Seven Pillars of Wisdom*, dedication: iBooks.

28 Faulkner, *Lawrence of Arabia's War*, 456.

29 Ibid., 463.

30 Rictor Norton, *My Dear Boy: Gay Love Letters through the Centuries* (San Francisco: Leyland Publications, 1998), 226.

8. The Bad Gays of Weimar Berlin

1   William L Shirer, *The Rise and Fall of the Third Reich: A History of Nazi Germany* (New York: Simon and Schuster, 2011), 106.

2   Ernst Röhm, foreword to *The Memoirs of Ernst Röhm*, trans. Eleanor Hancock (Barnsley, UK: Frontline Books, 2012), iBooks.

3   Ibid., chap. 1, iBooks.

4   Ibid., chap. 2, iBooks.

5   See Klaus Gietinger, *The Murder of Rosa Luxemburg*, trans. Loren Balhorn (London: Verso, 2019).

6   Shirer, *Rise and Fall of the Third Reich*, 35.

7   Ibid.

8   Laurie Marhoefer, *Sex and the Weimar Republic: German Homosexual Emancipation and the Rise of the Nazis* (Toronto: University of Toronto Press, 2015), 151.

9   Laurie Marhoefer, 'Queer Fascism and the End of Gay History', *NOTCHES* (blog), 19 June 2018, notchesblog.com.

10 Ibid.

11 Ibid.

12 Andrew Wackerfuss, *Stormtrooper Families: Homosexuality and Community in the Early Nazi Movement* (New York: Harrington Park Press, 2015).

13 Marhoefer, *Sex and the Weimar Republic*, 20.

14 Claudia Bruns, 'Eros, Macht und Männlichkeit. Männerbündische Konstruktionen in der deutschen Jugendbewegung zwischen Emanzipation und Reaktion', in: *Historische Jugendforschung. Jahrbuch des Archivs der deutschen Jugendbewegung* N.F. 7 (2010): 27.

15 Bruns, 'Eros, Macht und Männlichkeit', 27–8.

16 Robert Deam Tobin, *Peripheral Desires: The German Discovery of Sex* (Philadelphia: University of Pennsylvania Press, 2015), 59.

17 John Graven Hughes and Heinz Linge, *Getting Hitler into Heaven* (London: Transworld, 1987), 44.

18 Röhm, *Memoirs*, chap. 16, iBooks.

19 Ibid.

20 Eleanor Hancock, '"Only the Real, the True, the Masculine Held Its Value": Ernst Röhm, Masculinity, and Male Homosexuality', *Journal of the History of Sexuality* 8, no. 4 (1998): 625.

21 Ibid., 625–6.

22 Portions of this chapter concerning Radszuweit, specifically the analyses of his pro-Nazi articles in his magazines and newspapers, are adapted from a blog post by Ben Miller originally published in 2017 on OutHistory.org: Ben Miller, 'In the Archives:

Friedrich Radszuweit and the False Security of Collaboration', OutHistory.Org (blog), 27 March 2017.

23 For a history of Radszuweit's Friendship League and its successors, see Javier Samper Vendrell, *The Seduction of Youth: Print Culture and Homosexual Rights in the Weimar Republic* (Toronto: University of Toronto Press, 2020).

24 Susan Stryker, *Transgender History* (Berkeley, CA: Seal Press, 2008), 56.

25 Matthew H. Birkhold, "A Lost Piece of Trans History," *Paris Review* (blog), 15 January 2019.

26 Marhoefer, *Sex and the Weimar Republic*, 14.

27 Ibid., 9.

28 Ibid., 120.

29 Ibid., 126–7.

30 Ibid., 113.

31 John Lauritsen, 'Kurt Hiller: A 1928 Gay Rights Speech', 1995, available at paganpressbooks.com.

32 Marhoefer, *Sex and the Weimar Republic*, 116.

33 Ibid., 121.

34 Ibid., 122.

35 Ibid., 131–3.

36 *Die Freundin*, 11 January 1931, Sammlung Friedrich Radszuweit, Box 6, Schwules Museum Berlin.

37 Ibid.

38 *Herrn Adolf Hitler, München*, *Die Freundin*, 12 August 1931, Sammlung Friedrich Radszuweit, Box 6, Schwules Museum Berlin.

39 *Herrn Adolf Hitler, München*.

40 *Die Freundin*, February 1931, Sammlung Friedrich Radszuweit, Box 6, Schwules Museum Berlin.

41 Marhoefer, *Sex and the Weimar Republic*, 151.

42 Ibid., 152.

43 Ibid., 155.

44 Ibid., 157.

45 Ibid., 146–7.

46 *Blätter für Menschenrecht, April/Mai 1932*, Sammlung Radszuweit, Box 2, Folder 1, Schwules Museum Berlin.

47 Ralf Dose, *Magnus Hirschfeld: The Origins of the Gay Liberation Movement* (New York: Monthly Review Press, 2014), 89.

48 Stryker, *Transgender History*, 56.

49 See Jules Gill-Peterson, *Histories of the Transgender Child* (Minneapolis: University of Minnesota Press, 2018).

50 Jana Funke, 'Navigating the Past: Sexuality, Race, and the Uses of the Primitive in Magnus Hirschfeld's The World Journey of a

Sexologist', in *Sex, Knowledge, and Receptions of the Past*, ed. Kate Fisher and Rebecca Langlands (Oxford: Oxford University Press, 2015), 112–3.

51 Ibid., 111.

52 Heike Bauer, *The Hirschfeld Archives: Violence, Death, and Modern Queer Culture* (Philadelphia: Temple University Press, 2017), 17.

53 Shirer, *The Rise and Fall of the Third Reich*, 181.

54 Ibid., 182.

55 Ibid., 183.

56 Ibid., 183.

57 Ibid., 190.

58 Ibid., 196.

59 Vereinsakte, Sammlung Radszuweit, Box 1, Schwules Museum Berlin.

60 Eric Marcus, 'Magnus Hirschfeld', Making Gay History, n.d., makinggayhistory.com.

61 Magnus-Hirschfeld Gesellschaft, 'Otto Reutter: Das Hirschfel-Lied', accessed 7 November, 2021, magnus-hirschfeld.de.

9. Margaret Mead

1 Paul Shankman, *The Trashing of Margaret Mead: Anatomy of an Anthropological Controversy* (Madison: University of Wisconsin Press, 2009).

2 Margaret Mead, *Coming of Age in Samoa: A Psychological Study of Primitive Youth for Western Civilisation* (New York: William Morrow and Company, 1928), 16, 14, 19.

3 Ibid., 13.

4 Ibid., 9–10.

5 Micaela di Leonardo, *Exotics at Home: Anthropologies, Others, American Modernity* (Chicago: University of Chicago Press, 2000), 10.

6 Mead, *Coming of Age in Samoa*, 13.

7 Ibid., 39.

8 Ibid., 8.

9 Nancy Lutkehaus, *Margaret Mead: The Making of an American Icon* (Princeton, NJ: Princeton University Press, 2011), 1.

10 See Lee D. Baker, *Anthropology and the Racial Politics of Culture* (Durham, NC: Duke University Press, 2010).

11 Joyce D. Hammond, 'Telling a Tale: Margaret Mead's Photographic Portraits of Fa'amotu, a Samoan Tupou', *Visual Anthropology* 16, no. 4 (2003): 342.

12 Mark Anderson, *From Boas to Black Power* (Stanford, CA: Stanford University Press, 2019), 17.

13 Lutkehaus, *Margaret Mead*, 29.

14 Quoted in Anderson, *From Boas to Black Power*, 5.

15 James Baldwin and Margaret Mead, *A Rap on Race* (New York: J. B. Lippincott, 1971), 18.

16 Lois W. Banner, *Intertwined Lives: Margaret Mead, Ruth Benedict, and Their Circle* (New York: Vintage Books, 2004), chap. 1, iBooks.

17 Di Leonardo, *Exotics at Home*, 169.

18 Lutkehaus, *Margaret Mead*, 29.

19 Ibid.

20 Ibid., 30.

21 Banner, *Intertwined Lives*, chap. 3, iBooks.

22 Ibid., chap. 1, iBooks.

23 Ibid., chap. 1, iBooks.

24 Ibid., chap. 1, iBooks.

25 Margaret Caffrey and Patricia Francis, introduction to *To Cherish the Life of the World: The Selected Letters of Margaret Mead* (New York: Basic Books, 2006), Kindle.

26 Lutkehaus, *Margaret Mead*, 38–9.

27 Ned Blackhawk and Isaiah Lorado Wilner, eds., *Indigenous Visions: Rediscovering the World of Franz Boas* (New Haven, CT: Yale University Press, 2018), ii.

28 Lois Banner, *Intertwined Lives*, chap. 7, iBooks.

29 Ibid., chap. 7, iBooks.

30 Ibid., chap. 7, iBooks.

31 Deborah G Plant, 'The Benedict-Hurston Connection', *CLA Journal* 46, no. 4 (2003): 436.

32 Banner, *Intertwined Lives*, chap. 7, iBooks.

33 Plant, 'The Benedict-Hurston Connection'.

34 Ibid.

35 Banner, *Intertwined Lives*, chap. 8, iBooks.

36 Ibid.

37 Banner, *Intertwined Lives*, chap. 9, iBooks.

38 Di Leonardo, *Exotics at Home*, 169.

39 Margaret Mead, *Growing up in New Guinea: A Comparative Study of Primitive Education* (New York: Perennial Classics, 2001), 4.

40 Ibid.

41 Ibid., 12.

42 Banner, *Intertwined Lives*, chap. 11, iBooks.

43 Ibid.

44 Ibid.

45 Mead, *To Cherish the Life of the World*, loc. 3316, Kindle.

46 Ibid., loc. 3394, Kindle.

47 Peter Mandler, *Return from the Natives: How Margaret Mead Won the Second World War and Lost the Cold War* (New Haven, CT: Yale University Press, 2013), 16.

48 Ibid., 19.

49 Esther Newton, *Margaret Mead Made Me Gay: Personal Essays, Public Ideas* (Durham, NC: Duke University Press, 2000), 1.

50 Ibid., 2.

51 Ibid., 3.

52 Ben Miller, 'Wofur Sind Wir Da? Harry Hay, Die Homosexuellenfrage, Und Das Erbe Des Marxismus', *Invertito: Jahrbuch Für Die Geschichte Der Homosexualitäten* 18 (September 2018): 40–68.

53 Peter Sigal, Zeb Tortorici, and Neil L. Whitehead, eds., *Ethnopornography: Sexuality, Colonialism, and Archival Knowledge* (Durham, NC: Duke University Press, 2020), 4.

54 Ibid., 7.

55 Ann Laura Stoler, *Carnal Knowledge and Imperial Power: Race and the Intimate in Colonial Rule* (Berkeley: University of California Press, 2003).

56 Peter Drucker, *Warped: Gay Normality and Queer Anti-Capitalism*, Historical Materialism 92 (Leiden, Netherlands: Brill, 2016), 8.

57 Mandler, *Return from the Natives*, 46.

58 Ibid., 60.

59 Idid., 81.

60 Ibid., 69.

61 David H. Price, *Threatening Anthropology: McCarthyism and the FBI's Surveillance of Activist Anthropologists* (Durham: Duke University Press, 2004), 258.

62 Ibid., 255.

63 Banner, *Intertwined Lives*, chap. 14, iBooks.

64 Lutkehaus, *Margaret Mead*, 72.

65 Mead, *Collected Letters*, loc. 3727, Kindle.

66 Lutkehaus, *Margaret Mead*, 73.

67 Mead, *Collected Letters*, loc. 4042, Kindle.

68 David Price, 'Anthropologists as Spies', thenation.com, 2 November 2000.

69 Glen Doss, 'The Controversial Margaret Mead', *Stars and Stripes*, 2 June 1972.

70 Margaret Mead, *Collected Letters*, loc. 4095, Kindle.

71 Shankman, *The Trashing of Margaret Mead*, 8.

72 Ibid., 9–10.

73 Ibid., 11–12.

74 Barbara Gullahorn-Holecek, *Papua New Guinea: Anthropology on Trial* (Ambrose Video Publishing, 1983), archive.org.

75 Michel Foucault, *The History of Sexuality, Volume 1: An Introduction*, trans. Robert Hurley (New York: Pantheon Books, 1978), 7.

76 The quote is, among other things, reproduced as the epigraph to Lutkehaus, *Margaret Mead*.

10. J. Edgar Hoover and Roy Cohn

1 Anthony Summers, *Official and Confidential: The Secret Life of J. Edgar Hoover* (New York: Random House, 2012), 8.

2 Curt Gentry, *J. Edgar Hoover: The Man and his Secrets* (New York: Plume, 1992), 65.

3 Douglas M Charles, *The FBI's Obscene File: J. Edgar Hoover and the Bureau's Crusade against Smut* (Lawrence: University Press of Kansas, 2012), 27.

4 Gentry, *J. Edgar Hoover*, 66.

5 Ibid., 65.

6 Ibid., 65.

7 Summers, *Official and Confidential*, 28.

8 Gentry, *J. Edgar Hoover*, 69.

9 Summers, *Official and Confidential*, 32.

10 Gentry, *J. Edgar Hoover*, 78.

11 Ibid., 81.

12 Summers, *Official and Confidential*, 56.

13 Ibid., 32.

14 Cookie Woolner, '"Have We a New Sex Problem Here?" Black Queer Women in the Early Great Migration', Process: A Blog for American History, 24 October 2017, processhistory.org.

15 William J. Maxwell, 'When Black Writers Were Public Enemy No. 1', Politico, 30 April 2015, politico.com.

16 Hannah K. Gold, 'Why Did the FBI Spy on James Baldwin?', The Intercept, 15 August 2015, theintercept.com.

17 Letter reproduced in Beverly Gage, 'What an Uncensored Letter to MLK Reveals', *New York Times*, 11 November 2014.

18 Summers, *Official and Confidential*, 244.

19 Ibid., 259.

20 Ibid., 244.

21 Ibid., 79.

22 Nicholas Von Hoffman, *Citizen Cohn* (New York: Bantam, 1988), 337.

23 Summers, *Official and Confidential*, 81.

24 Ibid., 431.

25 Ibid., 431.

26 Ibid., 84.

27 Ibid., 255.

28 Ibid., 82.

29 Ibid., 252.

30 David K. Johnson, *The Lavender Scare* (Chicago: University Of Chicago Press, 2004), 11.

31 Summers, *Official and Confidential*, 56.

32 Von Hoffman, *Citizen Cohn*, 50.

33 Ibid., 53.

34 Ibid., 57.

35 Ibid., 59.

36 Ibid., 67.

37 Ibid., 69.

38 Ibid., 75.

39 Ibid., 91.

40 Walter Schneir and Miriam Schneir, *Invitation to an Inquest* (Garden City, NY:, Doubleday, 1965), 277.

41 Ibid., 193.

42 Ibid., 254.

43 Roy M. Cohn and Sidney Zion, *The Autobiography of Roy Cohn* (Secaucus, NJ: Lyle Stuart, 1988), 77.

44 Richard H. Rovere, *Senator Joseph McCarthy* (New York, Harper & Row, 1973), 125.

45 Summers, *Official and Confidential*, 181.

46 Ibid., 182.

47 Rovere, *Senator Joseph McCarthy*, 188.

48 Randy Shilts, *Conduct Unbecoming* (New York: Ballantine Books, 1994), 16.

49 Johnson, *The Lavender Scare*, 21.

50 Ibid., 31.

51 Ibid., 34.

52 John D'Emilio, *Sexual Politics, Sexual Communities: The Making of a Homosexual Minority in the United States* (Chicago: University of Chicago Press, 1983), 65.

53 Rovere, *Senator Joseph McCarthy*, 8.

54 Johnson, *The Lavender Scare*, 73.

55 Ibid., 166.

56 Naoko Shibusawa, 'The Lavender Scare and Empire: Rethinking Cold War Antigay Politics', *Diplomatic History* 36, no. 4 (2012): 723–52.

57 Cohn and Zion, *The Autobiography of Roy Cohn*, 51.

58 Rovere, *Senator Joseph McCarthy*, 32.
59 Ibid., 201.
60 Ibid., 203.
61 Ibid., 207.
62 Cohn and Zion, *The Autobiography of Roy Cohn*, 243.
63 Ibid., 236.
64 Von Hoffman, *Citizen Kohn*, 444.
65 Cohn and Zion, *The Autobiography of Roy Cohn*, 236.
66 Ibid., 244.
67 Von Hoffman, *Citizen Kohn*, 448.
68 Tony Kushner, *Angels in America: A Gay Fantasia on National Themes* (New York: Theatre Communications Group, 2003), 51.
69 Von Hoffman, *Citizen Kohn*, 456.
70 Ibid., 460.
71 Ibid., 16.
72 Ibid., 17.
73 Isaac Butler and Dan Kois, '"Eight Loving Arms and All those Suckers": How *Angels in America* Put Roy Cohn into the Definitive Story of AIDS', *New York Magazine*, February 2018, vulture.com.

11. Yukio Mishima

1 Nobuko Albery, 'Nobuko Albery Salutes the Ghost of Mishima, Novelist and Suicide', *London Review of Books*, 1 August 1985.
2 John Nathan, *Mishima: A Biography* (Boston: Little, Brown, 1974), 7.
3 Ibid., 7.
4 Henry Scott-Stokes, *The Life and Death of Yukio Mishima* (New York: Farrar, Straus and Giroux, 1974), 60.
5 Yukio Mishima, *Confessions of a Mask* (London: Peter Owen, 2007), 5.
6 Nathan, *Mishima*, 8.
7 Marguerite Yourcenar, *Mishima: A Vision of the Void* (New York: Farrar Strauss, and Giroux, 1986), 13.
8 Nathan, *Mishima*, 9.
9 Mishima, *Confessions of a Mask*, 16.
10 Ibid., 19.
11 Ibid., 12.
12 Ibid., 14.
13 Carl E Rollyson, ed., *Novelists with Gay and Lesbian Themes* (Ipswich, MA: Salem Press, 2012), 146.

14 Edmund White, *Genet* (London: Vintage, 2004), 322.

15 Louis Crompton, *Homosexuality and Civilization* (Cambridge, MA: Belknap Press of Harvard University Press, 2003), 413.

16 Ibid., 412.

17 Ibid., 420.

18 Ibid., 426.

19 Ibid., 425.

20 Gregory M Pflugfelder, *Cartographies of Desire: Male-Male Sexuality in Japanese Discourse, 1600–1950* (Berkeley: University of California Press, 1999), 153.

21 Ibid., 255.

22 Mishima, *Confessions of a Mask*, 241.

23 Nathan, *Mishima*, 16.

24 Ibid., 19.

25 Ibid., 23.

26 Yukio Mishima, 'Forest in Full Flower', as cited in Nathan, *Mishima*, 42.

27 Scott-Stokes, *The Life and Death of Yukio Mishima*, 89.

28 Ibid., 93.

29 Ibid., 106.

30 Nathan, *Mishima*, 55.

31 Scott-Stokes, *The Life and Death of Yukio Mishima*, 106.

32 Nathan, *Mishima*, 147.

33 Ibid., 112.

34 Ibid., 141.

35 Ibid., 106.

36 Mishima, *Confessions of a Mark*, 39.

37 Yukio Mishima, cited in Nathan, *Mishima*, 163.

38 Yukio Mishima, cited in ibid., 165.

39 Nathan, *Mishima*, 125.

40 Yukio Mishima, *Sun and Steel*, cited in ibid., 237.

41 Nathan, *Mishima*, 230.

42 Ibid., 271.

43 Ibid., 273.

44 Ibid., 279.

45 Ibid., 281.

12. Philip Johnson

1 Mark Joseph Stern, 'The Glass House as Gay Space: Exploring the Intersection of Homosexuality and Architecture', *Inquiries Journal* 4, no. 6 (2012).

2 See David K Johnson, *The Lavender Scare: The Cold War*

Persecution of Gays and Lesbians in the Federal Government (Chicago: University of Chicago Press, 2006).

3 Eve Kosofsky Sedgwick, *Epistemology of the Closet* (Berkeley: University of California Press, 1990), 1.

4 Ibid., 22.

5 See Michelangelo Signorile, *Queer in America: Sex, the Media, and the Closets of Power* (New York: Random House, 1993).

6 Alex Beam, *Broken Glass: Mies van der Rohe, Edith Farnsworth, and the Fight over a Modernist Masterpiece* (New York: Random House, 2020), chap. 11, iBooks.

7 Nicolai Ouroussoff, 'Through a Glass, Clearly, a Modernist's Questing Spirit', *New York Times*, 6 July 2007.

8 Franz Schulze, *Philip Johnson: Life and Work* (Chicago: University Of Chicago Press, 1996), 27.

9 Ibid., 31.

10 Ibid., 35.

11 See Martin Duberman, *The Worlds of Lincoln Kirstein* (Chicago: Northwestern University Press, 2008).

12 Mark Lamster, *The Man in the Glass House: Philip Johnson, Architect of the Modern Century* (Boston: Little, Brown, 2018), chap. 2, iBooks.

13 Schulze, *Philip Johnson*, 48.

14 Ibid., 50–1.

15 Lamster, *Man in the Glass House*, chap. 3, iBooks.

16 Ibid.

17 Ibid.

18 Schulze, *Philip Johnson*, 56.

19 Ibid., 55.

20 Lamster, *Man in the Glass House*, chap. 3, iBooks.

21 Ibid., chap. 4, iBooks.

22 Ibid.

23 Schulze, *Philip Johnson*, 89.

24 Lamster, *Man in the Glass House*, chap. 5, iBooks.

25 Ibid.

26 Ibid.

27 Ibid.

28 Ibid.

29 Ibid.

30 Ibid.

31 Ibid., chap. 7.

32 Ibid.

33 Ibid.

34 Ibid.

35 Ibid.

36 Ibid.

37 Joan Ockman, 'The Figurehead: On Monumentality and Nihilism in Philip Johnson's Life and Work', in *Philip Johnson: The Constancy of Change*, ed. Emmanuel Petit (New Haven, CT: Yale University Press, 2009), 88–9.

38 Kazys Varnelis, ed., *The Philip Johnson Tapes: Interviews by Robert A.M. Stern* (New York: The Monacelli Press, 2008).

39 Charles Kaiser, *The Gay Metropolis: The Landmark History of Gay Life in America* (New York: Grove Press, 2007), 213.

40 Ibid., 214.

41 Ibid., 213.

42 Emmanuel Petit, introduction to *Philip Johnson: The Constancy of Change*, 2.

43 Nikil Saval, 'Philip Johnson, the Man Who Made Architecture Amoral', *New Yorker*, 12 December 2018.

44 Petit, introduction to *Philip Johnson*, 2.

45 Paul Goldberger, 'A Major Monument of Post-modernism', *New York Times*, 31 March 1978.

46 Philip Johnson, 'Re-Building', *New York Times*, 28 December 1978.

47 Ibid.

48 John W Cook and Heinrich Klotz, *Conversations with Architects* (New York: Holt Rinehart & Winston, 1975), 35.

49 Ibid., 36.

50 Ibid., 36.

51 Lamster, *Man In The Glass House*, chap. 13, iBooks.

52 'The Architect Who Flirted With Fascism', *Deutsche Welle*, 28 January 2005.

53 Lamster, *Man in the Glass House*, chap. 17, iBooks.

54 Herbert Muschamp, 'Architecture Review; Philip Johnson Geometry in an Advertising Wrapper,' *New York Times*, 5 March 1998.

55 Johnson Study Group, 'Open Letter', 27 November 2020.

56 Alex Greenberger, 'MoMA's Philip Johnson Problem: How to Address the Architect's Legacy?', *ARTnews* (blog), 25 March 2021.

57 Lamster, *The Man In The Glass House*, prologue, iBooks.

58 Ibid.

59 Paul Goldberger, 'Obituary: Philip Johnson, 98, a Monumental Force on US Architectural Scene', *New York Times*, 27 January 2005.

13. Ronnie Kray

1 John Pearson, *The Profession of Violence: The Rise and Fall of the Kray Twins* (London: William Collins, 2015), 20.
2 Ibid., 22.
3 Reg Kray and Ron Kray with Fred Dinenage, *Our Story* (London: Pan, 1989), 3.
4 Ibid., 5.
5 Ibid., 3.
6 Fergus Linnane, *London's Underworld: Three Centuries of Vice and Crime* (London: Robson, 2004), 116.
7 Ibid., 120.
8 Matt Houlbrook, *Queer London: Perils and Pleasures in the Sexual Metropolis, 1918–1957* (Chicago: University of Chicago Press, 2005), 88.
9 Pearson, *The Profession of Violence*, 33.
10 Kray and Kray, *Our Story*, 22.
11 Ibid., 25.
12 Pearson, *The Profession of Violence*, 104.
13 Ibid., 77.
14 Ibid., 81.
15 Kray and Kray, *Our Story*, 28.
16 Ibid., 29.
17 Ibid., 31.
18 Ibid., 34.
19 Pearson, *The Profession of Violence*, 153.
20 Brian Lewis, *Wolfenden's Witnesses: Homosexuality in Postwar Britain* (London: Palgrave Macmillan, 2016), 271.
21 Ibid., 275.
22 Houlbrook, *Queer London*, 36.
23 Tom Driberg, *Ruling Passions* (London; New York: Quartet Books, 1978), 145.
24 Francis Wheen, *The Soul of Indiscretion: Tom Driberg – Poet, Philanderer, Legislator and Outlaw* (London: Fourth Estate, 1990), 191.
25 Driberg, *Ruling Passions*, 143.
26 Wheen, *The Soul of Indiscretion*, 350.
27 Pearson, *The Profession of Violence*, 197.
28 Wheen, *The Soul of Indiscretion*, 350.
29 Ibid., 350.
30 Cahal Milmo, 'Ronnie Kray's Association with Tory Peer and Fellow "Hunter of Young Men" Led to MI5 Investigation and Government Panic', *Independent*, 23 October 2015.
31 Pearson, *The Profession of Violence*, 201.

32 Ron Kray, *My Story* (London: Pan, 1993), 45.

33 Pearson, *The Profession of Violence*, 164.

34 John Pearson, *Notorious: The Immortal Legend of the Kray Twins* (London: Random House, 2011), 51.

14. Pim Fortuyn

1 'United in Anger' is the name of Jim Hubbard's excellent documentary. *United in Anger: A History of ACT UP*, directed by Jim Hubbard (New York: New York State Council on the Arts and the Ford Foundation, 2012).

2 Sarah Schulman, *Let the Record Show: A Political History of ACT UP New York, 1987–1993* (New York: Farrar, Straus and Giroux, 2021), 191.

3 Ibid., xxii.

4 Ibid., 345.

5 Ibid., 498.

6 Huub Dijstelbloem, 'Missing in Action: Inclusion and Exclusion in the First Days of AIDS in the Netherlands', *Sociology of Health and Illness* 36, no. 8 (2014): 1156–70.

7 Benjamin H Shepard, 'The Queer/Gay Assimilationist Split: The Suits vs. the Sluts', *Monthly Review* 53, no. 1 (2001).

8 David J. Bos, '"Equal Rites before the Law": Religious Celebrations of Same-Sex Relationships in the Netherlands, 1960s–1990s', *Theology and Sexuality* 23, no. 3 (2017): 188–208.

9 Ibid.

10 Andrew D. J. Shield, 'The Legacies of the Stonewall Riots in Denmark and the Netherlands', *History Workshop Journal* 89 (2020): 193–206.

11 Nathaniel Frank, *Awakening: How Gays and Lesbians Brought Marriage Equality to America* (Cambridge, MA: Belknap Press of Harvard University Press, 2017), 140.

12 Ibid., 359.

13 Merijn Oudenampsen, *The Rise of the Dutch New Right: An Intellectual History of the Rightward Shift in Dutch Politics* (Abingdon, Oxon, UK: Routledge, 2020), 115.

14 Andrew Osborn, 'Dutch Fall for Gay Mr Right', *Observer*, 14 April 2002.

15 Andrew D. J. Shield, *Immigrants in the Sexual Revolution: Perceptions and Participation in Northwest Europe* (London: Palgrave Macmillan, 2017), 14.

16 Ibid., 15.

17 Ibid., 73–4, 151.

18 Gloria Wekker, *White Innocence: Paradoxes of Colonialism and Race* (Durham, NC: Duke University Press, 2016), 112–13.

19 Ibid., 114.

20 Elizabeth Kolbert, 'Beyond Tolerance – What Did the Dutch See in Pim Fortuyn?," *New Yorker*, 1 September 2002.

21 Shield, *Immigrants in the Sexual Revolution*, 249.

22 Wekker, *White Innocence*, 119.

23 Jasbir K. Puar, *Terrorist Assemblages: Homonationalism in Queer Times* (Durham, NC: Duke University Press, 2007), xi.

24 Wekker, *White Innocence*, 128.

25 Shield, *Immigrants in the Sexual Revolution*, 248.

26 Paul van de Laar and Arie van der Schoor, 'Rotterdam's Superdiversity from a Historical Perspective (1600–1980)', in *Coming to Terms with Superdiversity: The Case of Rotterdam*, ed. Peter Scholten, Maurice Crul, and Paul van de Laar (Cham, Switzerland: Springer International Publishing, 2019), 21–55.

27 Ibid.

28 Ibid.

29 Oudenampsen, *The Rise of the Dutch New Right*, 117–18.

30 Stefan Dudink, 'A Queer Nodal Point: Homosexuality in Dutch Debates on Islam and Multiculturalism', *Sexualities* 20, no. 1–2 (2017): 3–23.

31 Julien van Ostaaijen, 'Local Politics, Populism and Pim Fortuyn in Rotterdam', in *Coming to Terms with Superdiversity: The Case of Rotterdam*, ed. Peter Scholten, Maurice Crul, and Paul van de Laar, IMISCOE Research Series (Cham: Springer International Publishing, 2019), 87–106.

32 Wekker, *White Innocence*, 128.

33 Kolbert, 'Beyond Tolerance'.

34 Van Ostaaijen, 'Local Politics, Populism, and Pim Fortuyn in Rotterdam'.

35 Wekker, *White Innocence*, 142.

36 Ibid., 143.

37 Kolbert, 'Beyond Tolerance'.

38 Wekker, *White Innocence*, 143.

39 Ibid., 141, 144.

40 Ibid., 152.

41 Oudenampsen, *The Rise of the Dutch New Right*, 2.

42 Frank Poorthuis en Hans Wansink, 'Pim Fortuyn op herhaling: "De islam is een achterlijke cultuur"', *de Volkskrant*, 5 May 2012.

43 'CDA wordt volgens peilingen tweede partij van Nederland', *Trouw*, 2 March 2002.

44   Kolbert, 'Beyond Tolerance'.

45   Ibid.

46   Ibid.

47   James Loeffler, 'The Problem With the "Judeo-Christian Tradition"', *Atlantic*, 1 August 2020.

48   Simon Coss, 'Profile – Gay Right Activist: Pim Fortuyn', Politico, 1 May 2002,.

49   Coss, 'Gay Right Activist'.

50   Oudenampsen, *The Rise of the Dutch New Right*, 149.

51   'Österreich: Toter Haider gewinnt Prozess zu seinem Sex-Leben', OTS.at, 18 November 2009.

52   Coss, 'Gay Rights Activist'.

53   Kirsty Lang, 'Obituary: Pim Fortuyn', *Guardian*, 7 May 2002.

54   Marlise Simons, 'Rightist Candidate in Netherlands Is Slain, and the Nation Is Stunned', *New York Times*, 7 May 2002.

55   Kolbert, 'Beyond Tolerance'.

56   Simons, 'Rightist Candidate in Netherlands Is Slain'.

57   Peter Jan Margry, 'The Murder of Pim Fortuyn and Collective Emotions Hype, Hysteria and Holiness in The Netherlands?', *Etnofoor* 16, no. 2 (2003): 110.

58   Ibid., 118.

59   Ibid., 124.

60   Wekker, *White Innocence*, 114.

61   Shield, *Immigrants in the Sexual Revolution*, 2.

62   Tjitske Akkerman, 'Anti-immigration Parties and the Defence of Liberal Values: The Exceptional Case of the List Pim Fortuyn', *Journal of Political Ideologies* 10, no. 3 (2005): 337–54.

63   Wouter Bos, 'Europe's Social Democrats, Solidarity and Muslim Immigration', The Globalist (blog), 9 December 2005, theglobalist.com.

64   Nicholas Watt, 'Dutch Recover Their Courage', *Guardian*, 22 November 2006.

65   Wekker, *White Innocence*, 115.

66   Marijn Niewenhuis, 'The Netherlands' Disgrace: Racism and Police Brutality', openDemocracy, 23 July 2015.

67   Ibid.

68   Ibid.

69   Leoni Schenk, 'Five Years after Mitch Henriquez: "Officers Are Still Barely Prosecuted"', Caribbean Network, 17 June 2020, caribbeannetwork.ntr.nl.

70   'End of Mission Statement of the Special Rapporteur on Contemporary Forms of Racism, Racial Discrimination, Xenophobia and Related Intolerance at the Conclusion of Her Mission to the

Kingdom of the Netherlands, The Hague', United Nations Office of the High Commissioner on Human Rights, 7 October 2019, ohchr.org.

71 Andrew Osborn, '"I Shot Fortuyn for Dutch Muslims", Says Accused,' *Guardian*, 28 March 2003.

Conclusion

1 See Roderick A. Ferguson, *One-Dimensional Queer* (Medford, MA: Polity, 2019).

2 Foucault, 'Friendship as a Way of Life', *Caring Labor: An Archive*, 18 November 2010.

3 These essays are collected in Allan Bérubé, *My Desire for History: Essays in Gay, Community, and Labor History*, eds John D'Emilio and Estelle B. Freedman (Chapel Hill, NC: University of North Carolina Press, 2011).

4 Leslie Feinberg, 'Street Transvestite Action Revolutionaries', *Worker's World*, 24 September 2006, workers.org.

5 See Tiffany N. Florvil, *Mobilizing Black Germany: Afro-German Women and the Making of a Transnational Movement* (Urbana: University of Illinois Press, 2020).

6 Larry Mitchell, *The Faggots and Their Friends between Revolutions* (Ithaca, N.Y.: Calamus Books, 1977), 3.

7 Ibid., 110.

Index

Index

Index